Jon E. Lewis is a historian and writer, whose books on history and military history are sold worldwide. He is also editor of many *The Mammoth Book of* anthologies, including the bestselling *On the Edge*.

Jon holds graduate and postgraduate degrees in history, and his work has appeared in *New Statesman*, the *Independent*, *Time Out* and the *Guardian*. He lives in Herefordshire with his partner and children.

Praise for Jon E. Lewis's previous books:

'A triumph.'

Saul David, author of *Victoria's Army*

'This thoughtful compilation . . . [is] almost unbearably moving.'

Guardian

'Compelling Tommy's-eye view of war.'

Daily Telegraph

'What a book. Five stars.'

Daily Express

SURVIVOR

The Autobiography

Edited by Jon E. Lewis

ROBINSON

Constable & Robinson Ltd
55–56 Russell Square
London WC1B 4HP
www.constablerobinson.com

First published in the UK as
The Mammoth Book of Endurance & Adventure
by Robinson, an imprint of Constable & Robinson Ltd, 2000

This edition published by Robinson, 2011

A copy of the British Library Cataloguing in
Publication Data is available from the British Library

ISBN: 978-1-84901-818-0

Printed and bound in the UK

1 3 5 7 9 10 8 6 4 2

CONTENTS

INTRODUCTION

'. . . in memories we were rich. We had pierced the veneer of outside things. We had "suffered, starved and triumphed, grovelled down yet grasped at glory, grown bigger in the bigness of the whole." We had seen God in his splendours, heard the text that nature renders. We had reached the naked soul of man.'

Sir Ernest Shackleton

Mankind has always been an adventurer. No sooner was he out of his African cradle, than he was questing to see what lay over the next horizon, along the next bend of the river. And there has probably always been an audience for his tales. It is easy enough to conjure up a scene of Early Adventurer entertaining his tribal band around the campfire; certainly the earliest recorded exploration, that of Harkhuf to the land of Yam in around 2300 BC, dates back almost to the invention of writing itself.

Today's modern audience, however, is more clamorous for adventure than its predecessors. The reasons are not hard to find. In a world made cosy by a cornucopia of consumer conveniences, people are endlessly trapped in humdrum routines and a surfeit of safety. Few of us would protest against it but all of us know that we have lost sight of something: human mettle, spirit in adversity, the ability to live dangerously. Those who have dared go outside the confines of civilization to pit themselves against

Nature remind us of what it is we are made of; their travails, to borrow the phrase of Antarctic explorer Sir Ernest Shackleton, enabling us to see 'the naked soul of man'. They may thrill us, but more importantly they illuminate us. We need them to do what they do.

Shackleton reminds us that the adventurer has other fascinations. In cynical times with very few heroes, he retains an heroic cast. And few were more heroic than Shackleton. As an explorer he was a failure, as a hero he was everything. A true believer in duty and service, he escaped Antarctica and then went back to rescue those in his charge. The 'boss' brought every man back safely. It's small wonder then that Shackleton is a curriculum item in business schools for those wanting to learn leadership skills.

By default, the majority of the eyewitness accounts collected in this book are by those who survived their personal tests of endurance, from Douglas Mawson struggling alone through an Antarctic blizzard to Charles Lindberg's fight against exhaustion aboard the *Spirit of St Louis*. They lived to bring home the tale. Sometimes, however, the records of the doomed have outlasted their authors, such as the harrowing last diaries found besides the corpse of R. F. Scott in Antarctica – the great white laboratory of endurance – and those of W. J. Wills in the desolate outback of Cooper's Creek. These diaries, aside from chronicling hardship and perseverance almost beyond imagination, also give a salutary lesson: Nature is not easily beaten.

If the public needs its adventurers, there remains the thundering question of what motivates the adventurer. Over time, the necessities of food, shelter, uninhabited land, trade, warfare and imperial ambition have all whipped adventurers across the unknown. So too, the chance for the big prize, fame and glory (there's nothing new about the lust for celebrity). In the centuries following the Enlightenment, adventure has frequently been dressed as the pursuit of knowledge, with expeditions to the ends, heights and depths of the world tasked with some scientific or geographical purpose. And yet, as the following pages secretly testify, the real *why*? Stimulating the modern adventurer is the exploration of an entirely different objective – the self *in extremis*. The proof of this is childishly easy, for almost all exploration in the last hundred years has, strictly speaking, been unnecessary, neither opening up new trade routes nor tracts of land to the touch of 'civilization'. The relationship between audience and adventurer, then, is purely symbiotic: the public desires adventurers so that they can vicariously experience their own 'naked soul'; fortuitously for the self-same public, some brave enough – or maybe foolish enough – men and women still feel a desire to test themselves to the limits.

It goes without saying that such a test should be a true endurance, one of mind and body. Endurance is usually conceived as sustained endeavour over time, but the meaning can be stretched to the maintenance of nerve and physical control over mere minutes of dangerous difficulty. Certainly, I have taken such licence in this book. Ekblaw's sledge ride over wafer-thin ice, Nick Danziger's gun-running jeep journey over the Afghan border, Charles Waterton's wrestle with a Guianese Cayman come to mind.

One of the necessary by-products of adventure is that it takes the adventurer – and thus the reader – to the last faraway places, where Nature still lives in unsullied magnificence (and deadly power). If this book is a chronicle of first-hand adventure, it is not least an anthology of white-knuckled travel writing. Sometimes, too, it is the travel writing of the highest art, such as Salomon Andrée's death-march diary across the Arctic, almost painterly in its depiction of the ice pack as a 'Magnificent Venetian landscape with canals between lofty hummock edges on both sides, water-square with ice-fountain and stairs down to the canals. Divine.'

The various terrains and elements of Nature have also served as the organizing principle of this book, from The Poles to The Air, via Mountains, Oceans and Rivers, Under the Ground, Deserts, and Jungles. This is a mere anthologist's contrivance.

None is more intrinsically perilous than another, they are all simply different. And all offer long odds for the adventurer determined upon the ultimate game of Man v Nature.

Jon E. Lewis, 2000

The Poles

LAST MAN WALKING

SIR DOUGLAS MAWSON
(1882–1958)

Australian geologist and Antarctic explorer. In September 1912 he set off with Dr Xavier Mertz, a Swiss mountaineer, and Lieutenant B.E.S. Ninnis, a British army officer, to explore King George V Land.

14 December 1912 When next I looked back, it was in response to the anxious gaze of Mertz who had turned round and halted in his tracks. Behind me nothing met the eye except my own sledge tracks running back in the distance. Where were Ninnis and his sledge?

I hastened back along the trail thinking that a rise in the ground obscured the view. There was no such good fortune, however, for I came to a gaping hole in the surface about eleven feet wide. The lid of the crevasse that had caused me so little thought had broken in; two sledge tracks led up to it on the far side – only one continued beyond.

Frantically waving to Mertz to bring up my sledge, upon which there was some alpine rope, I leaned over and shouted into the dark depths below. No sound came back but the moaning of a dog, caught on a shelf just visible one hundred and fifty feet below. The poor creature appeared to have a broken back, for it was attempting to sit up with the front part of its body, while the hinder portion lay limp. Another dog lay motionless by its side. Close by was what appeared in the gloom to be the remains of the tent and a canvas food tank containing a fortnight's supply.

We broke back the edge of the hard snow lid and, secured by a rope, took turns leaning over, calling into the darkness in the hope that our companion might be still alive. For three hours we called unceasingly but no answering sound came back. The dog had ceased to moan and lay without a movement. A chill draught rose out of the abyss. We felt that there was no hope.

It was difficult to realize that Ninnis, who was a young giant in build, so jovial and so real but a few minutes before, should thus have vanished without even a sound. It seemed so incredible that we half expected, on turning round, to find him standing there.

Why had the first sledge escaped? It seemed that I had been fortunate, as my sledge had crossed diagonally, with a greater chance of breaking the lid. The sledges were within thirty pounds of the same weight. The explanation appeared to be that Ninnis had walked by the side of his sledge, whereas I had crossed it sitting on the sledge. The whole weight of a man's body bearing on his foot is a formidable load, and no doubt was sufficient to smash the arch of the roof.

By means of a fishing line we ascertained that it was one hundred and fifty feet sheer to the ledge upon which the remains were seen; on either side the crevasse descended into blackness. It seemed so very far down there and the dogs looked so small that we got out the field-glass to complete the scrutiny of the depths.

All our available rope was tied together but the total length was insufficient to reach the ledge, and any idea of going below to investigate and to secure some of the food had to be abandoned.

Later in the afternoon Mertz and I went on to a higher point in order to obtain a better view of our surroundings and to see if anything helpful lay ahead. In that direction, however, the prospect of reaching the sea, where lay chances of obtaining seal and penguin meat, was hopeless on account of the appalling manner in which the coastal slopes were shattered. At a point two thousand four hundred feet above sea-level and three hundred and fifteen and three-quarter miles eastward from the Hut, a complete set of observations was taken.

We returned to the crevasse to consider what was to be done and prepare for the future. At regular intervals we called down into those dark depths in case our companion might not have been killed outright, and, in the meantime, have become unconscious. There was no reply.

A weight was lowered on the fishing line as far as the dog which had earlier shown some signs of life, but there was no response. All were dead, swallowed up in an instant . . .

At 9 p.m. we stood by the side of the crevasse and I read the burial service. Then Mertz shook me by the hand with a short 'Thank you!' and we turned away to harness up the dogs . . .

The night of the 6th [January 1913] was long and wearisome as I tossed about sleeplessly, mindful that for both of us our chances of reaching succour were now slipping silently and relentlessly away. I was aching to get on, but there could be no question of abandoning my companion whose condition now set the pace.

The morning of 7 January opened with better weather, for there was little wind and no snow falling; even the sun appeared gleaming through the clouds.

In view of the seriousness of the position it had been agreed overnight that at all costs we would go on in the morning, sledge-sailing with Mertz in his bag strapped on the sledge. It was therefore a doubly sad blow that morning to find that my companion was again touched with dysentery and so weak as to be quite helpless. After tucking him into the bag again, I slid into my own in order to kill time and keep warm, for the cold had a new sting about it in those days of want.

At 10 a.m. hearing a rustle from my companion's bag I rose to find him in a fit. Shortly afterwards he became normal and exchanged a few words, but did not appear to realize that anything out of the way had happened.

The information that this incident conveyed fell upon me like a thunderbolt, for it was certain that my companion was in a very serious state with little hope of any alleviation, for he was already unable to assimilate the meagre foods available.

There was no prospect of proceeding so I settled myself to stand by my stricken comrade and ease his sufferings as far as possible. It would require a miracle to bring him round to a fit travelling condition, but I prayed that it might be granted.

After noon he improved and drank some thick cocoa and soup.

Later in the afternoon he had several more fits and then, becoming delirious, talked incoherently until midnight. Most of that time his strength returned and he struggled to climb out of the sleeping-bag, keeping me very busy tucking him in again. About midnight he appeared to doze off to sleep and with a feeling of relief I slid down into my own bag, not to sleep, though weary enough, but to get warm again and to think matters over. After a couple of hours, having felt no movement, I stretched out my arm and found that my comrade was stiff in death. He had been accepted into 'the peace that passeth all understanding'.

It was unutterably sad that he should have perished thus, after the splendid work he had accomplished not only on that particular sledging journey but throughout the expedition. No one could have done better. Favoured with a generous and lovable character, he had been a general favourite amongst all the members of the expedition. Now all was over, he had done his duty and passed on. All that remained was his mortal frame which, toggled up in his sleeping-bag, still offered some sense of companionship as I threw myself down for the remainder of the night, revolving in my mind all that lay behind and the chances of the future.

Outside the bowl of chaos was brimming with drift-snow and as I lay in the sleeping-bag beside my dead companion I wondered how, in such conditions, I would manage to break and pitch camp single-handed. There appeared to be little hope of reaching the Hut, still one hundred miles away. It was easy to sleep in the bag, and the weather was cruel outside. But inaction is hard to bear and I braced myself together determined to put up a good fight.

Failing to reach the Hut it would be something done if I managed to get to some prominent point likely to catch the eye of a search-party, where a cairn might be erected and our diaries cached. So I commenced to modify the sledge and camping gear to meet fresh requirements.

The sky remained clouded, but the wind fell off to a calm which lasted several hours. I took the opportunity to set to work on the sledge, sawing it in halves with a pocket tool and discarding the rear section. A mast was made out of one of the rails no longer required, and a spar was cut from the other. Finally, the load was cut down to a minimum by the elimination of all but the barest necessities, the abandoned articles including, sad to relate, all that remained of the exposed photographic films.

Late that evening, the 8th, I took the body of Mertz, still toggled up in his bag, outside the tent, piled snow blocks around it and raised a rough cross made of the two discarded halves of the sledge runners.

On 9 January the weather was overcast and fairly thick drift was flying in a gale of wind, reaching about fifty miles an hour. As certain matters still required attention and my chances of re-erecting the tent were rather doubtful . . . the start was delayed.

Part of the time that day was occupied with cutting up a waterproof clothes-bag and Mertz's Burberry jacket and sewing them together to form a sail. Before retiring to rest in the evening I read through the burial service and put the finishing touches on the grave.

10 January arrived in a turmoil of wind and thick drift. The start was still further delayed. I spent part of the time in reckoning up the food remaining and in cooking the rest of the dog meat, this latter operation serving the good object of lightening the load, in that the kerosene for the purpose was consumed there and then and had not to be dragged forward for subsequent use. Late in the afternoon the wind fell and the sun peered amongst the clouds just as I was in the middle of a long job riveting and lashing the broken shovel.

The next day, 11 January, a beautiful, calm day of sunshine, I set out over a good surface with a slight down grade.

From the start my feet felt curiously lumpy and sore. They had become so painful after a mile of walking that I decided to examine them on the spot, sitting in the lee of the sledge in brilliant sunshine. I had not had my socks off for some days for, while lying in camp, it had not seemed necessary. On taking off the third and inner pair of socks the sight of my feet gave me quite a shock, for the thickened skin of the soles had separated in each case as a complete layer, and abundant watery fluid had escaped saturating the sock. The new skin beneath was very much abraded and raw. Several of my toes had commenced to blacken and fester near the tips and the nails were puffed and loose.

I began to wonder if there was ever to be a day without some special disappointment. However, there was nothing to be done but make the best of it. I smeared the new skin and the raw surfaces with lanoline, of which there was fortunately a good store, and then with the aid of bandages bound the old skin casts back in place, for these were comfortable and soft in contact with the abraded surface. Over the bandages were slipped six pairs of thick woollen socks, then fur boots and finally crampon over-shoes. The latter, having large stiff soles, spread the weight nicely and saved my feet from the jagged ice encountered shortly afterwards.

So glorious was it to feel the sun on one's skin after being without it for so long that I next removed most of my clothing and bathed my body in the rays until my flesh fairly tingled – a wonderful sensation which spread throughout my whole person, and made me feel stronger and happier . . .

17 January A start was made at 8 a.m. and the pulling proved more easy than on the previous day. Some two miles had been negotiated in safety when an event occurred which, but for a miracle, would have terminated the story then and there. Never have I come so near to an end; never has anyone more miraculously escaped.

I was hauling the sledge through deep snow up a fairly steep sloop when my feet broke through into a crevasse. Fortunately as I fell I caught my weight with my arms on the edge and did not plunge in further than the thighs. The outline of the crevasse did not show through the blanket of snow on the surface, but an idea of the trend was obtained with a stick. I decided to try a crossing about fifty yards further along, hoping that there it would be better bridged. Alas! it took an unexpected turn catching me unawares. This time I shot through the centre of the bridge in a flash, but the latter part of the fall was decelerated by the friction of the harness ropes which, as the sledge ran up, sawed back into the thick compact snow forming the margin of the lid. Having seen my comrades perish in diverse ways and having lost hope of ever reaching the Hut, I had already many times speculated on what the end would be like. So it happened that as I fell through into the crevasse the thought 'so this is the end' blazed up in my mind, for it was to be expected that the next moment the sledge would follow through, crash on my head and all go to the unseen bottom. But the unexpected happened and the sledge held, the deep snow acting as a brake.

In the moment that elapsed before the rope ceased to descend, delaying the issue, a great regret swept through my mind, namely, that after having stinted myself so assiduously in order to save food, I should pass on now to eternity without the satisfaction of what remained – to such an extent does food take possession of one under such circumstances. Realizing that the sledge was holding I began to look around. The crevasse was somewhat over six feet wide and sheer walled, descending into blue depths below. My clothes, which, with a view to ventilation, had been but loosely secured, were now stuffed with snow broken from the roof, and very chilly it was. Above at the other end of the four-teen-foot rope, was the daylight seen through the hole in the lid.

In my weak condition, the prospect of climbing out seemed very poor indeed, but in a few moments the struggle was begun. A great effort brought a knot in the rope within my grasp, and, after a moment's rest, I was able to draw myself up and reach another, and, at length, hauled my body on to the overhanging snow-lid. Then, when all appeared to be well and before I could get to quite solid ground, a further section of the lid gave way, precipitating me once more to the full length of the rope.

There, exhausted, weak and chilled, hanging freely in space and slowly turning round as the rope twisted one way and the other, I felt that I had done my utmost and failed, that I had no more strength to try again and that all was over except the passing. It was to be a miserable and slow end and I reflected with disappointment that there was in my pocket no antidote to speed matters; but there always remained the alternative of slipping from the harness. There on the brink of the great Beyond I well remember how I looked forward to the peace of the great release – how almost excited I was at the prospect of the unknown to be unveiled. From those flights of mind I came back to earth, and remembering how Providence had miraculously brought me so far, felt that nothing was impossible and determined to act up to Service's lines:

> Just have one more try – it's dead easy to die,
> It's the keeping-on-living that's hard.

My strength was fast ebbing; in a few minutes it would be too late. It was the occasion for a supreme attempt. Fired by the passion that burns the blood in the act of strife, new power seemed to come as I applied myself to one last tremendous effort. The struggle occupied some time, but I slowly worked upward to the surface. This time emerging feet first, still clinging to the rope, I pushed myself out extended at full length on the lid and then shuffled safely on to the solid ground at the side. Then came the reaction from the great nerve strain and lying there alongside the sledge my mind faded into a blank.

When consciousness returned it was a full hour or two later, for I was partly covered with newly fallen snow and numb with the cold. I took at least three hours to erect the tent, get things snugly inside and clear the snow from my clothes. Between each movement, almost, I had to rest. Then reclining in luxury in the sleeping-bag I ate a little food and thought matters over. It was a time when the mood of the Persian philosopher appealed to me:

> Unborn To-morrow and dead Yesterday,
> Why fret about them if To-day be sweet?

I was confronted with this problem: whether it was better to enjoy life for a few days, sleeping and eating my fill until the provisions gave out, or to 'plug on' again in hunger with the prospect of plunging at any moment into eternity without the supreme satisfaction and pleasure of the food. While thus cogitating an idea presented itself which greatly improved the prospects and clinched the decision to go ahead. It was to construct a ladder from a length of alpine rope that remained; one end was to be secured to the bow of the sledge and the other carried over my left shoulder and loosely attached to the sledge harness. Thus if I fell into a crevasse again, provided the sledge was not also engulfed, it would be easy for me, even though weakened by starvation, to scramble out by the ladder.

Notwithstanding the possibilities of the rope-ladder, I could not sleep properly, for my nerves had been overtaxed. All night long considerable wind and drift continued.

On the 19th it was overcast and light snow falling; very dispiriting conditions after the experience of the day before, but I resolved to go ahead and leave the rest to Providence . . .

29 January I was travelling along on an even down grade and was wondering how long the two pounds of food which remained would last, when something dark loomed through the haze of the drift a short distance away to the right. All sorts of possibilities raced through my mind as I headed the sledge for it. The unexpected had happened – in thick weather I had run fairly into a cairn of snow blocks erected by McLean, Hodgeman and Hurley, who had been out searching for my party. On the top of the mound, outlined in black bunting, was a bag of food, left on the chance that it might be picked up by us. In a tin was a note stating the bearing and distance of the mound from Aladdin's Cave (E. 30° S., distance twenty-three miles), and mentioning that the ship had arrived at the Hut and was waiting, and had brought the news that Amundsen had reached the Pole, and that Scott was remaining another year in Antarctica.

It certainly was remarkably good fortune that I had come upon the depot of food; a few hundred yards to either side and it would have been lost to sight in the drift. On reading the note carefully I found that I had just missed by six hours what would have been crowning good luck, for it appeared that the search party had left the mound at 8 a.m. that very day . . . It was about 2 p.m. when I reached it. Thus, during the night of the 28th our camps had been only some five miles apart.

Hauling down the bag of food I tore it open in the lee of the cairn and in my greed scattered the contents about on the ground. Having partaken heartily of frozen pemmican, I stuffed my pocket, bundled the rest into a bag on the sledge and started off in high glee, stimulated in body and mind. As I left the depot there appeared to be nothing on earth that could prevent me reaching the Hut within a couple of days, but a fresh obstacle with which I had not reckoned was to arise and cause further delay, leading to far-reaching results.

It happened that after several hours' march the surface changed from snow to polished névé and then to slippery ice. I could scarcely keep on my feet at all, falling every few moments and bruising my emaciated self until I expected to see my bones burst through the clothes. How I regretted having abandoned those crampons after crossing the Mertz Glacier; shod with them, all would be easy.

With nothing but finnesko on the feet, to walk over such a sloping surface would have been difficult enough in the wind without any other hindrance; with the sledge sidling down the slope and tugging at one, it was quite impossible. I found that I had made too far to the east and to reach Aladdin's Cave had unfortunately to strike across the wind.

Before giving up, I even tried crawling on my hands and knees.

However, the day's run, fourteen miles, was by no means a poor one.

Having erected the tent I set to work to improvise crampons. With this object in view the theodolite case was cut up, providing two flat pieces of wood into which were stuck as many screws and nails as could be procured by dismantling the sledgemeter and the theodolite itself. In the repair-bag there were still a few ice-nails which at this time were of great use.

Late the next day, the wind which had risen in the night fell off and a start was made westwards over the ice slopes with the pieces of nail-studded wood lashed to my feet. A glorious expanse of sea lay to the north and several recognizable points on the coast were clearly in view to east and west.

The crampons were not a complete success for they gradually broke up, lasting only a distance of six miles . . .

A blizzard was in full career on 31 January and I spent all day and most of the night on the crampons. On 1 February the wind and drift had subsided late in the afternoon, and I got under way expecting great things from the new crampons. The beacon marking Aladdin's Cave was clearly visible as a black dot on the ice slopes to the west.

At 7 p.m. that haven within the ice was attained. It took but a few moments to dig away the snow and throw back the canvas flap sealing the entrance. A moment later I slid down inside, arriving amidst familiar surroundings. Something unusual in one corner caught the eye – three oranges and a pineapple – circumstantial evidence of the arrival of the *Aurora*.

The improvised crampons had given way and were squeezing my feet painfully. I rummaged about amongst a pile of food-bags hoping to find some crampons or leather boots, but was disappointed, so there was nothing left but to repair the damaged ones. That done and a drink of hot milk having been prepared I packed up to make a start for the Hut. On climbing out of the cave imagine my disappointment at finding a strong wind and drift had risen. To have attempted the descent of the five and a half miles of steep ice slope to the Hut with such inadequate and fragile crampons, weak as I still was, would have been only as a last resort. So I camped in the comfortable cave and hoped for better weather next day.

But the blizzard droned on night and day for over a week with never a break. Think of my feelings as I sat within the cave, so near and yet so far from the Hut, impatient and anxious, ready to spring out and take the trail at a moment's notice. Improvements to the crampons kept me busy for a time; then, as there was a couple of old boxes lying about, I set to work and constructed a second emergency pair in case the others should break up during the descent. I tried the makeshift crampons on the ice outside, but was disappointed to find that they had not sufficient grip to face the wind, so had to abandon the idea of attempting the descent during the continuance of the blizzard. Nevertheless, by February 8 my anxiety as to what was happening at the Hut reached such a pitch that I resolved to try the passage in spite of everything, having worked out a plan whereby I was to sit on the sledge and sail down as far as possible.

Whilst these preparations were in progress the wind slackened. At last the longed-for event was to be realized. I snatched a hasty meal and set off. Before a couple of miles had been covered the wind had fallen off altogether, and after that it was gloriously calm and clear.

I had reached within one and a half miles of the Hut and there was no sign of the *Aurora* lying in the offing. I was comforted with the thought that she might still be at the anchorage and have swung inshore so as to be hidden under the ice cliffs. But even as I gazed about seeking for a clue, a speck on the north-west horizon caught my eye and my hopes went down. It looked like a distant ship – Was it the *Aurora*? Well, what matter! the long journey was at an end – a terrible chapter of my life was concluded!

Then the rocks around winter quarters began to come into view; part of the basin of the Boat Harbour appeared, and lo! there were human figures! They almost seemed unreal – was it all a dream? No, indeed, for after a brief moment one of them observed me and waved an arm – I replied – there was a commotion and they all ran towards the Hut. Then they were lost, hidden by the crest of the first steep slope. It almost seemed to me that they had run away to hide.

Minutes passed as I slowly descended trailing the sledge. Then a head rose over the brow of the hill and there was Bickerton, breathless after a long run uphill. I expect for a while he wondered which of us it was. Soon we had shaken hands and he knew all in a few brief words, I for my part learning that the ship had left earlier that very day.

THE BLOW

RICHARD EVELYN BYRD
(1888–1957)

American aviator and explorer, the first man to make an aeroplane flight over the North Pole, and later the first to overfly the South Pole. In 1933–4 Byrd spent five months alone in the Bolling Advance Weather Base – a rudimentary hut, its name notwithstanding – at 80.08° South during the polar winter.

Out of the cold and out of the east came the wind. It came on gradually, as if the sheer weight of the cold were almost too much to be moved. On the night of the 21st the barometer started down. The night was black as a thunderhead when I made my first trip topside; and a tension in the wind, a bulking of shadows in the night indicated that a new storm centre was forming. Next morning, glad of an excuse to stay underground, I worked a long time on the Escape Tunnel by the light of a red candle standing in a snow recess. That day I pushed the emergency exit to a distance of twenty-two feet, the farthest it was ever to go. My stint done, I sat down on a box, thinking how beautiful was the red of the candle, how white the rough-hewn snow. Soon I became aware of an increasing clatter of the anemometer cups. Realizing that the wind was picking up, I went topside to make sure that everything was secured. It is a queer experience to watch a blizzard rise. First there is the wind, rising out of nowhere. Then the Barrier unwrenches itself from quietude; and the surface, which just before had seemed as hard and polished as metal, begins to run like a making sea. Sometimes, if the wind strikes hard, the drift comes across the Barrier like a hurrying white cloud, tossed hundreds of feet in the air. Other times the growth is gradual. You become conscious of a general slithering movement on all sides. The air fills with tiny scraping and sliding and rustling sounds as the first loose crystals stir. In a little while they are moving as solidly as an incoming tide, which creams over the ankles, then surges to the waist, and finally is at the throat. I have walked in drift so thick as not to be able to see a foot ahead of me; yet, when I glanced up, I could see the stars shining through the thin layer just overhead.

Smoking tendrils were creeping up the anemometer pole when I finished my inspection. I hurriedly made the trapdoor fast, as a sailor might batten down a hatch; and knowing that my ship was well secured, I retired to the cabin to ride out the storm. It could not reach me, hidden deep in the Barrier crust; nevertheless the sounds came down. The gale sobbed in the ventilators, shook the stovepipe until I thought it would be jerked out by the roots, pounded the roof with sledgehammer blows. I could actually feel the suction effect through the pervious snow. A breeze flickered in the room and the tunnels. The candles wavered and went out. My only light was the feeble storm lantern.

Even so, I didn't have any idea how really bad it was until I went aloft for an observation. As I pushed back the trapdoor, the drift met me like a moving wall. It was only a few steps from the ladder to the instrument shelter, but it seemed more like a mile. The air came at me in snowy rushes; I breasted it as I might a heavy surf. No night had ever seemed so dark. The beam from the flashlight was choked in its throat; I could not see my hand before my face.

My windproofs were caked with drift by the time I got below. I had a vague feeling that something had changed while I was gone, but what, I couldn't tell. Presently I noticed that the shack was appreciably colder. Raising the stove lid, I was surprised to find that the fire was out, though the tank was half full. I decided that I must have turned off the valve unconsciously before going aloft; but, when I put a match to the burner, the draught down the pipe blew out the flame. The wind, then, must have killed the fire. I got it going again, and watched it carefully.

The blizzard vaulted to gale force. Above the roar the deep, taut thrumming note of the radio antenna and the anemometer guy wires reminded me of wind in a ship's rigging. The wind direction trace turned scratchy on the sheet; no doubt drift had short-circuited the electric contacts, I decided. Realizing that it was hopeless to attempt to try to keep them clear, I let the instrument be. There were other ways of getting the wind direction. I tied a handkerchief to a bamboo pole and ran it through the outlet ventilator; with a flashlight I could tell which way the cloth was whipped. I did this at hourly intervals, noting any change of direction on the sheet. But by 2 o'clock in the morning I had had enough of this periscope sighting. If I expected to sleep and at the same time maintain the continuity of the records, I had no choice but to clean the contact points.

The wind was blowing hard then. The Barrier shook from the concussions overhead; and the noise was as if the entire physical world were tearing itself to pieces. I could scarcely heave the trap-door open. The instant it came clear I was plunged into a blinding smother. I came out crawling, clinging to the handle of the door until I made sure of my bearings. Then I let the door fall shut, not wanting the tunnel filled with drift. To see was impossible. Millions of tiny pellets exploded in my eyes, stinging like BB shot. It was even hard to breathe, because snow instantly clogged the mouth and nostrils. I made my way towards the anemometer pole on hands and knees, scared that I might be bowled off my feet if I stood erect; one false step and I should be lost for ever.

I found the pole all right; but not until my head collided with a cleat. I managed to climb it, too, though ten million ghosts were tearing at me, ramming their thumbs into my eyes. But the errand was useless. Drift as thick as this would mess up the contact points as quickly as they were cleared; besides, the wind cups were spinning so fast that I stood a good chance of losing a couple of fingers in the process. Coming down the pole, I had a sense of being whirled violently through the air, with no control over my movements. The trapdoor was completely buried when I found it again, after scraping around for some time with my mittens. I pulled at the handle, first with one hand, then with both. It did not give. It's a tight fit, anyway, I mumbled to myself. The drift has probably wedged the corners. Standing astride the hatch, I braced myself and heaved with all my strength. I might just as well have tried hoisting the Barrier.

Panic took me then, I must confess. Reason fled. I clawed at the three-foot square of timber like a madman. I beat on it with my fists, trying to shake the snow loose; and, when that did no good, I lay flat on my belly and pulled until my hands went weak from cold and weariness. Then I crooked my elbow, put my face down, and said over and over again, You damn fool, you damn fool. Here for weeks I had been defending myself against the danger of being penned inside the shack; instead, I was now locked out; and nothing could be worse, especially since I had only a wool parka and pants under my wind-proofs. Just two feet below was sanctuary – warmth, food, tools, all the means of survival. All these things were an arm's length away, but I was powerless to reach them.

There is something extravagantly insensate about an Antarctic blizzard at night. Its vindictiveness cannot be measured on an anemometer sheet. It is more than just wind; it is a solid wall of snow moving at gale force, pounding like surf.* The whole malevolent rush is concentrated upon you as upon a personal enemy. In the senseless explosion of sound you are reduced to a crawling thing on the margin of a disintegrating world; you can't see, you can't hear, you can hardly move. The lungs gasp after the air

---

* Because of this blinding, suffocating drift, in the Antarctic winds of only moderate velocity have the punishing force of full-fledged hurricanes elsewhere.

sucked out of them, and the brain is shaken. Nothing in the world will so quickly isolate a man.

Half-frozen, I stabbed toward one of the ventilators, a few feet away. My mittens touched something round and cold. Cupping it in my hands, I pulled myself up. This was the outlet ventilator. Just why, I don't know – but instinct made me kneel and press my face against the opening. Nothing in the room was visible, but a dim patch of light illuminated the floor, and warmth rose up to my face. That steadied me.

Still kneeling, I turned my back to the blizzard and considered what might be done. I thought of breaking in the windows in the roof, but they lay two feet down in hard crust, and were reinforced with wire besides. If I only had something to dig with, I could break the crust and stamp the windows in with my feet. The pipe cupped between my hands supplied the first inspiration; maybe I could use that to dig with. It, too, was wedged tight; I pulled until my arms ached, without budging it; I had lost all track of time, and the despairing thought came to me that I was lost in a task without an end. Then I remembered the shovel. A week before, after levelling drift from the last light blow, I had stabbed a shovel handle up in the crust somewhere to leeward. That shovel would save me. But how to find it in the avalanche of the blizzard?

I lay down and stretched out full length. Still holding the pipe, I thrashed around with my feet, but pummelled only empty air. Then I worked back to the hatch. The hard edges at the opening provided another grip, and again I stretched out and kicked. Again no luck. I dared not let go until I had something else familiar to cling to. My foot came up against the other ventilator pipe. I edged back to that, and from the new anchorage repeated the manoeuvre. This time my ankle struck something hard. When I felt it and recognized the handle, I wanted to caress it.

Embracing this thrice-blessed tool, I inched back to the trapdoor. The handle of the shovel was just small enough to pass under the little wooden bridge which served as a grip. I got both hands on the shovel and tried to wrench the door up; my strength was not enough, however. So I lay down flat on my belly and worked my shoulders under the shovel. Then I heaved, the door sprang open, and I rolled down the shaft. When I tumbled into the light and warmth of the room, I kept thinking, How wonderful, how perfectly wonderful.

My wrist watch had stopped; the chronometers showed that I had been gone just under an hour. The stove had blown out again, but I did not bother to light it. Enough warmth remained for me to undress. I was exhausted; it was all I could do to hoist myself into the bunk. But I did not sleep at first. The blizzard scuffled and pounded gigantically overhead; and my mind refused to drop the thought of what I might still be doing if the shovel hadn't been there. Still struggling, probably. Or maybe not. There are harder ways to die than freezing to death. The lush numbness and the peace that lulls the mind when the ears cease listening to the blizzard's ridiculous noise, could make death seem easy.

ADRIFT ON THE ICE

SALOMON ANDRÉE
(1854–97)

Swedish balloonist. An attempt to fly over the North Pole in 1897 ended after three days when Andrée and his two companions were obliged to make a forced landing on the ice pack. For months the balloonists held out, before eventually perishing. Andrée's diary was not found until 1929.

12 July 1897 Although we could have thrown out ballast, and although the wind might, perhaps, carry us to Greenland, we determined to be content with standing still. We have been obliged to throw out very much ballast today and have not had any sleep nor been allowed any rest from the repeated bumpings, and we probably could not have stood it much longer. All three of us must have a rest, and I sent Strindb. and Fr. to bed at 11.20 o'cl. (5567), and I mean to let them sleep until 6 or 7 o'cl. if I can manage to keep watch until then. Then I shall try to get some rest myself. If either of them should succumb it might be because I had tired them out.

It is not a little strange to be floating here above the Polar Sea. To be the first that have floated here in a balloon. How soon, I wonder, shall we have successors? Shall we be thought mad or will our example be followed? I cannot deny but that all three of us are dominated by a feeling of pride. We think we can well face death, having done what we have done. Is not the whole, perhaps, the expression of an extremely strong sense of individuality which cannot bear the thought of living and dying like a man in the ranks, forgotten by coming generations? Is this ambition?

The rattling of the guidelines in the snow and the flapping of the sails are the only sounds heard, except the whining in the basket.

14 July 11 o'cl. p.m. we jumped out of the balloon. The landing Worn out and famished but 7 hours' hard work had to be done before we could recreate ourselves.

22 July 6.45 p.m. break camp. Nisse's sledge turned over and lay there in the water. 4hr. march. Night-camp. Sunshine beautiful ice . . .

23 July Break camp 2 p.m. Difficulties at once. Astr. obs. meteorol. Follow bear-tracks. Ferrying across with the sledges extremely risky. 4 little auks 2 ivory gulls 1 fulmar. Weather misty and windy. Snow moister. The leads more difficult. The hummocks inconsiderable. Ice on the pools. Tenting at 11 p.m. in lee of a big hummock. Nisse's cooking exp. bread, rousseau, butter, pease, soup-tablets. Hammarspik's poems. 24/7 broke camp 2.10 o'cl. several bad leads and ice-humps. The travelling bad and we were extremely fatigued. Dangerous ferryings and violent twistings, etc., of the sledges among the hummocks, etc. Followed the edge of a large lead almost the whole time.

25 July Breaking camp delayed by rain. New method of travelling: along leads and on smoother ice, wet snow and bad going. Gull with red belly. Wings blue underneath and above. Dark ring around neck. Seals often in openings, never in herds. Talked rot about seals. Nisse fell in and was in imminent danger of drowning. He was dried and wrung out and dressed in knickerbockers. Stopped short at a lead.

Load on my sledge the 26th on altering load:

		(before)
	Kilo	lbs.
4 ice-planks	8.50	18.7
3 bamboo-p (oles)	2.00	4.4
1 carrying-ring plank	1.00	2.2
1 boat-hook	1.50	3.3
1 bottom-tarpauling	1.00	2.2
1 sack private	17.5	38.5
1 △ basket	29.00	64.–
1 pot boot-grease	3.5	7.75
1 hose	3.5	7.75
1 large press	8.00	17.5
1 shovel and 1 reserve cross-piece	1.8	4.–
1 basket with contents	65.00	143.–
1 d:o	66.5	146.–
	208.8	459.3
Grapnel with rope	2.00	4.4
	210.8	463.7

26 July at o'cl. p.m. we began with the rafting. 1 big & 1 little bear visit during night around the tent. Northerly wind, hurra. Place-determination Long. 30° 15'–30° 47' and Lat. 82° 36'. Strindberg's bear. Bear-beef immensely good. Meat 1 hour in sea water then all well. Sledges broken. Iron-sheathing as experiment. Mending and examination of weight and considerable reduction. Revision of plan of journey. No time for sledge-pulling. Equipment for 45 days. Strange feelings and great indulgence in food on making reduction. To sleep at last about 7 a.m. on the 27 July.

28 July 8 p.m. turned out. Sheathing sledges. Begin with snow-shoes. Repair of Fraenkel's gear. Paradise; large smooth ice-floes without hummocks or leads or more melted snow-water than was needed for drinking. '*Parade-ice*' Fr. 'what old mammy sends us is always confoundedly good, anyway.' Terrible underfoot to begin with but in the evening magnificent ice and magnificent weather. The wind is felt much but is always welcome when it drives towards SE. Today we have crossed a number of bear-tracks but not a single lead. Now however we have come to a broad beast which we must get [. . .] tomorrow. Now we have turned in 12 o'cl. noon the 29th after having thus been at work 16 hours. We learn the poor man's way: to make use of *everything*. We also learn the art of living from one day to the other.

Describe in detail. Difficulties with the ice, the hummocks, melted snow-water, the (melted snow) pools and the leads and the floes of broken ice.

31 July 5 o'cl. a.m. start. 'Tramp' on our knees in deep snow. 'Tramp – tramp' on our knees. Discoverer of attractions of flopping = Nisse. Cut our way. The constant fog prevents us from choosing good road. Ever since the start we have been in very difficult country. The Polar dist. is certainly the birthplace of the principle of the greatest stumbling-blocks. 10 leads during the first 6 hours.

2 August 12 o'cl. midd. We broke camp. The last bear-meat was cut into small pieces so that it might at least *look like* being a lot. Thickness of ice 1.2 m (3.96 ft). Scarcely an hour after breaking camp we got a new bear. It was an old worn-out male animal with rotten teeth. I brought it down by a shot in the chest at a distance of 38 m (125 ft) S-g and Fr-l both fired outers. Clear calm and hot the whole day but the country extraordinarily difficult. I do not think we made 2 km (2,200 yds) in 10 hours. Axe destroyed. 1 skua visible and 2 gulls circling around the body of the bear. We did not get into our berths before 2 a.m. the 3 Aug. I washed my face for the first time since the 11 July and in the evening I mended a stocking. We hope that one bear will be enticed to follow us by the remains of the one shot, and so on so that we shall always have fresh meat at our heels. This time we took from the one we shot the fillet too (close in to the back) and the kidneys (1½ kilo

– 3¼ lbs) and the tongue and ribs. The 3 Aug. at 12 o'cl. we rose after being much plagued by the heat in the tent. We have determined to 'lie outdoors' today ... It is so warm that we do the pulling without any coats on. The ice horrible. Clothes-drying on a large scale. I made a fork for Fraenkel.

5 *August* Stocktaking of provisions

Hard bread 11b. of 1.1 (2.4 lbs)	12.1 (20.4 lbs)
12 biscuits 12 bl of	15.5 (34.1 lbs)
+5 Mellin's food	15.00 (33 lbs)
Butter 17 b. of 900 (2 lbs)	15.30 (34 lbs)
Chocolate powder 9 b. of 1 (2.2 lbs) extr.	9.00 (20 lbs)
Milk 10 b. of 250 (½ lb)	2.5 (5 lbs)
Lact scr. 10 b. of	2.5 (5 lbs)
Pemmican	3.0 (6.5lbs)
Sugar	5.00 (11lbs)
1 tin Stauffer prep	4.5 (10 lbs)
Coffee	2.00 (4.5 lbs)
1 tin chocolate	
3 b. Lime-juice tablets	
Whortleberry jam	1.00 (2.2 lbs)
9 tins sardines	
3 tins paste	
Soup tablets 3½ tins	
2 bottles syrup	
1 bottle port-wine	
6 snowflake	
Flour	1.00 (2.2 lbs)

This stocktaking shows that we must be careful especially with the bread.

Temp. falling still lower and each degree makes us creep deeper down into the sleeping-sack. Bad day today the first with course N 40° W = Seven Islands.

9 August [. . .] At 7.30 o'cl. I saw a hummock formed in a lane which was at right angles to the direction of the wind which led to a pressure. The country consists of large uneven fields full of brown ice small hummocks with snow-sludge and water-pools but not many large sea-leads. It is extremely tiring. F. has diarrhoea for 2nd time and there does not seem much left of his moral strength. The sweet-water leads were often not so very 'sweet' to cross. A black guillemot visible. A fine beautiful bear approached us but fled before we had a chance to shoot. This was a great grief for us and a pity too for soon we shall have no more bear's meat left. S. and F. went after him but in vain. We were tired out and F. was ill. I gave him opium for the diarrhoea. Afterwards we had several hours' work getting S.'s gun in order. Its mechanism is dreadfully carelessly constructed. We have been awake and busy for 18 hours when at 8 o'cl. p.m. we creep down into the sleeping-sack. The course always S 40° W. The 10 at 6.10 o'cl. a.m. all up. Load on *my sledge*

1 little sack	3.5	(7.7 lbs)
1 front basket	37.1	81.7
1 rear basket	37.3	82.
1 private sack	15.5	34
1 medicine chest	9.00	20
1 tent	9.0	20
2 tentp	1.5	3.3
Meat	5.0	11
	117.9	259.7
1 gun	1.6	3.5
	119.5	263.2
1 b. ammunition . . .	6.5	14.3
	126.0 kilo	277.5 lbs
1 sext.	2.2	4.8
1 sack	6.0 photog.	13.2
	134.2	295.5

The ground extraordinarily difficult. Absolutely untrafficable sludge-pools encountered today. they consist of broad channels filled with small lumps of ice and snow? Neither sledge nor boat can be moved forward there. In consequence of the place-determination given above the course was altered to S 50° W (to the Seven Islands). It is remarkable that we have travelled so far in latitude in spite of the wind having been right against us for several days. In consequence of our having come below 82 we have today had a feast with sardines for dinner and a Stauffer-cake for supper. The going today has been good although the road is bad. We assume that we have gone 3 kilometers (1.8 mile) or possib. 2 minutes . . .

11 August was a regular Tycho Brahe-day [unlucky day]. At once in the morning I came into the water and so did my sledge so that nearly everything became wet through. S. ran in to F.'s sledge and broke the boat with the grapnel. All the sledges turned somersaults repeatedly during the course of the day. Mine was twice turned completely up and down. The going was good but the country terrible . . . A peculiar incident happened on crossing a lead. We stood quite at a loss what to do for the edges of the ice were wretched and the channel so shallow that the boat could not float. Our ordinary methods failed us alto-gether. Then while we were speaking the ice-floe broke beneath Fraenkel and so we obtained a bit of ice of considerable size and with the assistance of this piece we then made the crossing quite cleverly. We have not been able to keep the course but have been obliged to go both to the north and to the east but endeavour to go S 50° W. Our distance today probably did not exceed 3.5 km. (2.1 miles).

At 4.30 p.m. our longitude was 30° E. At midday our latitude was 81° 54′ 7. F. thought he saw land and it was really so like land that we changed the course in that direction but it was found to be merely a peculiarly shaped large hummock.

13 August 5 p.m. start ... Tried in vain to get a seal. The ice reasonably good. In a fissure found a little fish which was pretty unafraid and seemed to be astonished at sight of us. I killed him with the shovel ... Just when we had passed the fissure S-g cried 'three bears'. We were at once in motion and full of excited expectation. Warned by our preceding disappointments we now went to work carefully. We concealed ourselves behind a hummock and waited but no bears came. Then I chose myself as a bait and crept forward along the plain whistling softly. The she-bear became attentive, came forward winding me but turned round again and lay down. At last it was too cold for me to lie immovably in the snow and then I called out to the others that we should rush up to the bears. We did so. Then the she-bear came towards me but was met by a shot which missed. I sprang up however and shot again while the bears that were fleeing stopped for a moment, then the she-bear was wounded at a distance of 80 paces but ran a little way whereupon I dropped her on the spot at 94 paces. My 4th shot dropped one cub. Then the third one ran but was wounded by Fraenkel and dropped by Strindberg who had had a longer way to go and so could not come up as quickly as I. There was great joy in the caravan and we cut our bears in pieces with pleasure and loaded our sledges with not less than 42 kilogrammes (138 lbs) i.e., with fresh meat for 23 days. Among the experiences we made with regard to the value of the parts of the bear it may be mentioned that we found the heart, brain and kidneys very palatable. The tongue too is well worth taking. The meat on the ribs is excellent. In the evening I shot an ivory gull. The work of cutting up the bears, etc. gave us so much to do that we did not march much this day. The wind has now swung round to SE so that we hope to drift westwards. Today the weather has been extremely beautiful and that is a good thing for otherwise the work would have been ticklish. When a bear is hit he brings out a roar and tries to flee as quick as he can. We have been butchers the whole day.

22 August [. . .] The country today has been terrible and I repeat what I wrote yesterday that we have not previously had such a large district with ice so pressed. There can scarcely be found a couple of square metres (yards) of ice which does not present evident traces of pressure and the entire country consisting of a boundless field of large and small hummocks. One cannot speak of any regularity among them. The leads today have been broken to pieces and the floes small, but in general it has been easy to get across. Now they are so frozen that neither ferrying nor rafting can now be employed. Today a lead changed just when we had come across it (5 minutes later and it would have been impossible) and we had an opportunity of seeing a very powerful pressing. The floes came at a great speed and there was a creaking round about us. It made a strange and magnificent impression. The day has been extremely beautiful. Perhaps the most beautiful we have had. With a specially clear horizon we have again tried to catch sight of Gillis Land but it is impossible to get a glimpse of any part of it. Our course has been S 60° W as on the previous days and the day's march has probably brought us about 3 min. in the direction of our course. The clear air was utilized by S-g to take lunar distances. He saw haloes on the snow . . . Magnificent Venetian landscape with canals between lofty hummock edges on both sides, water-square with ice-fountain and stairs down to the canals. Divine. Bear-ham several days old exquisite. I massaged F.'s foot. He had been pulling so that his knee went out of joint but it slipped in again but he had no bad effects of it. S-g had a pain in one toe, cause still unknown.

29 August [. . .] The ice as before but the leads are still very extensive and broke so that they are very difficult to cross. It now begins to feel cold. We have seen a bear today but unfortunately he went off at a gallop when he saw that he was noticed. S.'s sledge badly broken and we could only just manage to mend it. We come slowly onwards and I imagine we shall have to make a late autumn journey to reach Mossel bay. The ice and the snow on it are becoming as hard as glass and it is difficult to pull the sledges across it. Today we have tried to go S 45° W as S.'s lunar observations showed that we were rather more to the westward than we had imagined. But to keep a tolerably steady course among the leads is on my word no easy task however. Tonight was the first time I thought of all the lovely things at home. S. and F. on the contrary have long spoken about it. The tent is now always covered with ice inside and the bottom, which is double, feels pretty hard when it is being rolled together. I sweep it clean morning and evening before and after the cooking.

30 August 5 o'cl. p.m. Start. The ice as before and the course too but this was hard to keep for the leads have been difficult to get across. Two Ross' gulls visible. At last we found ourselves on a floe from which we could not come without rafting. As we had not more than 20 min. left of our march-time we determined to pitch our tent and see if the ice possibly moved during the night. Scarcely had we erected the tent before S. cried out 'a bear on top of us'. A bear then stood 10 paces from him. I was lying inside the tent sweeping the floor and so could do nothing but F. who was outside caught hold of a gun and gave the bear a shot that made him turn, badly wounded. To save cartridges he was allowed to run a bit but at last he had to be finished off with 3 more shots. The bear however had managed to get down into a broad lead and rolled himself about there but he could not swim far. I threw a grapnel past him and brought him in to the edge of the ice. This however was so thin that we hardly dared to stand on it but at last I succeeded in putting a noose around his neck and one around a foreleg. S. prised with a boat-hook and so we hauled him up on to the ice pretty easily. The situation was photographed and the bear was cut up. Once more we have 30 kilo (66 lbs) of meat, i.e. meat for 14 days if we calculate 0.9 kilo (2 lbs) each morning and evening and 300 (11 oz) for dinner. These quantities are carried next to the body so as not to be frozen. Two Ross' gulls visible.

31 August [. . .] The sun touched the horizon at midnight. The landscape on fire. The snow a sea of fire. The country fairly good. We could for the first time over broad new ice. First I crept across on all fours to test if it would hold. Then we went across in several places. One ferrying had to be made. The leads were passable but the ice was in lovely movement. It is fine to work the sledges onward through the middle of the crashing ice-pressures round about us. Sometimes a lead closes just when we need it, sometimes it opens suddenly the moment before or after a crossing. I had diarrhoea badly perhaps in consequence of a chill. F.'s sledge badly broken and had to be repaired on the spot. In the evening I took both morphine and opium . . .

3 September [. . .] Today we found ourselves surrounded by broad water-channels of great extent and found ourselves obliged to trust ourselves entirely to the boat. We succeeded in loading everything on it and then rowed for 3 hours at a pretty good pace towards the Seven Islands (our goal). It was with a rather solemn feeling when at 1h 50 o'cl. p.m. we began this new way of travelling gliding slowly over the mirror-like surface of the water between large ice-floes loaded with giant-like hummocks. Only the shriek of ivory gulls and the splashing of the seals when they dived and the short orders of the steersman broke the silence. We knew that we were moving onwards more quickly than usual and at every turn of the leads we asked ourselves in silence if we might not possibly journey on in this glorious way to the end. We called it glorious for the everlasting hauling of the sledges had become tiring I fancy the last few days and it would be a great relief for us to travel some days in another way. But at 5 o'cl. our joy came to an end; we then entered a bay in the ice which immediately afterwards was closed by a floe so that we could go neither onwards nor backwards. We were satisfied however for things had gone well, the boat was excellent and there was room for all our luggage.

9 September [. . .] Our meat supply is beginning to come to an end and we shoot two ivory gulls to supplement it. We do not like to shoot unless we can get at least two ivory gulls at one shot. They are delicate birds but I think they cost a lot of ammunition. For the last few days F. has had a pain in his left foot. I give him massage morning and evening and rub on liniment. Today (the 9 in p.m.) I have opened a large pus-blister washed it with sublimate solution and put on a bandage. Now I hope it will heal for it is hard for us to be without F.'s full strength. This is more than needful with our trying work. Our attacks of diarrhoea seem to have stopped. Yesterday I had a motion for the first time for at least 4 days but in spite of that did not notice any diarrhoea. The amount of the excretion was moderate and of normal consistence. F. has frequent motions and the consistence seems to be rather fluid but he does not complain of pains in the stomach and of diarrhoea as he has done almost constantly before . . .

Just now I had to leave off writing in order to fire a shot and drop two ivory gulls. Such birds always gather around our camp. Oh if we could shoot a seal or a bear just now. We need it so much . . . 6 o'cl.

F.'s foot is now so bad that he cannot pull his sledge but can only help by pushing. S. and I take it in turns to go back and bring up F.'s sledge. This tries our strength. We could not manage more than 6 hours' march especially as the country was extremely difficult. Just when we stopped I happened to fall into the water, for an ice-floe which to all appearance and on being tested with the boat-hook seemed to be solid and on which I jumped down proved to consist of nothing but a hard mass of ice-sludge which went to pieces when I landed on it. I flung myself on my back and floated thus until the others reached me a couple of oars with the help of which I crawled up again . . .

17 September Since I wrote last in my diary much has changed in truth. We laboured onwards with the sledges in the ordinary way but found at last that the new-fallen snow's and character did not allow us to continue quickly enough. F.'s foot which still did not allow him to pull compelled me and S. to go back in turns and pull forward F.'s sledge too. One of S.'s feet was also a little out of order. Our meat was almost at an end and the crossings between the floes became more and more difficult in consequence of the ice-sludge. But above all we found that the current and the wind irresistibly carried us down into the jaws between North East Land and Frans Joseph's Land and that we had not the least chance to reach North East Land. It was during the 12th and 13th Sept. when we were obliged to lie still on account of violent NW wind that we at last discovered the necessity of submitting to the inevitable, i.e. and wintering on the ice . . .

Our first resolution was to work our way across to a neighbouring ice-floe which was bigger and stronger and richer in ice-humps than that on which we were, which was low and small and full of saltwater pools, showing that it was composed of small pieces which would probably easily separate in the spring. We came to the new floe by rafting with the boat and soon found a suitable building-plot consisting of a large piece of ice which we hollowed out to some extent. The sides and the parts that were missing we supplied by filling up with blocks of ice and snow over which we threw water and thus made solid and durable. On the 15th we at last succeeded in getting a seal, as I had the luck to put a ball right through its head so that it was killed on the spot and could easily be brought 'ashore'.

Every part of the seal tastes very nice (fried). We are especially fond of the meat and the blubber. May we but shoot some score of seals so that we can save ourselves. The bears seem to have disappeared and of other game there are visible only ivory gulls, which, it is true, are not to be despised, but which cost too much ammunition. The ivory gulls come and sit on the roof of the tent. Remarkably enough the fulmars seem to have disappeared and of other birds only a little auk or possibly a young black guillemot have been visible during the last few days. F.'s foot is better now but will hardly be well before a couple of weeks. S.'s feet are also bad. I have made in order a landing-net to catch plankton or anything else that can be found in the water we shall see how it succeeds; a fortunate result of the attempt may I think somewhat improve our difficult position. Our humour is pretty good although joking and smiling are not of ordinary occurrence. My young comrades hold out better than I had ventured to hope. The fact that during the last few days we have drifted towards the south at such a rate contributed essentially I think to keeping up our courage. Our latitude on the 12 Sept. was 81° 21' and on the 15th we had drifted with a strong NW wind down to 80° 45'. Longitude in the latter case is I am certain considerably more easterly. Thus our drift in 72 hours amounts to about ⅔ of a degree of latitude and since then the wind has blown fresh from the same or a more northerly direction. Possibly we may be able to drive far southwards quickly enough and obtain our nourishment from the sea. Perhaps too it will not be so cold on the sea as on the land. He who lives will see. Now it is time to work. The day has been a remarkable one for us by our having seen land today for the first time since 11 July. It is undoubtedly New Iceland that we have had before our eyes . . .

There is no question of our attempting to go on shore for the entire island seems to be one single block of ice with a glacier border. It appears however not to be absolutely inaccessible on the east and west points. We saw a bear under the land and in the water I saw a couple of flocks (of 4) of those 'black guillemot youngsters'. I think a couple of little auks were also visible. The ivory gulls are seen half a score together. On the other hand the water seems to be poor in small animals for dragging gave no result (landing-net). A seal was seen but it was much terrified. We have seen no walrus. Our arrival at New Iceland is remarkable because it points to a colossal drift viz. of more than 1 degree of latitude since 12 Sept. If we drift in this way some weeks more perhaps we may save ourselves on one of the islands east of Spitzbergen. It makes us feel anxious that we have not more game within shooting-distance. Our provisions must soon and richly be supplemented if we are to have any prospect of being able to hold out for a time.

19 September [. . .] Today S. has been very busy house-building in accordance with a method he has invented. This consists of snow and fresh water being mixed after which the entire mass is built up into a wall and allowed to freeze. The work is both solid and neat. In a couple of days we shall probably have the baking-oven (i.e., the sleeping room) ready . . . The thickness of the ice of our floe at 'the great cargo-quay' has been measured and found to be 1.4–1.3–1.5m (4.6–4.3–4.95 ft) . . .

23 September Today all three of us have been working busily on the hut cementing together ice-blocks. We have got on very well and the hut now begins to take form a little. After a couple more days of such weather and work it should not take long until we are able to move in. We can probably carry our supplies in there the day after tomorrow. This is very necessary, as mortar we employ snow mixed with water and of this mass, which is handled by S. with great skill he is also making a vaulted roof over the last parts between the walls. We have now a very good arrangement of the day with 8 hours' work beginning with 2½ hours' work, thereupon breakfast ¾ and afterwards work until 4.45 o'cl. when we dine and take supper in one meal. We have now also tried the meat of the great seal and have found that it tastes excellent. One of the very best improvements in the cooking is that of adding blood to the sauce for the steak. This makes it thick and it tastes as if we had bread. I cannot believe but that blood contains much carbohydrate, for our craving for bread is considerably less since we began to use blood in the food. We all think so. We have also found everything eatable both as regards bear, great seal, seal and ivory gull (bear-liver of course excepted). For want of time we have not yet been able to cut up and weigh our animal but I think we now have meat and ham until on in the spring. We must however shoot more so as to be able to have larger rations and to get more fuel and light.

29 September [. . .] Our floe is diminished in a somewhat alarming degree close to our hut. The ice pressings bring the shores closer and closer to us. But we have a large and old hummock between the hut and the shore and hope that this will stop the pressure. This sounds magnificent when there is pressure but otherwise it does not appeal to us.

Thickn. of ice 1.1–1.2–1.5–1.9 (3.6–3.9–4.95–6.27 ft) have been measured by a new fissure which has arisen in our floe. Yesterday evening the 28 we moved into our hut which was christened 'the home'. We lay there last night and found it rather nice. But it will become much better of course. We must have the meat inside to protect ourselves against the bears. The ice in N.I. glacier is evidently stratified in a horizontal direction. The day before yesterday it rained a great part of the day which I suppose ought to be considered extremely remarkable at this time of the year and in this degree of latitude.

1 October [. . .] The 1 Oct. was a good day. The evening was as divinely beautiful as one could wish. The water was allied with small animals and a bevy of 7 black-white 'guillemots youngsters' were swimming there. A couple of seals were seen too. The work with the hut went on well and we thought that we should have the outside ready by the 2nd. But then something else happened. At 5.30 o'cl. (local time) in the morning of the 2nd we heard a crash and thunder and water streamed into the hut and when rushed out we found that our large beautiful floe had been splintered into a number of little floes and that one fissure had divided the floe just outside the wall of the hut. The floe that remained to us had a diam. of only 24 metre (80 ft) and one wall of the hut might be said rather to hang from the roof than to support it. This was a great alteration in our position and our prospects. The hut and the floe could not give us shelter and still we were obliged to stay there for the present at least. We were frivolous enough to lie in the hut the following night too. Perhaps it was because the day was rather tiring. Our belongings were scattered among several blocks and these were driving here and there so that we had to hurry. Two bear-bodies, representing provisions for 3–4 months were lying on a separate floe and so on. Luckily the weather was beautiful so that we could work in haste. No one had lost courage; with such comrades one should be able to manage under, I may say, any circumstances.

The loss of the ice-hut proved a catastrophe that the trio were unable to recover from. Although they landed on White Island on 5 October, they expired several days later, probably from hypothermia.

88° SOUTH

SIR ERNEST SHACKLETON
(1874–1922)

Irish-born explorer. In 1908 he led a British attempt on the Pole, 90° South.

29 December Yesterday I wrote that we hoped to do fifteen miles today, but such is the variable character of this surface that one cannot prophesy with any certainty an hour ahead. A strong southerly wind, with from 44° to 49° of frost, combined with the effect of short rations, made our distance 12 miles 600 yards instead. We have reached an altitude of 10,310 ft, and an uphill gradient gave us one of the most severe pulls for ten hours that would be possible. It looks serious, for we must increase the food if we are to get on at all, and we must risk a depot at seventy miles off the Pole and dash for it then. Our sledge is badly strained, and on the abominably bad surface of soft snow is dreadfully hard to move. I have been suffering from a bad headache all day, and Adams also was worried by the cold. I think that these headaches are a form of mountain sickness, due to our high altitude. The others have bled from the nose, and that must relieve them. Physical effort is always trying at a high altitude, and we are straining at the harness all day, sometimes slipping in the soft snow that overlies the hard sastrugi. My head is very bad. The sensation is as though the nerves were being twisted up with a corkscrew and then pulled out. Marshall took our temperature tonight, and we are all at about 94°, but in spite of this we are getting south. We are only 198 miles off our goal now. If the rise would stop the cold would not matter, but it is hard to know what is man's limit. We have only 150 lb per man to pull, but it is more severe work than the 250 lb per man up the glacier was. The Pole is hard to get.

30 December We only did 4 miles 100 yards today. We started at 7 a.m., but had to camp at 11 a.m., a blizzard springing up from the south. It is more than annoying. I cannot express my feelings. We were pulling at last on a level surface, but very soft snow, when at about 10 a.m. the south wind and drift commenced to increase, and at 11 a.m. it was so bad that we had to camp. And here all day we have been lying in our sleeping-bags trying to keep warm and listening to the threshing drift on the tent-side. I am in the cooking-tent, and the wind comes through, it is so thin. Our precious food is going and the time also, and it is so important to us to get on. We lie here and think of how to make things better, but we cannot reduce food now, and the only thing will be to rush all possible at the end. We will do and are doing all humanly possible. It is with Providence to help us.

31 December The last day of the old year, and the hardest day we have had almost, pushing through soft snow uphill with a strong head wind and drift all day. The temperature is minus 7° Fahr., and our altitude is 10,477 ft above sea-level. The altitude is trying. My head has been very bad all day, and we are all feeling the short food, but still we are getting south. We are in latitude 86° 54′ South tonight, but we have only three weeks' food and two weeks' biscuit to do nearly 500 geographical miles. We can only do our best. Too tired to write more tonight. We all get iced-up about our faces, and are on the verge of frostbite all the time. Please God the weather will be fine during the next fourteen days. Then all will be well. The distance today was eleven miles.

NOTE If we had only known that we were going to get such cold weather as we were at this time experiencing, we would have kept a pair of scissors to trim our beards. The moisture from the condensation of one's breath accumulated on the beard and trickled down on to the Burberry blouse. Then it froze into a sheet of ice inside, and it became very painful to pull the Burberry off in camp. Little troubles of this sort would have seemed less serious to us if we had been able to get a decent feed at the end of the day's work, but we were very hungry. We thought of food most of the time. The chocolate certainly seemed better than the cheese, because the two spoonfuls of cheese per man allowed under our scale of diet would not last as long as the two sticks of chocolate. We did not have both at the same meal. We had the bad luck at this time to strike a tin in which the biscuits were thin and overbaked. Under ordinary circumstances they would probably have tasted rather better than the other biscuits, but we wanted bulk. We soaked them in our tea so that they would swell up and appear larger, but if one soaked a biscuit too much, the sensation of biting something was lost, and the food seemed to disappear much too easily.

1 January 1909 Head too bad to write much. We did 11 miles 900 yards (statute) today, and the latitude at 6 p.m. was 87° 6½' South, so we have beaten North and South records. Struggling uphill all day in very soft snow. Everyone done up and weak from want of food. When we camped at 6 p.m. fine warm weather, thank God. Only 172½ miles from the Pole. The height above sea-level, now 10,755 ft, makes all work difficult. Surface seems to be better ahead. I do trust it will be so tomorrow.

2 January Terribly hard work today. We started at 6.45 a.m. with a fairly good surface, which soon became very soft. We were sinking in over our ankles, and our broken sledge, by running sideways, added to the drag. We have been going uphill all day, and tonight are 11,034 ft above sea-level. It has taken us all day to do 10 miles 450 yards, though the weights are fairly light. A cold wind, with a temperature of minus 14° Fahr., goes right through us now, as we are weakening from want of food, and the high altitude makes every movement an effort, especially if we stumble on the march. My head is giving me trouble all the time. Wild seems the most fit of us. God knows we are doing all we can, but the outlook is serious if this surface continues and the plateau gets higher, for we are not travelling fast enough to make our food spin out and get back to our depot in time. I cannot think of failure yet. I must look at the matter sensibly and consider the lives of those who are with me. I feel that if we go on too far it will be impossible to get back over this surface, and then all the results will be lost to the world. We can now definitely locate the South Pole on the highest plateau in the world, and our geological work and meteorology will be of the greatest use to science; but all this is not the Pole. Man can only do his best, and we have arrayed against us the strongest forces of nature. This cutting south wind with drift plays the mischief with us, and after ten hours of struggling against it one pannikin of food with two biscuits and a cup of cocoa does not warm one up much. I must think over the situation carefully tomorrow, for time is going on and food is going also.

3 January Started at 6.55 a.m., cloudy but fairly warm. The temperature was minus 8° Fahr. at noon. We had a terrible surface all the morning, and did only 5 miles 100 yards. A meridian altitude gave us latitude 87° 22′ South at noon. The surface was better in the afternoon, and we did six geographical miles. The temperature at 6 p.m. was minus 11° Fahr. It was an uphill pull towards the evening, and we camped at 6.20 p.m., the altitude being 11,220 ft above the sea. Tomorrow we must risk making a depot on the plateau, and make a dash for it, but even then, if this surface continues, we will be two weeks in carrying it through.

4 January The end is in sight. We can only go for three more days at the most, for we are weakening rapidly. Short food and a blizzard wind from the south, with driving drift, at a temperature of

47° of frost, have plainly told us today that we are reaching our limit, for we were so done up at noon with cold that the clinical thermometer failed to register the temperature of three of us at 94°. We started at 7.40 a.m., leaving a depot on this great wide plateau, a risk that only this case justified, and one that my comrades agreed to, as they have to every one so far, with the same cheerfulness and regardlessness of self that have been the means of our getting as far as we have done so far. Pathetically small looked the bamboo, one of the tent poles, with a bit of bag sewn on as a flag, to mark our stock of provisions, which has to take us back to our depot, one hundred and fifty miles north. We lost sight of it in half an hour, and are now trusting to our footprints in the snow to guide us back to each bamboo until we pick up the depot again. I trust that the weather will keep clear. Today we have done 12½ geographical miles, and with only 70 lb per man to pull it is as hard, even harder, work than the 100 odd lb was yesterday, and far harder than the 250 lb. were three weeks ago, when we were climbing the glacier. This, I consider, is a clear indication of our failing strength. The main thing against us is the altitude of 11,200 ft and the biting wind. Our faces are cut, and our feet and hands are always on the verge of frostbite. Our fingers, indeed, often go, but we get them round more or less. I have great trouble with two fingers on my left hand. They had been badly jammed when we were getting the motor up over the ice face at winter quarters, and the circulation is not good. Our boots now are pretty well worn out, and we have to halt at times to pick the snow out of the soles. Our stock of sennegrass is nearly exhausted, so we have to use the same frozen stuff day after day. Another trouble is that the lamp-wick with which we tie the finnesko is chafed through, and we have to tie knots in it. These knots catch the snow under our feet, making a lump that has to be cleared every now and then. I am of the opinion that to sledge even in the height of summer on this plateau, we should have at least forty ounces of food a day per man, and we are on short rations of the ordinary allowance of thirty-two ounces. We depoted our extra underclothing to save weight about three weeks ago, and are now in the same clothes night and day. One suit of underclothing, shirt and guernsey, and our thin Burberries, now all patched. When we get up in the morning, out of the wet bag, our Burberries become like a coat of mail at once, and our heads and beards get iced-up with the moisture when breathing on the march. There is half a gale blowing dead in our teeth all the time. We hope to reach within 100 geographical miles of the Pole; under the circumstances we can expect to do very little more. I am confident that the Pole lies on the great plateau we have discovered, miles and miles from any outstanding land. The temperature tonight is minus 24° Fahr.

5 January Today head wind and drift again, with 50° of frost, and a terrible surface. We have been marching through 8 in of snow, covering sharp sastrugi, which plays havoc with our feet, but we have done 13⅓ geographical miles, for we increased our food, seeing that it was absolutely necessary to do this to enable us to accomplish anything. I realise that the food we have been having has not been sufficient to keep up our strength, let alone supply the wastage caused by exertion, and now we must try to keep warmth in us, though our strength is being used up. Our temperatures at 5 a.m. were 94° Fahr. We got away at 7 a.m. sharp and marched till noon, then from 1 p.m. sharp till 6 p.m. All being in one tent makes our campwork slower, for we are so cramped for room, and we get up at 4.40 a.m. so as to get away by 7 a.m. Two of us have to stand outside the tent at night until things are squared up inside, and we find it cold work. Hunger grips us hard, and the food supply is very small. My head still gives me great trouble. I began by wishing that my worst enemy had it instead of myself, but now I don't wish even my worst enemy to have such a headache; still, it is no use talking about it. Self is a subject that most of us are fluent on. We find the utmost difficulty in carrying through the day, and we can only go for two or three more days. Never once had the temperature been above zero since we got on to the plateau, though this is the height of summer. We have done our best, and we thank God for having allowed us to get so far.

6 January This must be our last outward march with the sledge and camp equipment. Tomorrow we must leave camp with some food, and push as far south as possible, and then plant the flag. Today's story is 57° of frost, with a strong blizzard and high drift; yet we marched 13 geographical miles through soft snow, being helped by extra food. This does not mean full rations, but a bigger ration than we have been having lately. The pony maize is all finished. The most trying day we have yet spent, our fingers and faces being frost-bitten continually. Tomorrow we will rush south with the flag. We are at 88°7′ South tonight. It is our last outward march. Blowing hard tonight. I would fail to explain my feelings if I tried to write them down, now that the end has come. There is only one thing that lightens the disappointment, and that is the feeling that we have done all we could. It is the forces of nature that have prevented us from going right through. I cannot write more.

7 January A blinding, shrieking blizzard all day, with the temperature ranging from 60° to 70° of frost. It has been impossible to leave the tent, which is snowed up on the lee side. We have been lying in our bags all day, only warm at food time, with fine snow making through the walls of the worn tent and covering our bags. We are greatly cramped. Adams is suffering from cramp every now and then. We are eating our valuable food without marching. The wind has been blowing eighty to ninety miles an hour. We can hardly sleep. Tomorrow I trust this will be over. Directly the wind drops we march as far south as possible, then plant the flag, and turn homeward. Our chief anxiety is lest our tracks may drift up, for to them we must trust mainly to find our depot; we have no land bearings in this great plain of snow. It is a serious risk that we have taken, but we had to play the game to the utmost, and Providence will look after us.

8 January Again all day in our bags, suffering considerably physically from cold hands and feet, and from hunger, but more mentally, for we cannot get on south, and we simply lie here shivering. Every now and then one of our party's feet go, and the unfortunate beggar has to take his leg out of the sleeping-bag and have his frozen foot nursed into life again by placing it inside the shirt, against the skin of his almost equally unfortunate neighbour. We must do something more to the south, even though the food is going, and we weaken lying in the cold, for with 72° of frost the wind cuts through our thin tent, and even the drift is finding its way in and on to our bags, which are wet enough as it is. Cramp is not uncommon every now and then, and the drift all round the tent has made it so small that there is hardly room for us at all. The wind has been blowing hard all day; some of the gusts must be over seventy or eighty miles an hour. This evening it seems as though it were going to ease down, and directly it does we shall be up and away south for a rush. I feel that this march must be our limit. We are so short of food, and at this high altitude, 11,600 ft, it is hard to keep any warmth in our bodies between the scanty meals. We have nothing to read now, having depoted our little books to save weight, and it is dreary work lying in the tent with nothing to read and too cold to write much in the diary.

9 January Our last day outwards. We have shot our bolt, and the tale is latitude 88° 23' South, longitude 162° East. The wind eased down at 1 a.m., and at 2 a.m. we were up and had breakfast. At 4 a.m. started south, with the Queen's Union Jack, a brass cylinder containing stamps and documents to place at the furthest south point, camera, glasses, and compass. At 9 a.m. we were in 88° 23' South, half running and half walking over a surface much hardened by the recent blizzard. It was strange for us to go along without the nightmare of a sledge dragging behind us. We hoisted Her Majesty's flag and the other Union Jack afterwards, and took possession of the plateau in the name of His Majesty. While the Union Jack blew out stiffly in the icy gale that cut us to the bone, we looked south with our powerful glasses, but could see nothing but the dead white snow plain. There was no break in the plateau as it extended towards the Pole, and we feel sure that the goal we have failed to reach lies on this plain. We stayed only a few minutes, and then, taking the Queen's flag and eating our scanty meal as we went, we hurried back and reached our camp about 3 p.m. We were so dead tired that we only did two hours' march in the afternoon and camped at 5.30 p.m. The temperature was minus 19° Fahr. Fortunately for us, our tracks were not obliterated by the blizzard; indeed, they stood up, making a trail easily followed. Homeward bound at last. Whatever regrets may be, we have done our best.

Four years later, Shackleton returned to Antarctica and led an epic of survival when his boat Endurance *was crushed in the ice (see pp. 175–194).*

THE MARCH TO FORT ENTERPRISE

SIR JOHN FRANKLIN
(1786–1847)

After a career in the Royal Navy, in which he fought with Nelson at Trafalgar, Franklin turned to Arctic exploration, and died searching for the elusive Northwest Passage. On a previous expedition along Canada's Arctic coast in 1821, Franklin and his team made one of the most dramatic survival marches in history.

25 October In the afternoon we had a heavy fall of snow, which continued all night. A small quantity of *tripe de roche* (lichen) was gathered; and Crédit, who had been hunting, brought in the antlers and backbone of a deer which had been killed in the summer. The wolves and birds of prey had picked them clean, but there still remained a quantity of the spinal marrow which they had not been able to extract. This, although putrid, was esteemed a valuable prize, and the spine being divided into portions, was distributed equally. After eating the marrow, which was so acrid as to excoriate the lips, we rendered the bones friable by burning, and ate them also.

On the following morning the ground was covered with snow to the depth of a foot and a half, and the weather was very stormy. These circumstances rendered the men again extremely despondent: a settled gloom hung over their countenances, and they refused to pick *tripe de roche*, choosing rather to go entirely without eating than to make any exertion. The party which went for gum returned early in the morning without having found any; but St Germain said he could still make the canoe with the willows, covered with canvas, and removed with Adam to a clump of willows for that purpose. Mr Back accompanied them to stimulate his exertion, as we feared the lowness of his spirits would cause him to be slow in his operations. Augustus went to fish at the rapid, but a large trout having carried away his bait, we had nothing to replace it . . .

The sensation of hunger was no longer felt by any of us, yet we were scarcely able to converse upon any other subject than the pleasures of eating. We were much indebted to Hepburn at this crisis. The officers were unable from weakness to gather *tripe de roche* themselves, and Samandré, who had acted as our cook on the journey from the coast, sharing in the despair of the rest of the Canadians, refused to make the slightest exertion. Hepburn, on the contrary, animated by a firm reliance on the beneficence of the Supreme Being, tempered with resignation to his will, was indefatigable in his exertions to serve us, and daily collected all the *tripe de roche* that was used in the officers' mess. Mr Hood could not partake of this miserable fare, and a partridge which had been reserved for him was, I lament to say, this day stolen by one of the men . . .

About noon Samandré coming up, informed us that Crédit and Vaillant could advance no further. Some willows being discovered in a valley near us, I proposed to halt the party there, whilst Dr Richardson went back to visit them. I hoped too, that when the sufferers received the information of a fire being kindled at so short a distance they would be cheered, and use their utmost efforts to reach it, but this proved a vain hope. The Doctor found Vaillant about a mile and a half in the rear, much exhausted with cold and fatigue. Having encouraged him to advance to the fire, after repeated solicitations he made the attempt, but fell down amongst the deep snow at every step. Leaving him in this situation, the Doctor went about half a mile farther back, to the spot where Crédit was said to have halted, and the track being nearly obliterated by the snow drift, it became unsafe for him to go further. Returning he passed Vaillant, who having moved only a few yards in his absence, had fallen down, was unable to rise, and could scarcely answer his questions. Being unable to afford him any effectual assistance, he hastened on to inform us of his situation. When J. B. Belanger had heard the melancholy account, he went immediately to aid Vaillant, and bring up his burden. Respecting Crédit, we were informed by Samandré, that he had stopped a short distance behind Vaillant, but that his intention was to return to the encampment of the preceding evening.

When Belanger came back with Vaillant's load, he informed us that he had found him lying on his back, benumbed with cold, and incapable of being roused. The stoutest men of the party were now earnestly entreated to bring him to the fire, but they declared themselves unequal to the task; and, on the contrary, urged me to allow them to throw down their loads, and proceed to Fort Enterprise with the utmost speed. A compliance with their desire would have caused the loss of the whole party, for the men were totally ignorant of the course to be pursued, and none of the officers, who could have directed the march, were sufficiently strong to keep up at the pace they would then walk; besides, even supposing them to have found their way, the strongest men would certainly have deserted the weak. Something, however, was absolutely necessary to be done, to relieve them as much as possible from their burdens, and the officers consulted on the subject. Mr Hood and Dr Richardson proposed to remain behind, with a single attendant, at the first place where sufficient wood and *tripe de roche* should be found for ten days' consumption; and that I should proceed as expeditiously as possible with the men to the house, and thence send them immediate relief. They strongly urged that this arrangement would contribute to the safety of the rest of the party, by relieving them from the burden of a tent, and several other articles; and that they might afford aid to Crédit, if he should unexpectedly come up. I was distressed beyond description at the thought of leaving them in such a dangerous situation, and for a long time combated their proposal; but they strenuously urged, that this step afforded the only chance of safety for the party, and I reluctantly acceded to it. The ammunition, of which we had a small barrel, was also to be left with them, and it was hoped that this deposit would be a strong inducement for the Indians to venture across the barren grounds to their aid. We communicated this resolution to the men, who were cheered at the slightest prospect of alleviation to their present miseries, and promised with great appearance of earnestness to return to those officers, upon the first supply of food.

The party then moved on; Vaillant's blanket and other necessaries were left in the track, at the request of the Canadians, without any hope, however, of his being able to reach them. After marching till dusk without seeing a favourable place for encamping, night compelled us to take shelter under the lee of a hill, amongst some willows, with which, after many attempts, we at length made a fire. It was not sufficient, however, to warm the whole party, much less to thaw our shoes; and the weather not permitting the gathering of *tripe de roche*, we had nothing to cook. The painful retrospection of the melancholy events of the day banished sleep, and we shuddered as we contemplated the dreadful effects of this bitterly cold night on our two companions, if still living. Some faint hopes were entertained of Crédit's surviving the storm, as he was provided with a good blanket, and had leather to eat.

The weather was mild next morning. We left the encampment at nine, and a little before noon came to a pretty extensive thicket of small willows, near which there appeared a supply of *tripe de roche* on the face of the rocks. At this place Dr Richardson and Mr Hood determined to remain, with John Hepburn, who volunteered to stop with them. The tent was securely pitched, a few willows collected, and the ammunition and all other articles were deposited, except each man's clothing, one tent, a sufficiency of ammunition for the journey, and the officers' journals. I had only one blanket, which was carried for me, and two pair of shoes. The offer was now made for any of the men, who felt themselves too weak to proceed, to remain with the officers, but none of them accepted it. Michel alone felt some inclination to do so. After we had united in thanksgiving and prayers to Almighty God, I separated from my companions, deeply afflicted that a train of melancholy circumstances should have demanded of me the severe trial of parting, in such a condition, from friends who had become endeared to me by their constant kindness and co-operation, and a participation of numerous sufferings. This trial I could not have been induced to undergo, but for the reasons they had so strongly urged the day before, to which my own judgement assented, and for the sanguine hope I felt of either finding a supply of provision at Fort Enterprise, or meeting the Indians in the immediate vicinity of that place, according to my arrangements with Mr Wentzel and Akaitcho. Previously to our starting, Peltier and Benoit repeated their promises, to return to them with provision, if any should be found at the house, or to guide the Indians to them, if any were met.

Greatly as Mr Hood was exhausted, and indeed, incapable as he must have proved, of encountering the fatigue of our very next day's journey, so that I felt his resolution to be prudent, I was sensible that his determination to remain was chiefly prompted by the disinterested and generous wish to remove impediments to the progress of the rest. Dr Richardson and Hepburn, who were both in a state of strength to keep pace with the men, besides this motive which they shared with him, were influenced in their resolution to remain, the former by the desire which had distinguished his character, throughout the Expedition, of devoting himself to the succour of the weak, and the latter by the zealous attachment he had ever shown towards his officers.

We set out without waiting to take any of the *tripe de roche*, and walking at a tolerable pace, in an hour arrived at a fine group of pines, about a mile and a quarter from the tent. We sincerely regretted not having seen these before we separated from our companions, as they would have been better supplied with fuel here, and there appeared to be more *tripe de roche* than where we had left them.

Descending afterwards into a more level country, we found the snow very deep, and the labour of wading through it so fatigued the whole party, that we were compelled to encamp, after a march of four miles and a half. Belanger and Michel were left far behind, and when they arrived at the encampment appeared quite exhausted. The former, bursting into tears, declared his inability to proceed, and begged me to let him go back next morning to the tent, and shortly afterwards Michel made the same request. I was in hopes they might recover a little strength by the night's rest, and therefore deferred giving any permission *until* morning. The sudden failure in the strength of these men cast a gloom over the rest, which I tried in vain to remove, by repeated assurances that the distance to Fort Enterprise was short, and that we should, in all probability, reach it in four days. Not being able to find any *tripe de roche*, we drank an infusion of the Labrador tea plant (*ledum palustre*), and ate a few morsels of burnt leather for supper. We were unable to raise the tent, and found its weight too great to carry it on, we, therefore, cut it up, and took a part of the canvass for a cover. The night was bitterly cold, and though we lay as close to each other as possible, having no shelter, we could not keep ourselves sufficiently warm to sleep. A strong gale came on after midnight, which increased the severity of the weather. In the morning Belanger and Michel renewed their request to be permitted to go back to the tent, assuring me they were still weaker than on the preceding evening, and less capable of going forward; and they urged, that the stopping at a place where there was a supply of *tripe de roche* was their only chance of preserving life; under these circumstances, I could not do otherwise than yield to their desire. I wrote a note to Dr Richardson and Mr Hood, informing them of the pines we had passed, and recommending their removing thither. Having found that Michel was carrying a considerable quantity of ammunition, I desired him to divide it among my party, leaving him only ten balls and a little shot, to kill any animals he might meet on his way to the tent. This man was very particular in his inquiries respecting the direction of the house, and the course we meant to pursue; he also said, that if he should be able, he would go and search for Vaillant and Crédit; and he requested my permission to take Vaillant's blanket, if he should find it, to which I agreed, and mentioned it in my notes to the officers.

Scarcely were these arrangements finished, before Perrault and Fontano were seized with a fit of dizziness, and betrayed other symptoms of extreme debility. Some tea was quickly prepared for them, and after drinking it, and eating a few morsels of burnt leather, they recovered, and expressed their desire to go forward; but the other men, alarmed at what they had just witnessed, became doubtful of their own strength, and, giving way to absolute dejection, declared their inability to move. I now earnestly pressed upon them the necessity of continuing our journey, as the only means of saving their own lives, as well as those of our friends at the tent; and, after much entreaty, got them to set out at ten a.m.: Belanger and Michel were left at the encampment, and proposed to start shortly afterwards. By the time we had gone about two hundred yards, Perrault became again dizzy, and desired us to halt, which we did, until he, recovering, offered to march on. Ten minutes more had hardly elapsed before he again desired us to stop, and, bursting into tears, declared he was totally exhausted, and unable to accompany us further. As the encampment was not more than a quarter of a mile distant, we recommended that he should return to it, and rejoin Belanger and Michel, whom we knew to be still there, from perceiving the smoke of a fresh fire; and because they had not made any preparation for starting when we quitted them. He readily acquiesced in the proposition, and having taken a friendly leave of each of us, and enjoined us to make all the haste we could in sending relief, he turned back, keeping his gun and ammunition. We watched him until he was nearly at the fire, and then proceeded. During these detentions, Augustus becoming impatient of the delay had walked on, and we lost sight of him. The labour we experienced in wading through the deep snow induced us to cross a moderate-sized lake, which lay in our track, but we found this operation far more harassing. As the surface of the ice was perfectly smooth, we slipped at almost every step, and were frequently blown down by the wind, with such force as to shake our whole frames.

Poor Fontano was completely exhausted by the labour of this traverse, and we made a halt until his strength was recruited, by which time the party was benumbed with cold. Proceeding again, he got on tolerably well for a little time; but being again seized with faintness and dizziness, he fell often, and at length exclaimed that he could go no further. We immediately stopped, and endeavoured to encourage him to persevere, until we should find some willows to encamp; he insisted, however, that he could not march any longer through this deep snow; and said, that if he should even reach our encampment this evening, he must be left there, provided *tripe de roche* could not be procured to recruit his strength. The poor man was overwhelmed with grief, and seemed desirous to remain at that spot. We were about two miles from the place where the other men had been left, and as the track to it was beaten, we proposed to him to return thither, as we thought it probable he would find the men still there; at any rate, he would be able to get fuel to keep him warm during the night; and, on the next day, he could follow their track to the officer's tent; and, should the path be covered by the snow, the pines we had passed yesterday would guide him, as they were yet in view.

I cannot describe my anguish on the occasion of separating from another companion under circumstances so distressing. There was, however, no alternative. The extreme debility of the rest of the party put the carrying him quite out of the question, as he himself admitted; and it was evident that the frequent delays he must occasion if he accompanied us, and did not gain strength, would endanger the lives of the whole. By returning he had the prospect of getting to the tent where *tripe de roche* could be obtained, which agreed with him better than with any other of the party, and which he was always very assiduous in gathering. After some hesitation, he determined on going back, and set out, having bid each of us farewell in the tenderest manner. We watched him with inexpressible anxiety for some time, and were rejoiced to find, though he got on slowly, that he kept on his legs better than before. Antonio Fontano was an Italian, and had served many years in De Meuron's regiment. He had spoken to me that very morning, and after his first attack of dizziness, about his father, and had begged, that should he survive, I would take him with me to England, and put him in the way of reaching home.

The party was now reduced to five persons, Adam, Peltier, Benoit, Samandré, and myself. Continuing the journey, we came, after an hour's walk, to some willows, and encamped under the shelter of a rock, having walked in the whole four miles and a half. We made an attempt to gather some *tripe de roche*, but could not, owing to the severity of the weather. Our supper, therefore, consisted of tea and a few morsels of leather.

Augustus did not make his appearance, but we felt no alarm at his absence, supposing he would go to the tent if he missed our track. Having fire, we procured a little sleep. Next morning the breeze was light and the weather mild, which enabled us to collect some *tripe de roche*, and to enjoy the only meal we had had for four days. We derived great benefit from it, and walked with considerably more ease than yesterday. Without the strength it supplied, we should certainly have been unable to oppose the strong breeze we met in the afternoon. After walking about five miles, we came upon the borders of Marten Lake, and were rejoiced to find it frozen, so that we could continue our course straight for Fort Enterprise. We encamped at the first rapid in Winter River amidst willows and alders; but these were so frozen, and the snow fell so thick, that the men had great difficulty in making a fire. This proving insufficient to warm us, or even thaw our shoes, and having no food to prepare, we crept under our blankets. The arrival in a well-known part raised the spirits of the men to a high pitch, and we kept up a cheerful conversation until sleep overpowered us. The night was very stormy, and the morning scarcely less so; but, being desirous to reach the house this day, we commenced our journey very early. We were gratified by the sight of a large herd of reindeer on the side of the hill near the track, but our only hunter, Adam, was too feeble to pursue them. Our shoes and garments were stiffened by the frost, and we walked in great pain until we arrived at some stunted pines, at which we halted, made a good fire, and procured the refreshment of tea. The weather becoming fine in the afternoon, we continued our journey, passed the Dog-rib Rock, and encamped among a clump of pines of considerable growth, about a mile further on. Here we enjoyed the comfort of a large fire, for the first time since our departure from the sea-coast; but this gratification was purchased at the expense of many severe falls in crossing a stony valley, to get at these trees. These was no *tripe de roche*, and we drank tea and ate some of our shoes for supper. Next morning, after taking the usual repast of tea, we proceeded to the house. Musing on what we were likely to find there, our minds were agitated between hope and fear, and, contrary to the custom we had kept up, of supporting our spirits by conversation, we went silently forward.

At length we reached Fort Enterprise, and to our infinite disappointment and grief found it a perfectly desolate habitation. There was no deposit of provision, no trace of the Indians, no letter from Mr Wentzel to point out where the Indians might be found. It would be impossible to describe our sensations after entering this miserable abode, and discovering how we had been neglected: the whole party shed tears, not so much for our own fate, as for that of our friends in the rear, whose lives depended entirely on our sending immediate relief from this place.

I found a note, however, from Mr Back, stating that he had reached the house two days before, and was going in search of the Indians, at a part where St Germain deemed it probable they might be found. If he was unsuccessful, he purposed walking to Fort Providence, and sending succour from thence; but he doubted whether either he or his party could perform the journey to that place in their present debilitated state. It was evident that any supply that could be sent from Fort Providence would be long in reaching us, neither could it be sufficient to enable us to afford any assistance to our companions behind, and that the only relief for them must be procured from the Indians. I resolved, therefore, on going also in search of them; but my companions were absolutely incapable of proceeding, and I thought by halting two or three days they might gather a little strength, whilst the delay would afford us the chance of learning whether Mr Back had seen the Indians.

We now looked round for the means of subsistence, and were gratified to find several deer skins, which had been thrown away during our former residence. The bones were gathered from the heap of ashes; these with the skins, and the addition of *tripe de roche*, we considered would support us tolerably well for a time. As to the house, the parchment being torn from the windows, the apartment we selected for our abode was exposed to all the rigour of the season. We endeavoured to exclude the wind as much as possible, by placing loose boards against the apertures. The temperature was now between 15° and 20° below zero. We procured fuel by pulling up the flooring of the other rooms, and water for cooking, by melting the snow. Whilst we were seated round the fire, singeing the deer skin for supper, we were rejoiced by the unexpected entrance of Augustus. He had followed quite a different course from ours, and the circumstance of his having found his way through a part of the country he had never been in before, must be considered a remarkable proof of sagacity. The unusual earliness of this winter became manifest to us from the state of things at this spot. Last year at the same season, and still later, there had been very little snow on the ground, and we were surrounded by vast herds of reindeer; now there were but few recent tracks of these animals, and the snow was upwards of two feet deep. Winter River was then open, now it was frozen two feet thick.

When I arose the following morning, my body and limbs were so swollen that I was unable to walk more than a few yards. Adam was in a still worse condition, being absolutely incapable of rising without assistance. My other companions happily experienced this inconvenience in a less degree, and went to collect bones, and some *tripe de roche*, which supplied us with two meals. The bones were quite acrid, and the soup extracted from them excoriated the mouth if taken alone, but it was somewhat milder when boiled with *tripe de roche*, and we even thought the mixture palatable, with the addition of salt, of which a cask had been fortunately left here in the spring. Augustus today set two fishing lines below the rapid. On his way thither he saw two deer, but had not strength to follow them.

On the 13th the wind blew violently from south-east, and the snow drifted so much that the party were confined to the house. In the afternoon of the following day Belanger arrived with a note from Mr Back, stating that he had seen no trace of the Indians, and desiring further instructions as to the course he should pursue. Belanger's situation, however, required our first care, as he came in almost speechless, and covered with ice, having fallen into a rapid, and, for the third time since we left the coast, narrowly escaped drowning. He did not recover sufficiently to answer our questions, until we had rubbed him for some time, changed his dress, and given him some warm soup. My companions nursed him with the greatest kindness, and the desire of restoring him to health, seemed to absorb all regard for their own situation. I witnessed with peculiar pleasure this conduct so different from that which they had recently pursued, when every tender feeling was suspended by the desire of self-preservation. They now no longer betrayed impatience or despondency, but were composed and cheerful, and had entirely given up the practice of swearing, to which the Canadian voyagers are so addicted.

I undertook the office of cooking, and insisted they should eat twice a day whenever food could be procured; but as I was too weak to pound the bones, Peltier agreed to do that in addition to his more fatiguing task of getting wood. We had a violent snow storm all the next day, and this gloomy weather increased the depression of spirits under which Adam and Samandré were labouring. Neither of them would quit their beds; and they scarcely ceased from shedding tears all day; in vain did Peltier and myself endeavour to cheer them. We had even to use much entreaty before they would take the meals we had prepared for them. Our situation was indeed distressing, but in comparison with that of our friends in the rear, we thought it happy. Their condition gave us unceasing solicitude, and was the principal subject of our conversation.

Though the weather was stormy on the 26th, Samandré assisted me to gather *tripe de roche*. Adam, who was very ill, and could not now be prevailed upon to eat this weed, subsisted principally on bones, though he also partook of the soup. The *tripe de roche* had hitherto afforded us our chief support, and we naturally felt great uneasiness at the prospect of being deprived of it, by its being so frozen as to render it impossible for us to gather it.

We perceived our strength decline every day, and every exertion began to be irksome; when we were once seated the greatest effort was necessary in order to rise, and we had frequently to lift each other from our seats; but even in this pitiable condition we conversed cheerfully, being sanguine as to the speedy arrival of the Indians. We calculated indeed that if they should be near the situation where they had remained last winter, our men would have reached them by this day. Having expended all the wood which we could procure from our present dwelling, without danger of its fall, Peltier began this day to pull down the partitions of the adjoining houses. Though these were only distant about twenty yards, yet the increase of labour in carrying the wood fatigued him so much, that by the evening he was exhausted. On the next day his weakness was such, especially in the arms, of which he chiefly complained, that he with difficulty lifted the hatchet; still he persevered, while Samandré and I assisted him in bringing in the wood, but our united strength could only collect sufficient to replenish the fire four times in the course of the day. As the insides of our mouths had become sore from eating the bone-soup, we relinquished the use of it, and now boiled the skin, which mode of dressing we found more palatable than frying it, as we had hitherto done.

On the 29th, Peltier felt his pains more severe, and could only cut a few pieces of wood. Samandré, who was still almost as weak, relieved him a little time, and I aided them in carrying in the wood. We endeavoured to pick some *tripe de roche*, but in vain, as it was entirely frozen. In turning up the snow, in searching for bones, I found several pieces of bark, which proved a valuable acquisition, as we were almost destitute of dry wood proper for kindling the fire. We saw a herd of reindeer sporting on the river, about half a mile from the house; they remained there a long time, but none of the party felt themselves strong enough to go after them, nor was there one of us who could have fired a gun without resting it.

Whilst we were seated round the fire this evening, discoursing about the anticipated relief, the conversation was suddenly interrupted by Peltier's exclaiming with joy, '*Ah! le monde!*' imagining that he heard the Indians in the other room; immediately afterwards, to his bitter disappointment, Dr Richardson and Hepburn entered, each carrying his bundle. Peltier, however, soon recovered himself enough to express his delight at their safe arrival, and his regret that their companions were not with them. When I saw them alone my own mind was instantly filled with apprehensions respecting my friend Hood, and our other companions, which were immediately confirmed by the Doctor's melancholy communication, that Mr Hood and Michel were dead. Perrault and Fontano had neither reached the tent, nor been heard of by them. This intelligence produced a melancholy despondency in the minds of my party, and on that account the particulars were deferred until another opportunity. We were all shocked at beholding the emaciated countenances of the Doctor and Hepburn, as they strongly evidenced their extremely debilitated state. The alteration in our appearance was equally distressing to them, for since the swellings had subsided we were little more than skin and bone. The Doctor particularly remarked the sepulchral tone of our voices, which he requested us to make more cheerful if possible, unconscious that his own partook of the same key.

Hepburn having shot a partridge, which was brought to the house, the Doctor tore out the feathers, and having held it to the fire a few minutes divided it into six portions. I and my three companions ravenously devoured our shares, as it was the first morsel of flesh any of us had tasted for thirty-one days, unless, indeed, the small grizzly particles which we found occasionally adhering to the pounded bones may be termed flesh. Our spirits were revived by this small supply, and the Doctor endeavoured to raise them still higher by the prospect of Hepburn's being able to kill a deer next day, as they had seen, and even fired at, several near the house. He endeavoured, too, to rouse us into some attention to the comfort of our apartment, and particularly to roll up, in the day, our blankets, which (expressly for the convenience of Adam and Samandré) we had been in the habit of leaving by the fire where we lay on them. The Doctor having brought his prayer book and testament, some prayers and psalms, and portions of scripture, appropriate to our situation, were read, and we retired to bed.

Next morning the Doctor and Hepburn went out early in search of deer; but though they saw several herds and fired some shots, they were not so fortunate as to kill any, being too weak to hold their guns steadily. The cold compelled the former to return soon, but Hepburn persisted until late in the evening.

My occupation was to search for skins under the snow, it being now our object immediately to get all that we could, but I had not strength to drag in more than two of those which were within twenty yards of the house, until the Doctor came and assisted me. We made up our stock to twenty-six, but several of them were putrid, and scarcely eatable, even by men suffering the extremity

of famine. Peltier and Samandré continued very weak and dispir-
ited, and they were unable to cut fire-wood. Hepburn had in
consequence that laborious task to perform after he came back.
The Doctor having scarified the swelled parts of Adam's body, a
large quantity of water flowed out, and he obtained some ease,
but still kept his bed . . .

I may here remark that, owing to our loss of flesh, the hard-
ness of the floor, from which we were only protected by a blanket,
produced soreness over the body, and especially those parts on
which the weight rested in lying, yet to turn ourselves for relief
was a matter of toil and difficulty. However, during this period,
and indeed all along, after the acute pains of hunger, which
lasted but three or four days, had subsided, we generally enjoyed
the comfort of a few hours' sleep. The dreams which for the most
part, but not always, accompanied it, were usually (though not
invariably) of a pleasant character, being very often about the
enjoyments of feasting. In the day-time we fell into the practice of
conversing on common and light subjects, although we sometimes discussed with seriousness and earnestness topics
connected with religion. We generally avoided speaking directly
of our present sufferings, or even of the prospect of relief. I
observed, that in proportion as our strength decayed, our minds
exhibited symptoms of weakness, evinced by a kind of unreason-
able pettishness with each other. Each of us thought the other
weaker in intellect than himself, and more in need of advice and
assistance. So trifling a circumstance as a change of place, recommended by one as being warmer and more comfortable, and
refused by the other from a dread of motion, frequently called
forth fretful expressions which were no sooner uttered than
atoned for, to be repeated perhaps in the course of a few minutes.
The same thing often occurred when we endeavoured to assist
each other in carrying wood to the fire; none of us were willing to
receive assistance, although the task was disproportioned to our
strength. On one of these occasions, Hepburn was so convinced
of this waywardness that he exclaimed, 'Dear me, if we are spared

to return to England, I wonder if we shall recover our understandings.'

7 *November* Adam had passed a restless night, being disquieted by gloomy apprehensions of approaching death, which we *tried* in vain to dispel. He was so low in the morning as to be scarcely able to speak. I remained in bed by his side, to cheer him as much as possible. The Doctor and Hepburn went to cut wood. They had hardly begun their labour when they were amazed at hearing the report of a musket. They could scarcely believe that there was really anyone near, until they heard a shout, and immediately espied three Indians close to the house. Adam and I heard the latter noise, and I was fearful that a part of the house had fallen upon one of my companions, a disaster which had in fact been thought not unlikely. My alarm was only momentary; Dr Richardson came in to communicate the joyful intelligence that relief had arrived.

THIN ICE

W. ELMER EKBLAW
(1882–1949)

*American geographer. He was a member of the 1913–1917 Crocker
Land Arctic Expedition, during which time he lived with the Eskimos of
Thule, northwest Greenland.*

Spring had come to Thule. The daily temperatures still sank below
freezing, but the daily sunlight approached the twenty-four hour
maximum. In the sunlit niches among the rocks, the snow was fast
evaporating. Every day the open water was breaking in towards
the land. The spring hunting was on. At the first opportunity,
Mene, Sechmann and I had set out from North Star Bay for a
hunting trip at Cape Parry.

When we arrived, we found other hunters already rendezvoused
there, comfortably quartered in snow houses along the shore and
well stocked with walrus and seal that they had killed. We stayed
with them three days and then started back towards North Star
Bay, hunting along the edge of the ice as we sledged southward
towards Saunders Island in the mouth of Wolstenholme Sound.

Halfway between Beechwood Point and the northern point of
Saunders Island, but well out to sea, we came upon a deep
re-entrant of the open water, where a large herd of walrus were
disporting themselves along the edge of a patch of hummocky
old ice – an irresistible lure for Mene and Sechmann, who would
not go on without a try at this game. By a stroke of good fortune

all too infrequent in an Eskimo hunter's experience, Mene sank his harpoon at the first cast deep into the flank of a big cow walrus that swam up to the low berg behind which he had stalked the herd.

In due time we 'landed' the huge carcass, cut it up on the ice and, after feeding the dogs all they could eat, set up our tent and made ready to turn in for a sleep, while the dogs settled the meal they had eaten. It was well after midnight. The sun had hardly set. In the soft night light, the pale moon swung high in the sky, almost invisible. Flocks of fulmars, guillemots and eiders, but lately returned to the north, winged their ways still farther northward. The sky was well-nigh cloudless, the water rippled calm and dark before our tent and the ice towards the land gleamed solid and white as far as we could see.

Yet Sechmann shook his head and seemed uneasy – the sky in the south did not please him. Mene and I could detect nothing dubious and made light of his fears. Tired as he was, Sechmann got into his sleeping-bag reluctantly and, while Mene and I made the most of the chance to rest, he kept restless vigil.

Early forenoon came. The sun had risen well into the sky when Sechmann called us urgently. We turned out at once. A grey glare hung in the sky over the open water seaward and gusts of eddying winds swirled the loose snow about. The dogs were stirring uneasily. Not a bird was in sight on the water or in the air.

But it was none of these signs that had alarmed Sechmann enough to call us; he directed our attention to a long, wraith-like horizontal pennant of cloud flung out like a weathervane from the tip of a lone monadnock rising high above the plateau back of North Star Bay. To the Polar Eskimo, this pennant of cloud is a dread warning of the approach of a violent southerly gale and storm that will carry the ice out to sea. The moment Mene, who knew full well its grave import, saw this, he excitedly yelled to us to waste not a single moment in getting away.

We untied our dogs and hitched them to the sledges in less

time than it takes to tell. We left our tent, our sleeping-bags, our heap of walrus meat and, with our whips snapping in angry staccato, raced away as fast as our well fed dogs could carry us. We headed straight for North Star Bay, dodging the patches of rough ice as best we could, straining our eyes for the smoothest going ahead, running behind our sledges to lighten the loads for the dogs. The dogs sensed the alarm we felt. As the wind strengthened and the snow sifting before it rose higher and struck harder, they increased their speed rather than slowed down.

For an hour or more we raced along, hardly calling a word to one another – Mene, with the biggest and best dogs, in the lead; Sechmann, with poorer dogs but a better driver, close behind Mene's sledge; and I close behind Sechmann, merely because my dogs would not let the others get away.

And then came the crisis.

Spread black and threatening before us, a dark lead of new, thin ice stretched across the whole sound. How wide it was, we could not see in the haze of wind-driven snow. How thin it was, we could readily see, as our killing-irons broke through it of their own weight. How far it extended, we could only guess, but probably it reached from shore to shore.

During our absence the ice had parted under the urge of the ebbing spring tide and had drifted seaward. The water had frozen again over the lead, but only a thin film of ice had formed – so recently that no frost had yet whitened it. There it lay, barring our way, a dark, treacherous band that we had to cross. We could not tarry a moment, for not far behind us the storm was rolling in, a dark mass of tumbling cloud and wind-tossed snow.

As Sechmann drew his dogs back from the lead for a good running start, Mene moved along the lead a half hundred yards and drew back a little farther than Sechmann had done and I took my position still farther along the lead and still farther back; for, as Sechmann explained, we must not strike the ice at the same time or near together.

As Mene and I held our dogs back to give Sechmann a chance

to get started, we waved to each other but neither spoke a word – our feelings were too tense. As Sechmann's dogs struck out across the thin ice, they spread wide apart in the line; low and swift, with feet wide-spread, they ran; astride and well back on his sledge, Sechmann cracked his whip fast and furiously, encouraging but not striking his dogs. It was easy to see that they realized as well as he the danger they faced. Beneath the runners of his sledge, the yielding ice bent down; it rose in a wave-like fold before and behind.

Almost before Sechmann's dogs had got well out on the thin ice, Mene's team was on its way towards the edge. As his sledge struck the dark band, I saw, as I had not seen with Sechmann's sledge, that, while the rounded front part of the runners was holding up on the ice as the dogs sped along, the sharp, square corners at the back were cutting through and little jets of water were spraying up on either side of the runner. The runners were actually cutting two narrow lanes through the ice.

My own dogs had already dashed forward and, as my sledge neared the black, thin ice, I dared hardly hope that it would hold me, for I weighed at least fifty pounds more than either Mene or Sechmann. But my runners were shod a quarter-inch wider and, though the ice bent deep under the sledge, this extra width carried my greater weight. My dogs were doing their best to keep pace with Mene's and Sechmann's, so I had no need of using my whip.

With my heart in my mouth, scarcely daring to breathe, I sat rigid, watching the water spraying out from the sides of both runners; at times half the runners were cutting through. If a dog had stumbled, or bumped into another, to slow the sledge a moment, we should have dropped through. But not a dog faltered; every one knew as well as I what would happen if he did. Never had my team made such speed. The first moments were the most perilous. The young ice was thin, but it was also smooth as glass and we gathered momentum as we raced on; yet, even so, the minutes seemed hours. The lead proved to be over half a mile wide and it seemed an age before we got across.

As he struck the solid ice, Sechmann gave a wild yell of relief; Mene gave another as he achieved it a moment later; but, until I had taken a breath or two, I could not even whisper. To them, particularly to Sechmann, who came from the hazardous ice of the Disko region, it was an old, oft-repeated adventure; to me – well, I vowed it was my last hazard over such thin ice.

We could not take time to greet each other and congratulate ourselves on the safe outcome of our decision. The storm still raged and there might be other such leads ahead. We could lose no time. We drove relentlessly on through the gathering blizzard and finally made shore just within Cape Abernathy. There we built a snow shelter and stayed till the storm swept by.

THE END

ROBERT FALCON SCOTT
(1868–1912)

British naval officer and explorer. He led the 1900–4 National Antarctic
Expedition, which explored the Ross Sea and discovered King Edward
VII Land. In 1910 Scott returned to the Antarctic in a bid to reach the
South Pole.

Night, 15 January It is wonderful to think that two long marches
would land us at the Pole. We left our depot today with nine days'
provisions, so that it ought to be a certain thing now, and the only
appalling possibility the sight of the Norwegian flag forestalling
ours. Little Bowers continues his indefatigable efforts to get good
sights, and it is wonderful how he works them up in his sleeping-
bag in our congested tent. (Minimum for night –27.5°.) Only 27
miles from the Pole. We *ought* to do it now.

Tuesday, 16 January Camp 68. Height 9,760. T –23.5°. The worst has
happened, or nearly the worst. We marched well in the morning
and covered 7½ miles. Noon sight showed us in Lat. 89° 42' S, and
we started off in high spirits in the afternoon, feeling that tomorrow would see us at our destination. About the second hour of the
march Bowers' sharp eyes detected what he thought was a cairn;
he was uneasy about it, but argued that it must be a sastrugus.
Half an hour later he detected a black speck ahead. Soon we knew
that this could not be a natural snow feature. We marched on,

found that it was a black flag tied to a sledge bearer; near by the remains of a camp; sledge tracks and ski tracks going and coming and the clear trace of dogs' paws – many dogs. This told us the whole story. The Norwegians have forestalled us and are first at the Pole. It is a terrible disappointment, and I am very sorry for my loyal companions. Many thoughts come and much discussion have we had. Tomorrow we must march on to the Pole and then hasten home with all the speed we can compass. All the day-dreams must go; it will be a wearisome return. Certainly we are descending in altitude – certainly also the Norwegians found an easy way up.

Wednesday, 17 January Camp 69. T –22° at start. Night –21°. The Pole. Yes, but under very different circumstances from those expected. We have had a horrible day – add to our disappointment a head wind 4 to 5,* with a temperature –22°, and companions labouring on with cold feet and hands.

We started at 7.30, none of us having slept much after the shock of our discovery. We followed the Norwegian sledge tracks for some way; as far as we make out there are only two men. In about three miles we passed two small cairns. Then the weather over-cast, and the tracks being increasingly drifted up and obviously going too far to the west, we decided to make straight for the Pole according to our calculations. At 12.30 Evans had such cold hands we camped for lunch – an excellent 'weekend' one. We had marched 7.4 miles. Lat. sight gave 89° 53′ 37″. We started out and did 6½ miles due south. Tonight little Bowers is laying himself out to get sights in terrible difficult circumstances; the wind is blowing hard, T –21°, and there is that curious damp, cold feeling in the air which chills one to the bone in no time. We have been descending again, I think, but there looks to be a rise ahead; otherwise there is very little that is different from the awful monotony of past days. Great God! this is an awful place and terrible enough for us to

---

* Half a gale. The velocity of wind is denoted by numbers (1–10).

have laboured to it without the reward of priority. Well, it is some-thing to have got here, and the wind may be our friend tomorrow. We have had a fat Polar hoosh in spite of our chagrin, and feel comfortable inside – added a small stick of chocolate and the queer taste of a cigarette brought by Wilson. Now for the run home and a desperate struggle. I wonder if we can do it.

Thursday morning, 18 January Decided after summing up all obser-vations that we were 3.5 miles away from the Pole – one mile beyond it and 3 to the right. More or less in this direction Bowers saw a cairn or tent.

We have just arrived at this tent, 2 miles from our camp, there-fore about 1½ miles from the Pole. In the tent we find a record of five Norwegians having been here, as follows:

Roald Amundsen
Olav Olavson Bjaaland
Hilmer Hanssen
Sverre H. Hassel
Oscar Wisting.   16 Dec. 1911

The tent is fine – a small compact affair supported by a single bamboo. A note from Amundsen, which I keep, asks me to forward a letter to King Haakon!

The following articles have been left in the tent: 3 half bags of reindeer containing a miscellaneous assortment of mits and sleep-ing socks, very various in description, a sextant, a Norwegian artificial horizon and a hypsometer without boiling-point ther-mometers, a sextant and hypsometer of English make.

Left a note to say I had visited the tent with companions; Bowers photographing and Wilson sketching. Since lunch we have marched 6.2 miles SSE by compass (i.e. northwards). Sights at lunch gave us ½ to ¾ of a mile from the Pole, so we call it the Pole Camp. (Temp. Lunch –21°.) We built a cairn, put up our poor slighted Union Jack, and photographed ourselves – mighty cold work all of it – less than ½ a mile south we saw stuck up an old underrunner of a sledge. This we commandeered as a yard for a floorcloth sail. I imagine it was intended to mark the exact spot of the Pole as near as the Norwegians could fix it. (Height 9,500.) A note attached talked of the tent as being 2 miles from the Pole. Wilson keeps the note. There is no doubt that our predecessors have made thoroughly sure of their mark and fully carried out their programme. I think the Pole is about 9,500 feet in height; this is remarkable, considering that in Lat. 88° we were about 10,500.

We carried the Union Jack about ¾ of a mile north with us and left it on a piece of stick as near as we could fix it. I fancy the Norwegians arrived at the pole on the 15th Dec. and left on the 17th, ahead of a date quoted by me in London as ideal, viz. Dec. 22. It looks as though the Norwegian party expected colder weather on the summit than they got; it could scarcely be otherwise from Shackleton's account. Well, we have turned our back now on the goal of our ambition and must face our 800 miles of solid dragging – and good-bye to most of the day-dreams!

Tuesday, 6 February Lunch 7,900; Supper 7,210. Temp –15° [R. 20]. We've had a horrid day and not covered good mileage. On turning out found sky overcast; a beastly position amidst crevasses. Luckily it cleared just before we started. We went straight for Mt Darwin, but in half an hour found ourselves amongst huge open chasms, unbridged, but not very deep, I think. We turned to the north between two, but to our chagrin they converged into chaotic disturbance. We had to retrace our steps for a mile or so, then struck to the west and got on to a confused sea of sastrugi, pulling very hard; we put up the sail, Evans's nose suffered, Wilson very cold, everything horrid. Camped for lunch in the sastrugi; the only comfort, things looked clearer to the west and we were obviously going downhill. In the afternoon we struggled on, got out of sastrugi and turned over on glazed surface, crossing many crevasses – very easy work on ski. Towards the end of the march we realised the certainty of maintaining a more or less straight course to the depot, and estimate distance 10 to 15 miles.

Food is low and weather uncertain, so that many hours of the day were anxious; but this evening, though we are not as far advanced as I expected, the outlook is much more promising. Evans is the chief anxiety now; his cuts and wounds suppurate, his nose looks very bad, and altogether he shows considerable signs of being played out. Things may mend for him on the glacier, and his wounds get some respite under warmer conditions. I am indeed glad to think we shall so soon have done with plateau conditions. It took us 27 days to reach the Pole and 21 days back – in all 48 days – nearly 7 weeks in low temperature with almost incessant wind . . .

Sunday, 11 February R. 25. Lunch Temp. +6.5°; Supper + 3.5°. The worst day we have had during the trip and greatly owing to our own fault. We started on a wretched surface with light SW wind, sail set, and pulling on ski – in a horrible light, which made everything look fantastic. As we went on the light got worse, and suddenly we found ourselves in pressure. Then came the fatal decision to steer east. We went on for 6 hours, hoping to do a good distance, which in fact I suppose we did, but for the last hour or two we pressed on into a regular trap. Getting on to a good surface we did not reduce our lunch meal, and thought all going well, but half an hour after lunch we got into the worst ice mess I have ever been in. For three hours we plunged on on ski, first thinking we were too much to the right, then too much to the left; meanwhile the disturbance got worse and my spirits received a very rude shock. There were times when it seemed almost impossible to find a way out of the awful turmoil in which we found ourselves. At length, arguing that there must be a way on our left, we plunged in that direction. It got worse, harder, more icy and crevassed. We could not manage our ski and pulled on foot, falling into crevasses every minute – most luckily with no bad accident. At length we saw a smoother slope towards the land, pushed for it, but knew it was a woefully long way from us. The turmoil changed in character, irregular crevassed surface giving way to huge chasms, closely packed and most difficult to cross. It was very heavy work, but we had grown desperate. We won through at 10 p.m. and I write after 12 hours on the march. I *think* we are on or about the right track now, but we are still a good number of miles from the depot, so we reduced rations tonight. We had three pemmican meals left and decided to make them into four. Tomorrow's lunch must serve for two if we do not make big progress. It was a test of our endurance on the march and our fitness with small supper. We have come through well. A good wind has come down the glacier which is clearing the sky and surface. Pray God the wind holds tomorrow.

Wednesday, 14 February There is no getting away from the fact that we are not pulling strong: probably none of us. Wilson's leg still troubles him and he doesn't like to trust himself on ski; but the worst case is Evans, who is giving us serious anxiety. This morning he suddenly disclosed a huge blister on his foot. It delayed us on the march, when he had to have his crampon readjusted. Sometimes I fear he is going from bad to worse, but I trust he will pick up again when we come to steady work on ski like this afternoon. He is hungry and so is Wilson. We can't risk opening out our food again, and as cook at present I am serving something under full allowance. We are inclined to get slack and slow with our camping arrangements, and small delays increase. I have talked of the matter tonight and hope for improvement. We cannot do distance without the hours. The next depot some 30 miles away and nearly 3 days' food in hand.

Saturday, 17 February A very terrible day. Evans looked a little better after a good sleep, and declared, as he always did, that he was quite well. He started in his place on the traces, but half an hour later worked his ski shoes adrift, and had to leave the sledge. The surface was awful, the soft recently fallen snow clogging the ski and runners at every step, the sledge groaning, the sky overcast, and the land hazy. We stopped after about one hour, and Evans came up again, but very slowly. Half an hour later he dropped out again on the same plea. He asked Bowers to lend him a piece of string. I cautioned him to come on as quickly as he could, and he answered cheerfully as I thought. We had to push on, and the remainder of us were forced to pull very hard, sweating heavily. Abreast the Monument Rock we stopped, and seeing Evans a long way astern, I camped for lunch. There was no alarm at first, and we prepared tea and our own meal, consuming the latter. After lunch, and Evans still not appearing, we looked out, to see him still afar off. By this time we were alarmed, and all four started back on ski. I was first to reach the poor man and shocked at his appearance; he was on his knees with clothing disarranged, hands uncovered and frostbitten, and a wild look in his eyes. Asked what was the matter, he replied with a slow speech that he didn't know, but thought he must have fainted. We got him on his feet, but after two or three steps he sank down again. He showed every sign of complete collapse. Wilson, Bowers and I went back for the sledge, whilst Oates remainded with him. When we returned he was practically unconscious, and when we got him into the tent quite comatose. He died quietly at 12.30 a.m. On discussing the symptoms we think he began to get weaker just before we reached the Pole, and that his downward path was accelerated first by the shock of his frostbitten fingers, and later by falls during rough travelling on the glacier, further by his loss of all confidence in himself. Wilson thinks it certain he must have injured his brain by a fall. It is a terrible thing to lose a companion in this way, but calm reflection shows that there could not have been a better ending to the terrible anxieties of the past week. Discussion of the situation at lunch yesterday shows us what a desperate pass we were in with a sick man on our hands so far from home . . .

Friday, 2 March Lunch. Misfortunes rarely come singly. We marched to the [Middle Barrier] depot fairly easily yesterday afternoon, and since that have suffered three distinct blows which have placed us in a bad position. First we found a shortage of oil; with most rigid economy it can scarce carry us to the next depot on this surface [71 miles away]. Second, Titus Oates disclosed his feet, the toes showing very bad indeed, evidently bitten by the late temperatures. The third blow came in the night, when the wind, which we had hailed with some joy, brought dark overcast weather. It fell below –40° in the night, and this morning it took 1½ hours to get our foot-gear on, but we got away before eight. We lost cairn and tracks together and made as steady as we could N by W, but have seen nothing. Worse was to come – the surface is simply awful. In spite of strong wind and full sail we have only done 5½ miles. We are in a *very* queer street, since there is no doubt we cannot do the extra marches and feel the cold horribly.

Monday, 5 March Lunch. Regret to say going from bad to worse. We got a slant of wind yesterday afternoon, and going on 5 hours we converted our wretched morning run of 3½ miles into something over 9. We went to bed on a cup of cocoa and pemmican solid with the chill off. (R. 47.) The result is telling on all, but mainly on Oates, whose feet are in a wretched condition. One swelled up tremendously last night and he is very lame this morning. We started march on tea and pemmican as last night – we pretend to prefer the pemmican this way. Marched for 5 hours this morning over a slightly better surface covered with high moundy sastrugi. Sledge capsized twice; we pulled on foot, covering about 5½ miles. We are two pony marches and 4 miles about from our depot. Our fuel dreadfully low and the poor soldier nearly done. It is pathetic enough because we can do nothing for him; more hot food might do a little, but only a little, I fear. We none of us expected these terribly low temperatures, and of the rest of us Wilson is feeling them most; mainly, I fear, from his self-sacrificing devotion in doctoring Oates's feet. We cannot help each other, each has enough to do to take care of himself. We get cold on the march when the trudging is heavy, and the wind pierces our worn garments. The others, all of them, are unendingly cheerful when in the tent. We mean to see the game through with a proper spirit, but it's tough work to be pulling harder than we ever pulled in our lives for long hours, and to feel that the progress is so slow. One can only say 'God help us!' and plod on our weary way, cold and very miserable, though outwardly cheerful. We talk of all sorts of subjects in the tent, not much of food now, since we decided to take the risk of running a full ration. We simply couldn't go hungry at this time.

Saturday, 10 March Things steadily downhill. Oates's foot worse. He has rare pluck and must know that he can never get through. He asked Wilson if he had a chance this morning, and of course Bill had to say he didn't know. In point of fact he has none. Apart from him, if he went under now, I doubt whether we could get through. With great care we might have a dog's chance, but no more. The weather conditions are awful, and our gear gets steadily more icy and difficult to manage. At the same time, of course, poor Titus is the greatest handicap. He keeps us waiting in the morning until we have partly lost the warming effect of our good breakfast, when the only wise policy is to be up and away at once; again at lunch. Poor chap! it is too pathetic to watch him; one cannot but try to cheer him up.

Yesterday we marched up the depot, Mt Hooper. Cold comfort. Shortage on our allowance all round . . .

Sunday, 11 March Titus Oates is very near the end, one feels. What we or he will do, God only knows. We discussed the matter after breakfast; he is a brave fine fellow and understands the situation, but he practically asked for advice. Nothing could be said but to urge him to march as long as he could. One satisfactory result to the discussion; I practically ordered Wilson to hand over the means of ending our troubles to us, so that any one of us may know how to do so. Wilson had no choice between doing so and our ransacking the medicine case. We have 30 opium tabloids apiece and he is left with a tube of morphine. So far the tragical side of our story.

The sky was completely overcast when we started this morning. We could see nothing, lost the tracks, and doubtless have been swaying a good deal since – 3.1 miles for the forenoon – terribly heavy dragging – expected it. Know that 6 miles is about the limit of our endurance now, if we get no help from wind or surfaces. We have 7 days' food and should be about 55 miles from One Ton Camp tonight, 6 x 7 = 42, leaving us 13 miles short of our distance, even if things get no worse. Meanwhile the season rapidly advances . . .

Wednesday, 14 March No doubt about the going downhill, but everything going wrong for us. Yesterday we woke to a strong northerly wind with temp. –37°. Couldn't face it, so remained in camp till 2, then did 5¼ miles. Wanted to march later, but party feeling the cold badly as the breeze (N) never took off entirely, and as the sun sank the temp. fell. Long time getting supper in dark.

This morning started with southerly breeze, set sail and passed another cairn at good speed; halfway, however, the wind shifted to W by S or WSW, blew through our wind clothes and into our mits. Poor Wilson horribly cold, could [not] get off ski for some time. Bowers and I practically made camp, and when we got into the tent at last we were all deadly cold. Then temp. now midday down –43° and the wind strong. We *must* go on, but now the making of every camp must be more difficult and dangerous. It must be near the end, but a pretty merciful end. Poor Oates got it again in the foot. I shudder to think what it will be like tomorrow. It is only with greatest pains rest of us keep off frostbites. No idea there could be temperatures like this at this time of year with such winds. Truly awful outside the tent. Must fight it out to the last biscuit, but can't reduce rations.

Friday, 16 March, or Saturday 17 Lost track of dates, but think the last correct. Tragedy all along the line. At lunch, the day before yesterday, poor Titus Oates said he couldn't go on; he proposed we should leave him in his sleeping-bag. That we could not do, and we induced him to come on, on the afternoon march. In spite of its awful nature for him he struggled on and we made a few miles. At night he was worse and we knew the end had come.

Should this be found I want these facts recorded. Oates's last thoughts were of his mother, but immediately before he took pride in thinking that his regiment would be pleased with the bold way in which he met his death. We can testify to his bravery. He has borne intense suffering for weeks without complaint, and to the very last was able and willing to discuss outside subjects. He did not – would not – give up hope till the very end. He was a brave soul. This was the end. He slept through the night before last, hoping not to wake; but he woke in the morning – yesterday. It was blowing a blizzard. He said, 'I am just going outside and may be some time.' He went out into the blizzard and we have not seen him since.

I take this opportunity of saying that we have stuck to our sick companions to the last. In case of Edgar Evans, when absolutely out of food and he lay insensible, the safety of the remainder seemed to demand his abandonment, but Providence mercifully removed him at this critical moment. He died a natural death, and we did not leave him till two hours after his death. We knew that poor Oates was walking to his death, but though we tried to dissuade him, we knew it was the act of a brave man and an English gentleman. We all hope to meet the end with a similar spirit, and assuredly the end is not far.

I can only write at lunch and then only occasionally. The cold is intense, –40° at midday. My companions are unendingly cheerful, but we are all on the verge of serious frostbites, and though we constantly talk of fetching through, I don't think any one of us believes it in his heart.

We are cold on the march now, and at all times except meals. Yesterday we had to lie up for a blizzard and today we move dreadfully slowly. We are at No. 14 pony camp, only two pony marches from One Ton Depot. We leave here our theodolite, a camera, and Oates's sleeping-bags. Diaries, etc., and geological specimens carried at Wilson's special request, will be found with us or on our sledge.

Sunday, 18 March Today, lunch, we are 21 miles from the depot. Ill fortune presses, but better may come. We have had more wind and drift from ahead yesterday; had to stop marching; wind NW, force 4, temp. –35°. No human being could face it, and we are worn out *nearly*.

My right foot has gone, nearly all the toes – two days ago I was proud possessor of best feet. These are the steps of my downfall. Like an ass I mixed a small spoonful of curry powder with my melted pemmican – it gave me violent indigestion. I lay awake and in pain all night; woke and felt done on the march; foot went and I didn't know it. A very small measure of neglect and I have a foot which is not pleasant to contemplate. Bowers takes first place in condition, but there is not much to choose after all. The others are still confident of getting through – or pretend to be – I don't know! We have the last *half* fill of oil in our primus and a very small quantity of spirit – this alone between us and thirst. The wind is fair for the moment, and that is perhaps a fact to help. The mileage would have seemed ridiculously small on our outward journey.

Monday, 19 March Lunch. We camped with difficulty last night and were dreadfully cold till after our supper of cold pemmican and biscuit and a half a pannikin of cocoa cooked over the spirit. Then, contrary to expectation, we got warm and all slept well. Today we started in the usual dragging manner. Sledge dreadfully heavy. We are 15½ miles from the depot and ought to get there in three days. What progress! We have two days' food, but barely a day's fuel. All our feet are getting bad – Wilson's best, my right foot worse, left all right. There is no chance to nurse one's feet till we can get hot food into us. Amputation is the least I can hope for now, but will the trouble spread? That is the serious question. The weather doesn't give us a chance – the wind from N to NW and –40° temp today.

Wednesday, 21 March Got within 11 miles of depot Monday night; had to lie up all yesterday in severe blizzard. Today forlorn hope, Wilson and Bowers going to depot for fuel.

22 and 23 Blizzard bad as ever – Wilson and Bowers unable to start – tomorrow last chance – no fuel and only one or two [rations] of food left – must be near the end. Have decided it shall be natural – we shall march for the depot with or without our effects and die in our tracks.

Thursday, 29 March Since the 21st we have had a continuous gale from WSW and SW. We had fuel to make two cups of tea apiece and bare food for two days on the 20th. Every day we have been ready to start for our depot 11 *miles* away, but outside the door of the tent it remains a scene of whirling drift. I do not think we can hope for any better things now. We shall stick it out to the end, but we are getting weaker, of course, and the end cannot be far.

It seems a pity, but I do not think I can write more.

R. SCOTT

Last entry.
For God's sake look after our people.

Mountains

DEATH ZONE

WALTER BONATTI
(1930–)

Italian mountaineer. Bonatti's 1955 solo ascent of the South-West Pillar of Petit Dru was one of the outstanding achievements of post-war European climbing. Five years later, on the Central Pillar of Mont Blanc, Bonatti was involved in one of European mountaineering's greatest tragedies.

After twenty-four hours of uninterrupted march, we spent our first night on the face, freezing but serene. At 3.30 a.m. on the Tuesday dawn broke; a great explosion of fire between the Matterhorn and Monte Rosa announced the sunrise. It seemed incredible but this hour was the coldest of all. We made some more tea, which was to be the last during our adventure. The Frenchmen called to us and proposed that I take the lead. I agreed and an hour later we again set off in this order: Bonatti, Gallieni and Oggioni on the first rope, Kohlman and Mazeaud on the second and Guillaume and Vielle on the third.

We climbed quickly and reached the base of the last pinnacle about noon instead of two o'clock as we had expected. We had noticed mist trailing overhead, but it had not worried us over-much considering the altitude we had now reached; we hoped to be able to reach the summit before any brewing storm should break. However the storm caught us just as Mazeaud and Kohlman were beginning to climb the last pinnacle. We had only about two hundred and fifty feet of overhanging monolith to climb to complete our climb on the Pillar and to reach the ridge which led to the summit of Mont Blanc.

We all gathered together on the few ledges there were. The snowstorm was now raging furiously; it was thundering and the lightning flashed around us. The air was saturated with electricity and the gusts of wind blew powdered snow into our faces, blinding us. We were at a height of nearly 15,000 feet on the Pillar, the lightning-conductor of Mont Blanc. We three Italians were squatting on a little ledge; the Frenchmen were in two groups. Then, without warning, Kohlman's face was grazed by a flash of lightning. He was blinded by the flash but Mazeaud with a leap caught hold of him and managed to support him. For some minutes Kohlman was almost paralysed. We looked for the coramine and Mazeaud made him gulp some down. At last the Frenchman recovered and we were able to settle down.

At this moment, with the storm raging, we were as follows: I was on one narrow ledge, with Oggioni and Gallieni; Vielle, Mazeaud and Guillaume were on another ledge beside us while Kohlman was by himself on a third and slightly larger one farther down to give him a chance of stretching out. It was perhaps here that his psychological tragedy began, though we did not know it at the time.

The summit of Mont Blanc was not more than twelve hours' climb away from us. Beyond the summit, after we had conquered the Pillar, the Vallot hut was waiting, a sure shelter; after that, it was an easy descent to Chamonix. A break in the clouds for half a day would have been enough for us to achieve this, but in fact we never reached the summit.

It began to grow darker. The storm was more and more violent. We shut ourselves into our little tent and could judge the strength of the storm only by the intensity of the thunderclaps. Sometimes our spirits rose when we thought them to be very far off, sometimes we lost heart when we thought them close to us. The lightning flashes blinded us even through the opaque tent. We were there, alive, yet unable to do anything against the furious outpouring of the elements. Around us, secured to the same pitons that supported us in space, hung all our equipment for the climb: pitons, crampons and ice-axes; better bait for the lightning could not be imagined. We would have liked to throw them away, but how could we either ascend or descend without them? No one spoke; everyone was wrapped up in his own thoughts.

Just as we were thinking for the nth time that we were at the mercy of fate, we felt as if some force wanted to tear off our legs. We had all been grazed by the lightning. We yelled wildly. But we were alive, though now we knew that the storm could reduce us all to ashes at any time it chose. We called to one another to find out if everyone was still all right. Then there was a terrifying lull, which we knew heralded a last concentration of electricity which would inevitably break loose around us.

A few moments later a shock, similar to the one we had already experienced, but even more violent, nearly threw us off the face. Amid the commotion and shouts I could hear one voice clearly. I heard: 'We must get away!' I don't know if it was Oggioni or Gallieni. The words were born of despair and mirrored our state of mind. I thought that we were lost and I believe that we all thought the same. I relived my whole life and in my mind's eye saw all those dear faces and places which I should certainly never see again. Though by now resigned to my fate. I felt sorry that during my life I had not been able to do all the things I had intended. These are sensations which last only for seconds, yet they are clear and seem incredibly long.

Miraculously, however, the storm seemed to be dying away in the distance. Now we could only hear the drumming of the frozen snow on the rubberised cloth which covered us. We remained inert and apathetic; we did not even look outside the tent, for outside it was already dark. No one spoke. We did not eat. We were indifferent to everything. The snow which was falling though it was a very serious matter for us, almost gave us a sense of relief. We had been saved from the lightning and were still alive. I had never before been on such a face in such a storm: there was no skill and no technique which could have saved us.

Our complete immobility and the long stay in the tent had stifled us. We tore away a piece of the cloth and breathed avidly. Our tent was now buried in the snow, and the warmth of our bodies had created inside it watery drops which were transformed, by the sudden changes in temperature, now into water and now into ice crystals. I did not want to look at my watch, so as not to be disappointed by the slow passage of time. We did not speak to one another. All that could be heard were moans due sometimes to the discomfort of our positions, sometimes to the cold and sometimes to the feeling of suffocation which tortured us. We knew nothing about the Frenchmen, but we could often hear similar noises from them.

The night passed and a milky radiance heralded Wednesday's dawn. Only then did we emerge from the tent and were amazed at the amount of snow which had fallen during the night. The Frenchmen beside us were quite buried in it. Kohlman, on the wider ledge, was already standing up and looked like a dark blotch against the incandescent horizon, which seemed to announce a splendid day. We were overcome by a feeling of joy; the enormous quantity of fallen snow and the terrible frost were harbingers of good weather. Soon all of us were out of the tent, ready to begin the last stretch. I took a few snaps and we dismantled the little tent. But just as we were packing it up we found ourselves – I still do not know where those mists could have come from – again enveloped in the snowstorm. The very strong wind made the fresh snow whirl around us; we could not tell if it were snowing or whether this was the work of the wind.

We once more took refuge in our tent and the Frenchmen did the same. This time we went farther down, to Kohlman's ledge, which was larger and where the three of us – Oggioni, Gallieni and myself – could be a little more comfortable. Kohlman climbed up a few feet to where we had passed the night. He took his own bivouac equipment with him, a down sleeping-bag covered with plastic cloth, which wrapped him like a mummy. We belayed ourselves to pitons and settled down to wait.

During a short break a little earlier I had noticed that the snow had fallen even at a low altitude. We could scarcely believe that after snowing so long, the storm could come back once more. The Frenchmen asked me what I intended to do. I replied that we would wait, always in the hope of being able to get to the summit, the shortest way to safety. We were not short of provisions or equipment and could stay where we were. At this time of year the bad weather could not last very much longer and the idea of so dangerous and complicated a descent in the midst of a snowstorm terrified us, since we could reach the summit in less than half a day.

Mazeaud and his companions were belayed to a piton about twenty feet above me. Kohlman was alongside them. Mazeaud, who had a certain leadership over his companions, exchanged a few words with me and proposed that we two should set out together as soon as a break in the weather made it possible. Our job would be to fix pitons and ropes up the last two hundred and fifty feet of overhang, so that our five companions could come up after us. We agreed on this, but the break never came. We ate a little ham, some roast meat and jam, but we could not drink anything because the storm made it impossible to light a fire to make tea with melted snow.

It went on snowing, hour after monotonous hour. Amid the thoughts which jostled one another in my mind, I tried to remember other occasions, similar to this, when I had been trapped in the mountains by bad weather. I remembered that snowstorms had never lasted more than a day or two. So I said to myself: 'One day has gone already. The snowstorm cannot last more than another twenty-four hours. It is only a question of lasting out one day longer and then we shall be able to start.'

To remain in this very uncomfortable position squashed one

against the other in a space which could hardly hold a single person, became more and more intolerable. We could not turn our heads, we could not lie on our sides and the constant slope made it seem that our spines would crack. In such conditions it is easy to fall prey to irritability. There were moments when we would have liked to tear off our covering, but woe to us had we done so! Oggioni, Gallieni and I talked; we talked of everything; memories, plans, hopes, friendships, happy and unhappy reminiscences, just to kill time and to keep ourselves occupied.

Oggioni said to me: 'Do you remember when we said in Peru: Will the day ever come when we shall be together on the Pillar?' He said it sarcastically, since at that time we thought that everything on our home mountains would be easier. Yet now we were in conditions similar to those we had found on the Rondoy, when we had had to master that peak in the midst of a snowstorm and had been without shelter for two days and two nights. Gallieni was our vitamin man; he gave us pills, especially of vitamins C and A, to make up for our lack of food. He gave them to the Frenchmen by a primitive sort of pulley which we had made out of ropes and added some of our provisions. The Frenchmen were a little short of food.

The problem of passing water then arose. It was not possible to go out of the tent. I suggested to Gallieni that he should sacrifice his plastic cap and we each used it in turn. It was a terrifying experience; we had to make all sorts of contortions and hold fast to one another not to fall over. The whole operation took half an hour; our legs were hanging in space and our clothes hampered us.

It was now Wednesday evening. It was snowing harder than ever. I asked Gallieni, who was near the edge: 'Where's the wind blowing from?' 'Still from the west,' he said. That meant a snowstorm. Mazeaud, full of vitality and initiative, shouted to me: 'As soon as it gets better, you and I ought to go. If you think it would be better to start towards the left, then we will certainly go that way.' Oggioni, who did not know French, asked me what

Mazeaud had been saying and I explained. He agreed but asked: 'Do you think it possible to get out by way of the summit even in this weather?' He knew that I could find the way down from the summit whatever the weather, as I had already done it several times before. I said: yes, but that we should have to stay where we were another night, since in my heart I felt almost certain that the snowstorm would end next day.

Our breath in the tent was transformed into watery vapour and we were wet through. I thought with terror about what might happen when the hard frost which always precedes good weather came and hoped I would be able to bear it. We would have to spend an hour or so warming ourselves in the sun before making the last assault. We could not sleep. Night came upon us almost unawares. We were all on edge. Gallieni began to speak of his young children. My thoughts were ten thousand feet farther down, with my loved ones, in the intimacy of my home. Oggioni talked of Portofino. He had never been there and said: 'We mountaineers are really unlucky . . . with all the lovely things there are in the world, we get caught up in this sort of thing . . .' Gallieni said: 'And to think that I have a cosy home in Milano Marittima and such a nice beach: you can jump into the warm water and don't even have to take the trouble to swim, it's so shallow . . . You can walk for miles and miles . . .' Oggioni hid his apprehension with jokes. To look at, he was the calmest of the lot of us. I was sure that he, other than myself, was the only one to be fully aware that our plight was desperate.

The night between Wednesday and Thursday passed. In the forenoon Mazeaud came into our tent, because the plastic cloth over the Frenchmen's sleeping-bags had split under the gusts of wind. We managed to arrange ourselves after a thousand contortions and so passed the day. We tried to keep up our spirits, telling ourselves that the next day – Friday – would be fine, but we were not greatly convinced. In my inmost self I was already considering which would be the safest manner of retreating down the way we had come; in my opinion it was now impossible to reach the summit of the Pillar. I did not mention this to my companions so as not to discourage them.

Mazeaud told me about the south-west pillar of the Petit Dru which he had made the previous week. We spoke of our pleasure at getting to know one another and in sharing this adventure. We promised to meet again one day at Courmayeur or Chamonix and to talk over today's experiences. Our thirst was intense and we had to quench it by eating snow. We made pellets of snow and kept gnawing at them. We thought longingly of a tap at home which would give us all the water we wanted at a turn. It was paradoxical that in the midst of so much snow we should have a burning thirst. The frozen snow made our mouths burn and very sore.

Thursday passed and night came. During the long hours of darkness Oggioni and I, who were farthest from the edge, suffered particularly from lack of air. To him alone I confided my intention of descending at all costs. He agreed, but was terrified at the idea. Thursday night also passed. We had to set the alarm for half-past three. When I heard it ringing I shouted to everyone: 'We must go down at all costs. We cannot stay here any longer, otherwise it will be too late and we will not have the strength.'

When dawn began to break on the Friday morning the storm had been raging incessantly for more than sixty hours. Mist and snow merged into an impenetrable curtain. We dismantled everything and left a certain amount of our equipment behind. I was without an ice-axe which one of my companions had let fall by mistake on the first day. We began the descent by double rope. We had decided that I must lead, preparing the rappels. Behind me came all the others: Mazeaud, whose task was to help anyone who needed it, then the others and finally Oggioni who, strong in his experience, would be last man and recover the ropes.

At exactly six I lowered myself into the grey and stormy void almost blindly, without knowing where I was going. I felt as if I were in a stormy sea. The snow flurries gave me a feeling of dizziness. I had to watch every detail and try to recognise every fold of the rock to find out where I was. The manoeuvre took a long time and waiting for the ropes and pitons to come down from above in order to make the next rappel took even longer. Sometimes we were all bunched together, belayed to a piton, four or five of us hanging in space. About halfway down the Pillar I was unable to find a place to stop when the double rope came to an end. With some difficulty because of the snow flurries I managed to make myself understood. I needed another rope to attach to the one I was holding on to. There were no holds; the snow had packed tight even under the overhangs. I tied the two ropes together with my bare hands and continued my descent into space. There was now a four-hundred-foot rope down which I was sliding like a spider.

It was now no longer possible to talk with any of the others. I was completely suspended, looking for a hold which I could not find. I was worried, partly because I did not know where I could halt in my descent, partly because an enormous overhang cut off all possibility of communicating with my companions who, higher up, were waiting for my signal. At last, after some acrobatic swings in space, I managed to land on an outcrop of rock. I shouted repeatedly through the storm, hoping that my companions would understand that they could begin their descent. At one moment I saw the rope ascending and thought that one of them was on it and had begun to descend. Then, suddenly, the rope slipped away from me and dissappeared from sight. I was left there, on an outcrop, secured by a cord to a piton, in the heart of the Pillar, without any means of continuing my descent and wondering if my companions would be able to find me or would descend in some other direction. I went on shouting at the top of my voice, hoping to be heard, so that, if nothing else, they could tell me where they were. Several moments of anxiety passed. At last a dark patch appeared near me; it was Mazeaud who had realised where I was and had come to join me.

Our rappels continued with the same rhythm. We were getting closer to the foot of the Pillar. We were frozen and soaked through.

Then, hearing the dull thuds of some snowfalls. I realised that we had reached the base of the Pillar. But by now it was late in the afternoon and all we could do that night was to prepare a camp on the Col de Peuterey, which forms the base of the Pillar. We set foot on the level but the snow was extraordinarily deep; sometimes we sank into it up to our chests. I made Mazeaud take the lead for a bit, followed by all the others. I stayed where I was to give the direction. At one time the group seemed to have foundered in a very deep snowdrift. I joined them and then took the lead again, setting out by instinct towards the spot I thought suitable for a camp. Though I could not see it, it was imprinted on my mind. Behind me was Oggioni with whom I discussed whether it would be better to chance the protection which a crevasse could give us rather than build an igloo, since the snow was unstable. This was not so important for us who had our tent as for the four Frenchmen who hadn't one. We decided on the crevasse and told the Frenchmen, who accepted our advice.

We made arrangements for our camp before the night between Friday and Saturday fell. We had been making rappels for twelve hours. Kohlman seemed the most exhausted of all of us. We put him in our tent. With what was left of a butane gas cylinder Guillaume prepared some hot tea and gave it to him. The cold was atrocious. The wind was blowing continually and made the snow whirl around us. That was the worst night of all. We divided what was left of the provisions; prunes, chocolate, sugar and a little meat, now frozen. Oggioni refused the meat, preferring the sweetstuffs. All the others, however, nibbled at it. Kohlman showed me his fingers; they were livid. I thought it a good idea to massage them with cooking alcohol, of which we still had plenty. I passed him the alcohol flask, but he put it to his mouth and began to gulp it down. It was a most ill-advised action, but I thought he must have mistaken it for drinking alcohol. I took the flask away from him, but not before he had swallowed a couple of gulps. Were we already on the brink of madness?

It was pitch dark. We were in an inferno. Everyone was moaning and shivering with cold. The wind howled and the snow fell more and more heavily. Every now and then we would shake the snow off the tent, otherwise it would have smothered us. I tried to light the spirit-stove but had to give up for lack of air and, as in the last few days, we had to eat snow to quench our thirst. We were desperate, but no one said a word. Finally Oggioni said to me: 'Let's make a vow: if we get out of this safely, let us forget that the Pillar even exists.' I said, 'Yes.'

The night passed slowly and despairingly. At the same time as on the day before, at half past three, at the sound of my little alarm, we rose from our uncomfortable resting place. We wanted to save time and to get out of that terrifying situation which seemed as if it would never come to an end. The night had added another eighteen inches of snow to what had been there before. We set out in the midst of the storm. We all seemed to have endured that terrible camp well enough. Now I no longer had to take counsel with my companions; they left everything to me and I felt the heavy responsibility of a guide who must bring everyone back safely by the only possible route, the very dangerous Roches Gruber. We had to get to the Gamba before evening, otherwise it would be all over for all of us.

Before starting, Robert Guillaume gave Kohlman a coramine injection. Meanwhile, I, followed by Oggioni and Gallieni, began to clear a burrow through the very deep snow in the direction of the route chosen for our descent. We were now on a single rope in this order: Bonatti, Oggioni, Gallieni, Mazeaud, Kohlman, Vielle and Guillaume. The face which precedes the Roches Gruber was heavily laden with fresh snow which might avalanche at any moment. I told my companions to hurry up and join me and to get into shelter so that I could hold on to a rope if an avalanche should catch me while I was cutting the channel which would lead us to the Roches Gruber. I managed to do so and called to the others to pass, one by one, but when it came to Vielle's turn he could not do it. He kept falling and rising again, with every sign of exhaustion. Guillaume was beside him and encouraged him. He took Vielle's rucksack which he had thrown away on the slope, but Vielle seemed deaf to all our appeals which became rougher and rougher.

Meanwhile I went on to prepare the first of a very long series of rappels down the Roches Gruber. The sky had cleared for a moment, but the fine spell only lasted a short time. I could hear my companions inciting Vielle who had still not got across the couloir. I shouted to them to hurry up and begin the descent if we didn't want to die up there. I was the farthest down and was waiting for Kohlman who had followed me. Half an hour passed. Not understanding the delay. I again went up the rope for a few feet to see what was happening. Gallieni told me that Vielle was exhausted, that he was unable to cross the couloir by himself. He asked me if it would be possible to slide him along the snow to lighten the fatigue of walking. I agreed and told him to act quickly, adding that at this pace not only would we not get to the Gamba hut, but we would not even get down the Roches Gruber.

I went down again and rejoined Kohlman. I gathered from the excited voices of my companions that they were putting their plan into effect. I went on waiting for one of them to lower himself to me. Another half hour passed and not only did no one come down to join me, but their voices began little by little to die away. I didn't know what to do. Must every rappel take as long as this? Once again I shinned up the rope a few feet, far enough to be able to see my companions. I asked them: 'Why don't you come down?' A voice, possibly Gallieni's, followed by that of Mazeaud, told me: 'Vielle is dying!' I was petrified. I could see before me the little group of friends gathered around Vielle's body, which looked like a dark, inert bundle on the white snow. He was belayed to the rock and wrapped in our tent-cover to prevent the crows from getting at him.

I went back to Kohlman without telling him anything. Several more minutes, perhaps twenty, passed; now I knew it was all over with Vielle. There were no more voices to be heard, only the sound of the wind. It had begun to snow again. This agony unbroken by any human word was terrible. I went up the rope again and saw my companions busy securing to a piton Vielle's body and Galleni's rucksack, full of superfluous things. There were no laments. It was then ten o'clock. I went back again to Kohlman and told him to hold fast. Then Mazeaud arrived, who told him in broken phrases what had happened. Kohlman was deeply affected, and wept.

We continued the rappel. Taking advantage of a moment when all six of us were hanging on the same piton, I advised the greatest possible speed if we did not want to share Vielle's fate. Oggioni, as always, was my right-hand man and took the rear. Like Mazeaud, Guillaume and myself, he was carrying a full rucksack. Mazeaud, the strongest and the acknowledged leader of the Frenchmen, had the job of keeping the others up to the mark.

Not quite an hour had passed when we heard voices. I was the farthest down the rope at the time and I thought they must be the voices of my companions above me. Soon, however, I was convinced that someone was searching for us on the glacier below. I shouted back and asked my companions to shout all together, so that they could hear us. From the cries which came from below I understood that they wanted to tell me something, but the gusts of wind prevented me from understanding. For my part, I was quite certain that down there they would not be able to understand what I was shouting, which was: where were they and could they hear us. We went on in better spirits. When we reached the end of the Roches Gruber; about half past three, I calculated that from the morning before, when we had begun the descent, we had made at least fifty rappels.

A brief break in the storm allowed us to see the whole surface of the chaotic Frêney glacier. What a lot of snow had fallen! There were no furrows in the snow, which meant that no rescue party had passed that way. Where had the voices come from? We could see no one and fell into a mood of the blackest despair. Perhaps it was all over for all of us. We had been sure that the voices had come from the foot of the Roches Gruber and that had given us strength to overcome the terrible difficulties and dangers of that exceedingly difficult passage. We were, however, alone at the foot of the rocks and we still had before us many unforeseeable dangers on our way to the Gamba hut.

The slow and exhausting descent of the glacier began. We refused to accept our bad luck. The snow was still very deep. Not even in winter climbs could I recall having met with so much. We left behind us not a trail but a burrow. Fortunately the mists were beginning to rise and visibility gradually improved. That made it possible for us to enter safely the labyrinth of crevasses which led to the Col de l'Innominata, the last serious difficulty on our way to safety. But the deep snow so slowed down our advances, that we despaired of being able to reach the base of the col while there was still daylight.

I felt faint with fatigue, physical suffering and cold, but refused to give up.

Our file grew longer. Oggioni was stumbling every few steps, at the end of his tether. He was without a rucksack, which he had handed over to Gallieni. Sometimes he was last man, sometimes last but one. We groped our way on to the glacier in complete disorder, drunk with fatigue. We were roped together, but each went his own way without heeding anything. I realised that in such conditions it would be very hard for us to reach the foot of the Col de l'Innominata in daylight. Gallieni, behind me, seemed the least exhausted. I decided to unrope myself and him in order to go ahead as quickly as we could and prepare the couloir of the Innominata, otherwise our companions would no longer be able to climb it. This task would have to be completed by nightfall.

Our companions followed in our tracks. Meanwhile I attacked the terrible ice which had encrusted the Col de l'Innominata. Guillaume had remained behind. Within half an hour it would be dark and we were still struggling to reach the col. Now we were again all roped together; myself, Gallieni, Oggioni, Mazeaud and Kohlman. Our only hope was to reach the rescue parties while we still had a little strength left. They alone might be able to save those left behind. It was pitch dark when I reached the Col de l'Innominata. It was Saturday evening, after nine o'clock, and we had been out for six days. The powdery snow driven by the wind had begun again and in the west we could see the flashes of an approaching thunderstorm. There was nowhere to fix a piton to anchor the rope which supported my four companions and I had to hold it on my shoulders. I urged them to hurry. But the operation was very long and desperate. Orders mingled with cries of pain and desperation. Behind Gallieni, Oggioni seemed unable to grip the rock. Gallieni tried to help him in every way he could, supported in his turn by the rope which I held on my shoulders. The two Frenchmen down at the end of the rope were shouting and raving.

It was chaos. Three hours passed and we were still at the same point. I could not move. Every so often there were tugs at the rope which nearly pulled me into space. The pain of the rope and the cold made me feel faint. But if I collapsed it meant the end for everyone. In all those three hours Oggioni had not been able to move. All encouragement was in vain. Now and then he would reply with a wail; he seemed to be in a sort of trance. He was attached by a karabiner to a piton, and would have to free himself from it to give us a chance of hauling him up. But he hadn't the strength and he was so exhausted that perhaps he was incapable of thinking. I would have liked to go down to him but that was impossible since I had to keep the rope, which was holding him as well as Gallieni, firmly on my shoulders. At last, not being able to do anything else, Gallieni made sure that Oggioni was firmly fixed to the piton, undid the rope that bound him to Oggioni and the Frenchmen and came up to join me and was thus able to carry on rapidly towards the rescue parties. Oggioni remained roped to the strong Mazeaud, to whom I shouted to wait and look after the others who would soon be rescued.

While we were doing this we saw Kohlman fumbling his way along the rope in the darkness on the ice-covered face. He was unroped. He came towards us and passed Mazeaud, Oggioni and

Gallieni with an energy born of desperation which bordered on madness. Gallieni, guessing his state, managed to grasp him and tie him to the rope. Soon all three of us reached the col. Kohlman told us he was hungry and thirsty and then went on: 'Where is the Gamba hut?' He was completely out of his senses, but we could not abandon him.

We roped him between us. Gallieni was the first to begin the descent, followed by Kohlman who seemed to have forgotten all the rules of prudence. The slope was very difficult, steep and covered with ice. For the first hundred and fifty feet we let ourselves slide along a fixed rope evidently left there by the rescue parties searching for two Swiss on the Pointe Gugliermina. Then we went on as best we could. But Kohlman became more and more dangerous. He let himself slide on his back, hanging on to the rope and without using his crampons. At the end of the rope he continued to hang there and I had to support him, which made it impossible for me to catch up with him. When at last the rope became lighter, after he had found some sort of foothold, an unexpected tug told me he had again broken away and exposed us all to the risk of falling.

Neither threats nor encouragements moved him. He shouted disconnected phrases, gesticulated, raved. We thought we should have managed to get down in an hour; with Kohlman, now delirious, that hour became three.

With God's help, we reached the bottom. We still had an hour before us to reach the Gamba hut over snowdrifts which presented neither dangers nor difficulties save for their depth. We began to recover our spirits and our only thought was how to reach the hut quickly when an unexpected incident delayed us. Gallieni had dropped one of his gloves. He bent down to recover it and tried to keep his hand warm by thrusting it into his jacket. Kohlman, who interpreted this movement as an attempt to draw a pistol, spread his arms and rushed on Gallieni, clasping him tightly and making him roll down the slope. Gallieni managed to break free and I tried to check their movements with the rope. Kohlman then hurled himself at me. I dodged and he fell and began to roll, writhing in delirium. He had completely lost his senses. Then he rose again and tried to rush at us. By pulling both ends of the rope, we managed to keep him at a distance. We were all three roped together and one of us could break free. We could not drag him with us and it was essential not to lose a minute.

To untie ourselves from him, we had first to undo the iced-up knots. We had no knife, yet we had to get away from our poor crazed companion. He was watching every movement, ready to launch himself at us. One at a time, keeping the rope taut with our teeth, we lowered our breeches so as to be able to slip the noose of rope about our waists over our hips. We succeeded in this without Kohlman realising what we were doing. Then I shouted to Gallieni: 'Let go and run!' and we rushed off, rolling on the snow. There was only one thing to do: we must get to the hut in time to tell the rescue squads. Kohlman, up there, was in no danger of falling. But, as it happened, the first squad only arrived in time to see him draw his last breath.

In this way we covered the last twelve hundred feet which still divided us from the Gamba hut. It was pitch dark. We only managed to find it because I knew this area as well as my own house. Gallieni followed me unhurt. We circled the hut, hammering on the windows with our fists. We had just reached the door when we heard heavy steps inside and a hand raised the latch. The door burst open; we saw the interior of the hut dimly lit by a small lamp. It was full of sleeping men. We stepped over several bodies without recognising anyone. Then suddenly one of the men leapt to his feet and shouted: 'Walter, is that you?' and there was a rush of people and we were suffocated by embraces.

'Be quick!' I shouted. 'There's one man still out there! The others are on the Innominata! Be quick!' It was three o'clock on Sunday morning. The storm was still raging. We stretched out on the table in the middle of the hut and the others took the frozen crampons from our feet, undressed us and gave us dry clothes and warm drinks. I fell into a heavy stupor. When I awoke about three hours had gone by. The bodies of my companions had been found, except Vielle. They told me that Oggioni was dead and I was filled with uncontrollable grief. Dear Mazeaud, the only one of them to be found alive, embraced me and wept with me.

COTOPAXI

SEBASTIAN SNOW
(1929–2001)

English explorer. Despite no previous climbing experience he scaled both Chimborazo (20,500 feet) and Cotopaxi (at 19,650 feet the world's highest volcano) in Ecuador in 1953.

At the base camp – about 15,800 feet – we met four other Ecuadorians – all very youthful, and associates of the *Neuvos Horizontes* organization, who on hearing of our plan to spend the night on the crater-lip of the volcano decided that opportunity was too good to be missed. This decision was frightening; we tried hard to dissuade them for there was a good chance of them freezing solid before morning could come again. They had only one tent – too awkward to carry up to the summit, and there were then – that auspicious evening – still four of them.

'What will you do then – when you get up there?' we asked.

'We will dig ourselves foxholes and curl up in our sleeping-bags.'

'You won't last the night, you won't wake in the morning. It's your responsibility; we'll have nothing to do with it.'

Next morning at eight o'clock we set out in two parties, on two separate ropes. My own party carried only emergency equipment – a little two-man tent, which one enters on all fours through a hole in the side; some preserved fruit, a thermos of coffee, chocolate biscuits and barley sugar. The other four had thin sleeping-bags and iron rations.

For the first half-hour after leaving camp climbing was of the scrambling nature, amounting to no more than a breathless trudge over loose, volcanic shale. The first moment came when we arrived at the snow-line – here both parties solemnly sat on an outcrop of rock and started getting out crampons – ice-spikes – and ropes. This was frightening, for neither of these articles had to my conscious knowledge graced either my feet or waist.

Edmundo led, with myself in the centre and Pépé in the rear. We climbed cautiously along a traverse in steady relays, Edmundo employing his ice-axe with dexterous precision to cut steps for those behind by which we made the slow ascent.

With infinite care he would cut steps ahead of him, climbing sometimes thirty feet at a time while Pépé and I would pay out the rope – I was not good at this and would frequently hold up progress by getting it entangled around the spikes in my crampons. When this happened I perspired with frantic embarrassment and that in its turn meant that moisture obscured my spectacles and goggles – and before we continued I had to take them off and wipe them both. This happened many times.

When Edmundo had proceeded about ten yards he would drive his ice-axe into the snow, belay the rope around it and again around his body for double security and then take the strain while I climbed up the steps towards him. Reaching him I would belay and he (Edmundo) would proceed upwards for another thirty feet hacking out further ice-steps until he would belay once more to allow Pépé to join me. Then the manoeuvre would be repeated all over again and in this way we painstakingly ascended the dome of the world's highest volcano. It was very tiring for Edmundo.

Although it was toilsome work, it was also dangerous, for we all knew that one moment's relaxation or carelessness might plunge all three of us a thousand feet headlong below. I was just beginning to properly understand what mountaineering meant.

We had been climbing in this manner for perhaps half an hour when suddenly there was a cry from the party behind. Turning, I expected to witness someone falling. But no! – they were all on their feet. Pépé shouted a question across the intervening furrow between the two parties – his voice sounded strangely sinister in the silence of the Andean mountain air. A very few seconds later a voice replied, 'Snow blindness', and the next moment two of them – one leading the other – were taking the first steps down towards the Base camp. Now there were two. The hand of Providence must have been upon us, for if this incident had not occurred when and where it did – this account would not have been written. But we did not then know what the future held.

We watched the two going slowly down for a few minutes then we turned and faced what would lie ahead. Now, as we started again, my leg muscles began to ache intolerably and I thought I could never go on. But I did, I did . . .

At about 18,000 feet we came upon the first of the two crevassed areas – most dangerous part of the climb.

The first crevasse loomed up ahead – a six-foot fissure which doubtless went down into unimaginable depths.

We halted. Pépé drove his ice-axe hard into the frozen snow, tested it, hitched the rope around it, and took the strain. A second later Edmundo had leapt across the gap – the soft vibration of his landing on the far side caused the snow overhangs at the treacherous and uneven edge to crumble and fall in little sparkling lumps into the crevasse. It was fascinating. Then came my turn. I waited while Edmundo had me belayed on his side. I was trembling – as he looked up from his work and nodded. I jumped. A leap of six feet is nothing at sea-level, it's an exertion at 18,000 feet with crampons encrusted with frozen snow to weight one's feet. I had never jumped a crevasse before. All across, we struggled on again, placing our feet carefully in the steps Edmundo cut, with such toil, ahead; the temperature was below zero, the wind was rising, the weather worsening. Where the slightest slip meant the loss of life, we crawled warily.

At this stage I called for very frequent rests for my lungs heaved like the bellows of the hearth, and my heart, wholly unaccustomed to extreme elevation, thundered, like an express train entering a long tunnel, my legs ached intolerably, as if I had a chronic fever. Edmundo and Pépé were very patient – but I sensed, rather than saw, through their dark goggles that they were worried – for time was running out, and it was absolutely essential we gain the crater before darkness came. I wondered if I would stick it out, but I had to – these men were risking their lives at my invitation, I could not let them down now.

Then suddenly, as so often happens when one is at the end of one's tether, something happened. Edmundo had come to a halt – frozen in his steps like a pointer in the snow. His experienced eyes had detected an unusual darker patch in the snow ahead which showed where frozen snow had formed a flimsy treacherous snow-bridge across the depths of a crevasse. To put foot on that bridge would have invited disaster. Again we jumped.

Now the snow was getting deeper, often above our thighs. The wind was still mounting; it moaned now. I wondered what it would be like on the crater, for down here it was almost the force of a gale as it drove frozen particles of snow into the uncovered parts of our faces like the points of a thousand pine-needles. The protective cream with which I had smothered every unprotected part did nothing to alleviate the pain. I had some more in my rucksack, but couldn't make the effort to do anything that was not automatic. At this point I believe all three of us were feeling the strain, resting every few yards, climbing up and up in a series of traverses, like an ambitious cyclist up a very steep gradient, tacking three or four yards one way then three or four back the other. So sheer was the climb that it was impossible to take it in a straight line. Our rate of ascent must have been well under 500 feet an hour – slower than that when the snow deepened.

Later the all-encompassing darkness began to close down upon us. The gale, still rising, whipped up the snow from the face of the mountain in a fury blizzard, blotting out everything ahead.

Edmundo was himself now stopping frequently – lying like a waif in the snow smitten with the unpredictable *soroche* (mountain sickness) that made him vomit continuously. Bravely he insisted on retaining the first place on the rope. But it was a mistake for isolated in his world of sickness he went off the course and all sense of direction left us. This was really my fault, for it was I who had insisted on frequent stops which initially had wasted the precious hours of light – now we were paying for my mistake.

I staggered on blindly wherever Edmundo was leading – in a world of gloom, wind and drifting snow that to me was very sinister. All my extremities were frozen numb, they somehow seemed to obey like robots. I thought my face was going to be marked, horribly, for life.

We were all near to exhaustion, struggling like automatons, our breath coming in short, deep gasps as the altitude increased. But we had to go forward. To stop and rest meant collapse, dying of exposure in the white graves our warm bodies would imprint for themselves too easily in the ever-deepening snow. I did not know how the others felt but I was now desperately alarmed – grateful for the darkness as it withheld the sight of my tears from the eyes of Pépé – Edmundo would not have noticed, he was too ill. My one desire was to sit and never to rise; I wanted to leave my bones where we were, but I lacked the courage. Fear, coupled with the encouragements of Pépé, kept me going. Pépé was wonderful.

Suddenly there was a shout of triumph from Edmundo. Through a gap in the curtain of the blizzard he caught sight, momentarily, of the craggy outlines of the crater-lip itself. A wave of extreme jubilation swept through the party. Cold, fatigue, irritation were temporarily forgotten. We almost ran those last few yards . . . or what seemed at first to be the last few yards.

But our run quickly became a walk again, the walk a drunken stagger. Another five . . . ten . . . fifteen minutes passed, and still the elusive silhouette of what we so longingly sought eluded us – or was it that our eyes could not properly focus?

Again I fell over the frozen lengths of rope to lie spreadeagled, hopelessly, in the deep snow. I knew I had to make the effort to get up . . . to get up and go on . . . to get up and go on. I repeated the simple phrase over and over again for my brain had become irrevocably fixed in one groove and the gramophone kept playing . . . 'Get up and go on,' with unbearable monotony. I got to my feet and was just starting again when through the howling gale another shout came from Edmundo. He had reached the crater of Cotopaxi.

We struggled to join him on the marginal strip of loose, black lava, some thirty feet wide, where there was no snow.

Now, with the external side of the volcano no longer providing shelter, we caught the full force of the gale that came from the east.

Pépé and I struggled to pitch the two-man tent among the boulders and stones on the black patch of lava which separated the unpredictable depths of the volcano from the icy, snow-covered slope we had so painfully ascended.

The only way we could erect the tent was by Pépé crawling in through the hole – like a participant in an obstacle race – and pushing up the hollow aluminium tent-pole from within. While outside, I, at the same moment, pulled out the base flaps to their full extent and hammered in the skewer-like stays. Poor Edmundo, too ill to take any active part, watched fascinated as though in the throes of a nightmare.

Somehow we got the fragile-looking shelter up at a ridiculously uneven angle, about five feet below the edge of the volcano, just sufficient to allow the worst of the raging wind to pass over the conical top of the canvas. Even so the pressure on the ground pegs was exacting, and before entering I dragged some heavy boulders into position to weight down the edges of the tent as I considered it probable we might find ourselves halfway down the way we had come before dawn. This was a great work at 19,650 feet, and once the boulders were in place, the hitherto two-man tent was reduced internally to a one-man dimension. Nevertheless we all three managed to ease ourselves inside together with our rucksacks, rope, crampons, etc. We scarcely expected sleep.

Edmundo, ill with mountain sickness, lay in an inert heap. Pépé and I huddled close together, cramped, cold, and exhausted. The only food we had was a small carton of dried prunes – the ascent had taken much longer than anticipated and we had eaten everything else. We had no stove to 'fabricate water'.

Meanwhile the remaining two of the other party had also reached the crater, and even now we could hear sounds like a blacksmith's forge some ten yards away. They were digging their graves with vigour, their ice-axes crunching into the frozen, stony lava. Would they be able to dig deep enough holes? I wondered.

Some ten minutes after the noises of human endeavour had altogether ceased – there was a cry – almost theatrical in its tragic intensity, brought to us as it was through the moaning gale. I nudged Pépé.

'They'll freeze to death out there,' I said. Whereupon I untied the flap by which we entered our tent and shouted. A minute or so passed before a wretched apparition dragging a sleeping-bag after him appeared in the doorway. Unceremoniously Pépé and I helped him in; he was almost on the verge of collapse. He was only eighteen and, I noticed, had no gloves. Why did he come? A few minutes later there was a further cry, and a little later another figure appeared at the entrance – we got him in as well. How we did so I don't know.

It was then about seven o'clock in the evening and for the next sixteen hours the two-man tent (reduced to one-man in capacity) bulged with five frozen human beings. It was suffocating, yet freezing, and I kept making involuntary little lunges at the roof in quest of oxygen. If I'd had a knife I would have cut a hole and stuck out my nose. Instead I ran my fingers over the cold, moist canvas and applied them to my forehead. It helped for a few short seconds – it was like a self-baptism. But a little later I stood it no longer and dived bodily for the entrance flap, untied it, and ejected my head dartingly like a cobra in the act of striking, but brought it back into the tent as suddenly for outside the cold was equally insupportable. When circulation died in our feet we rubbed each other feverishly; two of us were too ill to bother. Perhaps they were fortunate – rubbing is very painful. We attempted two songs – they died as soon as they came to our lips. Two of us devoured the prunes, one did not want them and the other two did not know, I suppose, we even had them. Oh, the lassitude!

Even when dawn came again and the wind had dropped we could not get out for a blanket of mist enveloped the entire mountain. We had to wait until nearly eleven o'clock before the sun broke through.

By this time Edmundo had slightly recovered. It was decided now that we were on the crater we must try to scale a dangerous ice and snow pinnacle that rose some 150 feet above the lip. It has never been climbed. Accordingly, after an intense struggle to separate and find our various 'dismembered' limbs, we crawled out and put on our boots and crampons. How hateful they were! Fearful objects that no longer seemed part of us.

Leaving the tent and the other two within it, we climbed the few feet to the crater, in enforced slow motion, and then walked carefully along the lip. The wind was unbelievably painful on our right cheeks. There was nothing to see within the 'chimney' – nothing but scurrying mist and general murkiness. We moved for perhaps a hundred yards before the eminence that was our immediate goal came into view. It looked horribly sheer and full of predatory cornices. Soon we reached its base, but the mist, suddenly, totally obscured it. We couldn't remain where we were – the wind cut through as if we had no bone structure. We took cover behind a low line of frozen *sèracs* – as though we were in a slit trench preparatory to a final assault. We remained crouched in this manner for twenty minutes without moving – the mist did not lift for more than a few seconds at a time. At last we could stand it no longer and we made our way back to the tent and hustled the others.

With the visibility again getting worse, we struck camp and started off down the mountain in two parties as before. We came upon the crevassed areas again; more dangerous this time for there had been a fresh fall of snow in the night and consequently many new 'bridges' had been created.

Suddenly I felt the snow move underfoot, shuddering and sliding away. Stupidly I had ventured on to one of the 'new bridges' although Edmundo ahead had missed it. I tried to throw myself forward to safety. Too late. I felt myself dropping, then happily came an agonizing jerk around the ribs, and the rope held.

It was Pépé who had saved me. Even as the snow gave way, expectant as ever, he had stopped dead in his tracks, driving his ice-axe hard into the ground, twisting the rope like lightning around and at the same time leaning back on his heels to take the strain.

But all I knew then as I hung suspended was an urgent shout from Pépé. I didn't understand all the words but knew well enough what they meant.

'Don't move! Whatever you do – don't move!'

I felt rather like a marionette on a string until I at last managed to get a firm grip on the marginal snow.

We reached the Base camp – at 15,800 feet – at about three o'clock on the same afternoon, spent the night, went down to Hacienda Ilitio next day, and from thence we walked on to the main trunk road at Lasso and there picked up a long-distance bus for Quito where we arrived at about ten o'clock the same evening. It had been a hectic thirty-six hours. I nearly broke down in the street outside the bus terminus while I awaited the arrival of a taxi. It was a very, very short wait perhaps of only fifteen minutes – but something within me broke and I lost the faculties of direction, decision, and initiative. I swayed towards the ground, but just as I was about to drop a cab appeared and I fell within into the back seat.

The residents of the *Residencia Lutetia* were not all in bed as I groped my way through the hall. Paul Feret extricated himself from a group of people collected around the warmth of the fire.

'Did you do it, Sebastian?'

'Yes.'

'The bit of the top?'

'No.'

Then Paul gave me an arm and I went to my room and fell into bed with all the clothes that had been around me on the crater. When I awoke to strong sunlight, I found someone had taken off my boots.

MIRROR, MIRROR

ED DRUMMOND
(1951–)

American rock-climber. In 1972 Drummond made the first ascent of Arch Wall on the North Face of Trollrygen. The climb took twenty days.

We reached Oslo in two days, nudging in under the shrouds of cloud spreading a thin fine rain upon toast-faced Norwegians and palefaces alike. It was the first rain for a month. Burning up to Romsdal on the bike, I found my cagoule was promiscuous in the rain, but Lindy, at the back of me, kept dry and fed me on choco-late and made me hum with her big hugs. I couldn't lean on her as I could my cold companion of other years who pulled on my neck: my rain-slimed haul bag, my meticulous Humpty Dumpty. She was continually delighted at new waterfalls; she flew oohs to my ears and near the end of the journey, my goggles crying with rain, I raised a soggy arm at the alp of cloud shearing up a white mile. 'That's the wall,' I roared. She gripped her hand on my arm, and yelled about the coming bend.

Where am I? I'm cold. Thin mists shift past, touching me. Where is she? She must have got out of the bag. I shake my head out, struggling to look. There is another near me, raw-red in the white air. Hugh! A dream. I'm not on the Romsdalhorn. That was a week ago. Lindy isn't here. This is the wall.

So. Three nights. Almost 1,000ft. Our second ledge, Luckys. Seven pitches and a paper-dry cag. Hugh's still in the bag,

113

sleeping the sleep of the just, sound as a foetus, on his first wall. During the past three years I had, in three summers and a spring, snailed the mile-long approach scree twenty-three times and twenty times I came back. Not this time. 'The Northern European Wall'; 'The Mourning Wall'; 'The Rurt Wall' (Realised Ultimate Reality Troll); 'The Lord of the Walls'; 'The Drummond Route' (if we said nothing they'd call it this); 'The Royal Wall', naw, what has Robbins ever done for you? You'll never level with him.

On our first cralk up to the wall – the scree is so steep that it's like trying to ski uphill – we had climbed the first slabs, 200ft or so, gritty, nasty, wobbling to extreme. There had been the snow pitch, cricket size, and the jokes about forgetting the ice-axes, using skyhooks and étriers as we had no crampons and the ice was marble. Then the 'schrund and my little leap; it was all fun. After three trips we'd brimmed the hauls and I'd climbed the third, a squirrelly free up a great crooked slab, funnelling to an upside-down squeeze chimney that made me squeak. Then we went down, Lindy, who'd come up to watch, and I, slowly, like two old people, while Hugh flew off to the river where he swam among the salmon; the fishermen had all gone home. We just promised us a swim when it was all over.

Returning, two days later, Hugh went first and the hauls went after, quite a while after. His first haul; his first artyfishyl; first hamouac; first air jumar (barring one from a tree in Mexico). Hugh was, slowly, going up the wall. So it was noon when I set out on the fourth pitch.

And it was seven in the evening when Hugh's jumars gritted their teeth to follow. What passed in those seven hours is unforgettable: my mouth, sock-hot; my larynx strangling for spit; a fine trembling as of a thin wind trembling through me. It began with a layback of 20ft, wonderful but for the iron stone around my neck – it was a struggle, favourite uncle, was it not? Then the footholds faded away and I muttered on nuts under this thin roof until the only way up was up.

There was a crack, not a crack crack, but a line, a cra . . . ; the start of a crack say. At any rate the bolts were in the haul bag and this was the third pitch of the NA Wall as far as I was concerned. My rurps curled up when I banged their heads and refused to sit still. After five fingernail knifeblades I got out my hook and sat on that, about as secure as the last angel to make it on to that pinhead. Then I struck dirt. Now dirt is okay if you can get dug in. I began and ended with a knifeblade which dangled sillily from my waist, and I was glad that it was not me that was holding the rope, for after four hours and 40ft I might have been caught napping. But Hugh wasn't and as it was I only went 15ft for the hook stuck and though it trembled it snapped not, O Dolt.

So then I had to free that bit, but after that it eased some. Nuts hammered in the dirt and at long last a ding dong bong. Hotheaded I'd reached a ledge, feeling a bit sorry for myself. 'No Ledges' we called it and it all hung out. There we had a pantomime in hammocks by head torch which was really not in the least bit funny. Hugh, as chattery as a parrot, floated above me in his one-point. He even said he was comfortable and had the cheek to take a shit. By a battery son et lumière I watched his anus line an angry eye; no voyeur but it might look my way. However, he missed me, my arms full of ropes like some deeply confused spider.

'Ed! Come on, it's light.'

Oh, God, awake already.

'Look at the sun.'

Why don't you go back to sleep?

'Unh uh.'

There and then I decided that if he was unable to lead the next pitch, then that was it. I'd led every pitch so far (didn't you want to?) and it was unthinkable that I'd lead all of them. Not bloody likely. I'd make that clear. I tortoised out. What are you smiling at? Rather him than me. I've had about bloody five minutes bloody sleep. 'Right, coming.'

It was strange to be there, sitting up in the hammock, feet stirring in the air over the side, opening the haul, fingers weaseling in the cold stuff bags, tramp-thankful for food in the hand. Eating quietly we heard the whipcrack of breaking ice in the gloomy cwm below and I'd yell 'hello' with a dervish fervour (wake up, Drummond, grow up, you can't go back). The echoes yodelled and I'd say to Hugh, 'He's there.'

'Who?' he'd ask.

'That bloke,' I'd tell him. 'Listen.' And I'd do it again and we'd both cackle like kids with a home-made phone.

By 7 a.m. I was ready to belay him. I wasn't laughing now. One more pitch and there would be no retreat. I moled into the cold rope bag, my arms up to my elbows, fingers fiddling for the iron sling. I had a krab, empty, ready on the belay to receive it. My fingers curled in the sling; I moved my arm gracefully, slowly (I was cold), to clip it into the krab before passing it up to him. If I drop the iron sling we'll have to go back down. From the end of my arm my little family of fingers waved at me. And it went, there, no, once, twice, there, oh, down, out, there, and under and into the heart of the icefield, clinking like lost money.

I couldn't believe it. Hugh was silent. I kept saying I was sorry. I didn't mean it. Not this time (How do you know?). I couldn't believe it. Hugh said nothing.

'I've done it now.'

Instantly, 'How long will it take you to get back up?'

He's got you now.

I got back by noon, gasping. I'd come down to earth. A 600ft abseil, my figure-of-eight sizzling my spits at it, and then a free jumar all the way back. I was furious. 'Right, belay on.'

His pitch was perfect after a bit. Dirty at first, then a cool, clean fist-lock crack. Iron out in the air like a bunch of weapons, he groped at the sky like something falling. All around a sea-sheer swell of wall, untouchable. Him the one sign of life.

Then the rain came. A dot in the eye. I heave for my cagoule, one eye on Hugh, an invisible drizzle blackening the rock. New noises fizz in. Twitters of water and Hugh is yelling for his cagoule, but I point out the time and that he's leaking already. Well, for a couple of hours I kept pushing boiled sweets in my mouth and

Hugh kept on moaning and kept on. After 150ft he had to stop and pin himself to the wall.

Early evening. There he hung, wringing himself like fresh washing. Thank God he had no cagoule, or we would both have been up there for the night, him perched above, if not on, my head like a great wet heron. The waterfalls would weep all night. 'Why wait for Godot?' I yelled up. He said, 'Eh?' so I said, 'Come on down, let's piss off.'

We stripped the ropes off the hauls, tied the lot together and down we went, happy as nuns in a car. A slalom down the scree and back before dark. Back in the camp hut we listened with Lindy, gladly, to the rain hissing outside while we kissed at a smug mug of tea and drooled on the food to come. That night I slept like a child.

Eight days later, well picked, we humped up the boulder-fields in epileptic sun showers, snagged at by cold-cutting winds. The days were getting shorter.

The bergschrund had rotted back and we had to go down inside the mouth. Our ropes were 20ft up the slabs, strung taut to a peg. I manteled up on this mica jug, massaging off the dust, feeling sick with this white pit under me, thirty feet deep, rocks in its dark, lurking.

When I had the end of the rope I dangled a bong on and looped it to him. Three times I threw and three times I missed; each time the bong tolled dolefully. 'Hey, our funeral knell,' I yelled, but he wasn't impressed.

Two and half jumehours later Hugh brooded on the haul eggs, sucking the sacred sweet, as I botched up the freeasy and awkwaid of the next pitch. When I warbled down about the ledge I'd found, he said he'd kiss me, but on arrival he didn't hold me to the treat. In fact, the first thing that he said was that the next pitch looked a bit steep for him and ordered me to do it. But since it was dark I could wait until tomorrow. Under the tube-tent, scarfed in cigar smoke, we crept to sleep like refugees.

Pitch 7 took me all the next day. It is 156ft long; our ropes were

150ft long, at a stretch. That last six feet to the belay cracks saw me lying flat on my face on the ledge, hammering like front-crawling. Hugh climbed up from his end, pulling the haul bags (one at a time, and there were three, each weighing over fifty pounds) on to his shoulder and then weightlifting them up so that I could get them through the pulley. Hugh studied Law at university.

So. Three nights. Almost 1,000ft. Lucky's Ledge is no longer important. A stab of butter, a jab of honey; the pumpernickel crumbling among your fingers, a steamy censer of tea, packing your bags, hurrying as a jostle of cumulus smudges out the sun and the stove starts to fizz the drizzle.

As I remember we made three pitches that day in a rain as insidious as gas. For two or three seconds, suddenly the valley would come like an answer, and we would stumble into conversation, then numb up, sullen with wet clothes and cold, clubbed feet. In the downpouring darkness I jumed up to Hugh, squatting on blocks, owl aloof. While he belayed me I hand-traversed down to a ledge on his left, where I backheeled and rubbled away for over half an hour, making the bed. We couldn't find pin placements for the tube tent, so we hung our bivi bags from the rope and crept into their red, wet dark.

Sneaking out the next day at noon like shell-less tortoises, I realised as we both emptied a gallon of fresh water from our bags, that it might be better to have the opening at the front rather than at the top of the bag. A point that had escaped me as I tried out the bag on the floor in front of the fire at home. Sneer not. Wasn't the first Whillans Box a plastic mac and a pram? The Drummond Cot would have its night in time. Well, we strung the tube tent as an awning, lit the stove, and wrung our pulpy feet out, sitting in the cloud, machine-gunned by water drops from the great roofs that crashed out over 200ft wide, a thousand feet above our heads. We wriggled a little in the tent, slowly gulping lumpy salami, a bit stunned, stuttering with cold.

At about four we took the hood off our heads and saw the valley for the first time in twenty hours: the curve of the railway line, the thin black line of the road, pastures of grass, the glitter of the river, the big stacks of corn like yellow firs. The red tractor a slow blood drop. Then we heard yells, names, my name, and saw a spot of orange jump at the toe of the scree. It was Lindy calling, calling, and I called for my favourite team: 'LindyLindy LindyLindy,' and the wall called with me. Hugh even asked if I was going out that night.

Morning. The fifth day. Cornflower blue skies, fiord-cold in the shade, and above us brooded a huge wing of white granite, its edge a thin black slab about as long and steep as the spire of Salisbury Cathedral. I had seen this from the scree. We go that way.

Two skyhooks raised me off the rubble, and dash, wobbling, for 10ft without protection – a necessary enema after the thirty-hour sit-in. Then I'm staring at a poor flare where I belt a nut. Little chains of sweat trickle down my back. I'm struggling to free climb and Hugh's not even looking. Jerkily I straggle to a ledge, not a word of wonder escaping his lips as I braille for holds and shake on to this ledge with a flurry of boots. With time against us I was doing all the leading. Hugh sat still on his stone throne while I squirmed about, greasing my palms with myself. Still, a cat may look, and he was the one rock, the one unshakeable, all the way there and back.

Abseiling down in the dying day, the bergschrund breaking its wave beneath my feet 1,500ft below in the cold ammonia air, the tube tent was a rush of bright flesh, raw on the ledge, and Hugh, his back bent, peering, was a black bird feeding at it. After a soup supper, watched by the smouldery eye of Hugh's cigar, I blew my harmonica, and brought tears of laughter to our eyes. We were doing okay. Hugh even said he liked to hear me play.

Two days later we were barely 300ft higher, and what I could see was not pretty. It looked as though, during the night, someone had pumped Hugh's foot up. His skin transparent as tracing paper, the foot was a mallet of flesh, the toes tiny buds; thalidomide. I didn't want to say too much. Perhaps the strain of his jumaring had done it, or the rotting wet when we were at Lucky's taking the waters. It was early yet; we had a long way to go. He said he just needed to rest it.

The ledge was lovely and I was glad to linger there. We spread ourselves around, Hugh blowing gently on his foot while I had a bath. A snip of cotton for a flannel, line for a towel, and a nip of antiseptic to give my spit a bit of bite. With behindsight I don't recommend the antiseptic neat, my dears. Let me tell you it wasn't a red face I had. The funny thing was it didn't hurt at the time I dabbed it, lovingly, my back turned while I blinked over the drop; but the day after, well, as they say, there hangs a tale.

A week later, his feet out like two heady cheeses in the dim pink light of the tent, Hugh has the mirror. He's checking on the stranger – the first time in twelve days, squeezing his pimples, humming some Neil Young song. For four days we've been in and out of this womb tube, harassed each time we go outside by the web of stuff bags breeding at the hole end. They are our other stomachs. We feel in them for our pots, our pottage, and our porter (although the porter is water since we've finished the orange). Cosmetics ended, we turn to draughts, drawing a board on the white insulating pad and inventing a set of signs for pieces and moves. So we pass an hour; doze, shift, fidget, sleep, talk, warn, fart, groan or cackle, plan, doze, and watch the light dissolve like a dye in the darkness. Snuggled together we are pre-eminently grateful that there is another here at the end of the day. We don't talk about failing and I hardly think about it now – we've been here so long it's a way of life. The pendulum's done now and the only sign I'm waiting for is a weather one. The valley in my mind is out of sight.

In raggy mists we moved quickly, leaving our hauls on the bivouac ledge. Hugh, some deflated astronaut, swam slowly up on jumars as though someone had taken the gravity away. Breezes whiffed up my cuffs and my icy cagoule etherised the back of my neck. After those two pitches. I frog-legged left, my numb hands bungling on the flat holds, to reach a little ledge from where I would go down to pendulum. After each pitch I was getting a bit desperate with the cold and I'd can-can to keep warm. Hugh, only 40ft away, was a white ghastly shadow.

Below us, Norway was at war. A volcanic pit of bursting water; the cwm boomed, a vat of slashed air. Stones howled around us and avalanching crashes trembled the wall. And I. Nothing could be seen in the gassing mist. No pendulum today.

Going back to our home, Hugh passed out into the cloud first, using the haul lines as a back rope to the bivouac ledge, which would otherwise have been impossible to return to because of the overhanging wall. When I got down he'd a brew ready which lit a fire, briefly, inside me. My thanks that it wasn't snowing just about made it.

During the night it snowed.

In the morning it was still falling, so we rolled over; better sleep on it. In the fitful sleep of that day I had my dream! The editor of *Mountain* had arrived at the foot of the scree and, with a foghorn or some kind of voice, had managed to wake me, telling me that he had come all the way from England to let me know what a great job I was doing for British rock-climbing (he never mentioned Hugh), and also how we were contributing to better Anglo-Norwegian political relations.

By the time I awoke he was gone but Hugh hadn't; he was just vanishing down the hole at the other end. My watch told 4 a.m. the night had gone. I oozed out of my pit to find lard-pale Hugh with the blue-black foot, sitting stinking in a skinful of sun. For half an hour we wallowed, exposing ourselves to the warm air. New creatures we were, able, if not to fly, at least to jumar, up there. And up there, today, I had to swing for it.

I try, flying, at 30ft below Hugh, then 50ft, then 80ft, then at over 100ft and I'm a bit too low so I jume up to about 95. 'Ed Leadlegs,' I tell him but only the wind hears me. I'm getting a bit tired; Hugh has given up asking me how I'm doing and he is just hanging, staring, his pipe alight – the wind brings a tang of it to me. No doubt he's thinking of his girl in Mexico.

The white wall is so steep here that I can barely keep hold of it when I crab myself right for the big swing. But my first swings wing me out into space away from the wall and I have to pirouette to miss smashing my back. This is ridiculous. Like a spider at puberty I toil but spin not. It's after 2 p.m. Lindy will be here soon.

When I've fingernailed back as far right as I can (and this time I manage about four feet more) I'm nearly 80ft away from the groove that I'm trying to reach.

I'm off, the white rushing past; out, out, away from the wall, way past the groove, out – I tread air, the valley at my feet. Hugh moons down, he's yelling something – can't hear a word he's saying – rushing, coming back, crashing in, wall falling on top of me, I kick, jab, bounce my boot, bounce out, floating, an easy trapeze. Then the unknown groove is running into my open arms and I strike at a flake and stick. Fingers leeching its crack.

I hung a nut in (my jumars attaching me to the rope are pulling me up), then I get an et. and stand in it. The nut stays put. Jumars down. Now put a knife under that block. The press of the block keeps it in as I weigh in on it. Out flips the nut. Whoops. I know I'm going to get there. I can't see Hugh but I know he's there. A tiny nut like a coin in a slot. Watch me. The knifeblade tinkles out. Thank you. The nut gleams a gold tooth at me. There you go. To climb is to know the universe is All Right. Then I clink a good pin in at a stretch. Can't get the nut now (it's still there). And then I'm in the groove, appalled at the sheer, clean walls around and below me, baying for breath, my heart chopping through my chest.

We have lost 100ft, but gained a narrow track of cracks that will, I believe, lead to the 'Arch Roof', the huge, square-cut over-hang that from the valley looks like an old press photo of the Loch Ness Monster. I saw a crack in 1970 through binoculars going out through the top of his head. 'Loch Ness Monster sighted on Troll Wall'. I'd out-yeti Whillans yet. Just before dark Hugh lands and goes on ahead to order dinner; we're eating out at the Traveller's Tube tonight, a farewell meal. The pendulum being done, our time was going and so must we.

But it snowed for two days.

On the thirteenth day the sun rubbed shoulders with us again, and Hugh jumared up at a snail sprint. He found that the yellow perlon he was on had rubbed through to half its core, so he tied that out with an overhand before I came up at a slow rush. Halfway up I worked loose a huge detached flake which had hung 100ft above our tent; it took me five minutes so we had no need to worry. We watch it bounce, bomb-bursting down to the cwm, and the walls applaud.

The crack above the pendulum's end was a nice smile for standard angles except where a ladder of loose flakes is propped. Bloody visions slump at the belay below me. Silence. Care. The hauls zoom out well clear.

The next two pitches, up a bulging, near-blind groove, were ecstasy. I had to free climb. The hooks were only for luck, and I was quick in the blue fields. Above, suddenly, two swifts flashed past, thuds of white. 'That's us,' I yelled to myself. Lindy may not have been here, but there she was. I could hear her, naming my name, and I flew slowly up. Four fine patches of ledgeless pleasure that day. In the dark Hugh jumared up to the Arch, me guiding his feet with my head torch.

But that night the sky shone no stars. Packs of black cloud massed. Not enough food to eat. A sweet or two. No cigar. And too late to fish for hammocks. All night, four hours, I squirmed in my seat sling. I speculated on recommending to the makers that they rename it the Iron Maiden, but it was too suitable an epitaph to laugh about. My hip is still numb from damaged nerves.

Came the morning I was thrashed. The sun did not exist. The roof over my head was a weight on my mind. Suddenly, over Vengetind the weather mountain, clouds boiled, whipping and exploding in avalanching chaos. Over Lillejfel, a low shoulder on the other side of the valley cauldron, a dinosaur mass of white cloud was rat-arrowing toward us. We could hardly run away; we were so cold and hungry we could hardly move.

I was scared as I moved out under the Arch, a clown without props, all these things were real, there were no nets here, only dear patient Hugh blowing on his fingers.

No man walks on air was all my thought as I melted out of sight, upside down for 40ft, my haul line dissolving in the mist. I couldn't feel that I was connected to anything solid. Fly sized, I mimed away under three giant inverted steps, lips. Not a single foothold, not a toehold in a hundred feet. Just over the final lip, in a single strand of crack, I pinned myself to a wall of water and started to land the hauls.

They must have seen me coming. I couldn't believe it. Raindrops ripped into me, making me wince. The cold rose an octave, catapulting hail into my face. The wind thrummed a hundred longbow cords. I could hardly see through my Chinese eyes. Only while I hauled could I stop shaking. My fingers, cut deeply at the tips, were almost helpless. People at upstairs windows watching a road accident in the street below. My feet were dying. My silent white hands.

Hugh came up for air, grinning. He'd had no idea down there. Up here he had the thing itself. Murdering, washing out more than ears. I led off, hardly knowing where, except that we couldn't stay there. I could only just open my karabiners with two hands. Sleet had settled thickly on the bunches of tie-offs. Both of us were really worried. Hugh cried up after an hour that he was getting frostbite. What could I say? I had to find a place for the night.

If you ever go there and have it the way we did, you'll know why we called it 'The Altar'. I remember the rush in the drowning dark to hang the tent, the moss churning to slush beneath our feet. Back to back, our backs to the wall, we slumped on three feet of ledge for three days. We had nothing to drink for the first two of those days; our haul bags were jammed below us and we were diseased with fatigue. Lice trickles of wet get everywhere.

I remember Hugh drinking the brown water that had collected

in his boots, instantly vomiting it out, and me silently mouthing the gluey water from my helmet. You didn't miss much. Hugh. He shared his food with me, some cheese and dates and a bag of sweets; rare fruits. After a day he had to piss and used quadrupled poly bags which I politely declined to use; I had no need. A day later my proud bladder was bursting. But sitting, propped in a wet bed of underwear, I was impotent. For over two hours I strained and grunted in scholastic passion. Hugh said it was trench penis. A sort of success went to my head, however, or rather on to and into my sleeping bag. After that I felt like some great baby, trapped in his wet cot, the air sickly with urine, and sleep would not come.

To get more room, both of us, we later confessed when there were witnesses present, developed strategies of delay while we shuffled the status quo. 'Could you sit forward a minute?' Or, 'Would you hold this for me?' At times I'd get Hugh to tuck my insulating pads around me to bluff off the cold stone. It was deeply satisfying to have someone do that. Grizzly, bristly Hugh: what a mother.

We wondered if this could continue for more than a week. But we didn't wonder what would happen if it did. We never talked about not finishing. (We were just over 1,000ft below the summit.) It was no longer a new route to us. It was not possible to consider anything else as real. There were no echoes from the valley. There was no valley. There was no one to call your name. No wall now; unhappy little solipsists, all we had was each other.

We began to get ratty, like children locked in a bedroom. An elbow scuffled against a back once or twice as we humped back to stop the slow slide off the ledge. A ton of silence rested on us like a public monument, for hours on end. I felt that this was all sterile. I ate food, wore out my clothes, used up my warmth, but earned nothing, made nothing. The art was chrysalising into artifice. A grubby routine. Trying not to die. Millions have the disease and know it not. My sleep a continual dream of hammering: banging in pins, clipping in, moving up, then back down, banging, banging, taking them out. A bit like having fleas. Searching for an ultimate belay. Unable to stop: the Holy Nail. My Dad, my dad, why hast thou forsaken me? At times I was pretty far gone.

But it wasn't all self-pity. We talked about the plight of the Trolls and could clearly see a long bony hairy arm poking under the tent, handing us a steaming pan of hot troll tea, and although nothing appeared in our anaesthetic dark, the idea lit a brief candle.

Three days later we were released.

Lindy yelled us out. A giant marigold sun beamed at us. Everywhere up here – and we could see hundreds of miles – was white, perfect, appalling. Across the river I could clearly make out scores of tourists, a distant litter of colour in one of the camping fields opposite the wall. Cars flashed their headlamps and horns bugled as we struggled into view and flagged them with our tent.

Then, quickly, the charging roar of an avalanche. I flattened to the wall. And then I spotted it, a helicopter, gunning in a stone's throw from the wall, a military green with yellow emblems. A gun poked from the window. 'Hugh, they're going to shoot us,' then, tearing his head up he saw it: an arm waving. We waved arms, heads, legs; danced, jigged, yelled, while they circled in and away like something from another world. Later we learned that it was Norwegian television, but we fluttered no blushes on the wall. The spell of our selves was broken.

Five hours later, after a long lovely 130ft of aid, intricate and out in space, I was on the final summit walls, the last roofs wiped with light, 700ft above me.

All that night, while a white moon sailed over our shoulders, we perched on our haul bags and cut off the blood to our already damaged feet, too exhausted to know. Sharing our last cigar while the nerves in our feet were suffocating to death, we shone in our hunger and smiled a while.

As soon as I put my weight on my foot in the new dawn I knew I'd had it. Hugh's foot was an unspeakable image, and I had to tell him when his heel was grounded inside his boot. He could hardly have his laces tied at all and I was terrified that one of his boots might drop off.

All that day the feeling was of having my boots being filled with boiling water that would trickle in between my toes and flood my soles. Then a sensation of shards of glass being wriggled into the balls of my feet. And upon each of my feet a dentist was at work, pulling my nails and slowly filing my toes. Then nothing but a rat-tatting heart when I stopped climbing. I would tremble like water in a faint breeze. I knew it was hypothermia. We had had no food for three days. Maybe it was two.

All the last day we called, a little hysterically I think, for someone on the summit; they were coming to meet us. Sitting fifteen feet below the top, with Hugh whimpering up on jumars I heard whispers . . . 'Keep quiet . . . wait until he comes over the top.'

There was no one there. Only, thank God, the sun. It seemed right in a way to meet only each other there. At the summit cairn Hugh sucked on his pipe while my tongue nippled at a crushed sweet that he had found in his pocket. We dozed warm as new cakes, in a high white world, above impenetrable clouds which had shut out the valley all day. We were terribly glad to be there. After midnight we collapsed into a coma of sleep, half a mile down in the boulder-field.

We met them the next morning, quite near the road; it must have been about half past eight. They were coming up to meet us. Lindy flew up the hill to hug me forever. I was Odysseus, with a small o, I was Ed, come back for the first time. Hugh grinned in his pain when I told the Norwegian journalists that his real name was Peer Gynt, and that he was an artist like Van Gogh, but that he had given a foot for the wall, instead of an ear to his girl.

On our last hobble, he had, before we met the others, found himself dreaming of the walks he used to have with his Dad, as a child, into the park to feed the ducks, and of the delights of playing marbles (we were both pocketing stones and rare bits from the summit on down). When we arrived in Andalsnes with our friends, I saw the apples burning on the boughs, glowy drops of gold and red (the green gargoyle buds, the little knuckle apples had lit while we were gone); and the postbox in its red skirt shouted to me as we turned the corner into town. Bodil washed Hugh's feet, sent for her doctor, and everyone in our house was alive and well. Only the Troll Wall gave me black looks, over the hill and far away at last. Black iceberg under eye-blue skies.

Back in England my feet were as irrefutable as war wounds. I was on my back for a month, and I had the cuttings from the Norwegian press, as precious as visas. But nowhere to get to.

THE LONG GRIND

SIR EDMUND HILLARY
(1919–2008)

*New Zealand mountaineer and explorer. A member of Sir John Hunt's
1953 Himalayan expedition, Hillary, together with Sherpa Tenzing,
made the first ascent of Everest.*

I looked at the way ahead. From our tent very steep slopes covered
with deep powder snow led up to a prominent snow shoulder on
the south-east ridge about a hundred feet above our heads. The
slopes were in the shade and breaking trail was going to be cold
work. Still a little worried about my boots, I asked Tenzing to lead
off. Always willing to do his share, and more than his share if
necessary, Tenzing scrambled past me and tackled the slope. With
powerful thrusts of his legs he forced his way up in knee-deep
snow. I gathered in the rope and followed along behind him.

We were climbing out over the tremendous South face of the
mountain, and below us snow chutes and rock ribs plummeted
thousands of feet down to the Western Cwm. Starting in the
morning straight on to exposed climbing is always trying for the
nerves, and this was no exception. In imagination I could feel my
heavy load dragging me backwards down the great slopes below;
I seemed clumsy and unstable and my breath was hurried and
uneven. But Tenzing was pursuing an irresistible course up the
slope, and I didn't have time to think too much. My muscles soon
warmed up to their work, my nerves relaxed and I dropped into

the old climbing rhythm and followed steadily up his tracks. As we gained a little height we moved into the rays of the sun, and although we could feel no appreciable warmth, we were greatly encouraged by its presence. Taking no rests, Tenzing ploughed his way up through the deep snow and led out on to the snow shoulder. We were now at a height of 28,000 feet. Towering directly above our heads was the South Summit – steep and formidable. And to the right were the enormous cornices of the summit ridge. We still had a long way to go.

Ahead of us the ridge was sharp and narrow, but rose at an easy angle. I felt warm and strong now, so took over the lead. First I investigated the ridge with my ice-axe. On the sharp crest of the ridge and on the right-hand side loose powder snow was lying dangerously over hard ice. Any attempt to climb on this would only produce an unpleasant slide down towards the Kangshung glacier. But the left-hand slope was better – it was still rather steep, but it had a firm surface of wind-blown powder snow into which our crampons would bite readily.

Taking every care, I moved along on to the left-hand side on the ridge. Everything seemed perfectly safe. With increased confidence, I took another step. Next moment I was almost thrown off balance as the wind-crust suddenly gave way and I sank through it up to my knee. It took me a little while to regain my breath. Then I gradually pulled my leg out of the hole. I was almost upright again when the wind-crust under the other foot gave way and I sank back with both legs enveloped in soft, loose snow to the knees. It was the mountaineer's curse – breakable crust. I forced my way along. Sometimes for a few careful steps I was on the surface, but usually the crust would break at the critical moment and I'd be up to my knees again. Though it was tiring and exasperating work, I felt I had plenty of strength in reserve. For half an hour I continued on in this uncomfortable fashion, with the violent balancing movements I was having to make completely destroying rhythm and breath. It was a great relief when the snow conditions improved and I was able to stay on the surface. I still kept down on the steep slopes on the left of the ridge, but plunged ahead and climbed steadily upwards. I came over a small crest and saw in front of me a tiny hollow in the ridge. And in this hollow lay two oxygen bottles almost completely covered with snow. It was Evans' and Bourdillon's dump.

I rushed forward into the hollow and knelt beside them. Wrenching one of the bottles out of its frozen bed I wiped the snow off its dial – it showed a thousand-pounds pressure – it was nearly a third full of oxygen. I checked the other – it was the same. This was great news. It meant that the oxygen we were carrying on our backs only had to get us back to these bottles instead of right down to the South Col. It gave us more than another hour of endurance. I explained this to Tenzing through my oxygen mask. I don't think he understood but he realized I was pleased about something and nodded enthusiastically.

I led off again. I knew there was plenty of hard work ahead and Tenzing could save his energies for that. The ridge climbed on upwards rather more steeply now, and then broadened out and shot up at a sharp angle to the foot of the enormous slope running up to the South Summit. I crossed over on to the right-hand side of the ridge and found the snow was firm there. I started chipping a long line of steps up to the foot of the great slope. Here we stamped out a platform for ourselves and I checked our oxygen. Everything seemed to be going well. I had a little more oxygen left than Tenzing, which meant I was obtaining a slightly lower flow rate from my set, but it wasn't enough to matter and there was nothing I could do about it anyway.

Ahead of us was a really formidable problem, and I stood in my steps and looked at it. Rising from our feet was an enormous slope slanting steeply down on the precipitous East face of Everest and climbing up with appalling steepness to the South Summit of the mountain 400 feet above us. The left-hand side of the slope was a most unsavoury mixture of steep loose rock and snow, which my New Zealand training immediately regarded with grave suspicion, but which in actual fact the rock-climbing Britons,

Evans and Bourdillon had ascended in much trepidation when on the first assault. The only other route was up the snow itself and still faintly discernible here and there were traces of the track made by the first assault party, who had come down it in preference to their line of ascent up the rocks. The snow route it was for us! There looked to be some tough work ahead, and as Tenzing had been taking it easy for a while I hard-heartedly waved him through. With his first six steps I realized that the work was going to be much harder than I had thought. His first two steps were on top of the snow, the third was up to his ankles and by the sixth he was up to his hips. But almost lying against the steep slope, he drove himself onwards, ploughing a track directly upwards. Even following in his steps was hard work, for the loose snow refused to pack into safe steps. After a long and valiant spell he was plainly in need of a rest, so I took over.

Immediately I realized that we were on dangerous ground. On this very steep slope the snow was soft and deep with little coherence. My ice-axe shaft sank into it without any support and we had no sort of a belay. The only factor that made it at all possible to progress was a thin crust of frozen snow which tied the whole slope together. But this crust was a poor support. I was forcing my way upwards, plunging deep steps through it, when suddenly with a dull breaking noise an area of crust all around me about six feet in diameter broke off into large sections and slid with me back through three or four steps. And then I stopped; but the crust gathering speed, slithered on out of sight. It was a nasty shock. My whole training told me that the slope was exceedingly dangerous, but at the same time I was saying to myself: 'Ed my boy, this is Everest – you've got to push it a bit harder!' My solar plexus was tight with fear as I ploughed on. Halfway up I stopped, exhausted. I could look down 10,000 feet between my legs, and I have never felt more insecure. Anxiously I waved Tenzing up to me.

'What do you think of it, Tenzing?' And the immediate response, 'Very bad, very dangerous!' 'Do you think we should go on?' and there came the familiar reply that never helped you

much but never let you down: 'Just as you wish!' I waved him on
to take a turn at leading. Changing the lead much more frequently
now, we made our unhappy way upwards, sometimes sliding
back and wiping out half a dozen steps, and never feeling confident that at any moment the whole slope might not avalanche. In
the hope of some sort of a belay we traversed a little towards the
rocks, but found no help in their smooth, holdless surfaces. We
plunged on upwards. And then I noticed that a little above us, the
left-hand rock ridge turned into snow and the snow looked firm
and safe. Laboriously and carefully we climbed across some steep
rock, and I sank my ice-axe shaft into the snow of the ridge. It
went in firm and hard. The pleasure of this safe belay after all the
uncertainty below was like a reprieve to a condemned man.
Strength flowed into my limbs, and I could feel my tense nerves
and muscles relaxing. I swung my ice-axe at the slope and started
chipping a line of steps upwards – it was very steep, but seemed
so gloriously safe. Tenzing, an inexpert but enthusiastic step
cutter, took a turn and chopped a haphazard line of steps up
another pitch. We were making fast time now and the slope was
starting to ease off. Tenzing gallantly waved me through, and
with a growing feeling of excitement I cramponed up some firm
slopes to the rounded top of the South Summit. It was only 9 a.m.

With intense interest I looked at the vital ridge leading to the
summit – the ridge about which Evans and Bourdillon had made
such gloomy forecasts. At first glance it was an exceedingly
impressive and indeed a frightening sight. In the narrow crest of
this ridge, the basic rock of the mountain had a thin capping of
snow and ice – ice that reached out over the East face in enormous
cornices, overhanging and treacherous, and only waiting for the
careless foot of the mountaineer to break off and crash 10,000 feet
to the Kangshung glacier. And from the cornices the snow
dropped steeply to the left to merge with the enormous rock bluffs
which towered 8,000 feet above the Western Cwm. It was impressive all right! But as I looked my fears started to lift a little. Surely
I could see a route there? For this snow slope on the left, although

very steep and exposed, was practically continuous for the first half of the ridge, although in places the great cornices reached hungrily across. If we could make a route along that snow slope, we could go quite a distance at least.

With a feeling almost of relief, I set to work with my ice-axe and cut a platform for myself just down off the top of the South Summit. Tenzing did the same, and then we removed our oxygen sets and sat down. The day was still remarkably fine, and we felt no discomfort through our thick layers of clothing from either wind or cold. We had a drink out of Tenzing's water bottle and then I checked our oxygen supplies. Tenzing's bottle was practically exhausted, but mine still had a little in it. As well as this, we each had a full bottle. I decided that the difficulties ahead would demand as light a weight on our backs as possible so determined to use only the full bottles. I removed Tenzing's empty bottle and my nearly empty one and laid them in the snow. With particular care I connected up our last bottles and tested to see that they were working efficiently. The needles on the dials were steady on 3,300 lb per square inch pressure – they were very full bottles holding just over 800 litres of oxygen each. At three litres a minute we consumed 180 litres an hour, and this meant a total endurance of nearly four and a half hours. This didn't seem much for the problems ahead, but I was determined if necessary to cut down to two litres a minute for the homeward trip.

I was greatly encouraged to find how, even at 28,700 feet and with no oxygen, I could work out slowly but clearly the problems of mental arithmetic that the oxygen supply demanded. A correct answer was imperative – any mistake could well mean a trip with no return. But we had no time to waste. I stood up and took a series of photographs in every direction, then thrust my camera back to its warm home inside my clothing. I heaved my now pleasantly light oxygen load on to my back and connected up my tubes. I did the same for Tenzing, and we were ready to go. I asked Tenzing to belay me and then, with a growing air of excitement, I cut a broad and safe line of steps down to the snow saddle below the South Summit. I wanted an easy route when we came back up here weak and tired. Tenzing came down the steps and joined me, and then belayed once again.

I moved along on to the steep snow slope on the left side of the ridge. With the first blow of my ice-axe my excitement increased. The snow to my astonishment – was crystalline and hard. A couple of rhythmical blows of the ice-axe produced a step that was big enough for our oversize high-altitude boots. But the best of all the steps were strong and safe. A little conscious of the great drops beneath me, I chipped a line of steps for the full length of the rope – forty feet – and then forced the shaft of my axe firmly into the snow. It made a fine belay and I looped the rope around it. I waved to Tenzing to join me, and as he moved slowly and carefully along the steps I took in the rope as I went on cutting steps. It was exhilarating work – the summit ridge of Everest, the crisp snow and the smooth easy blows of the ice-axe all combined to make me feel a greater sense of power than I had ever felt at great altitudes before. I went on cutting for rope length after rope length.

We were now approaching a point where one of the great cornices was encroaching on to our slope. We'd have to go down to the rocks to avoid it. I cut a line of steps steeply down the slope to a small ledge on top of the rocks. There wasn't much room, but it made a reasonably safe stance. I waved to Tenzing to join me. As he came down to me I realized there was something wrong with him. I had been so absorbed in the technical problems of the ridge that I hadn't thought much about Tenzing, except for a vague feeling that he seemed to move along the steps with unnecessary slowness. But now it was quite obvious that he was not only moving extremely slowly, but he was breathing quickly and with difficulty and was in considerable distress. I immediately suspected his oxygen set and helped him down on to the ledge so that I could examine it. The first thing I noticed was that from the outlet of his face-mask there were hanging some long icicles. I looked at it more closely and found that the outlet tube – about two inches in diameter – was almost completely blocked up with ice. This was preventing Tenzing from exhaling freely and must have made it extremely unpleasant for him. Fortunately the outlet tube was made of rubber and by manipulating this with my hand I was able to release all the ice and let it fall out. The valves started operating and Tenzing was given immediate relief. Just as a check I examined my own set and found that it too, had partly frozen up in the outlet tube, but not sufficiently to have affected me a great deal. I removed the ice out of it without a great deal of trouble. Automatically I looked at our pressure gauges – just over 2,900 lb (2,900 lb was just over 700 litres; 180 into 700 was about 4) – we had nearly four hours' endurance left. That meant we weren't going badly.

I looked at the route ahead. This next piece wasn't going to be easy. Our rock ledge was perched right on top of the enormous bluff running down into the Western Cwm. In fact, almost under my feet, I could see the dirty patch on the floor of the Cwm which I knew was Camp IV. In a sudden urge to escape our isolation I waved and shouted and then as suddenly stopped as I realized my foolishness. Against the vast expanse of Everest, 8,000 feet above them we'd be quite invisible to the best binoculars. I turned back to the problem ahead. The rock was far too steep to attempt to drop down and go around this pitch. The only thing to do was to try to shuffle along the ledge and cut handholds in the bulging ice that was trying to push me off it. Held on a tight rope by Tenzing, I cut a few handholds and then thrust my ice-axe as hard as I could into the solid snow and ice. Using this to take my weight I moved quickly along the ledge. It proved easier than I had anticipated. A few more handholds, another quick swing across them, and I was able to cut a line of steps up on to a safe slope and chop out a roomy terrace from which to belay Tenzing as he climbed up to me.

We were now fast approaching the most formidable obstacle on the ridge – a great rock step. This step had always been visible in aerial photographs, and in 1951 on the Everest Reconnaissance we had seen it quite clearly with glasses from Thyangboche. We had always thought of it as the obstacle on the ridge which could well spell defeat. I cut a line of steps across the last snow slope, and then commenced traversing over a steep rock slab that led to the foot of the great step. The holds were small and hard to see, and I brushed my snow-glasses away from my eyes. Immediately I was blinded by a bitter wind sweeping across the ridge and laden with particles of ice. I hastily replaced my glasses and blinked away the ice and tears until I could see again. But it made me realize how efficient was our clothing in protecting us from the rigours of even a fine day at 29,000 feet. Still half blinded, I climbed across the slab, and then dropped down into a tiny snow hollow at the foot of the step. And here Tenzing joined me.

I looked anxiously up at the rocks. Planted squarely across the ridge in a vertical bluff, they looked extremely difficult, and I knew that our strength and ability to climb steep rock at this altitude would be severely limited. I examined the route out to the left. By dropping fifty or a hundred feet over steep slabs, we might be able to get around the bottom of the bluff, but there was no indication that we'd be able to climb back on to the ridge again. And to lose any height now might be fatal. Search as I could, I was unable to see an easy route up to the step or, in fact, any route at all. Finally, in desperation I examined the right-hand end of the bluff. Attached to this and overhanging the precipitous East face was a large cornice. This cornice, in preparation for its inevitable crash down the mountainside, had started to lose its grip on the rock, and a long narrow vertical crack had been formed between the rock and the ice. The crack was large enough to take the human frame, and though it offered little security, it was at least a route. I quickly made up my mind – Tenzing had an excellent belay and we must be near the top – it was worth a try.

Before attempting the pitch, I produced my camera once again. I had no confidence that I would be able to climb this crack, and with a surge of competitive pride which unfortunately afflicts even mountaineers, I determined to have proof that at least we had reached a good deal higher than the South Summit. I took a few photographs and then made another rapid check of the oxygen – 2,550 lb pressure. (2,550 from 3,300 leaves 750. 750 over 3,300 is about two-ninths. Two ninths off 800 litres leaves about 600 litres. 600 divided by 180 is nearly 3½.) Three and a half hours to go. I examined Tenzing's belay to make sure it was a good one and then slowly crawled inside the crack.

In front of me was the rock wall, vertical but with a few promising holds. Behind me was the ice wall of the cornice, glittering and hard but cracked here and there. I took a hold on the rock in front and then jammed one of my crampons hard into the ice behind. Leaning back with my oxygen set on the ice, I slowly levered myself upwards. Searching feverishly with my spare boot, I found a tiny ledge on the rock and took some of the weight off my other leg. Leaning back on the cornice, I fought to regain my breath. Constantly at the back of my mind was the fear that the cornice might break off, and my nerves were taut with suspense. But slowly I forced my way up – wriggling and jambing and using every little hold. In one place I managed to force my ice-axe into a crack in the ice, and this gave me the necessary purchase to get over a holdless stretch. And then I found a solid foothold in a hollow in the ice, and next moment I was reaching over the top of the rock and pulling myself to safety. The rope came tight – its forty feet had been barely enough.

I lay on the little rock ledge panting furiously. Gradually it dawned on me that I was up the step, and I felt a glow of pride and determination that completely subdued my temporary feelings of weakness. For the first time on the whole expedition I really knew I was going to get to the top. 'It will have to be pretty tough to stop us now' was my thought. But I couldn't entirely ignore the feeling of astonishment and wonder that I'd been able to get up such a difficulty at 29,000 feet even with oxygen.

When I was breathing more evenly I stood up and leaning over the edge, waved to Tenzing to come up. He moved into the crack and I gathered in the rope and took some of his weight. Then he, in turn, commenced to struggle and jam and force his way up until I was able to pull him to safety – gasping for breath. We rested for a moment. Above us the ridge continued on as before – enormous overhanging cornices on the right and steep snow slopes on the left running down to the rock bluffs. But the angle of the snow slopes was easing off. I went on chipping a line of steps, but thought it safe enough for us to move together in order to save time. The ridge rose up in a great series of snakelike undulations which bore away to the right, each one concealing the next. I had no idea where the top was. I'd cut a line of steps around the side of one undulation and another would come into view. We were getting desperately tired now and Tenzing was going very slowly. I'd been cutting steps for almost two hours, and my back and arms were starting to tire. I tried cramponing along the slope without cutting steps, but my feet slipped uncomfortably down the slope. I went on cutting. We seemed to have been going for a very long time and my confidence was fast evaporating. Bump followed bump with maddening regularity. A patch of shingle barred our way, and I climbed dully up it and started cutting steps around another bump. And then I realized that this was the last bump, for ahead of me the ridge dropped steeply away in a great corniced curve, and out in the distance. I could see the pastel shades and fleecy clouds of the highlands of Tibet.

To my right a slender snow ridge climbed up to a snowy dome about forty feet above our heads. But all the way along the ridge the thought had haunted me that the summit might be the crest of a cornice. It was too late to take risks now. I asked Tenzing to belay me strongly, and I started cutting a cautious line of steps up the ridge. Peering from side to side and thrusting with my ice-axe, I tried to discover a possible cornice, but everything seemed solid and firm. I waved Tenzing up to me. A few more whacks of the ice-axe, a few very weary steps, and we were on the summit of Everest.

It was 11.30 a.m. My first sensation was one of relief – relief that the long grind was over; that the summit had been reached before our oxygen supplies had dropped to a critical level; and relief that in the end the mountain had been kind to us in having a pleasantly rounded cone for its summit instead of a fearsome and unapproachable cornice. But mixed with the relief was a vague sense of astonishment that I should have been the lucky one to attain the ambition of so many brave and determined climbers. It seemed difficult at first to grasp that we'd got there. I was too tired and too conscious of the long way down to safety really to feel any great elation. But as the fact of our success thrust itself more clearly into my mind, I felt a quiet glow of satisfaction spread through my body – a satisfaction less vociferous but more powerful than I had ever felt on a mountain top before. I turned and looked at Tenzing. Even beneath his oxygen mask and the icicles hanging from his hair, I could see his infectious grin of sheer delight.

EXTREME DANGER

MAURICE HERZOG
(1919–)

*French climber. In 1950 Herzog led the first conquest of Annapurna,
reaching the summit himself along with Louis Lachenal. It was the first
8,000-metre peak to be scaled. On the descent, the monsoon broke
around the French team, producing appalling weather; several of the
expedition were attacked by frostbite – particularly Herzog himself, who
had lost his gloves near the summit – and snow-blindness.*

I hurried everyone up; we must get down – that was our first
objective. As for the equipment, well it could not be helped; we
simply must be off the mountain before the next onslaught of the
monsoon. For those of us with frostbitten limbs it was a matter of
hours. I chose Aila and Sarki to escort Rébuffat, Lachenal and
myself. I tried to make the two Sherpas understand that they must
watch me very closely and hold me on a short rope. For some
unknown reason, neither Lachenal nor Rébuffat wished to rope.

While we started down, Schatz, with Angtharkay and Pansy,
went up to fetch Terray who had remained on the glacier above.
Schatz was master of the situation – none of the others were
capable of taking the slightest initiative. After a hard struggle, he
found Terray:

'You can get ready in a minute,' he said.

'I'm beginning to feel my feet again,' replied Terray, now more
amenable to reason.

'I'm going to have a look in the crevasse. Maurice couldn't find the camera and it's got all the shots he took high up.'

Terray made no reply; he had not really understood, and it was only several days later that we fully realised Schatz's heroism. He spent a long time searching the snow at the bottom of the cavern, while Terray began to get anxious; at last he returned triumphantly carrying the camera which contained the views taken from the summit. He also found my ice-axe and various other things, but no cine-camera, so our last film shots would stop at 23,000 feet.

Then the descent began. Angtharkay was magnificent, going first and cutting comfortable steps for Terray. Schatz, coming down last, carefully safeguarded the whole party.

Our first group was advancing slowly. The snow was soft and we sank in up to our knees. Lachenal grew worse: he frequently stopped and moaned about his feet. Rébuffat was a few yards behind me.

I was concerned at the abnormal heat, and feared that bad weather would put an end here and now to the epic of Annapurna. It is said that mountaineers have a sixth sense that warns them of danger – suddenly I became aware of danger through every pore of my body. There was a feeling in the atmosphere that could not be ignored. Yesterday it had snowed heavily, and the heat was now working on these great masses of snow which were on the point of sliding off. Nothing in Europe can give any idea of the force of these avalanches. They roll down over a distance of miles and are preceded by a blast that destroys everything in its path.

The glare was so terrific that without glasses it would have been impossible to keep one's eyes open. By good luck we were fairly well spaced out, so that the risk was diminished. The Sherpas no longer remembered the different pitches, and often with great difficulty, I had to take the lead and be let down on the end of the rope to find the right way. I had no crampons and I could not grasp an axe. We lost height far too slowly for my liking, and it worried me to see my Sherpas going so slowly and carefully and at the same time so insecurely. In actual fact they went very well, but I was so impatient I could no longer judge their performance fairly.

Lachenal was a long way behind us and every time I turned round he was sitting down in the track. He, too, was affected by snow-blindness, though not as badly as Terray and Rébuffat, and found difficulty in seeing his way. Rébuffat went ahead by guess-work, with agony in his face, but he kept on. We crossed the couloir without incident, and I congratulated myself that we had passed the danger zone.

The sun was at its height, the weather brilliant and the colours magnificent. Never had the mountains appeared to me so majestic as in this moment of extreme danger.

All at once a crack appeared in the snow under the feet of the Sherpas, and grew longer and wider. A mad notion flashed into my head – to climb up the slope at speed and reach solid ground. Then I was lifted up by a super-human force, and as the Sherpas disappeared before my eyes, I went head over heels. I could not see what was happening. My head hit the ice. In spite of my efforts I could no longer breathe, and a violent blow on my left thigh caused me acute pain. I turned round and round like a puppet. In a flash I saw the blinding light of the sun through the snow which was pouring past my eyes. The rope joining me to Sarki and Aila curled round my neck – the Sherpas shooting down the slope beneath would shortly strangle me, and the pain was unbearable. Again and again I crashed into solid ice as I went hurtling from one serac to another, and the snow crushed me down. The rope tightened round my neck and brought me to a stop. Before I had recovered my wits I began to pass water, violently and uncontrollably.

I opened my eyes to find myself hanging head downwards, with the rope round my neck and my left leg in a sort of hatchway of blue ice. I put out my elbows towards the walls in an attempt to stop the unbearable pendulum motion which sent me from one side to the other, and caught a glimpse of the final slopes of the couloir beneath me. My breathing steadied and I blessed the rope which had stood the strain of the shock.

I simply *had* to try to get myself out. My feet and hands were numb, but I was able to make use of some little nicks in the wall. There was room for at least the edges of my boots. By frenzied, jerky movements I succeeded in freeing my left leg from the rope and then managed to right myself and to climb up a yard or two. After every move I stopped, convinced that I had come to the end of my physical strength, and that in a second I should have to let go.

One more desperate effort, and I gained a few inches – I pulled on the rope and felt something give at the other end – no doubt the bodies of the Sherpas. I called, but hardly a whisper issued from my lips. There was a death-like silence. Where was Gaston?

Conscious of a shadow, as from a passing cloud, I looked up instinctively; and lo and behold! two scared black faces were framed against the circle of blue sky. Aila and Sarki! They were safe and sound, and at once set to work to rescue me. I was incapable of giving them the slightest advice. Aila disappeared, leaving Sarki alone at the edge of the hole; they began to pull on the rope, slowly, so as not to hurt me, and I was hauled up with a power and steadiness that gave me fresh courage. At last I was out. I collapsed on the snow.

The rope had caught over a ridge of ice and we had been suspended on either side; by good luck the weight of the two Sherpas and my own had balanced. If we had not been checked like this we should have hurtled down another 1,500 feet. There was chaos all around us. Where was Rébuffat? I was mortally anxious, for he was unroped. Looking up I caught sight of him less than a hundred yards away:

'Anything broken?' he called out to me.

I was greatly relieved, but I had no strength to reply. Lying flat, and semi-conscious, I gazed at the wreckage about me with unseeing eyes. We had been carried down for about 500 feet. It was not a healthy place to linger in – suppose another avalanche should fall! I instructed the Sherpas:

'Now – Doctor Sahib. Quick, very quick!'

By gestures I tried to make them understand that they must hold me very firmly. In doing this I found that my left arm was practically useless. I could not move it at all; the elbow had seized up – was it broken? We should see later. Now, we must push on to Oudot.

Rébuffat started down to join us, moving slowly; he had to place his feet by feel alone, and seeing him walk like this made my heart ache; he, too, had fallen, and he must have struck something with his jaw, for blood was oozing from the corners of his mouth. Like me, he had lost his glasses and we were forced to shut our eyes. Aila had an old spare pair which did very well for me, and without a second's hesitation Sarki gave his own to Rébuffat.

We had to get down at once. The Sherpas helped me up, and I advanced as best I could, reeling about in the most alarming fashion, but they realised now that they must hold me from behind. I skirted round the avalanche to our old track which started again a little farther on.

We now came to the first wall. How on earth should we get down? Again, I asked the Sherpas to hold me firmly:

'*Hold me well because . . .*'

And I showed them my hands.

'Yes, sir,' they replied together like good pupils. I came to the piton; the fixed rope attached to it hung down the wall and I had to hold on to it – there was no other way. It was terrible; my wooden feet kept slipping on the ice wall, and I could not grasp the thin line in my hands. Without letting go I endeavoured to wind it round them, but they were swollen and the skin broke in several places. Great strips of it came away and stuck to the rope and the flesh was laid bare. Yet I had to go on down; I could not give up halfway.

'Aila! *Pay attention! . . . Pay attention!*'

To save my hands I now let the rope slide over my good forearm and lowered myself like this in jerks. On reaching the bottom I fell about three feet, and the rope wrenched my forearm and wrists.

The jolt was severe and affected my feet. I heard a queer crack and supposed I must have broken something – no doubt it was the frostbite that prevented me from feeling any pain.

Rébuffat and the Sherpas came down and we went on, but it all seemed to take an unconscionably long time, and the plateau of Camp II seemed a long way off. I was just about at the limit of my strength. Every minute I felt like giving up; and why, anyway, should I go on when for me everything was over? My conscience was quite easy: everyone was safe, and the others would all get down. Far away below I could see the tents. Just one more hour – I gave myself one more hour and then, wherever I was, I would lie down in the snow. I would let myself go, peacefully. I would be through with it all, and could sleep content.

Setting this limit somehow cheered me on. I kept slipping, and on the steep slope the Sherpas could hardly hold me – it was miraculous that they did. The track stopped above a drop – the second and bigger of the walls we had equipped with a fixed rope. I tried to make up my mind, but I could not begin to see how I was going to get down. I pulled off the glove I had on one hand, and the red silk scarf that hid the other, which was covered in blood. This time everything was at stake – and my fingers could just look after themselves. I placed Sarki and Aila on the stance from which I had been accustomed to belay them, and where the two of them would be able to take the strain of my rope by standing firmly braced against each other. I tried to take hold of the fixed rope; both my hands were bleeding, but I had no pity to spare for myself and I took the rope between my thumb and forefinger, and started off. At the first move I was faced at once with a painful decision: if I let go, we should fall to the bottom: if I held on, what would remain of my hands? I decided to hold on.

Every inch was a torture I was resolved to ignore. The sight of my hands made me feel sick; the flesh was laid bare and red, and the rope was covered with blood. I tried not to tear the strips right off: other accidents had taught me that one must preserve these bits to hasten the healing process later on. I tried to save my hands by braking with my stomach, my shoulders, and every other possible point of contact. When would this agony come to an end?

I came down to the nose of ice which I myself had cut away with my axe on the ascent. I felt about with my legs – it was all hard. There was no snow beneath. I was not yet down. In panic I called up to the Sherpas:

'Quick . . . Aila . . . Sarki . . . !'

They let my rope out more quickly and the friction on the fixed rope increased.

My hands were in a ghastly state. It felt as though all the flesh was being torn off. At last I was aware of something beneath my feet – the ledge. I had made it! I had to go along it now, always held by the rope; only three yards, but they were the trickiest of all. It was over. I collapsed, up to the waist in snow, and no longer conscious of time.

When I half-opened my eyes Rébuffat and the Sherpas were beside me, and I could distinctly see black dots moving about near the tents of Camp II. Sarki spoke to me, and pointed out two Sherpas coming up to meet us. They were still a long way off, but all the same it cheered me up.

I had to rouse myself; things were getting worse and worse. The frostbite seemed to be gaining ground – up to my calves and my elbows. Sarki put my glasses on for me again, although the weather had turned grey. He put one glove on as best he could; but my left hand was in such a frightful state that it made him sick to look at it, and he tried to hide it in my red scarf.

The fantastic descent continued and I was sure that every step would be my last. Through the swirling mist I sometimes caught glimpses of the two Sherpas coming up. They had already reached the base of the avalanche cone, and when, from the little platform I had just reached, I saw them stop there, it sapped all my courage.

Snow began to fall, and we now had to make a long traverse over very unsafe ground where it was difficult to safeguard anyone: then, fifty yards farther, we came to the avalanche cone. I recognised Phutharkay and Angdawa mounting rapidly towards us. Evidently they expected bad news, and Angdawa must have been thinking of his two brothers, Aila and Pansy. The former was with us all right – he could see him in the flesh – but what about Pansy? Even at this distance they started up a conversation, and by the time we reached them they knew everything. I heaved a deep sigh of relief. I felt now as if I had laid down a burden so heavy that I had nearly given way beneath it. Phutharkay was beside me, smiling affectionately. How can anyone call such people 'primitive', or say that the rigours of their existence take away all sense of pity? The Sherpas rushed towards me, put down their sacks, uncorked their flasks. Ah, just to drink a few mouthfuls! Nothing more. It had all been such a long time . . .

Phutharkay lowered his eyes to my hands and lifted them again, almost with embarrassment. With infinite sorrow, he whispered: 'Poor Bara Sahib – Ah . . .'

These reinforcements gave me a fresh access of courage, and Camp II was near. Phutharkay supported me, and Angdawa safeguarded us both. Phutharkay was smaller than I, and I hung on round his neck and leant on his shoulders, gripping him close. This contact comforted me and his warmth gave me strength. I staggered down with little jerky steps, leaning more and more on Phutharkay. Would I ever have the strength to make it even with his help? Summoning what seemed my very last ounce of energy, I begged Phutharkay to give me yet more help. He took my glasses off and I could see better then. Just a few more steps – the very last . . .

My friends all rallied round – they took off my gloves and my cagoule and settled me into a tent already prepared to receive us. I found this simplification intensely comforting: I appreciated my new existence which, though it would be short-lived, was for the moment so easy and pleasant. In spite of the threatening weather the others were not long in arriving: Rébuffat was the first – his toes were frostbitten, which made it difficult for him to walk and he looked ghastly, with a trickle of blood from his lips, and signs of suffering writ large on his face. They undressed him, and put him in a tent to await treatment.

Lachenal was still a long way off. Blind, exhausted, with his frostbitten feet, how could he manage to follow such a rough and dangerous track? In fact, he got over the little crevasse by letting himself slide down on his bottom. Couzy caught up with him on his way down and, although desperately weary himself, gave him invaluable assistance.

Lionel Terray followed closely behind them, held on a rope by Schatz, who was still in fine fettle. The little group drew nearer to the camp. The first man to arrive was Terray, and Marcel Ichac went up towards the great cone to meet him. Terray's appearance was pitiful. He was blind, and clung to Angtharkay as he walked. He had a huge beard and his face was distorted by pain into a dreadful grin. This 'strong man', this elemental force of nature who could barely drag himself along, cried out:

'But I'm still all right. If I could see properly, I'd come down by myself.'

When he reached camp Oudot and Noyelle were aghast. Once so strong, he was now helpless and exhausted. His appearance moved them almost to tears.

Immediately after, Schatz and Couzy arrived, and then Lachenal, practically carried by two Sherpas. From a distance it looked as though he was pedalling along in the air, for he threw his legs out in front in a most disordered way. His head lolled backwards and was covered with a bandage. His features were lined with fatigue and spoke of suffering and sacrifice. He could not have gone on for another hour. Like myself, he had set a limit which had helped him to hold on until now. And yet Biscante, at such a moment, still had the spirit to say to Ichac:

'Want to see how a Chamonix guide comes down from the Himalaya?'

Ichac's only reply was to hold out to him a piece of sugar soaked in adrenalin.

It was painful to watch Terray groping for the tent six inches from his nose: he held both hands out in front of him feeling for obstacles. He was helped in, and he lay down; then Lachenal, too, was laid on an air mattress.

Everyone was now off the mountain and assembled at Camp II. But in what a state! It was Oudot's turn to take the initiative, and he made a rapid tour of inspection. Faced with the appalling sight that we presented, his countenance reflected, now the consternation of the friend, now the surgeon's impersonal severity.

He examined me first. My limbs were numb up to well beyond the ankles and wrists. My hands were in a frightful condition; there was practically no skin left, the little that remained was black, and long strips dangled down. My fingers were both swollen and distorted. My feet were scarcely any better: the entire soles were brown and violet, and completely without feeling. The arm which was hurting me, and which I was afraid might be broken, did not appear to be seriously injured, and my neck was all right.

I was anxious to have Oudot's first impression.

'What do you think of it all?' I asked him, ready to hear the worst.

'It's pretty serious. You'll probably lose part of your feet and hands. At present I can't say more than that.'

'Do you think you'll be able to save something?'

'Yes, I'm sure of it. I'll do all I can.'

This was not encouraging, and I was convinced that my feet and hands would have to be amputated.

Oudot took my blood pressure and seemed rather concerned. There was no pressure in the right arm, and the needle did not respond at all on my left arm. On my legs the needle oscillated slightly, indicating a restricted flow of blood. After putting a dressing over my eyes to prevent the onset of ophthalmia; he said:

'I'm going to see Lachenal. I'll come back in a moment and give you some injections. I used them during the war and it's the only treatment that's any use with frostbite. See you presently.'

Lachenal's condition was slightly less serious. His hands were not affected, and the black discolouration of his feet did not extend beyond the toes, but the sinister colour reappeared on his heels. He would very likely lose his toes, but that would probably not prevent him from climbing, and from continuing to practise his profession as a guide.

Rébuffat's condition was much less serious. His feet were pink except for two small grey patches on his toes. Ichac massaged him with Dolpyo for two hours and this appeared to relieve him; his eyes were still painful, but that was only a matter of two or three days. Terray was unscathed: like Rébuffat he was suffering from ophthalmia – most painful, but only a temporary affliction. Couzy was very weak, and would have to be considered out of action. That was the balance sheet.

Night fell gradually. Oudot made his preparations, requisitioned Ichac and Schatz as nurses, and Camp II was turned into a hospital. In cold and discomfort, and to the accompaniment of continual avalanches, these men fought late into the night to save their friends. Armed with torches, they passed from tent to tent, bending over the wounded and giving them emergency treatment, at this minute camp, perched 20,000 feet up on the flanks of one of the highest mountains in the world.

Oudot made ready to give me arterial injections. The lamp shone feebly and in the semi-darkness Ichac sterilised the syringes as best he could with ether. Before starting operations, Oudot explained:

'I am going to inject novocaine into your femoral and brachial arteries.'

As I could not see a thing with the bandage over my eyes, he touched with his finger the places where he would insert the needle: both groins and in the bends of my elbows.

'It's going to hurt. Perhaps I shan't get the right place first shot. But in any case you mustn't move, particularly when I have got into the artery.'

I was not at all reassured by these preparations; I had always had a horror of injections. But it would have to be done, it was the only thing possible.

'Go ahead,' I said to Oudot, 'but warn me when you are going to stab.'

Anyhow, perhaps it would not hurt all that much in my present condition. I heard the murmur of voices – Oudot asking if something was ready, and Ichac answering: 'Here you are. Got it?'

Oudot ran his fingers over my skin. I felt an acute pain in the groin and my legs began to tremble; I tried to control myself. He had to try again, for the artery rolled away from the needle. Another stab, and my whole body was seized with convulsions, I stiffened when I should have relaxed, and felt all my nerves in revolt.

'Gently!' I could not help myself.

Oudot began again: my blood was extremely thick and clotted in the needle.

'Your blood is black – it's like black pudding,' he said in amazement.

'That's got it!' This time he had succeeded in spite of my howls which, I knew very well, made the operation all the more difficult to perform. The needle was now in position:

'Don't move!' Oudot shouted at me. Then to Ichac:

'Hand it over!'

Ichac passed him the syringe; I felt the needle moving in my flesh and the liquid began to flow into the artery. I should never, until then, have believed so much pain to be possible. I tried to brace myself to the utmost to keep myself from trembling: it simply had to be successful! The liquid went on flowing in.

'Can you feel any warmth?' asked Oudot, brusquely, while he was changing the syringe. Again the liquid went in; I gritted my teeth.

'Does it feel warm?'

Oudot was insistent – the point was evidently crucial; yet still I felt nothing. Several times the syringe was emptied, filled up, and emptied again:

'Now, do you feel anything?'

'I seem to feel a little warmth, but it's not very definite.'

Was it auto-suggestion? The needle was withdrawn abruptly,

and while Ichac sterilised the instruments. I had a few moments respite.

'It's excruciating, the way it hurts,' I said, just as if Oudot needed telling!

'Yes, I know, but we must go on.'

Oudot amputated the ends of all Herzog's fingers and toes. Herzog never climbed again, but turned instead to politics, becoming the French Minister of Sport.

DOG DAYS

A. J. BARRINGTON
(DATES UNKNOWN)

New Zealand gold-digger. In 1863 he led a prospecting party to north-east Otago.

21 *April* Very heavy rain has now set in and every appearance of its continuing. This is the heaviest rain I have seen since I left Victoria. The lake has risen four feet today, and the rivers are at a fearful height. Nothing to eat since a small snack this morning. There is nothing at all that we can find here eatable – no fern root, no spear-grass, no annis, or any vegetable whatever; nothing but stones, timber and water. I am certain we can get payable gold here if we can only get to work. It continued to rain at a fearful rate during the four following days, and flooded the lake and river, entirely precluding any work. Obtained just sufficient game to keep life in us, only after great hardships and difficulties.

26 *April* Foggy morning; cleared up about 12; put our blankets out to dry. One of the boys started early this morning to look after some game, but returned without any. Have but about 4lbs oatmeal now, and are 80 miles from the Wakatip in a straight line, but it will take us twice 80 to get there. My two mates made up their minds to start back again the first fine day we get, but I do not fancy going back the same route. I have tried all I know to induce them to continue east with me, as we cannot be more than

30 miles from the west river running into Lake Hawea, which lies NE from the Wanaka Lake, and which I believe to be the centre of the golden line of country, as the farther we get eastward the better we find the gold, and it is not half the distance that it is to the Wakatip. They however refused, and I then said I should go alone, which I was afterwards sorry I did not do, as I believe we had got almost to the end of the chain of mountains which runs north to Jackson's Bay from the Wakatip. If I had had a dog nothing should have prevented me from going alone, as I know it cannot be a worse road than we have had coming here.

27 April Turned out early and tore up one of my blankets to make shirts, as my clothes were worn out in the bush. The river and creeks so high that we cannot cross any of them; the smallest stream a few days since is now impassable.

28 April Rained till night, when it cleared up. Made a good fire and dried our clothes, ready for a start back in the morning, should it be fine. We are all very weak for the want of sufficient food. If we could travel we could always get sufficient food, but it is having to camp in wet weather that kills us.

29 April Packed up a few things which we cannot do well without, leaving behind picks, shovels, tin dishes, gimlets, nails, spokeshave, chisels, and several other things, which made our swags much lighter, but they felt just as heavy, on account of our weak state. We got a few miles up the river south, and had a good feed on some paradise ducks that we shot, turned in and felt much refreshed. The place we left this morning is situated about half a mile east of the river, lies due south from Jackson's Bay, and 30 miles east of the coast.

30 April Continued on our course up the river – a very bushy sideling of a steep mountain gorge, with the white foam of the river some hundreds of feet below us – jumping from one precipice to another, which under any other circumstances would have looked pretty. We did not, however, stop long to admire it, as then it looked hideous. Toiled away till night, when we had a hard matter to find a piece of ground 6 ft square on which to pitch the tent, and harder still to light a fire and cook four magpies we had shot on the road.

1 May Got up the river a few miles and came to a precipice and a very large and deep waterfall. It took us a long time to ascend, but we succeeded after many difficulties and dangers, our lives many times depending on a few blades of grass, which grow out of the face of the rocks. After a few miles further we came to a nice flat, where we could see there was any amount of game. Camped here the following day, hunting.

3 May Crossed the river and up the saddle, which leads up the side of a large burnt mountain; in gaining the top of which we had a few hours of fearful danger. The stones are so soft or rotten that we could not tell the moment our feet would give way and down we should go several hundred feet. At one time we were two hours getting twenty yards. Reached the top at one p.m. Ran it along south, which way our course lay, till near dark, then camped at the side of a little creek running down the side of the mountain higher up. There are three small lakes on this mountain nearly of the same size, with a few ducks on them.

4 May Made an early start, but it commenced raining about 10 a.m. and continued so all day. I lost the run of my mates all of a sudden, I having kept a little lower down on the side of the mountain. I thought nothing of it at the time, as we had often parted and met together again, but this time I cooeyed and got no answer. Thinking they were ahead I hurried on, but left them behind. Cooeyed all the way as I went, but got no answer. Could see the river down under me in the flat; got down, waited for an hour, but no sign of them; fired two guns hoping they would hear them, but no answer; so I gave them up, thinking that they had crossed along the side and over the mountain more to the eastward. I proceeded to follow up the river all the afternoon and shot one blue mountain duck, which I may say is all the provisions I have. I am very badly fitted for the road before me, having no dog and every appearance of a week or two's rain, as at every change of the moon we have had a week's rain lately, sometimes more. I have about three-quarters of a pound of oatmeal and a long weary road to travel. Travelled all the afternoon up the river; saw several creeks coming in, with quartz reefs showing and quartz boulders, and every indication of gold, but did not stop, as I had nothing to try a bit of dirt with. Still continued walking. Camped.

5 May I am camped on the side of a mountain by the side of a foaming creek, the rain coming down in torrents; cannot light a fire. Got two little ducks, but cannot cook them; had raw oatmeal for breakfast; have had nothing since yesterday morning, and walked all day, then pitched the tent and turned in with wet clothes and blankets. Got a fire at night, cooked one of my little ducks and ate it.

6 May Still raining, with snow mixed. I am certain this is snow on the mountains; if so I shall have a hard matter to get over. Very cold; could not sleep last night, my teeth cracking together all night with cold, and cramp in my legs. I do not feel at all well. The rats stole my little duck, which I intended for this day's food. This is the first day I have been heartily sick of the country. Nothing to eat; cannot light a fire; all my clothes and blankets wet. I am indeed miserable.

7 May Turned out and had a look; any amount of snow on the surrounding hills, and still snowing fast and freezing. Turned in again; slept all day, or rather stopped in bed.

8 May Still snowing and no sign of a change; no food.

9 May Turned out early; any amount of snow in the night. I do not know what to do now. I intended to have started this morning, wet or dry, snow or rain, but I am completely jammed in. I cannot move; snow falling thick and fast. Whether to go back and follow the river round to Plenty Lake, or to try and get over the mountains to Mineral Creek is a consideration which I cannot decide on. Night coming on again; nothing to eat, and fearfully cold.

10 May Turned out early; wrung the tent and clothes as well as I could, packed up and tried to go right up the mountain to the eastward, in hopes of seeing a smoke from my mates' fire, knowing they cannot be far off; but after toiling hard for half a day and falling in the snow head-first some hundreds of times, found it impossible to get up. Had to start away for the river again, and try and get up to its head and over the saddle. I have not eaten anything now for several days. There is a little spear-grass here; if I could get a fire to boil, or rather roast it, I think I could pass a day or two, but even that is forbidden. It is now snowing; two feet six inches solid snow by my tent, and I believe there is a deal more on the mountain. Turned into my wet blankets again for another night's misery.

11 May Could not sleep a minute all night; had to keep my legs and feet constantly in motion to keep the blood in circulation, and if I stopped a minute my feet felt dead with cold, and I should have the cramp in my legs. My clothes are still wet; there can be very little heat in me, or my clothes would dry sleeping in them all night; I must try and get a fire before I leave here if possible, to dry my blankets and flannels or another night like last will cook me. Rain, snow, and sleet, very heavy all day. Tried hard to get a fire, but could not; turned in again to my wet blankets.

12 May Rain and sleet very heavy; looks very bad; cannot get out of the tent; I do not know what is to be done, so turn into my wet blankets again to keep me warm, for it is fearful cold, thinking of Edward Dunmore and the 'Maori Hen'. If I have to stop here a few days more I shall be just as bad. (By the bye, I forgot to mention that I made every enquiry possible about the 'Maori Hen', but could not hear whether he got to Fox's or not.) I have had one little duck to eat for the last six days, yet strange to say I do not feel hungry. This will not do much longer, but on the side of a mountain covered with three or four feet of snow it is a hard matter to get food of any description. Went out in the afternoon to try and shoot something, but could not see anything to shoot – not even a robin. Found a root of spear-grass, ate some of it but could not enjoy it raw; then turned in for another night's rocking about.

13 May Turned out this morning with the intention of making a start, but the weather is so bad I am afraid to stir, it is raining heavily and the snow is thawing a little.

14 May Turned out early; wrung the tent and other things, which were very wet, packed up once more, and made a start. Got on very well for about half a mile, when my legs began to fail me, and I found I could not get more than twenty yards at a spell. Toiled away till I saw by the sun it was nearly noon, and I had not got one mile away from the timber where I was camped, and was completely done, so there was nothing for it but desert my swag or die here. The former idea I carried into effect. I threw away everything but my blankets, gun, and a little powder and shot, which was my only dependence. Amongst the things I abandoned was a couple of specimens which we got in the Little River, and a small parcel of gold, which we found in prospecting, with maps, books, etc., all of which I have before mentioned. After throwing away my swag I had a very hard task to get up the hill, as there was over two feet snow and very soft. I kept slipping and falling, till at length I arrived at the top of the saddle and saw a creek at the other side, and a grassy flat about a mile long and half a mile wide. I got to the river by sundown, and was going to the west end of the flat to camp, and try to get a duck or something to eat; but on looking up the creek I saw a smoke, which I went to and found my mates camped there. They were surprised to see me. I was greatly reduced since they saw me, and was very weak – just able to put one foot before another. I asked them if they had anything to eat; they said they had had nothing that day, but they started hunting, and got two Maori hens which they gave me, and with the heat of the fire I was much refreshed.

15 May Rained all day till noon. Miserable living; we are just alive and very weak.

16 May Turned out and started up the creek with nothing to eat; walked all day up right-hand branch of Wild Dog Creek; shot two magpies at noon and ate them raw, which refreshed us much at the time. We reached a long way up by night and camped under an overhanging rock, just under the snow. Nothing to eat but a little grass root: fearfully cold.

17 May Started early to try and get over the snow and down the other side. Had a fearful hard day's toil. Here is about a mile long of pure ice, as clear as crystal; you can see down into it several fathoms, just like looking down into the blue ocean, and no such thing as walking on it. We had to go round several times to where there was a little fresh snow lying on it, to be able to get along. At length made the foot of the saddle, and then we had some climbing to do to get up the mountain, which was covered with frost and snow, at an angle of 75 degrees. I was so weak that I thought I must give in, but I ate plenty of the little snowberries which grow under the snow. They helped us on a good deal, and we reached the top about 2 p.m. What a sight then met our eyes! Nothing but mountains of snow as far as we could see, in every direction but west. We got down by powerful exertion. At one time Simonin was behind me; I heard him sing out 'Look out', I turned round and he was coming down the snow at a fearful rate, head first, on his back. He held the gun in one hand, but had to let it go, when both he and the gun passed me at the rate of a swallow, and did not stop till they reached a little flat about two miles down, with a fall of 1,000 feet. I thought he was killed, but he was all right, with the exception of being a little frightened. We got down to the head of the flat and camped. Such a day I hope never to see again.

18 May Snow and sleet all day. Tried to get away, but had to camp again about six miles down the gorge. Had to camp under a rock, in a foot of snow. No fire, wet clothes, and nothing to eat. Hard times.

19 May Turned out early and started down the gorge, which took us all day. Snow and rain all day. Reached the flat at dark and camped in the bush with two feet of snow. Had a fearful job to light a fire. Fearfully cold night; our feet frostbitten and very sore.

20 May Rain and snow. Could not stir out before the evening, when it turned out fine and we went hunting. Night very cold; snowing hard again and freezing.

21 May Travelled down a large flat and entered into the heaviest and steepest gorge* I ever saw. Here we were very near losing Farrell. He volunteered to be lowered down by a flax rope on to a rock about 14 feet over the water, and thus pass our swags across; but when he got halfway down the rope broke and away he went into a fearful boiling eddy in the creek. I looked but could not see him anywhere for over a minute and a half, when I saw him rise just at the top of the precipice and seize at another rock, which he succeeded in catching hold of and getting upon. If he had gone

---

* The gorge of the Olivine River, into which Forgotten River flows.

4 ft farther, he would have been dashed down a precipice 200 ft so that he would never have been seen any more. Camped that night on the bare stones by the side of the creek. Nothing for a bed and nothing to eat. Very cold.

22 May Made a start early. Saw the Plenty Lake. Could not make out where we were till we got near the flat; then could see the Wild Dog River, and knew we were about halfway between the two lakes. Just able to walk, but very weak. Caught two kakapo and two magpies, and had a better supper than we had had for many a day.

23 May Went out early to shoot something for breakfast, but could get nothing. Kept close to the left-hand range, going down towards Poverty Lake.

24 May Kept on down the side of the range, hunting as we went along.

25 May Turned out before daylight to try and shoot some kakas, which were over us in the high trees, as the pine is an immense height; these birds come here to roost at night, and fly away to the mountains at daylight. Could not see them; got to our old camp on Poverty Lake by sundown. Camped and had a good supper. Feel much refreshed but our feet are very sore; all our toes are covered with running sores; Simonin's feet are not bad; I believe mine are far the worst. I do hope we shall get a few days fine weather, so as to enable us to get into the Wakatip once more.

26 May Another change in the weather. Rain again. Cannot get out of the tent. Nothing to eat all day.

27 May Rain again all day. We shall be worse off than ever if this weather continues. We are very weak and no chance of any fish or game here as we are now on an island, on account of the lake rising all round us and running back into the lagoons. Got a little fern root.

28 May Rain in torrents again. I do not know what we shall do. This is the third day again and nothing to eat but a bit of fern root. We cannot get out of the tent; the water is rising slowly but surely.

29 May This is the most miserable day of my existence. We had to turn out last night at 10 o'clock, and the water rose so fast that we could not get anything away but our blankets. Had to wade to the side of the range up to our middles in water. We tied the powder and guns and a few other things up to the ridge pole, afraid to carry them away in case of getting them wet. The night was very dark and before [we rea]ched the hill I got up to my arms in water. [I thought] I should never get across, but we reached the land safe about a quarter of a mile distant. Had to walk up and down all night, the rain still pouring down. If this night does not kill us we shall never die. Daylight broke upon us, each looking for the other and wondering that we are all alive. Got a fire this morning: kept it going all day, but could not get back to our tent, as there is ten feet of water to go through, so we shall have another night, which I hope will be fine or we shall perish.

30 May Fine morning. Did not rain much all night. I cut my blanket in two, to make a tent of one half of it, and slept by the fire very comfortably, considering our situation. Farrell crossed to the tent up to his middle in water this morning, and brought the two guns and some powder, and shot a duck, which came up swimming in the lake. We also shot a little kaka, which we boiled with some fern root, for the first meal we have had in four days.

31 May Whilst in the act of packing up, I saw a rat which the dog had killed in the night. I never picked up a nugget of gold during the last ten years with more satisfaction than I picked him up, put him in the fire, and roasted him just as he was, then cut him in three parts, which we pronounced the sweetest bit of meat we ever ate. Proceeded up the side of the range, very weak and tired, and the bush wet. Camped about one-third of the way up the range with clothes wet. Could not get a fire.

1 June Started early, to try and get over today. Camped about two miles from the saddle. Raining, very weak, and our feet awfully painful.

2 June Got over the saddle through the snow and down to Kakapo Flat,* where we expected to stop a day or two and get plenty of game; but the flat was covered with snow, and consequently the birds do not come down out of the range at night, but stop under the rocks and in the timber in the warmest place. Caught one kakapo and one Maori hen, which we cooked for supper under a rock, where we camped about 10 o'clock. It rained all the remainder of the day. Went hunting, but the dog would not work, as he had had a bird that morning and eaten it.

3 June Continued on our road (feet getting worse) through the snow up the creek. Crossed over the flat and down to our old camp at the head of Mineral Creek. Caught one Maori hen and cooked it for supper, or rather for thirty-six hours' food for three men. Went to bed very weak and bad.

4 June Continued our course down the creek, made the old camp at the west foot of the dividing range, so tired that we would give all the world to be at the other side of it. Weather likely to be wet. Got three Maori hens, which is indeed a treat. Went to bed in good spirits, hoping we shall have good weather to get over the range, as that is all that troubles us. We know if we were over the divide

---

* Alabaster Pass.

we can get to the Wakatip if we do not get anything more to eat, as it is all downhill afterwards.

5 June Got down to the edge of the bush, when it commenced raining, with a heavy thick fog on the mountain. We consulted as to whether we should go on or not, the weather looking so bad. Camped. Rained all day. Caught one kakapo; very poor store to carry us over the divide. My feet are in an awful mess, and nothing to put on them but Maori hen fat. I do not think we shall be able to get over; we are three skeletons just alive.

6 June Packed up once more to cross the divide if possible. If we cannot cross, we shall have to follow the creek down to the Awarua River, from thence to the Kakapo Lake, down to the sea, and stop there all the winter if possible. We are now six days coming from Poverty Lake, which I have done in one day before now. Got up to the head of the timber by night, and camped under a rock.

7 June Raining very heavy this morning. This is the worst of all to be caught here, where we cannot get anything to eat. Commenced to snow at noon, and has every appearance of a heavy fall; so we must start. Did not get up a mile when we were up to our knees in soft snow; the higher we ascended the deeper it got, and we could scarcely see each other ten yards off. However we managed it after a long time, and when we got on top the snow was first-rate to walk on – just hard enough to keep us up, and down this side was beautiful, till we came within a mile of the bottom, when the snow became very soft, and we were till eight o'clock at night before we got down to our old camp, where we camped on three feet of snow. Our blankets and clothes all wet.

8 June Snowed all night. Made a start down the creek, tumbling and rolling over rocks and stones, sometimes wholly disappearing in the snow, till we got down a few miles. Saw some kakas in a tree; my gun was too wet to be used, so Simonin got one of his barrels in the humour and shot seven of them, which saved our dog, as we had agreed to kill and eat him this afternoon. Still snowing. We here camped and cooked six of them. Had a good dinner and dried our clothes a little. Commenced to rain very hard again.

9 June Rained heavily all day. Cooked our remaining bird. I went up the creek in the afternoon but could not see anything. Our feet are breaking out in fresh places, and are very sore.

10 June Rain again. I wonder if we shall ever reach the Wakatip – only two and a half days' tramp even in our state, and yet we cannot get a fine day, or anything to eat. If fasting and praying is of any value to sinners, we ought soon to become saints, for we have had enough of it lately. Cleared up about noon, when we made a start and got down a few miles further to our old camp.

11 June Got nearly to the Dart and in sight of the Wakatip, which was indeed a welcome sight to us. We caught plenty of Maori hens and had a good feast – happy once more, even under our circumstances. Nearly skeletons, and can scarcely put one foot before the other.

12 June Turned out in good spirits, hoping this will be the last day of our hardships. Started down the Dart. Feet bad, and the gravel hurt them very much. Got down to the Island and heard some person shooting; crossed over to see who it was, and found the captain of Mr Rees's yacht and his mate, who were up pigeon shooting. We asked them to send a boat across to the other side of the Dart to fetch us when they returned, as they would be down before we should. They said they would either send a boat for us or come and fetch us themselves. We arrived at the Lake just at sundown; made a fire and commenced firing guns, which were answered from the township. In the course of an hour five of the boys came across for us in Mr Barrett's whale boat. We were invited by Mr Reid, at the station, to come up and stop there for a while till we got better. From thence we went to Frankton Hospital where, with the constant care and attention we receive, we hope to be soon recovered.

ACROSS THE GREAT DIVIDE

MERIWETHER LEWIS &
WILLIAM CLARK
(1774–1809) & (1770–1838)

*American soldiers and explorers. In 1803, Lewis and Clark were
appointed co-commanders of the US Corps of Discovery with instructions to explore the continent from the Missouri River to the Pacific
Ocean – a vast unknown territory known as 'Louisiana', recently
purchased by the US from France. Their subsequent 'Voyage of
Discovery' lasted 28 months, covered 8,000 miles, and was chronicled in
Lewis and Clark's expedition journals.*

[Lewis] *Monday, 26 August 1805* [Shoshone indian camp, Rocky
Mountains] I found it a folly to think of attemp[t]ing to decend
this river [the Snake] in canoes and therefore determined to
commence the purchase of horses in the morning from the indians
in order to carry into execution the design we had formed of
passing the rocky Mountains. I now informed Cameahwait of my
intended expedition overland to the great river which lay in the
plains beyond the mountains and told him that I wished to
purchase 20 horses of himself and his people to convey our
baggage. He observed that the Minnetares had stolen a great
number of their horses this spring but hoped his people would
spear me the number I wished. I also asked a guide, he observed
that he had no doubt but the old man who was with Capt. C.
would accompany us if we wished him and that he was better

informed of the country than any of them. Matters being thus far arranged I directed the fiddle to be played and the party danced very merily much to the amusement and gratification of the natives, though I must confess that the state of my own mind at this moment did not well accord with the prevailing mirth as I somewhat feared that the caprice of the indians might suddenly induce them to withhold their horses from us without which my hopes of prosicuting my voyage to advantage was lost; however I determined to keep the indians in a good humour if possible, and to loose no time in obtaining the necessary number of horses. I directed the hunters to turn out early in the morning and indeavor to obtain some meat. I had nothing but a little parched corn to eat this evening.

[Clark] *Thursday, 29 August 1805* I left our baggage in possession of 2 men and proceeded on up to join Capt. Lewis at the upper Village of Snake Indians where I arrived at 1 oClock found him much engaged in Councelling and attempting to purchase a fiew more horses. I Spoke to the Indians on various Subjects endeavoring to impress on theire minds the advantage it would be to them for to sell us horses and expedite the [*our*] journey the nearest and best way possibly that we might return as soon as possible and winter with them at Some place where there was plenty of buffalow, our wish is to get a horse for each man to carry our baggage and for Some of the men to ride occasionally, The horses are handsom and much acustomed to be changed as to their Parsture, we cannot calculate on their carrying large loads & feed on the Grass which we may calculate on finding in the Mountain thro' which we may expect to pass on our rout.

[Clark] *Friday, 30 August 1805* finding that we Could purchase no more horse[s] than we had for our goods &c. (and those not a Sufficient number for each of our Party to have one which is our wish) I Gave my Fuzee to one of the men & Sold his musket for a horse which Completed us to 29 total horses, we Purchased pack cords Made Saddles & Set out on our rout down the [*Lemhi*] river by land guided by my old guide [and] one other who joined him, the old gu[i]de's 3 Sons followed him, before we Set out our hunters killed three Deer proceeded on 12 Miles and encamped on the river South Side.

at the time we Set out from the Indian Camps the greater Part of the Band Set out over to the waters of the Missouri. we had great attention paid to the horses, as they were nearly all Sore Backs, and Several pore, & young Those horses are indifferent, maney Sore backs and others not acustomed to pack, and as we cannot put large loads on them are Compelled to purchase as maney as we can to take our Small proportion of baggage of the Parties, (& Eate if necessary) Proceeded on 12 Miles to day.

[Clark] *Monday, 2 September 1805* proceeded on up the Creek, proceded on thro' thickets in which we were obliged to Cut a road, over rockey hill Sides where our horses were in [per]peteal danger of Slipping to their certain distruction & up & Down Steep hills, where Several horses fell, Some turned over, and others Sliped down Steep hill Sides, one horse Crippeled & 2 gave out.

[Clark] *Tuesday, 3 September 1805* hills high & rockey on each Side, in the after part of the day the high mountains closed the Creek on each Side and obliged us to take on the Steep Sides of those Mountains, So Steep that the horses Could Scur[ce]ly keep from Slipping down, Several sliped & Injured themselves verry much, with great dificuelty we made [blank space in MS.] miles & Encamped on a branch of the Creek we assended after crossing Several Steep points & one mountain, but little to eate

The mouintains to the East Covered with Snow. we met with a great misfortune, in haveing our last Th[er]mometer broken, by accident. This day we passed over emence hils and Some of the worst roads that ever horses passed, our horses frequently fell Snow about 2 inches deep when it began to rain which terminated in a Sleet [storm].

Tuesday, 3 September 1805

N. 25.° W. 2½	Miles to a Small fork on the left Hilley and thick assending
N. 15.° W. 2	miles to a fork on the right assending
N. 22.°W. 2½	miles to a fork on the left passing one on the left Several Spring runs on the right Stoney hills & much falling timber
N. 18.° E. 2	miles passing over Steep points & winding ridges to a high Point passed a run on the right
N. 32.° W. 2	miles to the top of a high hill passed 2 runs from the left, passing on the Side of a Steep ridge. no road
N. 40.° W 3	miles leaveing the waters of the Creek to
14	the right & passing over a high pine Mountn. o the head of a Drean running to the left

[Clark] *Wednesday, 4 September 1805* a verry cold morning every thing wet and frosed, Groun[d] covered with Snow, we assended a mountain & took a Divideing ridge* which we kept for Several Miles & fell on the head of a Creek which appeared to run the Course we wished to go

prosued our Course down the Creek to the forks about 5 miles where we met a part[y] of the Tushepau nation, of 33 Lodges about 80 men 400 Total and at least 500 horses, those people rec[e]ved us friendly, threw white robes over our Sholders & Smoked in the pipes of peace, we Encamped with them & found them friendly but nothing but berries to eate a part of which they gave us, those Indians are well dressed with Skin shirts & robes, they [are] Stout & light complected more So than Common for Indians, The Chief harangued untill late at night, Smoked in our pipe and appeared Satisfied. I was the first white man who ever wer on the waters of this river.

---

* Lost Trail Pass into Montana on the west slope of the Continental Divide.

[Clark] *Thursday, 5 September 1805* we assembled the Chiefs & warriers and Spoke to them (with much dificuel[t]y as what we Said had to pass through Several languages before it got into theirs, which is a gugling kind of language Spoken much thro the throught [throat]) we informed them who we were, where we came from, where bound and for what purpose &c. &c. and requested to purchase & exchange a fiew horses with them, in the Course of the day I purchased 11 horses & exchanged 7 for which we gave a fiew articles of merchendize, those people possess ellegant horses.

[Clark] *Friday, 6 September 1805* took a Vocabelary of the language listened our loads & packed up, rained contd. untill 12 oClock

all our horses purchased of the flat heads (*oote-lash-shutes*) we Secured well for fear of their leaveing of us, and Watched them all night for fear of their leaving us or the Indians prosuing & Steeling them.

[Lewis] *Monday, 9 September 1805* two of our hunters have arrived, one of them brought with him a redheaded woodpecker of the large kind common to the U States. this is the first of the kind I have seen since I left the Illinois. just as we were seting out Drewyer arrived with two deer. we continued our rout down the valley about 4 miles and crossed the river; it is hear a handsome stream about 100 yards wide and affords a considerable quantity of very clear water, the banks are low and it's bed entirely gravel. the stream appears navigable, but from the circumstance of their being no sammon in it I believe that there must be a considerable fall in it below. our guide could not inform us where this river* discharged itself into the columbia river, he informed us that it continues it's course along the mountains to the N as far as he knew it and that not very distant from where we then were it

---

* Bitterroot River, originally named Clark's River by the explorers.

formed a junction with a stream nearly as large as itself which took it's rise in the mountains near the Missouri to the East of us and passed through an extensive valley generally open prarie which forms an excellent pass to the missouri. the point of the Missouri where this Indian pass intersects it, is about 30 miles above the *gates of the rocky mountain,* or the place where the valley of the Missouri first widens into an extensive plain after entering the rockey Mountains. the guide informed us that a man might pass to the Missouri from hence by that rout in four days.

we continued our rout down the W. side of the river about 5 miles further and encamped on a large creek which falls in on the West. as our guide inform[ed] me that we should leave the river at this place and the weather appearing settled and fair I determined to halt the next day rest our horses and take some scelestial Observations. we called this Creek *Travellers rest.*

[Clark] *Wednesday, 11 September 1805* proceeded on up the *Travellers rest Creek* accompanied by the Flat head Indian about 7 miles our guide tels us a fine large roade passes up this river to the Missouri. The loss of 2 of our horses detained us unl. 3 oClock P.M. our *Flat head* Indian being restless thought proper to leave us and proceed on alone, Sent out the hunters to hunt in advance as usial. (we have Selected 4 of the best hunters to go in advance to hunt for the party. This arrangement has been made long since)

Encamped at Some old Indian Lodges, nothing killed this evening hills on the right high & ruged, the mountains on the left high & Covered with Snow. The day Verry worm.

[Clark] *Thursday, 12 September 1805* The road through this hilley Countrey is verry bad passing over hills & thro' Steep hollows, over falling timber &c. &c. continued on & passed Some most intolerable road on the Sides of the Steep Stoney mountains, which might be avoided by keeping up the Creek which is thickly covered with under groth & falling timber, Crossed a Mountain 8 miles with out water & encamped on a hill Side on the Creek after

Decending a long Steep mountain, Some of our Party did not get up untill 10 oClock P M.

[Clark] *Thursday (Saturday), 14 September* 1805 a verry high Steep mountain for 9 miles to a large fork from the left which appears to head in the Snow toped mountains we Encamped opposit a Small Island at the mouth of a branch on the right side of the river which is at this place 80 yards wide, Swift and Stoney, here we were compelled to kill a Colt for our men & Selves to eat for the want of meat & we named the South fork Colt killed Creek, and this river we Call *Flat head* River the flat head name is Koos koos ke The Mountains which we passed to day much worst than yesterday the last excessively bad & thickly Strowed with falling timber & Pine Spruce fur Hackmatak & Tamerack, Steep & Stoney our men and horses much fatigued.

[Clark] *Wednesday (Sunday), 15 September 1805* Several horses Sliped and roled down Steep hills which hurt them verry much the one which Carried my desk & Small trunk Turned over & roled down a mountain for 40 yards & lodged against a tree, broke the Desk the horse escaped and appeared but little hurt Some others very much hurt, from this point I observed a range of high mountains Covered with Snow from SE to SW with their tops bald or void of timber,

after two hours delay we proceeded on up the mountain Steep & ruged as usial, more timber near the top, when we arrived at the top As we Conceved, we could find no water and Concluded to Camp and make use of the Snow we found on the top to cook the remns. of our Colt & make our Supe, evening verry cold and cloudy. Two of our horses gave out, pore and too much hurt to proceed on and left in the rear. nothing killed to day except 2 Phests.

From this mountain I could observe high ruged mountains in every direction as far as I could see. with the greatest exertion we could only make 12 miles up this mountain.

[Clark] *Saturday (Monday), 16 September 1805* began to Snow about 3 hours before Day and continued all day the Snow in the morning 4 inches deep on the old Snow, and by night we found it from 6 to 8 inches deep, I walked in front to keep the road and found great dificuelty in keeping it as in maney places the Snow had entirely filled up the track, and obliged me to hunt Several minits for the track, at 12 oClock we halted on the top of the mountain to worm & dry our Selves a little as well as to let our horses rest and graze a little on Some long grass which I observed, (*on*) The (*South*) Knobs Steep hill Sides & falling timber Continue to day, and a thickly timbered Countrey of 8 different kinds of pine, which are so covered with Snow, that in passing thro' them we are continually covered with Snow.

I have been wet and as cold in every part as I ever was in my life, indeed I was at one time fearfull my feet would freeze in the thin Mockirsons which I wore, after a Short Delay in the middle of the Day, I took one man and proceeded on as fast as I could about 6 miles to a Small branch passing to the right, halted and built fires for the party agains[t] their arrival which was at Dusk, verry cold and much fatigued, we Encamped at this Branch in a thickly timbered bottom which was scurcely large enough for us to lie leavil, men all wet cold and hungary. Killed a Second Colt which we all Suped hartily on and thought it fine meat.

[Lewis] *Wednesday, 18 September 1805* Cap Clark set out this morning to go a head with six hunters. there being no game in these mountains we concluded it would be better for one of us to take the hunters and hurry on to the leavel country a head and there hunt and provide some provisions while the other remained with and brought on the party. the latter of these was my part; accordingly I directed the horses to be gotten up early being determined to force my march as much as the abilities of our horses would permit.

this morning we finished the remainder of our last coult. we dined & suped on a skant proportion of portable soupe, a few canesters of which, a little bears oil and about 20 lbs of candles form our stock of provision, the only resources being our guns & packhorses. the first is but a poor dependance in our present situation where there is nothing upon earth ex[c]ept ourselves and a few small pheasants, small grey Squirrels, and a blue bird of the vulter kind about the size of a turtle dove or jay bird.

[Clark] *Monday (Wednesday), 18 September 1805* I proceeded on in advance with Six hunters to try and find deer or Something to kill.

[Lewis] *Thursday, 19 September 1805* Fraziers horse fell from this road in the evening, and roled with his load near a hundred yards into the Creek. we all expected that the horse was killed but to our astonishment when the load was taken off him he arose to his feet & appeared to be but little injured, in 20 minutes he proceeded with his load. this was the most wonderfull escape I ever witnessed, the hill down which he roled was almost perpendicular and broken by large irregular and broken rocks.

we took a small quantity of portable soup, and retired to rest much fatiegued. several of the men are unwell of the disentary. brakings out, or irruptions of the Skin, have also been common with us for some time.

[Clark] *Tuesday (Thursday), 19 September 1805* Set our early proceeded on up the [*Hungry*] Creek passing through a Small glade at 6 miles at which place we found a horse. I derected him killed and hung up for the party after takeing a brackfast off for our Selves which we thought fine.

[Lewis] *Friday, 20 September 1805* This morning my attention was called to a species of bird which I had never seen before. It was reather larger than a robbin, tho' much it's form and action. the colours were a blueish brown on the back the wings and tale black, as wass a stripe above the croop 3 4 of an inch wide in front of the neck, and two others of the same colour passed from it's eyes back along the sides of the head. the top of the head, neck brest and belley and butts of the wing were of a fine yellowish brick reed [red]. it was feeding on the buries of a species of shoe-make or ash which grows common in [this] country & which I first observed on 2d. of this month. I have also observed two birds of a blue colour both of which I believe to be of the haulk or vulter kind. the one of a blue shining colour with a very high tuft of feathers on the head a long tale, it feeds on flesh the beak and feet black. it's note is chă-ăh, chă-ăh. it is about the size of a pigeon, and in shape and action resembles the jay bird.

Three species of Pheasants, a large black species, with some white feathers irregularly scattered on the brest neck and belley – a smaller kind of a dark uniform colour with a red stripe above the eye, and a brown and yellow species that a gooddeel resembles the phesant common to the Atlantic States.

we were detained this morning untill ten oclock in consequence of not being enabled to collect our horses. we had proceeded about 2 Miles when we found the greater part of a horse which Capt. Clark had met with and killed for us. he informed me by note that he should proceed as fast as possible to the leavel country which lay to the SW of us, which we discovered from the heights of the mountains on the 19th there he intended to hunt until our arrival. at one oclock we halted on a small branch runing to the left and made a hearty meal on our horse beef much to the comfort of our hungry stomachs. here I learnt that one of the Packhorses with his load was missing and immediately dispatched Baptiest Lapage who had charge of him, to surch for him. he returned at 3 OC. without the horse. The load of the horse was of considerable value consisting of merchandize and all my stock of winter cloathing. I therefore dispatched two of my best woodsmen in surch of him, and proceeded with the party.

our road was much obstructed by fallen timber particularly in the evening. we encamped on a ridge where ther was but little grass for our horses, and at a distance from water. however we obtained as much as served our culinary purposes and suped on our beef. the soil as you leave the heights of the mountains becomes gradually more fertile. the land through which we passed this evening is of an excellent quality tho' very broken, it is a dark grey soil. a grey free stone appearing in large masses above the earth in many places. saw the hucklebury, honeysuckle, and alder common to the Atlantic states, also a kind of honeysuckle which bears a white bury and rises about 4 feet high not common but to the western side of the rockey mountains. a growth which resembles the choke cherry bears a black bury with a single stone of sweetish taste, it rises to the hight of 8 or 10 feet and grows in thick clumps. the Arborvita is also common and grows to an immence size, being from 2 to 6 feet in diameter.

[Clark] *Wednesday (Friday), 20 September 1805* I set out early and proceeded on through a Countrey as ruged as usial at 12 miles decended the mountain to a level pine Countrey proceeded on through a butifull Countrey for three miles to a Small Plain in which I found maney Indian lodges,* a man Came out to meet me, & Conducted me to a large Spacious Lodge which he told me (by Signs) was the Lodge of his great Chief who had Set out 3 days previous with all the Warriers of the nation to war on a South West derection & would return in 15 or 18 days. the fiew men that were left in the Village and great numbers of women geathered around me with much apparent signs of fear, and apr. pleased they those people gave us a Small piece of Buffalow meat, Some dried Salmon beries & roots in different States, Some round and much like an onion which they call Pas she co [*quamash. the Bread or Cake is called Pas-shi-co*] Sweet, of this they make bread & Supe they also gave us, the bread made of this root all of which we eate hartily, I gave them a fiew Small articles as preasents, and proceeded on with a Chief to his Village 2 miles in the Same Plain,

---

* At Weippe, Idaho.

† The Chopunnish, or Nez Perces, were located on the Salmon and Snake rivers.

where we were treated kindly in their way and continued with them all night Those two Villages consist of about 30 double lodges, but fiew men a number of women & children, they call themselves *Cho pun-nish* or *Pierced noses†* Their diolect appears verry different from the flat heads, [*Tushapaws*], altho origineally the Same people.

Emence quantity of the [*quawmash or*] *Pas-shi-co* root gathered & in piles about the plain, those roots grow much like an onion in marshey places the seed are in triangular Shells, on the Stalk. they sweat them in the following manner i.e. dig a large hole 3 feet deep, cover the bottom with Split wood on the top of which they lay Small Stones of about 3 or 4 Inches thick, a Second layer of

Splited wood & Set the whole on fire which heats the Stones, after the fire is extinguished they lay grass & mud mixed on the Stones, on that dry grass which Supports the Pâsh-shi-co root a thin Coat of the Same grass is laid on the top, a Small fire is kept when necessary in the Center of the kill &c.

I find myself verry unwell all the evening from eateing the fish & roots too freely Sent out hunters they killed nothing.

[Lewis] *Saturday, 21 September 1805* we killed a few Pheasants, and I killed a prarie woolf which together with the ballance of our horse beef and some crawfish which we obtained in the creek enabled us to make one more hearty meal, not knowing where the next was to be found.

the Arborvita increases in quantity and size. I saw several sticks today large enough to form eligant perogues of at least 45 feet in length. I find myself growing weak for the want of food and most of the men complain of a similar deficiency, and have fallen off very much.

[Clark] *Thursday (Saturday), 21 September 1805* A fine Morning Sent out all the hunters in different directions to hunt deer, I my self delayed with the Chief to prevent Suspision and to Collect by Signs as much information as possible about the river and Countrey in advance. The Chief drew me a kind of chart of the river, and informed me that a greater Chief than himself was fishing at the river half a days march from his Village called the twisted hare [hair], and that the river forked a little below his Camp and at a long distance below & below 2 large forks one from the left & the other from the right the river passed thro' the mountains at which place was a great fall of the Water passing through the rocks, at those falls white people lived from whome they precured the white Beeds & Brass &c. which the womin wore.

I am verry sick to day and puke which relive me.

[Lewis] *Sunday, 2 September 1805* Notwithstanding my positive directions to hubble the horses last evening one of the men neglected to comply. he plead[ed] ignorance of the order. this neglect however detained us untill ½ after eleven OCk. at which time we renewed our march, our course being about west. We had proceeded about two and a half miles when we met Reubin Fields one of our hunters, whom Capt. Clark had dispatched to meet us with some dryed fish and roots that he had procured from a band of Indians, whose lodges were about eight miles in advance. I ordered the party to halt for the purpose of taking some refreshment. I divided the fish roots and buries, and was happy to find a sufficiency to satisfy compleatly all our appetites. the pleasure I now felt in having tryumphed over the rockey Mountains and decending once more to a level and fertile country where there was every rational hope of finding a comfortable subsistence for myself and party can be more readily conceived than expressed, nor was the flattering prospect of the final success of the expedition less pleasing. on our approach to the village which consisted of eighteen lodges most of the women fled to the neighbouring woods on horseback with their children, a circumstance I did not expect as Capt. Clark had previously been with them and informed them of our pacific intentions towards them and also the time at which we should most probably arrive. the men and none of what we had stowed inside the cabin. We ourselves had stripped the raft of everything of real value, which now lay in safety on the top of the great sun-smitten rock inside the reef.

Since I had jumped off the raft, I had genuinely missed the sight of all the pilot fish wriggling in front of our bows. Now the great balsa logs lay right up on the reef in six inches of water, and brown sea slugs lay writhing under the bows. The pilot fish were gone. The dolphins were gone. Only unknown flat fish with peacock patterns and blunt tails wriggled inquisitively in and out between the logs. We had arrived in a new world. Johannes had left his hole. He had doubtless found another lurking-place here.

I took a last look round on board the wreck, and caught sight of a little baby palm in a flattened basket. It projected from an eye in a coconut to a length of eighteen inches, and two roots stuck out below. I waded in towards the island with the nut in my hand. A little way ahead I saw Knut wading happily landwards with a model of the raft, which he had made with much labour on the voyage, under his arm. We soon passed Bengt. He was a splendid steward. With a lump on his forehead and sea water dripping from his beard, he was walking bent double pushing a box, which danced along before him every time the breakers outside sent a stream over into the lagoon. He lifted the lid proudly. It was the kitchen box, and in it were the Primus and cooking utensils in good order.

I shall never forget that wade across the reef towards the heavenly palm island that grew larger as it came to meet us. When I reached the sunny sand beach, I slipped off my shoes and thrust my bare toes down into the warm, bone-dry sand. It was as though I enjoyed the sight of every footprint which dug itself into the virgin sand beach that led up to the palm trunks. Soon the palm-tops closed over my head, and I went on, right in towards the centre of the tiny island. Green coconuts hung under the palm-tufts, and some luxuriant bushes were thickly covered with snow-white blossoms, which smelt so sweet and seductive that I felt quite faint. In the interior of the island two quite tame terns flew about my shoulders. They were as white and light as wisps of cloud. Small lizards shot away from my feet, and the most important inhabitants of the island were large blood-red hermit crabs; which lumbered along in every direction with stolen snail-shells as large as eggs adhering to their soft hinder-parts.

I was completely overwhelmed. I sank down on my knees and thrust my fingers deep down into the dry warm sand.

The voyage was over. We were all alive. We had run ashore on a small uninhabited South Sea island. And what an island! Torstein came in, flung away a sack, threw himself flat on his back and looked up at the palm-tops and the white birds, light as down, which circled noiselessly just above us. Soon we were all six lying there. Herman, always energetic, climbed up a small palm and pulled down a cluster of large green coconuts. We cut off their soft tops, as if they were eggs, with our machete knives, and poured down our throats the most delicious refreshing drink in the world – sweet, cold milk from young and seedless palm fruit. On the reef outside resounded the monotonous drumbeats from the guard at the gates of paradise.

'Purgatory was a bit damp,' said Bengt, 'but heaven was more or less as I'd imagined it.'

We stretched ourselves luxuriously on the ground and smiled up at the white trade wind clouds drifting by westward up above the palm-tops. Now we were no longer following them helplessly; now we lay on a fixed, motionless island, really in Polynesia.

And as we lay and stretched ourselves, the breakers outside us rumbled like a train, to and fro, to and fro all along the horizon.

Bengt was right; this was heaven.

ATLANTIC ORDEAL

ALAIN BOMBARD
(1924–2005)

French scientist who sailed across the Atlantic in a rubber dingy to test his theory that castaways could survive in an open boat by obtaining food – in the shape of fish and plankton – from the sea itself, and drinking sea water in limited quantities.

'Land! Land!' is the cry of the castaway when he sights the first coast. My cry on 11 November was 'Rain! Rain!'

I had noticed for some time that the surface of the sea had become strangely calm, exactly as if it were sleeked down with oil, and suddenly I realised why: 'Rain! Here comes the rain,' I cried aloud.

I stripped ready for it, so that I could wash all the salt off my body, and then sat down on one of the floats. I stretched out the tent on my knees, and held between my legs an inflatable rubber mattress, capable of holding some fifteen gallons of water. I waited. Like the sound of a soda syphon, monstrously magnified, I heard advancing from far away the noise of water beating on water. I must have waited nearly twenty minutes, watching the slow approach of this manna from heaven. The waves were flattened under the weight of the rain and the wind buffeted me as the squall hit the boat. The cloud passed over slowly, writhing with the vertical turbulence of a small cyclone. I was drenched in a tropical downpour, which rapidly filled the tent sheet and made it sag with the weight between my knees. I plunged my head in it and as quickly spat the water out again. It was impregnated with salt from the tent and I let it all spill overboard. At the second fill, although the water tasted strongly of rubber, it was like nectar. I washed myself voluptuously. The squall did not last long, but the rainfall was tremendous. Not only did I drink my fill that day, but I was able to store three or four gallons in my rubber mattress. I was going to have a gurgling pillow, but each night my reserve of water was going to renew my hopes for the next day. Even if I had nothing to eat, even if I caught no fish, I at least had something to drink.

For three weeks I had not had a drop of fresh water, only the liquid I pressed from my fish, but my reactions were perfectly normal, just the marvellous sensation of swallowing a real drink at last. My skin was still in good order, although much affected by the salt, my mucous membranes had not dried, and my urine had remained normal in quantity, smell and colour. I had proved conclusively that a castaway could live for three weeks (and even longer, because I could have continued perfectly well) without fresh water. It is true that Providence was to spare me the ordeal of having to rely again on the flat, insipid fish juice. From that day on I always had enough rainwater to slake my thirst. It sometimes seemed as if my stock was about to run out, but a shower always came in time.

I found that it was impossible to wash the salt out of my clothes and bedding, and I had to remain until the end 'a man of salt water' (as the Polynesians say of people who live off the sea) completely encrusted with it until the day of my arrival.

The day of the rain brought me both pleasure and perturbation. The pleasure consisted in a new sort of bird, an attractive creature called, in English, I believe, a white-tailed tropic bird, and which the French call a *paille-cul*. It looks like a white dove with a black beak and has a long quill in its tail, which, with an impertinent air, it uses as an elevator. I rummaged quickly for my raft book, written for the use of castaways, and read that the appearance of this bird did not necessarily mean that one was near land. But as it could only come from the American continent, being completely unknown in the Old World, it was a good sign. For the first time, I had met a bird which came, without a shadow of doubt, from my destination.

This pleasant interlude was succeeded at about two o'clock in the afternoon by twelve hours of terror, which lasted until two the next morning. Just as I was peacefully reading a little Aeschylus, there was a violent blow on the rudder: 'That's another shark,' I thought, and looked up. What I saw was a large swordfish of undeniably menacing aspect. He was following the dinghy at a distance of about twenty feet, seemingly in a rage, his dorsal fin raised like hackles. In one of his feints round the boat, he had collided with my rudder oar. I found I had a determined enemy. If I only succeeded in wounding him he would surely attack again, and that would be the end of L'Hérétique. What was worse, as I was hurriedly getting my harpoon ready, a clumsy movement knocked it into the sea. It was my last one. Now I was disarmed. I fixed my pocket knife on to my underwater gun as a makeshift bayonet, determined to sell my life dearly if he attacked in earnest.

This intolerable anxiety lasted twelve long hours. As night fell I could follow the swordfish's movements by his luminous wake and the noise his dorsal fin made cutting the water. Several times his back bumped the underside of the dinghy, but he still seemed a little afraid of me. He never approached from ahead, and every time he came at me he changed course at the last moment before striking the floats. I came to believe that he was frightened, probably as frightened as I was. Every living creature possesses some means of defence, but it must perturb an attacker not to know what it is. In the early hours of the morning his wake disappeared, but I spent a sleepless night.

One of the lulls in this encounter brought a minor relief, which I interpreted as a message from the land. It was one of those little glass floats used on fishing nets, encrusted with little shellfish, cirripedia and other sorts of barnacle. It had clearly been in the water a long time, but it was a sign of human life.

It was an exhausting day, and by the time it was over I was utterly miserable. It rained so hard during the night that I thought I was going to have too much fresh water, after having gone without it for so long. I wrote: 'It would really be too much if I drowned in fresh water, but that is what is going to happen if this downpour goes on. I have enough for a month. My God, what a cloudburst! What is more, the sea is rising. A pale sun poked through this morning, but it is still raining.'

Another excitement was what I took to be my first clump of Sargasso seaweed. In fact, it was a magnificent jellyfish, the float blue and violet, of the type known as a Portuguese man-of-war. Its long treacherous filaments, hanging to a considerable depth, can cause dangerous stings, which often develop into ulcers.

I realised after one or two wakeful nights, how essential it was to get a good sleep: 'Forty-eight hours without sleep, and I am utterly depressed; the ordeal is really beginning to get me down. Moreover, the sea is infested with tunny and swordfish. I can see them leaping all round me. I do not mind the tunny and the birds so much, but the swordfish are a real menace. Am making good speed, but would willingly add another five or six days to the voyage if I could rest up in comparative calm. This dark, forbidding sea has a depressing effect.' It really seemed as if the sea was in mourning. It was as black as ink, flecked from time to time by a white crest, which the plankton made luminous by night. It looked like an evening dress with occasional white flowers, or a Japanese mourning robe. Not a star to be seen and the low sky seemed about to crush me. I realised the full meaning of the term 'heavy weather'; it felt like a physical weight on my shoulders.

At five o'clock on 12 November I noted: 'Rain and yet more rain, this is more than I can stand. But I wonder if I am not nearer the coast than I think, as there are several more birds. There are ten round me at the same time, and my bird book says that more than six mean that one is not more than a hundred or two hundred miles from the coast.' Little did I think that I was only just over a hundred miles away from the Cape Verde Islands.

During the night of 12 and 13 November, I had another visit from a shark, or at least so I hoped. There was no way of telling whether it was a shark or a swordfish. Every time a shark appeared during the day, I felt perfectly safe. I gave it the ritual clout on the nose and off it went. But during the night, fearing that one of those devilish creatures might spear me with his sword, I was no longer able to be so bold. I had to remain watchfully awake, trying to identify the intruder, and waiting wide-eyed for it to make off. Sleep was effectively banished. And often it seemed that sharks or other creatures were playing some sort of ball-game during the night with my dinghy, without my daring to interfere.

It was still raining in torrents. Under such a deluge I was obliged to stretch the tent right over my head, but it formed great pockets of water which trickled down through the gaps. After a certain time, the weight threatened to break the guy ropes, and I had to push from underneath to spill the water overboard. It must be difficult to realise the sacrifice involved for a castaway in thus jettisoning his reserve of fresh water. Even without sharks and swordfish, sleep had become practically impossible. The rain thundered down and every quarter of an hour or so I had to heave it overboard. An unbelievable quantity of water fell on the tent and trickled through every crevice.

I began to believe, in a confused sort of way, in the active hostility of certain inanimate objects. I might decide to write up the log or work out some calculations. I would sit down, with a pencil ready at hand. I only needed to turn round for ten seconds, and it found some means of disappearing. It was like a mild form of persecution mania, although up till then I had always been able to meet such annoyances with good humour, thinking of the similar misfortunes suffered by the *Three Men in a Boat*.

'*Friday, 14 November* The last forty-eight hours have been the worst of the voyage. I am covered with little spots and my tongue is coated. I do not like the look of things at all. The storm has been short and violent. Was obliged to put out the sea anchor for several hours, but hoisted sail again at about 9.30. Raining in sheets and everything soaked through. Morale still fairly good, but I am starting to get physically tired of the perpetual wetness, which there is no sun to dry. I do not think I have lost a great deal of time, but it is impossible to determine my latitude as I can see neither sun nor stars, and another of these confounded rainstorms is blowing up from the horizon. The sea is calmer, but yesterday I shipped plenty. They say, "fine weather follows rain". I can hardly wait for it.'

During the night a tremendous wave, catching me by the stern, carried me along at great speed and then flooded *L'Hérétique*, at the same time breaking my rudder oar. The dinghy immediately turned broadside on and my sail started to flap in a sinister manner, straining at my rough stitches. I plunged forward to gather it in, but stumbled against the tent and tore a great rent near the top of one of the poles. There would be no way of mending it properly and it happened just as I had to battle for life with the waves. I threw out both my sea anchors. Docilely, *L'Hérétique* turned her stern to my normal course and faced up to her assailants. By this time I was at the end of my strength and, accepting all the risks, I decided that sleep was the first necessity. I fastened up the tent as close as I could and made up my mind to sleep for twenty-four hours, whatever the weather did and whatever happened.

The squalls continued for another ten hours, during which my eggshell craft behaved admirably. But the danger was not yet passed. The worst moments came after the wind had dropped, while the sea continued to rage. The wind seemed to enforce a sort of discipline on the sea, propelling the waves without giving them time to break: left to themselves, they were much less disciplined. They broke with all their force in every direction, overwhelming everything in their path.

'*Saturday, 15 November, 13.30* Taking advantage of the rain to do a little writing. Have only two rudder oars left. Hope they will hold out. Rain has been coming down in torrents since ten o'clock yesterday evening, no sign of the sun; am wet through. Everything is soaked and I have no means of drying a thing, my sleeping-bag looks like a wet sack. No hope of taking my position. The weather was so bad during the night that I wondered for a time if I had not drifted into the Doldrums. Fortunately there is no doubt that the trade wind is still with me. Making good time, almost too fast for comfort. Still worried about the sail. When will the weather clear up? There was one patch of blue sky in the west, but the wind is from the east. Perhaps tomorrow will be better, but I am going to have another thick night. About seven o'clock this morning an aircraft flew over me quite low. Tried to signal it, but my torch would not work. First sign of human life since 3 November, hope there will be more. Sky to the west now clearing rapidly, difficult to understand why.'

There was a sort of battle in the sky the whole day between the two fronts of good and bad weather. I called it the fight between the blue and the black. It started with the appearance in the west of a little patch of blue, no bigger than a gendarme's cap, as the French song has it, and there seemed little hope of it growing. The black clouds, impenetrable as ink, seemed fully conscious of their power, and marched in serried ranks to attack the tiny blue intruder, but the blue patch seemed to call up rein-forcements on its wings, and in a few hours to the south and north, that is to say to my left and right, several more blue patches had appeared, all seemingly about to be engulfed in the great black flood advancing towards them. But where the clouds concentrated on frontal attacks, the blue of the sky used infiltra-tion tactics, breaking up the mass of black until the good weather predominated. By four o'clock in the afternoon its victory was clear. 'Thank God for the sun! I am covered with little spots, but the sun is back.' Little did I know that the most troublesome part of my voyage was about to begin.

I had not the faintest idea where I was. With no sun for three days I was in a state of complete ignorance, and on Sunday the 16th when I got my sextant ready, I was in a fever of apprehension. By a miracle I had not drifted much to the south. I was still on latitude 16° 59′, which passes to the north of Guadeloupe. That vital point was settled, but my boat looked like a battlefield. My hat had blown off in the storm and all I now had as protection for my head was a little white floppy thing, made out of waterproofed linen, quite inadequate in such a climate. The tent was torn in two places and although the dinghy seemed to have suffered no damage, everything in it was drenched. Even after the long sunny days which were now to come, the night dew continued to re-impregnate my warm clothes and sleeping-bag, so I was never again to know a dry night until I touched land.

A disturbing incident then showed that I could not afford to relax my vigilance for one moment. During the storm, I had tried to protect the after part of L'Hérétique from the breaking waves by trailing a large piece of rubberised cloth fixed firmly to the ends of my two floats. This seemed to divert the force of the waves as they broke behind me. Even though the storm had died down, I saw no point in removing this protection. But the following night, a frightful noise brought me out of my sleeping-bag at one bound. My protective tail was no longer there. The piece of cloth had been torn away. I checked anxiously that the floats had not been damaged and that they were still firmly inflated. Some creature which I never saw, probably attracted by the vivid yellow colour of the cloth which hung down between the floats, had torn it off by jumping out of the water. This it had done with such precision that there was no other visible sign of its attack.

Like the boat, I too had taken a buffering. I was much weakened and every movement made me terribly tired, rather like the period after my long fast in the Mediterranean. I was much thinner, but was more worried about the state of my skin. My whole body was covered with tiny red spots. At first they were little more than surface discolorations, not perceptible to the touch, but in a day or two they became hard lumps that finally developed into pustules. I was mortally afraid of a bad attack of boils, which, in the condition I was in, would have had serious consequences. The pain alone would have proved unbearable and I would no longer have been able to sit or lie down.

The only medicament I had to treat such an outbreak was mercurochrome, which made me look as if I was covered in blood. During the night the pain became very bad and I could not bear anything in contact with my skin. The least little abrasion seemed to turn septic and I had to disinfect them all very carefully. The skin under my nails was all inflamed, and small pockets of pus, very painful, formed under half of them. I had to lance them without an anaesthetic. I could probably have used some of the penicillin I had on board, but I wanted to keep up my medical observations with a minimum of treatment for as long as I could stand it. My feet were peeling in great strips and in three days I lost the nails from four toes.

I would never have been able to hold out if the deck had not been made of wood, which I regard as an essential piece of equipment in a life raft. Without it I would have developed gangrene or, at the very least, serious arterial trouble.

For the time being my ailments were still localised. My blood pressure remained good and I was still perspiring normally. In spite of that, I greeted with relief the victorious sun which appeared on the 16th, expecting it to cure the effects of the constant humidity which I had endured. I did not know that the sun was to cause even worse ordeals during the cruel twenty-seven days which were to follow.

The castaway must never give way to despair, and should always remember, when things seem at their worst, that 'something will turn up' and his situation may be changed. But neither should he let himself become too hopeful; it never does to forget that however unbearable an ordeal may seem, there may be another to come which will efface the memory of the first. If a toothache becomes intolerable, it might almost seem a relief to exchange it for an earache. With a really bad pain in the ear, the memory of the toothache becomes a distinctly lesser evil. The best advice that I can give is that whether things go well or ill, the castaway must try to maintain a measure of detachment. The days of rain had been bad enough, but what followed, in spite of the rosy future the sun at first seemed to promise, was to seem much worse.

THE CATARACTS OF THE ZAÏRE

JOHN BLASHFORD-SNELL
(1936–)

British soldier and explorer. During 1975–6 Blashford-Snell led the Zaïre River Expedition, which marked the centenary of H. M. Stanley's historic trek through Central Africa.

Following my bout of malaria I was also struck with some pretty uncomfortable dysentery, but by New Year's Day I was fit again, the boats had been made ready, the engines tested, the crews briefed and a great crowd gathered on the Island of Mimosa near the capital to watch our fight with Kinsuka, first of the thirty-two cataracts of the Livingstone Falls that cover more than 200 miles between Kinshasa and the Atlantic. Assisting us on much of the stretch were the two Hamilton water jet boats. They had been designed in New Zealand and built in Britain. These 220 horsepower, fast and highly manoeuvrable craft were to be a vital part of the forthcoming operation.

At 11.00 hours *La Vision* passed easily through the narrows where the river had now been constricted from something like nine miles wide to one mile across. Running down a smooth tongue of water, the inflatables skirted the line of tossing twenty-foot waves that rose and fell in the centre of the river. Acting as rescue boats the jet craft lay in the lee of weed-covered boulders. Gerry Pass and Eric Rankin, the Survival–Anglia television team, had been positioned on one of these tiny islands to get a really first-rate shot of the drama, which they did when *David Gestetner* appeared with her white ensign fluttering. On the shore an elderly English lady missionary, overcome with emotion, is said to have burst into tears and then fainted at the sight. However, I put this down to the fact that the *Gestetner*'s crew were Royal Marines!

As the boat crossed the first fall, her stern engine struck a submerged rock which hurled it upwards off its wooden transom. The flaying propeller sliced through the neoprene fabric of the stern compartment, which deflated immediately. Aboard the jet we could not understand the cause of the trouble, but we could see the great raft was being swept out of control into the angry wave towers that we knew must be avoided at all costs. In a second Jon Hamilton, our skipper, had opened the throttle and driven the eighteen-foot boat straight into the pounding mounds of coffee-coloured water.

I could see Mike Gambier in the water; his white crash helmet and red life jacket showing clearly, he bobbed amongst the flying spray. Our sister jet, driven by Ralph Brown, was already making for him with a scramble-net down the side. Lieutenant Nigel Armitage-Smith was standing by to pull him in. The deafening roar of water and engines drowned all commands. Everyone was acting instinctively now. *David Gestetner*'s skipper was trying to pass us a line, his face contorted as he yelled against the din.

Suddenly I heard Ken Mason yell, 'Watch out!' I looked up and saw an enormous wave had flung the crippled *Gestetner* forward and upward, straight towards us. For a moment she towered above, riding a fearsome wall of falling white water, and then came crashing down with a great 'ponk' right across us. For a second we were locked together in the tempest, but then we managed to wriggle from beneath and circle our quarry once again. This time we succeeded in taking the line and were soon dragging the craft like a stricken whale towards Monkey Island, where we managed to do the necessary emergency repairs. In fact, we were probably the first men ever to reach this large jungle-covered island, isolated in the middle of the rapids.

The next day, with all well again, we set off downriver. Rapid followed rapid as we cautiously felt our way through the treacherous waters that gurgled and swirled between the banks of black rock. To get the necessary supplies into the boats meant relays of overland teams working outwards from the capital in our very tired Land-Rovers and a few Toyota trucks that had been kindly lent to us. Wildlife was not much in evidence but on 2 January we did come across some islands literally alive with huge bats. There were thousands of them festooning the trees, and when I fired a flare from my signal pistol, the hideous creatures took off and showered us with their excreta. It is interesting that Stanley reported great flocks of birds in this area; I think that in fact he saw these colonies of bats. They must have had a twelve-inch wing span, and were obviously of value to the Zaïrois because we could see nets set up on tall poles at the side of the river to catch them.

In the days that followed we shot more rapids and avoided the most ferocious waves and water I've ever met. For each the drill was the same: air reconnaissance by Beaver, then the jets would take the skippers ahead to examine the heaving inconsistent flood and the swirling whirlpools that went up to thirty yards across. On either side vertical cliffs of red rock rose for hundreds of feet and fish eagles shrieked their yodelling cries as we passed. Meanwhile, our support teams worked day and night to get fuel and supplies into us over the deeply rutted tracks. In my log for Friday, 3 January I recorded a typical day's sailing:

Major rapids navigated were Inkisi and then the dreaded Borboro. Later we navigated an unnamed rapid which was not too severe. The river continues to drop and has fallen approximately 30 centimetres in twenty-four hours. Borboro was the most formidable rapid we have yet tackled. I did not dare to take the Avon S400s through manned and so ordered them to be towed by jets into centre of current and released without crews. This did not work as there is such a strong counter-current going upstream that they were continuously driven back, but, after some skilful manoeuvring, we got them through. Went through myself in Jet I with Tac HQ; waves enormous, about nine metres high. Just as we left rapid a great boiling mass of water erupted with a deep rumbling sound right beside us; it was some two metres in height. When it subsided the water began to spin wildly and as it accelerated a vortex appeared in the centre and I gazed down into a horrific whirlpool some thirty metres across and three metres deep in the centre. The river around us had gone mad, waves breaking, rocks flashing by and all the 220 horse-power of the jet's engine were called upon to drag us from the grip of this revolving cavern. As we left it the hole closed up again and the surface became a sheet of fast-moving water. Similarly, another giant whirlpool appeared on our right and another ahead. The river was wild and it was almost as if some unseen force was trying to pluck us downwards.

On 6 January we reached Isangila, the falls that had forced Stanley to abandon his boats and march over the mountains to the sea. Here I decided reluctantly to move the giant rafts overland as far as the Yalala Falls, leaving the jets and the Avon dinghies to tackle the ferocious stream alone. The giant craft simply hadn't got the power to manoeuvre in these rushing currents and boiling water. In no time, one of the dinghies was ripped open from stem to stern on razor-sharp rocks and Jim Masters was injured. That night it took 900 stitches and a gallon of Araldite adhesive to repair the damaged boat. Jim drank a little J & B and recovered!

It was late afternoon when our jets entered the relatively clear passage that would take us through the terrible Isangila cataract. We were halfway down when I saw two gigantic waves converging on our bows. With a crash they struck simultaneously, hurling the 3,000-pound boat upwards. I fell across Jon Hamilton, knocking him momentarily from the wheel, and out of the corner of my eye I saw Pam almost go over the side. Then as we hit the water again there was another huge wave towering ahead of us. For a moment I thought we were done for. It was a monster. The wall of water smashed over us blotting out the daylight; somehow we were still afloat. There was a strange silence; the engine had died. Ahead a line of black rocks rose like dragon's teeth on the lip of a fall and we were being swept straight towards them. Jon tried desperately to start the engine, his face creased with concern. Fortunately on the third attempt it fired. It only stuttered for a minute, but it was long enough for us to get into an eddy behind a huge boulder, where we could hold position whilst the electric bilge pumps baled us out.

Finally even the jets were halted by shallows and reefs at the Inga Rapid, but with two more short portages and some excellent warping with long ropes, we got the amazing Avon recce boats through to the foot of the biggest obstacle in the entire river, Yalala. A mile of water boiling over terraces and through jagged rocks at frightening speed greeted us. Meanwhile our giant rafts had been carried by a Zaïre army lorry to within two miles of the river. Here we regrouped. Some of us had marched over the crystal mountains just as Stanley's men had done. We experienced the same elephant grass, endless rolling hills, ridges and sharp, suet-coloured quartz rocks underfoot that give these highlands its name. We too stumbled and fell on the slippery boulders at the river's edge. Ken Mason suffered a badly ripped arm and I injured my back. Porters, descendants of the people who had helped Stanley, assisted us.

At last we all came to the Yalala Falls, where the sappers were already clearing a way for us to carry the giant boats down to the river. For three days we toiled in the blistering heat with pick, spade and crowbar, and even some highly unstable dynamite, to clear the boulders and get the giant rafts to the water. Supporting us during this operation was our American officer, Captain Tom Mabe. Tom and his colleague, Sergeant John Connor, had come with us throughout the journey. Both were in the US Special Forces and were useful members of our team, although I fear at times we must have driven them mad. Tom had managed to get hold of the explosive, but it was delivered at the Inga dam construction site and had to be driven to the river over a bumpy track.

It was late at night when Pam, Ken and I set out in a Land-Rover with at least two broken springs. In the back were large boxes of sticky, sweating dynamite and one crate of whisky. The vehicle lights didn't work particularly well and as we motored along the rutted road in the night, Ken began to ask about the dangers of premature initiation. We soon convinced him that our journey was likened to that shown so graphically in the film, *The Wages of Fear*.

'Oh my God,' he said, seizing a bottle of J & B from the back and clutching it between his legs.

'What on earth are you doing?' asked Pam.

'Well, I may as well get drunk and protect my courting tackle at the same time,' rejoined our jovial photographer as we bounced along with our lethal cargo. The nervous tension made us roar with laughter and swig deep gulps of the bottle.

Pam at this point looked very much like a boy, with her hair covered in mud and her shirt in grease. In fact some Italian engineers whom we had met had referred to her as 'Fred the mechanic' and I don't think they really understood that she was a girl. Earlier in the expedition a chief had greeted her with '*Bonjour, monsieur*', but her confidence was restored when we discovered he was almost blind!

Finally, with sixty porters beneath each huge boat, we moved them like giant caterpillars down a 1,000-foot slope to the river. Here we joined up with the Avon dinghies that had been portaged or controlled by lines through the surging white water towards us. Now only three rapids barred our way to the sea, but with up to sixteen million gallons per second pouring through a gorge which had narrowed the river to a bare 400 yards, the power can be imagined. Indeed the depth here was probably about 140 feet at high water. The river seemed to be alive with great boiling bubbles rushing up from the depths and erupting on the surface.

Then as quickly as they came they were replaced by whirlpools and swirling currents.

Our porters, many of them Angolan refugees and some almost certainly Freedom Fighters, came with gifts of sugarcane wine and fruit to see us off, but the river was not going to let us get away unscathed yet.

In the final rapid, *La Vision*, my flagship, was momentarily trapped in a whirlpool, like a cork in a washtub, being bent downwards and spun round and round with engines screaming. Before I could stop them coming down Alun Davies's Avon was capsized by a fifteen-foot wave. The upturned boat with its crew of three clinging to it was swept towards a yawning whirlpool. The jets at this point had been sent back to Kinshasa, and from where I was situated 1,000 yards downriver, I couldn't see what had happened. However the following recce boat saw the accident and its skipper, Neil Rickards, a Royal Marine corporal, decided to have a go. Taking his own small craft through the mountains of tossing water, he managed to get right into the whirlpool and circle around inside it, rather like a motorcyclist in a 'wall of death' at a fairground. In the centre of this swirling mass he could see Alun's capsized Avon with its crew of three still clinging on frantically to the lifeline. Eventually, by going the same way that the water was revolving, Neil managed to get his craft alongside the stricken boat so that Bob Powell and Somue, one of the ZLOs, could pull the three men to safety. Then he circled up again in the same direction that the water was turning and out of the top. As they left he looked back and was just in time to see the upturned craft disappear down the vortex. Downriver, I was surprised a few moments later when the capsized boat bobbed up from the river bed beside me. The engine was smashed to pieces, the floorboards wrecked and there appeared to be no survivors. But the crew had all been saved thanks to Neil's courage and skill, for which he was later awarded the Queen's Gallantry Medal and made one of Britain's 'Men of the Year'.

Two days later we reached the little seaport of Banana and at dusk our strange fleet, which had set out almost four months before in the centre of Africa, sailed into the setting sun. Basil, in cassock and surplice, held an improvised cross and beneath the flags of the nations represented in our team, he conducted a simple service. Under our hulls the water heaved gently. Strangely, it no longer tugged and pulled at us; there was no current, for we were now in the Atlantic.

RACE AGAINST TIME

SIR RANULPH FIENNES
(1944–)

*English soldier-explorer. During 1979–82 he led the first circumpolar
navigation of the earth.*

With the outboards repaired and Bryn looking happier, we set out
from Russian Mission [Alaska] on a blustery morning. I noticed
with surprise that no boats were out or about, nor was there any
other sign of life. This was especially strange since it was the
middle of the salmon run, the short annual period when a healthy
income could be made on the river.

I received some nasty little shocks during the morning and
took quite a bit of water in the aluminium boat. The inflatables
could happily fill to the brim with water and carry on floating
high, but any water in my dinghy had to be removed at once.
Draining was only possible when moving fast enough to tip the
bows up, then a clumsy wooden bung could be removed from a
hole near the base of the transom. Unless the plug was replaced
after draining, this hole could cause the boat to leak rapidly as
soon as she slowed down and returned to a level plane. Lose the
bung and things could get tricky.

Until noon the confused state of the river made me cautious
but not alarmed. I noticed a pall of dust in the sky further upriver
but when we reached the area where I thought I had seen it, there
was nothing there. Just a trick of the light it seemed.

But some fifteen miles short of Holy Cross we entered a long narrow valley heavily forested on either side where the dust cloud effect was again evident. At the entrance to the valley an Eskimo fishing village nestled on one bank, its river boats drawn well up above the shingle bank. Two men watched us pass. I waved. There was no response but a slight shaking of the head from the older of the two.

The water began to career about, striking with miniature breakers against the rock walls on the rim of each minor curve. But still I felt no undue threat beyond the normal swell and undulation of the great river's forces. As I nosed further out into the northerly-bearing valley, an unseen surge moved against the right side of my boat and almost tipped me off my plank seat by the tiller.

With little warning, waves unlike any I had seen except in sizeable rapids seemed to grow out of the water like boils erupting from the riverbed. Breaking into a sweat, for I have a healthy fear of rough water, I steered quickly for the nearest bank. This was unfortunately the 'cut' bank, indicating that side of the river where the faster current runs. 'Lee' banks are very often low and dressed with gentle sand slopes for there the water is quiet. Where the river flows down a straight stretch, cut and lee banks may alternate on either side depending on the configuration of the riverbed.

Dust clouds emanated from the cut bank as I made to escape the central turmoil. It was as though a dragon breathed there. As I closed with the bank, a pine tree toppled over and crashed into the river. Then another and, with it, a whole section of the bank itself collapsed. The roar of my outboard drowned all other sounds and the forces of destruction which gnawed at the river's banks operated in silence as far as I was concerned. This added to the sinister, almost slow-motion appearance of the phenomenon, for such it was to me. I could not at the time grasp what was happening. I had, after all, boated up or down thousands of miles of wild rivers in North America and never once experienced this.

Also, my private, long-nurtured idea of the Yukon was of a slow wide river as gentle as the Thames.

Above the collapsed bank I saw that the forest, from under-growth to the very tops of the giant pines, was bent over and alive with movement. A great wind was at work, although in my hooded suit on the boat I could feel nothing.

For a moment I hovered in indecision. The waves in the middle of the river, some 600 yards wide at this point, were totally unin-viting yet any minute my boat was liable to disappear under a falling pine, should I remain close in. There was no question of landing. No question of trying to turn broadside on and then head back downstream. My boat climbed and fell like a wild thing; shook as though in a mastiff's jaws, then veered towards the crumbling cut bank in response to unseen suction.

Ahead the river narrowed into a bottleneck, the banks grew steeper and the chaotic waves of the river's spine here extended almost clear across our front. Between standing waves and crum-bling bank, I glimpsed a sag in the water. It was fleetingly possible to see the river actually mounting in height the further away it was from the bank. I had often heard that the centre of a river can be several feet higher than at the edges given sufficient flow and force, but never before had I clearly viewed the effect. It was distinctly off-putting.

I pushed with both hands on the tiller and the boat, reluctantly, edged away from the cut bank and began to head obliquely across the river. Perhaps things were better on the far side. But to get there I had to pass through the middle of the river, where the turbulence was greatest and the hydraulic waves so close together that my boat no sooner fell down the face of one than the next raced curling above me. It needed just one brief error on the tiller and I would add critically to the ten inches of silt-laden water already swilling around my feet. I would sink within seconds.

From the corner of my eye I noticed Bryn had seen my dilemma and moved his inflatable as close as the turmoil allowed. When I sink, I thought, Bryn's boat will be my only chance. 'As big as houses' I remembered the state trooper's warning. I could see why such an exaggeration might come about. These waves were no more than four or five feet high yet their configuration, violence and closeness would make any local riverboat a death trap for its inmates.

Before another wave could swamp my wallowing craft I turned broadside on to the hydraulics, applied full throttle and headed straight into the maelstrom in the centre of the river. Whether sheer luck or the shape of the waves saved me I do not know, but no more water came inboard. Much of the time it was like surf-riding along the forward face of a breaker, then a violent incline and sideways surge as the old wave passed beneath and the next one thrust at the little tin hull.

An edge of exhilaration broke through the sticky fear which till then held me in thrall. For the first time since entering the turbulence I realised there was a chance of getting through and began to experience the old thrill of rapids riding from the days long past when we had tackled far greater waves from the comparative safety of unsinkable inflatables.

How long it took to cross the river was impossible to gauge but gradually the waves grew less fierce and less close and then there was quiet water but for the outwash from the rough stuff. Ahead I could see, between waves and lee bank, a lane of smooth water edged by sand. Bryn and then Charlie emerged from the waves like bucking broncos. Both were smiling for my narrow escape had not gone unnoticed.

There were other stretches where conditions were tricky but never a patch on that first windy valley. That night we stopped in Holy Cross and the keeper of the travellers' lodge, Luke Demientieff, told us we were lucky to be alive. We had been travelling north in the first big southerly blow of the year in winds exceeding seventy knots.

'Even paddle steamers,' he said, 'would not, in the old days, venture at such a time.'

We had covered the worst stretch of the river in the worst

possible conditions and, as far as the riverside folk were concerned, we were quite mad. When I asked him how anyone should know or care that we had passed, Luke said: 'It only needs one pair of eyes from one riverside shack to see you go by for the radio phones all along the river to start buzzing. When you passed the old huts at Paimuit and entered the slough by Great Paimuit Island the word was about you were goners.' He paused and added with a chuckle, 'Still we're pleased you made it to the lodge after all. Business has been poor lately.'

RIDING A GUIANESE CAYMAN

CHARLES WATERTON
(1782–1865)

English naturalist and explorer. He spent a decade from 1812 collecting specimens in South America.

The day was now declining apace, and the Indian had made his instrument to take the cayman. It was very simple. There were four pieces of tough hard wood, a foot long, and about as thick as your little finger, and barbed at both ends; they were tied round the end of the rope, in such a manner, that if you conceive the rope to be an arrow, these four sticks would form the arrow's head; so that one end of the four united sticks answered to the point of the arrowhead, while the other ends of the sticks expanded at equal distances round the rope. Now it is evident that, if the cayman swallowed this (the other end of the rope, which was thirty yards long, being fastened to a tree), the more he pulled, the faster the barbs would stick into his stomach. This wooden hook, if you may so call it, was well baited with the flesh of the acouri, and the entrails were twisted round the rope for about a foot above it.

Nearly a mile from where we had our hammocks, the sand-bank was steep and abrupt, and the river very still and deep; there the Indian pricked a stick into the sand. It was two feet long, and on its extremity was fixed the machine; it hung suspended about a foot from the water, and the end of the rope was made fast to a stake driven well into the sand.

The Indian then took the empty shell of a land tortoise and gave it some heavy blows with an axe. I asked him why he did that. He said it was to let the cayman hear that something was going on. In fact the Indian meant it as the cayman's dinner-bell. Having done this, we went back to the hammocks, not intending to visit it again till morning. During the night, the jaguars roared and grumbled in the forest, as though the world was going wrong with them, and at intervals we could hear the distant cayman. The roaring of the jaguars was awful; but it was music to the dismal noise of these hideous and malicious reptiles.

About half past five in the morning the Indian stole off silently to take a look at the bait. On arriving at the place he set up a tremendous shout. We all jumped out of our hammocks and ran to him. The Indians got there before me, for they had no clothes to put on, and I lost two minutes in looking for my trousers and in slipping into them.

We found a cayman, ten feet and a half long, fast to the end of the rope. Nothing now remained to do but to get him out of the water without injuring his scales – *hoc opus, hic labor*. We mustered strong: there were three Indians from the creek; there were my own Indian Yan, Daddy Quashi, the negro from Mrs Peterson's, James, Mr R. Edmonstone's man, whom I was instructing to preserve birds, and, lastly, myself.

I informed the Indians that it was my intention to draw him quietly out of the water, and then secure him. They looked and stared at each other, and said I might do it myself, but they would have no hand in it; the cayman would worry some of us. On saying this, *consedere duces*, they squatted on their hams with the most perfect indifference.

The Indians of these wilds have never been subject to the least restraint, and I knew enough of them to be aware that if I tried to force them against their will they would take off, and leave me and my presents unheeded, and never return.

Daddy Quashi was for applying to our guns, as usual, considering them our best and safest friends. I immediately offered to knock him down for his cowardice, and he shrank back, begging that I would be cautious, and not get myself worried, and apologizing for his own want of resolution. My Indian was now in conversation with the others, and they asked if I would allow them to shoot a dozen arrows into the cayman, and thus disable him. This would have ruined all. I had come above three hundred miles on purpose to get a cayman uninjured, and not to carry back a mutilated specimen. I rejected their proposition with firmness, and darted a disdainful eye upon the Indians.

Daddy Quashi was again beginning to remonstrate, and I chased him on the sandbank for a quarter of a mile. He told me afterwards, he thought he should have dropped down dead with fright; for he was firmly persuaded, if I had caught him, I should have bundled him into the cayman's jaws. Here, then, we stood in silence, like a calm before a thunderstorm. '*Hoc res summa loco. Scinditur in contraria vulgus.*' They wanted to kill him, and I wanted to take him alive.

I now walked up and down the sand, revolving a dozen projects in my head. The canoe was at a considerable distance, and I ordered the people to bring it round to the place where we were. The mast was eight feet long, and not much thicker than my wrist. I took it out of the canoe, and wrapped the sail round the end of it. Now it appeared clear to me, that if I went down upon one knee, and held the mast in the same position as the soldier holds his bayonet when rushing to the charge, I could force it down the cayman's throat, should he come open-mouthed at me. When this was told to the Indians, they brightened up, and said they would help me to pull him out of the river.

'Brave squad!' said I to myself, '"*Audax omnia perpeti,*" now that you have got me betwixt yourselves and danger.' I then mustered all hands for the last time before the battle. We were, four South American savages, two negroes from Africa, a creole from Trinidad, and myself, a white man from Yorkshire – in fact, a little tower of Babel group, in dress, no dress, address and language.

Daddy Quashi hung in the rear. I showed him a large Spanish

knife, which I always carried in the waistband of my trousers: it spoke volumes to him, and he shrugged up his shoulders in absolute despair. The sun was just peeping over the high forests on the eastern hills, as if coming to look on and bid us act with becoming fortitude. I placed all the people at the end of the rope, and ordered them to pull till the cayman appeared on the surface of the water; and then, should he plunge, to slacken the rope and let him go again into the deep.

I now took the mast of the canoe in my hand (the sail being tied round the end of the mast) and sank down upon one knee, about four yards from the water's edge, determining to thrust it down his throat in case he gave me an opportunity. I certainly felt somewhat uncomfortable in this situation, and I thought of Cerberus on the other side of the Styx ferry. The people pulled the cayman to the surface; he plunged furiously as soon as he arrived in these upper regions, and immediately went below again on their slackening the rope. I saw enough not to fall in love at first sight. I now told them we would run all risks, and have him on land immediately. They pulled again, and out he came – 'monstrum horrendum, informe'. This was an interesting moment. I kept my position firmly, with my eye fixed steadfast on him.

By this time the cayman was within two yards of me. I saw he was in a state of fear and perturbation. I instantly dropped the mast, sprang up, and jumped on his back, turning half round as I vaulted, so that I gained my seat with my face in a right position. I immediately seized his forelegs, and by main force twisted them on his back; thus they served me for a bridle.

He now seemed to have recovered from his surprise, and probably fancying himself in hostile company, he began to plunge furiously, and lashed the sand with his long and powerful tail. I was out of reach of the strokes of it by being near his head. He continued to plunge and strike, and made my seat very uncomfortable. It must have been a fine sight for an unoccupied spectator.

The people roared out in triumph, and were so vociferous that it was some time before they heard me tell them to pull me and my beast of burden further inland. I was apprehensive the rope might break, and then there would have been every chance of going down to the regions under water with the cayman. That would have been more perilous than Arion's marine morning ride: '*Delphini insidens vada cærula suleat Arion.*'

The people now dragged us above forty yards on the sand: it was the first and last time I was ever on a cayman's back. Should it be asked how I managed to keep my seat, I would answer, I hunted some years with Lord Darlington's foxhounds.

After repeated attempts to regain his liberty, the cayman gave in, and became tranquil through exhaustion. I now managed to tie up his jaws, and firmly secured his forefeet in the position I had held them. We had now another severe struggle for superiority, but he was soon overcome, and again remained quiet. While some of the people were pressing upon his head and shoulders, I threw myself on his tail, and by keeping it down to the sand, prevented him from kicking up another dust. He was finally conveyed to the canoe, and then to the place where we had suspended our hammocks. There I cut his throat, and, after breakfast was over, commenced the dissection.

RIVER OF DOUBT

THEODORE ROOSEVELT
(1858–1919)

President of the USA. After withdrawing from politics in 1912, he went to Brazil and, two years later, made the first descent of a previously unknown tributary of the Amazon, subsequently named Rio Roosevelt. He was accompanied on the expedition by his son Kermit, and the Brazilian explorer Candido Rondon.

On the morning of 22 March we started in our six canoes. We made ten kilometres. Twenty minutes after starting we came to the first rapids. Here everyone walked except the three best paddlers, who took the canoes down in succession – an hour's job. Soon after this we struck a bees' nest in the top of a tree overhanging the river; our steersman climbed out and robbed it, but, alas! lost the honey on the way back. We came to a small steep fall, which we did not dare run in our overladen, clumsy, and cranky dugouts. Fortunately we were able to follow a deep canal which led off for a kilometre, returning just below the falls, fifty yards from where it had started. Then, having been in the boats and in motion only one hour and a half, we came to a long stretch of rapids which it took us six hours to descend, and we camped at the foot. Everything was taken out of the canoes, and they were run down in succession. At one difficult and perilous place they were let down by ropes; and even thus we almost lost one.

We went down the right bank. On the opposite bank was an

Indian village, evidently inhabited only during the dry season. The marks on the stumps of trees showed that these Indians had axes and knives; and there were old fields in which maize, beans, and cotton had been grown. The forest dripped and steamed. Rubber trees were plentiful. At one point the tops of a group of tall trees were covered with yellow-white blossoms. Others bore red blossoms. Many of the big trees, of different kinds, were buttressed at the base with great thin walls of wood. Others, including both palms and ordinary trees, showed an even stranger peculiarity. The trunk, near the base, but sometimes six or eight feet from the ground, was split into a dozen or twenty branches or small trunks which sloped outwards in a tent-like shape, each becoming a root. The larger trees of this type looked as if their trunks were seated on the tops of the pole-frames of Indian tepees. At one point in the stream, to our great surprise, we saw a flying-fish. It skimmed the water like a swallow for over twenty yards.

Although we made only ten kilometres we worked hard all day. The last canoes were brought down and moored to the bank at nightfall. Our tents were pitched in the darkness.

Next day we made thirteen kilometres. We ran, all told, a little over an hour and three-quarters. Seven hours were spent in getting past a series of rapids at which the portage, over rocky and difficult ground, was a kilometre long. The canoes were run down empty – a hazardous run, in which one of them upset.

Yet while we were actually on the river, paddling and floating downstream along the reaches of swift, smooth water, it was very lovely. When we started in the morning, the day was overcast and the air was heavy with vapour. Ahead of us the shrouded river stretched between dim walls of forest, half-seen in the mist. Then the sun burned up the fog, and loomed through it in a red splendour that changed first to gold and then to molten white. In the dazzling light, under the brilliant blue of the sky, every detail of the magnificent forest was vivid to the eye: the great trees, the network of bush-ropes, the caverns of greenery, where thick-leaved vines covered all things else. Wherever there was a hidden

boulder the surface of the current was broken by waves. In one place in midstream, a pyramidal rock thrust itself six feet above the surface of the river. On the banks we found fresh Indian sign.

In the morning, just before leaving this camp, a tapir swam across stream a little way above us, but unfortunately we could not get a shot at it. An ample supply of tapir beef would have meant much to us. We had started with fifty days' rations, but this by no means meant full rations, in the sense of giving every man all he wanted to eat. We had two meals a day, and were on rather short commons – both our mess and the camaradas' – except when we got plenty of palm-tops. For our mess we had the boxes chosen by Fiala, each containing a day's rations for six men, our number. But we made each box last a day and a half, or at times two days, and in addition we gave some of the food to the camaradas. It was only on the rare occasions when we had killed some monkeys or curássows, or caught some fish, that everybody had enough. We would have welcomed that tapir. So far the game, fish and fruit had been too scarce to be an element of weight in our food supply. In an exploring trip like ours, through a difficult and utterly unknown country, especially if densely forested, there is little time to halt, and game cannot be counted on. It is only in lands like our own West thirty years ago, like South Africa in the middle of the last century, like East Africa today, that game can be made the chief food supply. On this trip our only substantial food supply from the country hitherto had been that furnished by the palm-tops. Two men were detailed every day to cut down palms for food.

A kilometre and a half after leaving this camp we came on a stretch of big rapids. The river here twists in loops, and we had heard the roaring of these rapids the previous afternoon. Then we passed out of earshot of them, but Antonio Correa, our best waterman, insisted all along that the roaring meant rapids worse than any we had encountered for some days. 'I was brought up in the water, and I know it like a fish, and all its sounds,' said he. He was right. We had to carry the loads nearly a kilometre that afternoon, and the canoes were pulled out on the bank so that they might be in readiness to be dragged overland next day. Rondon, Lyra, Kermit and Antonio Correa explored both sides of the river. On the opposite or left bank they found the mouth of a considerable river, bigger than the Rio Kermit, flowing in from the west and making its entrance in the middle of the rapids. This river we christened the Taunay, in honour of a distinguished Brazilian, an explorer, a soldier, a senator, who was also a writer of note. Kermit had with him two of his novels, and I had read one of his books dealing with a disastrous retreat during the Paraguayan war.

Next morning, the 25th, the canoes were brought down. A path was chopped for them and rollers laid; and halfway down the rapids Lyra and Kermit, who were overseeing the work as well as doing their share of the pushing and hauling, got them into a canal of smooth water, which saved much severe labour. As our food supply lowered we were constantly more desirous of economizing the strength of the men. One day more would complete a month since we had embarked on the Dúvida – as we had started in February, the lunar and calendar months coincided. We had used up over half our provisions. We had come only a trifle over 160 kilometres, thanks to the character and number of the rapids. We believed we had three or four times the distance yet to go before coming to a part of the river where we might hope to meet assistance, either from rubber-gatherers or from Pyrineus, if he were really coming up the river which we were going down. If the rapids continued to be as they had been it could not be much more than three weeks before we were in straits for food, aside from the ever-present danger of accident in the rapids; and if our progress were no faster than it had been – and we were straining to do our best – we would in such event still have several hundreds of kilometres of unknown river before us. We could not even hazard a guess at what *was in front* . . .

Two of our men were down with fever. Another man, Julio, a fellow of powerful frame, was utterly, worthless, being an inborn, lazy shirker with the heart of a ferocious cur in the body of a bullock. The others were good men, some of them very good indeed. They were under the immediate supervision of Pedrinho Craveiro, who was *first class in every way* . . .

In mid-afternoon we were once more in the canoes; but we had paddled with the current only a few minutes, we had gone only a kilometre, when the roar of rapids in front again forced us to haul up to the bank. As usual, Rondon, Lyra and Kermit, with Antonio Correa, explored both sides while camp was being pitched. The rapids were longer and of steeper descent than the last, but on the opposite or western side there was a passage down which we thought we could get the empty dugouts at the cost of dragging them only a few yards at one spot. The loads were to be carried down the hither bank, for a kilometre, to the smooth water. The river foamed between great rounded masses of rock, and at one point there was a sheer fall of six or eight feet. We found and ate wild pineapples. Wild beans were in flower. At dinner we had a toucan and a couple of parrots, which were very good.

All next day was spent by Lyra in superintending our three best watermen as they took the canoes down the west side of the rapids, to the foot, at the spot to which the camp had meantime been shifted. In the forest some of the huge sipas, or rope vines, which were as big as cables, bore clusters of fragrant flowers. The men found several honey-trees, and fruits of various kinds, and small coconuts; they chopped down an ample number of palms for the palm-cabbage; and most important of all, they gathered a quantity of big Brazil nuts, which when roasted tasted like the best of chestnuts, and are nutritious; and they caught a number of big piranhas, which were good eating. So we all had a feast, and everybody had enough to eat and was happy . . .

Next morning we went about three kilometres before coming to some steep hills, beautiful to look upon, clad as they were in dense, tall, tropical forest, but ominous of new rapids. Sure enough, at their foot we had to haul up and prepare for a long portage. The canoes we ran down empty. Even so, we were within an ace of losing two, the lashed couple in which I ordinarily journeyed. In a sharp bend of the rapids, between two big curls, they were swept among the boulders and under the matted branches which stretched out from the bank. They filled, and the racing current pinned them where they were, one partly on the other. All of us had to help get them clear. Their fastenings were chopped asunder with axes. Kermit and half a dozen of the men, stripped to the skin, made their way to a small rock island in the little falls just above the canoes, and let down a rope which we tied to the outermost canoe. The rest of us, up to our armpits and barely able to keep our footing as we slipped and stumbled among the boulders in the swift current lifted and shoved, while Kermit and his men pulled the rope and fastened the slack to a half-submerged tree. Each canoe in succession was hauled up the little rock island, baled, and then taken down in safety by two paddlers. It was nearly four o'clock before we were again ready to start, having been delayed by a rainstorm so heavy that we could not see across the river. Ten minutes' run took us to the head of another series of rapids; the exploring party returned with the news that we had an all day's job ahead of us; and we made camp in the rain, which did not matter much, as we were already drenched through. It was impossible with the wet wood, to make a fire sufficiently hot to dry all our soggy things, for the rain was still falling. A tapir was seen from our boat, but, as at the moment we were being whisked round in a complete circle by a whirlpool, I did not myself see it in time to shoot.

Next morning we went down a kilometre, and then landed on the other side of the river. The canoes were run down, and the loads carried to the other side of a little river coming in from the west, which Colonel Rondon christened Cherrie River. Across this we went on a bridge consisting of a huge tree felled by Macario, one of our best men. Here we camped, while Rondon, Lyra, Kermit and Antonio Correa explored what was ahead. They were absent until mid-afternoon. Then they returned with the news that we were among ranges of low mountains, utterly different in formation from the high plateau region to which the first rapids, those we had come to on 2 March, belonged. Through the first range of these mountains the river ran in a gorge, some three kilometres long, immediately ahead of us. The ground was so rough and steep that it would be impossible to drag the canoes over it and difficult enough to carry the loads; and the rapids were so bad, containing several falls, one of at least ten metres in height, that it was doubtful how many of the canoes we could get down them. Kermit, who was the only man with much experience of rope work, was the only man who believed we could get the canoes down at all; and it was, of course, possible that we should have to build new ones at the foot to supply the place of any that were lost or left behind. In view of the length and character of the portage, and of all the unpleasant possibilities that were ahead, and of the need of keeping every pound of food, it was necessary to reduce weight in every possible way and to throw away everything except the barest necessities.

We thought we had reduced our baggage before, but now we cut to the bone. We kept the fly for all six of us to sleep under. Kermit's shoes had gone, thanks to the amount of work in the water which he had been doing; and he took the pair I had been wearing, while I put on my spare pair. In addition to the clothes I wore, I kept one set of pyjamas, a spare pair of drawers, a spare pair of socks, half a dozen handkerchiefs, my wash kit, my pocket medicine-case, and a little bag containing my spare spectacles, gun-grease, some adhesive plaster, some needles and thread, the 'fly-dope', and my purse and letter of credit, to be used at Manaos. All of these went into the bag containing my cot, blanket, and mosquito net. I also carried a cartridge bag containing my cartridges, head net, and gauntlets. Kermit cut down even closer, and the others about as close.

The last three days of March we spent in getting to the foot of the rapids in this gorge. Lyra and Kermit, with four of the best watermen, handled the empty canoes. The work was not only difficult and laborious, in the extreme, but hazardous, for the walls of the gorge were so sheer that at the worst places they had to cling to narrow shelves on the face of the rock, while letting the canoes down with ropes. Meanwhile Rondon surveyed and cut a trail for the burden-bearers, and superintended the portage of the loads. The rocky sides of the gorge were too steep for laden men to attempt to traverse them. Accordingly the trail had to go over the top of the mountain, both the ascent and the descent of the rock-strewn, forest-clad slopes being very steep. It was hard work to carry loads over such a trail. From the top of the mountain, through an opening in the trees on the edge of a cliff, there was a beautiful view of the country ahead. All around and in front of us there were ranges of low mountains about the height of the lower ridges of the Alleghanies. Their sides were steep and they were covered with the matted growth of the tropical forest. Our next camping place at the foot of the gorge, was almost beneath us, and from thence the river ran in a straight line, flecked with white water, for about a kilometre. Then it disappeared behind and between mountain ridges, which we supposed meant further rapids. It was a view well worth seeing but, beautiful although the country ahead of us was, its character was such as to promise further hardships, difficulty, and exhausting labour, and especially further delay; and delay was a serious matter to men whose food supply was beginning to run short, whose equipment was reduced to the minimum, who for a month, with the utmost toil, had made very slow progress, and who had no idea of either the distance or the difficulties of the route in front of them . . .

During this portage the weather favoured us. We were coming towards the close of the rainy season. On the last day of the month, when we moved camp to the foot of the gorge, there was a thunderstorm but on the whole we were not bothered by rain until the last night when it rained heavily, driving under the fly so as to wet my cot and bedding. However, I slept comfortably enough, rolled in the damp blanket. Without the blanket I should have been uncomfortable; a blanket is a necessity for health. On the third day Lyra and Kermit, with their daring and hard-working watermen after wearing labour, succeeded in getting five canoes through the worst of the rapids to the chief fall. The sixth, which was frail and weak, had its bottom beaten out on the jagged rocks of the broken water. On this night, although I thought I had put my clothes out of reach, both the termites and the carregadores ants got at them, ate holes in one boot, ate one leg of my drawers, and riddled my handkerchief; and I now had nothing to replace anything that was destroyed.

Next day Lyra, Kermit and their camaradas brought the five canoes that were left down to camp. They had in four days accomplished a work of incredible labour and of the utmost importance; for at the first glance it had seemed an absolute impossibility to avoid abandoning the canoes when we found that the river sank into a cataract-broken torrent at the bottom of a canyon-like gorge between steep mountains. On 2 April we once more started, wondering how soon we should strike other rapids in the mountains ahead, and whether in any reasonable time we should, as the aneroid indicated, be so low down that we should necessarily be in a plain where we could make a journey of at least a few days without rapids. We had been exactly a month going through an uninterrupted succession of rapids. During that month we had come only about 110 kilometres, and had descended nearly 150 metres – the figures are approximate but fairly accurate. We had lost four of the canoes with which we started, and one other, which we had built, and the life of one man; and the life of a dog which by its death had, in all probability, saved the life of Colonel Rondon. In a straight line northward, towards our supposed destination, we had not made more than a mile and a quarter a day; at the cost of bitter toil for most of the party, of much risk for some of the party, and of some risk and some hardship for all the party. Most of the camaradas were downhearted, naturally enough, and occasionally asked one of us if we really believed that we should ever get out alive, and we had to cheer them up as best we could.

There was no change in our work for the time being. We made but three kilometres that day. Most of the party walked all the time, but the dugouts carried the luggage until we struck the head of the series of rapids which were to take up the next two or three days. The river rushed through a wild gorge, a chasm or canyon, between two mountains. Its sides were very steep, mere rock walls, although in most places so covered with the luxuriant growth of the trees and bushes that clung in the crevices, and with green moss, that the naked rock was hardly seen. Rondon, Lyra and Kermit, who were in front, found a small level spot with a beach of sand, and sent back word to camp there while they spent several hours in exploring the country ahead. The canoes were run down empty, and the loads carried painfully along the face of the cliffs; so bad was the trail that I found it rather hard to follow although carrying nothing but my rifle and cartridge bag. The explorers returned with the information that the mountains stretched ahead of us, and that there were rapids as far as they had gone. We could only hope that the aneroid was not hopelessly out of kilter and that we should, therefore, fairly soon find ourselves in comparatively level country. The severe toil, on a rather limited food supply, was telling on the strength as well as on the spirits of the men; Lyra and Kermit in addition to their other work, performed as much actual physical labour as any of them.

Next day, 3 April, we began the descent of these sinister rapids of the chasm. Colonel Rondon had gone to the summit of the mountain in order to find a better trail for the burden-bearers, but it was hopeless, and they had to go along the face of the cliffs . . .

Lyra, Kermit and Cherrie, with four of the men, worked the canoes halfway down the canyon. Again and again it was touch and go whether they could get past a given point. At one spot the channel of the furious torrent was only fifteen yards across. One canoe was lost, so that of the seven with which we had started only two were left. Cherrie laboured with the other men at times, and also stood as guard over them, for, while actually working, of course no one could carry a rifle. Kermit's experience in bridge building was invaluable in enabling him to do the rope work by which alone it was possible to get the canoes down the canyon. He and Lyra had now been in the water for days. Their clothes were never dry. Their shoes were rotten. The bruises on their feet and legs had become sores. On their bodies some of the insect bites had become festering wounds, as indeed was the case with all of us. Poisonous ants, biting flies, ticks, wasps, bees, were a perpetual torment. However, no one had yet been bitten by a venomous serpent, a scorpion, or a centipede although we had killed all of the three within camp limits.

Under such conditions whatever is evil in men's natures comes to the front. On this day a strange and terrible tragedy occurred. One of the camaradas, a man of pure European blood, was the man named Julio of whom I have already spoken. He was a very powerful fellow and had been importunately eager to come on the expedition and he had the reputation of being a good worker. But, like so many men of higher standing, he had had no idea of what such an expedition really meant, and under the strain of toil, hardship and danger his nature showed its true depths of selfishness, cowardice and ferocity. He shirked all work. He shammed sickness. Nothing could make him do his share; and yet unlike his self-respecting fellows he was always shamelessly begging for favours. Kermit was the only one of our party who smoked, and he was continually giving a little tobacco to some of the camaradas, who worked especially well under him. The good men did not ask for it but Julio, who shirked every labour, was always, and always in vain, demanding it. Colonel Rondon, Lyra and Kermit each tried to get work out of him, and in order to do anything with him had to threaten to leave him in the wilderness. He threw all his tasks on his comrades and, moreover, he stole their food as well as ours. On such an expedition the theft of food comes next to murder as a crime, and should by rights be punished as such. We could not trust him to cut down palms or gather nuts, because he would stay out and eat what ought to have gone into the common store. Finally, the men on several occasions themselves detected him stealing their food. Alone of the whole party, and thanks to the stolen food, he had kept in full flesh and bodily vigour.

One of our best men was a huge negro named Paixão – Paishon – a corporal and acting sergeant in the engineer corps. He had, by the way, literally torn his trousers to pieces, so that he wore only the tatters of a pair of old drawers until I gave him my spare trousers when we lightened loads. He was a stern disciplinarian. One evening he detected Julio stealing food and smashed him in the mouth. Julio came crying to us, his face working with fear and malignant hatred; but after investigation he was told that he had got off uncommonly lightly. The men had three or four carbines, which were sometimes carried by those who were not their owners.

On this morning, at the outset of the portage, Pedrinho discovered Julio stealing some of the men's dried meat. Shortly afterwards Paishon rebuked him for, as usual, lagging behind. By this time we had reached the place where the canoes were tied to the bank and then taken down one at a time. We were sitting down waiting for the last loads to be brought along the trail. Pedrinho was still in the camp we had left. Paishon had just brought in a load, left it on the ground with his carbine beside it, and returned on the trail for another load. Julio came in, put down his load, picked up the carbine, and walked back on the trail, muttering to himself but showing no excitement. We thought nothing of it, for he was always muttering; and occassionally one of the men saw a monkey or big bird and tried to shoot it, so it was never surprising to see a man with a carbine.

In a minute we heard a shot; and in a short time three or four of the men came up the trail to tell us that Paishon was dead, having been shot by Julio, who had fled into the woods. Colonel Rondon and Lyra were ahead; I sent a messenger for them, directed Cherrie and Kermit to stay where they were and guard the canoes and provisions, and started down the trail with the doctor – an absolutely cool and plucky man with a revolver but no rifle – and a couple of the camaradas. We soon passed the dead body of poor Paishon. He lay in a huddle, in a pool of his own blood, where he had fallen, shot through the heart. I feared that Julio had run amuck, and intended merely to take more lives before he died, and that he would begin with Pedrinho, who was alone and unarmed in the camp we had left. Accordingly I pushed on, followed by my companions, looking sharply right and left; but when we came to the camp the doctor quietly walked by me, remarking: 'My eyes are better than yours, Colonel; if he is in sight I'll point him out to you, as you have the rifle.' However, he was not there, and the others soon joined us with the welcome news that they had found the carbine.

The murderer had stood to one side of the path and killed his victim, when a dozen paces off, with deliberate and malignant purpose. Then evidently his murderous hatred had at once given way to his innate cowardice, and, perhaps hearing someone coming along the path, he fled in panic terror into the wilderness. A tree had knocked the carbine from his hand. His footsteps showed that after going some rods he had started to return, doubtless for the carbine, but had fled again, probably because the body had then been discovered. It was questionable whether or not he would live to reach the Indian villages, which were probably his goal. He was not a man to feel remorse – never a common feeling; but surely that murderer was in a living hell, as, with fever and famine leering at him from the shadows, he made his way through the empty desolation of the wilderness. Franca, the cook, quoted out of the melancholy proverbial philosophy of the people the proverb: 'No man knows the heart of anyone,' and then expressed with deep conviction a weird ghostly belief I had never encountered before: Paishon is following Julio now, and will follow him until he dies; 'Paishon fell forward on his hands and knees, and when a murdered man falls like that his ghost will follow the slayer as long as the slayer lives' . . .

We buried him beside the place where he fell. With axes and knives the camaradas dug a shallow grave, while we stood by with bared heads. Then reverently and carefully we lifted the poor body, which but half an hour before had been so full of vigorous life. Colonel Rondon and I bore the head and shoulders.

We laid him in the grave, and heaped a mound over him, and put a rude cross at his head. We fired a volley for a brave and loyal soldier, who had died doing his duty. Then we left him for ever, under the great trees beside the lonely river.

That day we got only halfway down the rapids. There was no good place to camp. But at the foot of one steep cliff there was a narrow, boulder-covered slope, where it was possible to sling hammocks and cook; and a slanting spot was found for my cot, which had sagged until by this time it looked like a broken backed centipede. It rained a little during the night but not enough to wet us much. Next day Lyra, Kermit and Cherrie finished their job, and brought the four remaining canoes to camp, one leaking badly from the battering on the rocks. We then went downstream a few hundred yards, and camped on the opposite side; it was not a good camping place, but it was better than the one we left.

The men were growing constantly weaker under the endless strain of exhausting labour. Kermit was having an attack of fever, and Lyra and Cherrie had touches of dysentery, but all three continued to work. While in the water trying to help with an upset canoe I had, by my own clumsiness, bruised my leg against a boulder, and the resulting inflammation was somewhat bothersome. I now had a sharp attack of fever, but, thanks to the excellent care of the doctor, was over it in about forty-eight hours; but Kermit's fever grew worse, and he too was unable to work for a day or two. We could walk over the portages, however. A good doctor is an absolute necessity on an exploring expedition in such a country as that we were in, under penalty of a frightful mortality among the members; and the necessary risks and hazards are so great, the chances of disaster so large, that there is no warrant for increasing them by the failure to take all feasible precautions.

The next day we made another long portage round some rapids, and camped at night still in the hot, wet, sunless atmosphere of the gorge. The following day, 6 April, we portaged past another set of rapids, which proved to be the last of the rapids of the chasm. For some kilometres we kept passing hills, and feared lest at any moment we might again find ourselves fronting another mountain gorge, with, in such case, further days of grinding and perilous labour ahead of us, while our men were disheartened, weak and sick. Most of them had already begun to have fever. Their condition was inevitable after over a month's uninterrupted work of the hardest kind in getting through the long series of rapids we had just passed; and a long further delay, accompanied by wearing labour, would have almost certainly meant that the weakest among our party would have begun to die. There were already two of the camaradas who were too weak to help the others, their condition being such as to cause us serious concern.

However, the hills gradually sank into a level plain and the river carried us through it at a rate that enabled us during the remainder of the day to reel off thirty-six kilometres, a record that for the first time held out promise. Twice tapirs swam the river while we passed but not near my canoe. However, the previous evening Cherrie had killed two monkeys and Kermit one, and we all had a few mouthfuls of fresh meat; we had already had a good soup made out of a turtle Kermit had caught. We had to portage by one short set of rapids, the unloaded canoes being brought down without difficulty. At last, at four in the afternoon, we came to the mouth of a big river running in from the right. We thought it was probably the Ananás, but, of course, could not be certain. It was less in volume than the one we had descended, but nearly as broad; its breadth at this point being ninety-five yards as against one hundred and twenty for the larger river. There were rapids ahead, immediately after the junction, which took place in latitude 10° 58′ south. We had come 216 kilometres all told, and were nearly north of where we had started. We camped on the point of land between the two rivers. It was extraordinary to realize that here about the eleventh degree we were on such a big river, utterly unknown to the cartographers and not indicated by even a hint on any map. We named this big tributary Rio Cardozo, after a gallant officer of the Commission who had died of beriberi just as our expedition began. We spent a day at this spot determining our exact position by the sun, and afterward by the stars, and sending on two men to explore the rapids in advance. They returned with the news that there were big cataracts in them, and that they would form an obstacle to our progress. They had also caught a huge siluroid fish, which furnished an excellent meal for everybody in camp. This evening at sunset the view across the broad river, from our camp where the two rivers joined, was very lovely; and for the first time we had an open space in front of and above us, so that after nightfall the stars and the great waxing moon were glorious overhead, and against the rocks in midstream the broken water gleamed like tossing silver . . .

Next day, 8 April, we made five kilometres only, as there was a succession of rapids. We had to carry the loads past two of them, but ran the canoes without difficulty, for on the west side were long canals of swift water through the forest. The river had been higher, but was still very high, and the current raced round the many islands that, at this point, divided the channel. At four we made camp at the head of another stretch of rapids, over which the Canadian canoes would have danced without shipping a teaspoonful of water but which our dugouts could only run empty. Cherrie killed three monkeys and Lyra caught two big piranhas so that we were again all of us well provided with dinner and breakfast. When a number of men, doing hard work, are most of the time on half-rations, they grow to take a lively interest in any reasonably full meal that does arrive.

On the 10th we repeated the proceedings: a short quick run; a few hundred metres' portage, occupying, however, at least a couple of hours; again a few minutes run; again other rapids. We again made less than five kilometres; in the two days we had been descending nearly a metre for every kilometre we made in advance and it hardly seemed as if this state of things could last, for the aneroid showed that we were getting very low down. How I longed for a big Maine birch-bark, such as that in which I once went down the Mattawamkeag at high water! It would have slipped down these rapids as a girl trips through a country dance.

But our loaded dugouts would have shoved their noses under every curl. The country was lovely. The wide river, now in one channel, now in several channels, wound among hills; the shower-freshened forest glistened in the sunlight; the many kinds of beautiful palm-fronds and the huge pacova-leaves stamped the peculiar look of the tropics on the whole landscape – it was like passing by water through a gigantic botanical garden. In the afternoon we got an elderly toucan, a piranha, and a reasonably edible side-necked river-turtle, so we had fresh meat again. We slept as usual in earshot of rapids. We had been out six weeks, and almost all the time we had been engaged in wearily working our way down and past rapid after rapid. Rapids are by far the most dangerous enemies of explorers and travellers who journey along these rivers.

Next day was a repetition of the same work. All the morning was spent in getting the loads to the foot of the rapids at the head of which we were encamped, down which the canoes were run empty. Then for thirty or forty minutes we ran down the swift, twisting river, the two lashed canoes almost coming to grief at one spot where a swirl of the current threw them against some trees on a small submerged island. Then we came to another set of rapids, carried the baggage down past them, and made camp long after dark in the rain – a good exercise in patience for those of us who were still suffering somewhat from fever. No one was in really buoyant health. For some weeks we had been sharing part of the contents of our boxes with the camaradas but our food was not very satisfying to them. They needed quantity, and the main-stay of each of their meals was a mass of palmitas; but on this day they had no time to cut down palms. We finally decided to run these rapids with the empty canoes, and they came down in safety. On such a trip it is highly undesirable to take any save necessary risks, for the consequences of disaster are too serious; and yet if no risks are taken the progress is so slow that disaster comes anyhow; and it is necessary perpetually to vary the terms of the perpetual working compromise between rashness and over caution. This night we had a very good fish to eat, a big silvery fellow called a pescada, of a kind we had not caught before.

One day Trigueiro failed to embark with the rest of us, and we had to camp where we were next day to find him. Easter Sunday we spent in the fashion with which we were altogether too familiar. We only ran in a clear course for ten minutes all told, and spent eight hours in portaging the loads past rapids down which the canoes were run; the balsa was almost swamped This day we caught twenty-eight big fish, mostly piranhas, and everybody had all he could eat for dinner, and for breakfast the following morning.

The forenoon of the following day was a repetition of this wearisome work; but late in the afternoon the river began to run in long quiet reaches. We made fifteen kilometres, and for the first time in several weeks camped where we did not hear the rapids. The silence was soothing and restful. The following day, 14 April, we made a good run of some thirty-two kilometres. We passed a little river which entered on our left. We ran two or three light rapids, and portaged the loads by another. The river ran in long and usually tranquil stretches. In the morning when we started the view was lovely. There was a mist, and for a couple of miles the great river, broad and quiet, ran between the high walls of tropical forest, the tops of the giant trees showing dim through the haze. Different members of the party caught many fish and shot a monkey and a couple of jacú-tinga – birds akin to a turkey, but the size of a fowl – so we again had a camp of plenty. The dry season was approaching, but there were still heavy, drenching rains. On this day the men found some new nuts of which they liked the taste, but the nuts proved unwholesome and half of the men were very sick and unable to work the following day. In the balsa only two were left fit to do anything, and Kermit plied a paddle all day long.

Accordingly, it was a rather sorry crew that embarked the following morning, 15 April. But it turned out a red-letter day. The day before, we had come across cuttings, a year old, which were probably but not certainly made by pioneer rubber-men. But on this day

– during which we made twenty-five kilometres – after running two hours and a half we found on the left bank a board on a post, with the initials J. A., to show the farthest-up point which a rubberman had reached and claimed as his own. An hour farther down we came on a newly built house in a little planted clearing and we cheered heartily. No one was at home, but the house, of palm-thatch, was clean and cool. A couple of dogs were on watch, and the belongings showed that a man, a woman and a child lived there, and had only just left. Another hour brought us to a similar house where dwelt an old black man, who showed the innate courtesy of the Brazilian peasant. We came on these rubber-men and their houses in about latitude 10° 24′.

In mid-afternoon we stopped at another clean, cool, picturesque house of palm-thatch. The inhabitants all fled at our approach, fearing an Indian raid; for they were absolutely unprepared to have any one come from the unknown regions upstream. They returned and were most hospitable and communicative, and we spent the night there. Said Antonio Correa to Kermit: 'It seems like a dream to be in a house again, and hear the voices of men and women, instead of being among those mountains and rapids.'

We had passed the period when there was a chance of peril, of disaster, to the whole expedition. There might be risk ahead to individuals, and some difficulties and annoyances for all of us; but there was no longer the least likelihood of any disaster to the expedition as a whole. We now no longer had to face continual anxiety, the need of constant economy with food, the duty of labour with no end in sight, and bitter uncertainty as to the future.

It was time to get out.

HOLED

STEVEN CALLAHAN
(1952–)

American yachtsman. In 1981 he entered the single-handed Mini-Transat race between England and Antigua, sailing a 21-foot yacht, Napoleon Solo.

My little boat continues to slice across undulating foothills that are rapidly growing into small mountains. The water that was sparkling clear now reflects the dark, threatening sky. Waves froth and spit at us as we carve around them towards the sinking sun. *Solo* is kept more or less on course by the electric automatic pilot. Its motor hums a fatiguing song as it constantly works overtime. Despite the occasional waterfalls that cascade across the deck, I am not too uncomfortable. I joke in front of my movie camera, gnaw on a greasy sausage, and belch in a Long John Silver croak: 'Aargh, matey, as you can see, we's havin' just fine weather. Course we could do with a bit o' wind.' I crawl up on the foredeck and stuff one of the jibs into its sack. Cold water runs down my spine and up my arms.

The sky grows darker as dusk approaches. When *Solo* slides into the wave troughs, the sun dips to the horizon. Dip, dip, and it finally drowns in the west. *Solo* slashes on into the night. The waves and wind seem to grow fiercer at night. I cannot see the waves far off – and then suddenly they are here, breaking and rushing down on us. Then they scurry away again into the shadow of the world almost before I am aware that they have struck.

For over ten thousand miles and one and a half Atlantic crossings, my ship and I have kept each other company. She has seen worse, much worse. If things significantly deteriorate, I can adopt storm tactics: reduce sail, and either heave to or run downwind. The pilot chart promises infrequent gales of minor intensity for this part of the south Atlantic and time of year. The wind can pipe up to force seven or so, enough to muss one's hair and guarantee a bathing on deck, but not enough to loosen one's dentures. In about two weeks I will be lying in the baking sun of the Caribbean with a cold rum punch in hand. *Solo* will be placidly anchored with sails furled beneath some palm-studded beach.

Fortunately I rarely have to be on deck; only to reef the sails or to change jibs. I have provided the boat with an inside steering and central control station. I sit beneath a Plexiglas hatch that looks like a boxy jet canopy. From here I can steer with an inside tiller, adjust the sails by reaching out through the open washboard to the cleats and winches beside the hatch, and keep watch, all at the same time. In addition, I can look at the chart on the table below me, chat on the radio beside me, or cook up a meal on the galley stove, all without leaving my seat. Despite the acrobatics of the sea, the cabin remains relatively comfortable. Save for an occasional drip of water feeling its way through the crevices of the hatch, my surroundings are dry. The air hangs heavy with the dampness of the coming storm, but the varnished wood of the cabin glows warmly in the soft light. The shapes contained in the wood grain become animals, people, companions. They calm me. The small amount of coffee that I manage to transfer from my lurching cup to my mouth warms me and props my eyes open. My stomach, made of some noncorroding, inexplodable and otherwise nonimpressionable alloy, does not yearn for a dry biscuit diet; instead, I eat heartily and plan for my birthday dinner two days from now. I can't bake a cake, having no oven, but I will have a go at chocolate crêpes. I'll stir a tin of rabbit I've saved into a curry, ignoring the French superstition that even the slightest mention of *lapin* assures a crew the most wretched luck.

Though I feel secure in my floating nest, the storm reawakens my caution, which has slumbered for a week. Each ten-foot wave that sweeps by contains more tons of water than I care to imagine. The wind whistles across the deck and through the rigging wires. Occasionally Solo's rear is kicked, and she brings her head to wind as if to see the striking bully. The jib luffs with a rustling rattle, then pulls taut as Solo turns off to continue on her way. Visions of a rogue wave snap into my mind. Caused by the coincidence of peaks travelling in different directions or at different speeds, a rogue can grow to four times the average wave height and could throw Solo about like a toy. Converging wave troughs can also form a canyon into which we could plunge. Often such anomalies flow from different directions, forming vertical cliffs from which seas tumble in liquid avalanches.

Six months ago Solo fell with a thunderous bang in just such a cascade off the Azores. The sky disappeared and nothing but green was visible across the deck hatch. The boat immediately righted and we sailed on, but it was a hard knock. My books and sextant leaped over the tall fiddle rails, smashing on the chart table and splintering its moldings. If they had not hit the table, they would have landed in my face. I was lucky that time; I must be more cautious.

Disaster at sea can happen in a moment, without warning, or it can come after long days of anticipation and fear. It does not always come when the sea is fiercest but may spring when waters lie as flat and imperturbable as a sheet of iron. Sailors may be struck down at any time, in calm or in storm, but the sea does not do it for hate or spite. She has no wrath to vent. Nor does she have a hand of kindness to extend. She is merely there, immense, powerful, and indifferent. I do not resent her indifference, or my comparative insignificance. Indeed, it is one of the main reasons I like to sail: the sea makes the insignificance of my own small self and of all humanity so poignant.

I watch Solo's boiling, phosphorescent wake as it dissipates among the somersaulting waves. 'Things could be worse,' I muse.

Then voices from the past speak to me. 'Each time you have chanted that phrase, things have inevitably gotten worse.' I think of the pilot chart figures, which are averages taken from ships' data. There might be some truth to the idea that charted estimates of gale strengths tend to be low. After all, if a captain hears of bad weather, he doesn't usually head his rust bucket for the centre of it in order to get some fresh air. No doubt I will be a bit uncomfortable for a few days.

I check my gear over and make sure all is as secure and shipshape as a floating fool can make it. I inspect the hull, deck, bulkheads, cabinetry, and all of the joints that hold my wooden jewellery box secure. The kettle is filled for coffee or steaming lemonade. A lump of chocolate is at hand beside the radio. All essential preparations have been made.

It is about 22.30 Greenwich Mean Time. The moon hangs full, white and motionless, undisturbed by the tempest and the tumultuous sea. If conditions continue to worsen, I will have to head more southerly. For the time being, I can do nothing more, so I lie down to rest. At 23.00 I get up and undress. I lie down again clothed only in a T-shirt. A watch circles my wrist, and around my neck is a slab of whale tooth on a string. It is the most I will wear the next two and a half months.

My boat slues around the rushing peaks, her keel clinging to the slopes like a mountain goat, her port side pressed down against the black, rolling ocean. I lie on my bunk, slung upon the lee canvas, hanging as if in a hammock.

BANG! A deafening explosion blankets the subtler sounds of torn wood fibre and rush of sea. I jump up. Water thunders over me as if I've suddenly been thrown into the path of a rampaging river. Forward, aft – where does it come from? Is half of the side gone? No time. I fumble with the knife I have sheathed by the chart table. Already the water is waist deep. The nose of the boat is dipping down. *Solo* comes to a halt as she begins a sickening dive. She's going down, down! My mind barks orders. Free the emergency package. My soul screams. You've lost her! I hold my breath, submerge, slash at the tie-downs that secure my emergency duffel. My heart is a pounding pile driver. The heavy work wrings the air from my lungs and my mind battles with my limbs for the opportunity to breathe. Terminal darkness and chaos surround me. Get out, get out, she's going down! In one rhythmic movement I rocket upwards, thrust the hatch forwards, and catapult my shaking body on to the deck, leaving my package of hope behind.

Less than thirty seconds have elapsed since impact. The bow points towards its grave at a hesitating low angle and the sea washes about my ankles. I cut the tie-downs that secure the raft canister. Thoughts flash about me like echoes in a cave. Perhaps I have waited too long. Perhaps it is time to die. Going down . . . die . . . lost without trace. I recall the life raft instructions: throw the bulky hundred pounds overboard before inflation. Who can manoeuvre such weight in the middle of a bucking circus ride? No time, quickly – she's going down! I yank. The first pull, then the second – nothing, nothing! This is it, the end of my life. Soon, it will come soon. I scream at the stubborn canister. 'Come on, you bastard!' The third pull comes up hard, and she blows with a bursting static *shush*. A wave sweeps over the entire deck, and I simply float the raft off. It thrashes about on the end of its painter. *Solo* has been transformed from a proper little ship to a submerged wreck in about one minute. I dive into the raft with the knife clenched in my teeth, buccaneer style, noticing that the movie camera mounted on the aft pulpit has been turned on. Its red eye winks at me. Who is directing this film? He isn't much on lighting but his flair for the dramatic is impressive.

Unmoving and unconcerned, the moon looks down upon us. Its lunar face is eclipsed by wisps of clouds that waft across it, dimming the shadow of *Solo*'s death. My instincts and training have carried me through the motions of survival, but now, as I have a moment to reflect, the full impact of the crash throbs in my head. Never have all of my senses seemed so sharp. My emotions are an incomprehensible mix. There is a wailing anguish that mourns the loss of my boat. There is a deep disappointment in myself for my failures. Overshadowing it all is the stark realization that what I think and feel will not matter much longer. My body shakes with cold. I am too far from civilization to have any hope of rescue.

In the space of a moment, myriad conversations and debates flash through my mind, as if a group of men are chattering within my skull. Some of them joke, finding comic relief in the camera's busily taking pictures that no one will ever see. Others stoke a furnace of fear. Fear becomes sustenance. Its energy feeds action. I must be careful. I fight blind panic: I do not want the power from my pumping adrenalin to lead to confused and counterproductive activity. I fight the urge to fall into catatonic hysteria: I do not want to sit frozen in fear until the end comes. Focus, I tell myself. Focus and get moving.

I see my vessel, my companion, my child, swallowed up like a crumb too small for the deep Atlantic to taste. Waves bury her and pass. *Solo*'s white decks emerge. She's not going down, not yet. Wait until she goes before cutting the painter. Even though I have added canned water and other gear to the raft's supplies, I will not live long without additional equipment. Wait and salvage everything you can. My body shakes even more with fright and cold, and my eyes sting from the salt. I must get some clothes, some cover, anything. I begin hacking off a piece of the mains'l. Don't cut the raft, be careful, careful. Once cut, the sailcloth rips off easily. The raft flips about as I pull the horseshoe life preserver and man-overboard pole off of *Solo*'s stern. Foam and sea continue to sweep across her, but she rises each time. My mind coaxes her. Please don't go, not yet, please stay up. The watertight compartments that I designed and installed have combined with pockets of air trapped inside of her. She fights back. Her jib snaps with loud report. Her hatch and rudder bang as the ocean beats her. Perhaps she will not sink after all. Her head is under but her rear hesitates like a child at the shore, unable to make the final plunge.

I ache with cold; the stench of rubber, plastic and talc fill my nostrils. *Solo* may sink any moment now, but I must get back inside. There isn't much time. I pull up to the side of the boat, climb aboard, and stand for a second feeling the strange sensation of being in the sea and on deck at the same time. Waves rear up and bury the boat, but time after time *Solo* struggles to the surface. How much battering will she take before water feels its way into the few remaining air spaces? How many moments are left before she will disappear for the last time?

Between towering crests that wash over me, I lower myself into the hatch. The water below is peaceful compared to the surrounding tempest. I duck into the watery tomb, and the hatch slams shut behind me with a crack. I feel for the emergency bag and cut away the lines that secure it. Waves wander by, engulf us, and move on. I gasp for air. The bag is freed but seems to weigh as much as the collected sins of the world. While struggling in the companionway, pushing and tugging to get the gear on deck, I fight the hatch, which beats against my back. Heaving the bag into the raft requires all the strength I have.

As it tumbles into the raft, I turn to re-enter the hatch. My hand turns aft and finds a piece of floating cushion wedged against the overhead. Jerking at it, I arise for a gulp of air. There is none. In that moment I feel as though the last breath in the galaxy has been breathed by someone else. The edge of the sea suddenly rips past. I see the surface shimmering like a thousand candles. Air splutters in, and I gasp as the clatter of *Solo* becomes muffled by the coming of the next wave.

I tie the cushion to the end of a halyard and let it float about while I submerge to retrieve my bed. Bundling up my wet sleeping bag is like capturing an armful of snakes. I slowly manage to shove, pull, and roll the bag into the raft. With the final piece of cushion, I fall in behind. I have successfully abandoned ship.

My God, *Solo* is still floating! I see her slowly rolling farther on to her side as I gather up items that float out of the cabin one by one: a cabbage, an empty Chock Full o' Nuts coffee can, and a box containing a few eggs. The eggs will probably not last long, but I take them anyway.

I am too exhausted to do any more. I will not part from *Solo*, but should she want to leave I must be able to let go. Seventy feet of ⅜ inch line, tied to the end of the mainsheet, allows me to drift well downwind. *Solo* disappears when we dip into the waves' troughs. Great foaming crests of water grind their way towards us. There is a churning up to windward like the surf on the shore. I hear it coming; I hear the clap and bang and snap that are *Solo*'s words to me, 'I'm here.' The raft rises to meet the head of the wave that rushes towards me. The froth and curl crash by just to port.

The entrance fly on the tent-type cover snaps with a ripping sound each time the Velcro seal is blown by the wind. I must turn the raft or a breaker may drive through the opening. While on a wave peak, I look aft at *Solo*'s deck mounting on the next swell. The sea rises smoothly from the dark, a giant sitting up after a sleep. There is a tight round opening in the opposite side of the tent. I stick myself through this observation port up to my waist. I must not let go of the rope to *Solo*, but I need to move it. I loop a rope through the mainsheet which trails from *Solo*'s deck and lead it back to the raft. One end of this I secure to the handline around the raft's perimeter. The other I wind around the handline and bring the tail through the observation port. If *Solo* sinks I can let go of this tail and we will slip apart. Wait – can't get back in . . . I'm stuck. I try to free myself from the canopy clutching my chest. The sea spits at me. Crests roar in the darkness. I twist and yank and fall back inside. The raft swings and presents the wall of the tent to the waves. Ha! A good joke, the wall of a tent against the sea, the sea that beats granite to sand.

With a slipknot I tie *Solo*'s line to the handhold webbing that encircles the inside of the raft. While frantically tying all of my equipment to the webbing, I hear rumbling well to windward. It must be a big wave to be heard so far off. I listen to its approach. A rush of water, then silence. I can feel it rising over me. There is a wrenching rubbery shriek from the raft as the wave bursts upon us and my space collapses in half. The windward side punches in and sends me flying across the raft. The top collapses and water shoots in everywhere. The impact is strengthened by the jerking painter, tied to my ship full of water, upwind from where the sea sprang. I'm going to die. Tonight. Here some 450 miles away from the nearest land. The sea will crush me, capsize me, and rob my body of heat and breath. I will be lost, and no one will even know until I'm weeks overdue.

I crawl back to windward, keeping one hand on the cord to *Solo*, the other hand clutching the handline. I huddle in my sodden sleeping-bag. Gallons of water slosh about in the bottom of the raft. I sit on the cushion, which insulates me from the icy floor. I'm shivering but begin to warm up. It is a time to wait, to listen, to think, to plan, and to fear.

As my raft and I rise to the crest of a wave. I can see *Solo* wallowing in the following trough. Then she rises against the face of the next wave as I plummet into the trough that had cradled her a moment before. She has rolled well over now, with her nose and starboard side under and her stern quarter fairly high. If only you will stay afloat until morning. I must see you again, must see the damage that I feel I have caused you. Why didn't I wait in the Canaries? Why didn't I soften up and relax? Why did I drive you to this so that I could complete my stupid goal of a double crossing? I'm sorry, my poor *Solo*.

I have swallowed a lot of salt and my throat is parched. Perhaps in the morning I can retrieve more gear, jugs of water, and some food. I plan every move and every priority. The loss of body heat is the most immediate danger, but the sleeping-bag may give me enough protection. Water is the first priority, then food. After that, whatever else I can grab. Ten gallons of water rest in the galley locker just under the companionway – forty to eighty days' worth of survival rations waiting for me just a hundred feet away. The raised stern quarter will make it easier to get aft. There are two large duffels in the aft cabin, hung on the top sides; one is full of food – about a month's worth – and the other is full of clothes. If I can dive down and swim forward, I may be able to pull my survival suit out of the fore-peak. I dream of how its thick neoprene will warm me up.

Waves continue to pound the raft, beating the side in, pouring in water. The tubes are as tight as teak logs, yet they are bent like spaghetti. Bailing with the coffee can again and again, I wonder how much one of these rafts can take and watch for signs of splitting.

A small overhead lamp lights my tiny new world. The memory of the crash, the rank odour of my surroundings, the pounding of the sea, the moaning wind, and my plan to reboard *Solo* in the morning roll over and over in my brain. Surely it will end soon.

5 February, day 1 I am lost about halfway between western Oshkosh and Nowhere City. I do not think the Atlantic has emptier waters. I am about 450 miles north of the Cape Verde Islands, but they stand across the wind. I can drift only in the direction she blows. Downwind, 450 miles separate me from the nearest shipping lanes. Caribbean islands are the closest possible landfall, eighteen hundred nautical miles away. Do not think of it. Plan for daylight, instead. I have hope if the raft lasts. Will it last? The sea continues to attack. It does not always give warning. Often the curl develops just before it strikes. The roar accompanies the crash, beating the raft, ripping at it.

I hear a growl a long way off, towards the heart of the storm. It builds like a crescendo, growing louder and louder until it consumes all of the air around me. The fist of Neptune strikes, and with its blast the raft is shot to a staggering halt. It squawks and screams, and then there is peace, as though we have passed into the realm of the afterlife where we cannot be further tortured.

Quickly I yank open the observation port and stick my head out. *Solo*'s jib is still snapping and her rudder clapping, but I am drifting away. Her electrics have fused together and the strobe light on the top of her mast blinks goodbye to me. I watch for a long time as the flashes of light become visible less often, knowing it is the last I will see of her, feeling as if I have lost a friend and a part of myself. An occasional flash appears, and then nothing. She is lost in the raging sea.

I pull up the line that had tied me to my friend, my hope for food and water and clothing. The rope is in one piece. Perhaps the loop I had tied in the mainsheet broke during the last shock. Or the knot; perhaps it was the knot. The vibration and surging might have shaken it loose. Or I may have made a mistake in tying it. I have tied thousands of bowlines; it is a process as familiar as turning a key. Still . . . No matter now. No regrets. I simply wonder if this has saved me. Did my tiny rubber home escape just before it was torn to pieces? Will being set adrift kill me in the end?

Somewhat relieved from the constant assault on the raft, I chide myself in a Humphrey Bogart fashion. Well, you're on your own now, kid. Mingled with the relief is fright, pain, remorse, apprehension, hope and hopelessness. My feelings are bundled up in a massive ball of inseparable confusion, devouring me as a black hole gobbles up light. I still ache with cold, and now my body is shot through with pain from wounds that I've not noticed before. I feel so vulnerable. There are no backup systems remaining, no place to bail out to, no more second chances. Mentally and physically, I feel as if all of the protection has been peeled away from my nerves and they lie completely exposed.

STORM

JOHN RIDGWAY & CHAY BLYTH
(1938–) & (1940–)

English soldiers. In 1966 they rowed the Atlantic in an open dory,
English Rose III.

By the end of my 'stag' the breeze had freshened to a steady wind, and when John next woke me to replace him at the oars a big sea was running and I had to shout to make myself heard above the noise of wind and waves.

John pointed to the sky. Heavy black clouds were racing low, overhead, and I felt the first big spots of rain on my face.

'I don't think I've made any headway at all in the last hour,' John bellowed in my ear. 'If anything, I've been losing ground.'

'Well, let me give it a try,' I shouted back. 'The wind's pretty strong, so perhaps the storm will blow over quickly.'

He shrugged his shoulders and crawled under the canvas. I did not really believe the storm would pass over quickly, but hated to admit right at the start that my two hours' slogging at the oars was not going to carry us more than a few yards nearer home. It was depressing to work so hard and know that gradually, hour by hour, the sea was pressing us back to the West.

The slamming jar of the waves on the end of the oars at the start of every stroke had an accumulative effect on both mind and body when the wind was in the East. It was a form of punch drunkenness. I found I could sit there for an hour without a single thought in my head and be so little aware of the soreness of my hands that my arms might have been ten yards long.

At those times the brain worked slowly, but the imagination was a vivid thing, and I terrified myself with thoughts of primeval creatures rising from the incredible depths to seize and destroy our boat. When in this condition neither of us wanted our food. The pummelling from the oars combined with fear and tiredness to kill our appetites.

That day marked the beginning of a new phase in our voyage. Far from passing over quickly, the storm lasted for nearly a week. For three days and nights we were unable to row and unable to sleep. We had both known fear many times before in our lives – but never anything like this. The sea was like something out of hell. Lacking keel, sail or motor, we could not keep 'Rosie's' head into the sea, and she thrashed piteously like a mad dog in convulsions. We knew that this could not be over tomorrow, or for many tomorrows. It was like being rubbed down with rough sandpaper.

By then we had lost track of how many storms there had been, knowing only that each one left us progressively weaker and one step nearer defeat. At 2 p.m. on 27 July we shipped oars and hauled the mildewed canvas canopy into place on its metal frame. There was no longer any use trying to disguise the fact that we were running into trouble.

The situation was already serious. That morning while trying to pick up a BBC news bulletin a freak wave had broken right over the boat and swamped our radio. We tried to persuade ourselves that it had only been temporarily put out of action. But neither of us really believed this.

'Perhaps when it's had a chance to dry out it will be all right,' said John. 'The water has probably got to the points and it is shorting out.'

'And if it doesn't work?'

'Then we'll just have to rely on the watches to time our sighting,' he said. 'I expect they're pretty accurate. And if they're not there's damn all we can do about it now.'

Until then we had been able to check and reset the watches by the radio time signals. They had never been more than a few seconds out. But in three weeks those seconds could mount up and eventually cause a serious error in calculating our position.

Our log notes were running to double the length of previous entries. We scribbled away in the hope that by writing down our problems we would unload some of the worry.

On Thursday, 28 July John wrote: 'As darkness falls it is apparent that we are unable to row any longer, as each changeover between men entails a swing off course, and the energy required to bring her back is too much.

'All the time we are slowly slipping back. As we eat our curry and drink our cocoa we decide to slip the sea anchor . . . We have been almost stationary for so long there are several small fishes under the boat, and as I put the sea anchor over Blyth tries to sniggle one in best Scottish fashion. The fish is about eight inches long and fairly deep and mottled brown and white in colour.

'We didn't catch it. Neither of us wanted our food. This was caused in me by an amalgamation of pure fear and seasickness. We now realise our position and are both simply afraid. With the sea anchor over we both curl up under the canopy in the stern – both wet before it started. The salt is extremely irritating to our skin, and the position very cramped and a nightmare for anyone who suffers from claustrophobia. A grim, grim day.'

My own log was equally stark. 'We have been rowing against this south-east wind now for three days,' I wrote. 'Now we've reduced it to one hour on and one hour sleeping. My hands are very sore indeed. I can't clench my fists. It seems all the tendons and muscles and all my fingers have been pulled. Before I start my hour's sleep I put lanoline on my hands, but they are so painful it doesn't seem to help. When I wake up it's a nightmare those first few minutes. My hands won't do anything. When you take a stroke you get this fantastic jerk on your arms and hands. How I pray the wind will change to the West.

'There's been some fish following us all day. When we throw

some paper over the side they dart out to it and then back to the stern. We rowed all day and then the seas gradually built up. At 10.00 GMT it was getting dark and the seas were very large by this time. We decided to put over the sea anchor. The first time for over a month or more – I can't really remember. The night was spent in the two sleeping positions. Very uncomfortable and not a great deal of sleep. I got soaked all down my legs and behind. The water rushed in under the canopy into my boots and down my trouser leg. This only happened once, but it was enough.

'We used water bags inflated as pillows and to put next to us where something would be sticking into us. I slept next to the pumps, but was very lucky. I only had to get up four times to pump out. I only hope the sea anchor holds the night.'

On 29 July we emerged only once from beneath the canvas canopy, and that was to check the sea anchor. To have lost it at that point would have been a disaster. For nothing could have stopped us being blown West with the wind, and we could easily have lost fifty miles.

We spent the day huddled together in the stern in a space measuring no more than five feet by four feet. John felt very sick and tried to sleep as much as possible.

The waves were like mountains and bigger than any we had seen up till then. Their tops were sliced flat by the wind, and they came towards us frighteningly fast and with a noise like a plane on full throttle. We learned to judge by their speed and sound which waves were going to pass under us, which would break into the boat and which would hit us smack on.

The constant battering of hundreds of pounds of falling water on the canvas canopy finally proved too much for the metal frame. It collapsed and introduced yet another form of personal discomfort. We tried to prop the edges up with two stout poles from our emergency kit. Every half minute or so the wind would lift the canvas. The poles would dislodge and the whole soggy mess would come tumbling down on our heads. We were driven almost to the point of hysteria.

Again I think it is worthwhile quoting from our logs to explain the full misery of that day. Nothing I can add now would so completely capture the events and feelings we experienced.

Wrote John: 'The sea anchor seems to hold well – I believe because it does not have a rigid ring at the mouth, but can "breathe" like a parachute.

'As night draws on we think of Samuelson and Harbo and how they rowed into a great easterly wind for two days and then lay exhausted at sea anchor – an exact parallel to our present circumstances. On the third night they were overturned. We believe *English Rose III* to be more seaworthy.

'Tonight we lie and wait – nothing could save us if we get into difficulties. No ship could get us off these seas, even if it arrived in time. We are completely in God's hands, at the mercy of the weather. All night the wind screams louder and louder and the sound of the sea becomes louder. We talked of many things, the night train to Scotland, the things we had done. And slowly we were overtaken by an enormous feeling of humility and the desire to return and try to live a better life.'

I noted a similar conclusion in my own log.

'We stayed in our beds all day. You really start thinking of the good things in your life. A lot of humble pie can easily be eaten in a situation like this. There's only one word for it – nightmare.

'We often think of Johnstone and where he is. How fortunate for him he has a cabin. If both boats make this I'll shake his hand. If he's having it the same as us, as he must, he's having it rough. We ate very little. No hot meals. We would have had to move everything to cook. The best way round this is to sleep. The sticks that kept the canopy up kept falling down. The wind would lift it a little and it would come down and hit us on the head about five times a minute. It would drive you to the point of getting angry – which I did. About 18.00 I got up to check the sea anchor. Okay. Pump out. I looked at the waves. They were huge. The biggest we've had so far. This must surely be the effect of the hurricane. It was almost white everywhere I looked.

'At 3.00 hours we were wakened by the storm. The wind howled and the waves crashed against the stern and bow. Whack! It would hit the boat – but "Rosie" took it all. What a boat this is, wonderful. The dorymen certainly knew what they were talking about.

'I pumped out very few times. Awful.

'You could hear the waves roar like an engine coming towards you, crash into you, then roar off into the night. Then the next one. Only one thing for it. Sleep then prayer. God comes close to you out here.

'You have three feet on each side of you. Then death.

'I have never been so frightened before as I am here. I pray tomorrow that it will change. During the night I get fantastic pains in the knees. It came from them being bent for so long.

'We are now both sleeping on the side which is away from the wind so that the side nearest the wind is higher and helps stop the water coming over the side.

'My feet are numb. This must be the effect of the cold and the canopy resting on top of them. This canopy is continually wet now, laying on top of me. I can't get away from it.'

The Lord must have heard our prayers, for early the next morning – Saturday, 30 July – the wind shifted to the North-west. We hauled in the sea anchor, and with the waves decreasing by the minute, we were soon racing eastwards with John on the oars.

But the sea had not finished with us yet. As the afternoon dragged past the wind swung round to the South, and by early evening we were in the grip of another storm, having had no chance to dry out and still reeling from tiredness and exposure.

The seas rapidly climbed to enormous proportions and life became a constant nightmare once more. For John the suffering was even more intense. He had developed a rash from knees to hips, and his neck was circled with salt water sores. the only thing in our first-aid kit which gave him any relief at all was foot powder – and we were already down to our last tin.

During the night it began to rain and the winds grew even fiercer. Dawn found us weakening rapidly and almost crying from lack of sleep. We were weary now to be finished, but home seemed so far away. There was a growing desperation in both of us to put an end to it – but that we were unable to do.

For four days we had been soaked to the skin. The salt water worked its way into our sores and John's rash, and every movement meant further pain and misery.

Again the wind veered round to the West, but the storm continued without a let-up, and we saw nature performing tricks which defy logic. Great mountains, covered in icing sugar, marched endlessly towards the East, and we, thank God, were dragged along with them.

It is difficult to say which was worst, being on or off watch. The choice: to crouch soaking wet under a pile of streaming canvas or sit in the open wrapped in a dripping blanket. John looked exhausted with dark, sunken eyes, and I dreaded to think how I must look.

So we crashed on and on. Nothing mattered but to keep on going. 'Rosie' seemed like a thing alive. We hung precariously for long moments, balancing on the crest of a wave, surfing eastward with a speed that was terrifying yet wonderful. The dory took a terrible battering – but seemed to be indestructible. This fight against nature was going the whole distance, with only one round to the elements. A small hand-painted plaque was ripped from our stern.

It had been fastened there by George Hitchcock, a Cape Codder who gave us tremendous assistance in preparing for the crossing.

It was while I was out with George, taking lessons in rowing, that it suddenly dawned on me just what we were attempting. I turned to him and said, 'Three thousand miles. What the hell have I done?'

He had scored these words on the plaque along with another quote: 'Let's get bloody rowing.' It was a phrase we used often in the days preceding our departure from Cape Cod.

'Let's get bloody rowing,' we said, 'and get on with the job.'

I missed that tiny plaque, that and a nine-year-old letter from my mother and the last letter from Maureen were very comforting in moments of strain. Also the verse which the dorymen put on one of the watertight compartment doors:

> When at last I sight the shore,
> And the fearful breakers roar,
> Fear not, He will pilot me.

This I believed in.

Under the Ground

THE ABYSS

NORBERT CASTERET
(1897–1987)

French speleologist. In 1952 Casteret led the exploration of the deepest known chasm on land, the Pierre Saint-Martin pothole in the Pyrenees, during the descent of which Marcel Loubens lost his life. Two years later, Casteret returned to Pierre Saint-Martin to recover Loubens's body and continue exploration of the abyss.

I reached Pierre Saint-Martin on 3 August 1954, a whole day in advance of my companions. Two Spanish *carabiniers* stood near the entry to the pothole. These men were wrapped in heavy cloaks, for the weather was grey and cold as it so often was throughout that dreary summer. They had been on guard for several days, taking turns of duty with four others under the command of a lieutenant.

At the bottom of the shake-hole (a depression about 30 feet deep giving access to the narrow opening of the shaft itself) I could see the wooden cross upon which, in 1952, we had painted these words: 'In the depths of this chasm lies Marcel Loubens, fallen on the battlefield of speleology.'

Wind, rain, snow and sun had obliterated much of the inscription, and I noticed that the first line 'In the depths of this chasm lies . . .' had completely vanished. The coincidence struck me, and I chose to regard it as a favourable omen of our purpose: Loubens would rest no more in that vast, cruel abyss; we would succeed in bringing up his body, and give it Christian burial at long last in the cemetery of his native village. We had given his parents a solemn promise to that effect in 1952.

4 *August* The sun rose in a cloudless sky; and while the last of our party hurried up from the valley to the camp, pitched at an altitude of 5,800 feet, the drone of approaching aircraft could be heard. As in 1953, the Air Force and Parachute Regiment at Pau had kindly agreed to deliver our heavier and more cumbersome gear by parachute.

Three Junkers machines made several journeys to drop some fifty loads. They fulfilled their task with incomparable skill; for in spite of strong winds and the slope on which we were assembled, the multi-coloured parachutes came down literally into our arms. A single tourist plane carrying a press photographer, together with an observation-aircraft circled overhead throughout the morning. The whole business, in fact, looked like an aerial display staged for the benefit of all – shepherds, sightseers, speleologists, French and Spanish police. The most important and most fragile load came down in twin parachutes joined together, and landed gently on the grass. This was the duralumin container; it measured 7 feet 6 inches in length, and was made at the École Pratique at Bagnères-de-Bigorre to Lépineux's design.

Later in the day a convoy of mules brought up the remainder of our gear, which we stored near the shepherd's hut. For the fifth successive year the hum of activity caused by our arrival had disturbed the solitude and silence of the Pyrenees.

Tents sprang up like mushrooms; packing cases that lay where they had fallen from the air were now collected by members of the team, and by a crowd of trippers who lent a willing hand but who were obliged to beat a hasty retreat on the approach of bad weather. Mist rose stealthily from the valley and enshrouded everything. Torrential rain driven by an icy wind brought the day to a miserable close; reminding us that we were indeed high up on the western Pyrenees, where the Atlantic gales provide an annual rainfall of something like ninety-six inches. Lévi had warned us in the circular letter before the expedition: 'Waterproof clothing will of course be no less essential in the surface camp than at the bottom of the chasm.'

5 and 6 August These were days of preparation, during which everyone worked hard at all kinds of jobs; laying telephone lines; erecting the heavy winding-gear at the mouth of the shaft; repairing tackle which had been damaged in transit; packing materials and foodstuffs for use underground. Last, but not least, our cooks got busy laying out their kitchen.

There were twenty members of the team. Most of us had not met for twelve months; for the Groupe Spéléologique de la Pierre Saint-Martin, which includes men from all over France and Belgium, makes a point of foregathering only once a year, on the occasion of its summer campaign.

6 August The Spanish lieutenant climbed up from his little camp 220 yards from the pothole. His manner was quite formal; he simply wanted a full list of the party. Then, to our absolute amazement he gave us official notice that the Spaniards would take no part in the expedition, and that we must confine ourselves to recovering Loubens's body – there must be no further attempt to explore the chasm.

By nightfall, Queffelec, with his assistants, Rossini, Isola, Accoce and Laisse, had got the winch into position. Pierre Louis, our official engineer, set a pulley-jack at the entry to the great vertical shaft. All was now ready, and the descent could begin.

I had again volunteered to go down first, both as a matter of principle and also to clear the cornices of fallen stone. This particular chasm, is still in process of formation; from year to year masses of rock break off from the walls and pile up in dangerous heaps on the balconies and smaller overhangs. Lépineux, however, had determined to lighten my task by cleaning the first platform, 257 feet down. He reached it without mishap, and set to work with an American army shovel, conversing with us over the telephone. Meanwhile I was at the receiving end, not far from the winch; I took note of all he said, and I must say it surprised me. Considering he had himself cleared this same balcony, which inclined sharply downwards, he was amazed by the amount of debris that had accumulated since 1953. He spent a good two hours throwing down lumps of rock; and I could hear his gasps of astonishment as he realized the extent to which the interior of the chasm had disintegrated.

You see, nothing can fall into the shaft from outside; the entrance is far too narrow, and opens like a dormer window in a vertical wall of rock. All this debris with which Lépineux had to deal came from *inside*, through 'chimneys' and smaller flues crammed with stones. These were gradually dislodged by the trickling water and erosion, and fell into the shaft.

As darkness fell it grew cold, a keen wind blew, and a dismal fog lay heavy on the mountain. 'Real Pierre Saint-Martin weather,' as someone had remarked as we returned to camp for the night. A small, solitary tent drowned in mist, and shaken by angry squalls, is not an enchanting or invigorating place.

Alone, rolled up in my sleeping-bag, I could still hear within me those subterranean avalanches hurtling downward, smashed to fragments at terrifying depths. I saw myself tomorrow, within a few short hours, hanging from a thread in that huge shaft which a Parisian journalist has so aptly described as 'the Eiffel Tower poised on the towers of Notre-Dame'.

7 *August* A bright, sunny day. I could hear sheep-bells in the neighbouring fold; there were voices too, one of them Etchebarre's. That worthy *gendarme* was busy sending radio messages by short-wave to Saint-Engrâce in the valley.

Attention was before long concentrated upon the shake-hole, where Queffelec shouted to his assistants and then asked in a tremendous voice: 'Anyone for the lift?' 'Shan't be long!' I called back, knowing to whom his question was directed. Then, while the rest of the party moved towards the chasm, I disappeared into a stone hut where the provisions were stored. Henri Périllous, our cook, was busied about many things; he was the least talkative, but one of the hardest working members of our crew. Throughout our stay at Pierre Saint-Martin this frail, retiring youth of eighteen, ever willing and ever smiling, fulfilled a crushing task. He was always on duty, cooking at all hours of the day and night, or carrying pails of water from a distant stream. In fact, Henry Périllous had often to go down to the winch in the middle of the night with food for hungry workers who could not leave their job.

'Henri,' I said, 'I'm going down in half an hour'; and the good fellow at once lit another stove* and prepared me an excellent lunch. (It was unlikely that I should have another hot meal for a week!) I had even to refuse a second course; there was too much of it, and I was going to need all my resources of mind and body for my journey down the shaft.

It was 10 a.m. by the time I reached the shake-hole.

Before going down on a rope-ladder, I stopped for a word with Queffelec and to cast an eye over the winding-gear. Its strength reassured me; but not being an engineer I understood little of its complicated mechanism. Queffelec drew me aside, and, lowering his normally loud voice, pointed to the new steel cable on its drum: 'It's not as good as last year's,' he said. 'It's quite safe, of course, but the strands are not so tightly wound. I warn you, you'll spin round like a top.' This was confirmed by the physicist, Labeyrie, who joined us at that moment. Well, if the technicians said so, I was in for an uncomfortable time. But why worry in advance? I put on a bold front and reached the bottom of the shake-hole, feeling like a gladiator in the arena. Other members of the team were waiting there to harness me and help me through the narrow entry to the shaft. This year I had given much thought to my wardrobe. A good deal of snow had fallen during the

---

* These stoves were fuelled with butane gas.

winter; the spring had been wet; and we anticipated that the cascade, which begins 722 feet below the surface, would be particularly heavy. Accordingly, I wore woollen underclothing and two suits of overalls, the first rubberized and the outer one of stout canvas. Finally I unfolded a large square of highly elastic sheet-rubber, in the centre of which I had cut a hole about the size of my fist. I passed my head through this hole, and was thus arrayed in a kind of *poncho* which covered me down to the waist and fitted close to my neck without strangling me.

The general effect, it seemed, was rather odd: the thing resembled a large white waterproof table napkin, and made me look like an outsize baby about to eat its porridge! As in 1953, it was Bidegain who helped me on with the heavy parachute harness; I was no more than a puppet in those powerful hands, which lifted me clean off the ground to make sure that the breast-strap was properly adjusted and would cause me no discomfort. Delteil busied himself with my helmet, inside which he adjusted the earphones. He inspected my breast-lamp, and carefully fastened the mouthpiece on each side of my neck. 'That's important,' he remarked; 'otherwise you can't make yourself heard properly. I know, because I've got a huge Adam's apple!'

And now Pierre Louis, attentive and methodical as ever, was waiting for me at the entrance to the shaft. With ritual precision he attached me to the end of the cable by means of a climber's snap-hook. Henceforward I was linked to the winding-gear and its attendants who waited only for a signal to lower me.

I have already explained that the opening which gives immediate access to the shaft is so narrow and inconveniently placed that you have to be something of an acrobat to get in at all. Although one cannot go down Pierre Saint-Martin without luggage, the kitbags which everyone carried slung from each of the suspension straps were too bulky to pass the opening in that position. One had therefore to slip through oneself, and then wait on a narrow ledge 13 feet down until the two bags were lowered on the end of a rope.

I had just entered and reached –13 when the sky above me was darkened. I was surprised, and looked up. I could scarcely believe my eyes. There was a perfectly colossal sack being pushed through the hole. In due course it landed at my side.

'Lévi,' I called up, 'I told you not to overload me; how do you expect me to clean up the shaft with all this tied round me?'

'I'm sorry,' he replied, 'but you'll have to forgive me. You know the chasm as well as I do, and you know how I go to work. One must be prepared for anything; you may be alone down there for several days, and that bag contains only your minimum requirements of tackle, food, and bedding.'

Another huge sack then arrived. Having to make the best of it, I hooked on these two monstrosities which were to weigh me down and prove a serious hindrance. Then I heard a suave voice from on high: 'Maestro, you've forgotten one small item'; and there appeared a heavy 6 ft 6 in board. It was Lépineux who bade me this gracious farewell. Reluctantly I tied the thing to my belt so that it would hang below me, and was just going to call 'Lower away!' when someone else spoke. This time it was a photographer, leaning over the edge and asking me to 'look up and smile nicely!' One must try to oblige everyone, and above all not disappoint the Press. I therefore looked up; but I feel sure my smile was somewhat formal and contracted!

At last I was free to take off. I gave the signal, and had travelled rather less than 65 feet when I came to a halt. 'What's up?' I asked. 'Oh, nothing much,' Queffelec replied; 'but we shall have to ask you to be patient for a few minutes while we change the motor.'

Change the motor! I thought at first he was joking, but he assured me that it was unavoidable.

'How long will you be?'

'Oh, twenty minutes to half an hour. Will you stay where you are or come up again?'

Without those damned bags and the board I would have remained where I was, hanging in mid-air. As it was, I asked to come up, though much against my inclination, for it was quite a business in itself, nor is it good for morale to stay proceedings at the last moment and have to begin all over again. The job of passing out my baggage and then extricating myself, not to mention the intense heat of the shake-hole, caused me to perspire heavily in my woollens and waterproof overalls – an unfortunate circumstance, considering that I would soon have to plunge once more into the icy chasm.

Sitting on the ground, tired and roasting in my shell, I kept quite still in order not to aggravate the perspiration. Bidegain came up with a look of mingled concern and amusement. 'Well, Casteret,' he asked, 'are you going to spend your fifty-seventh birthday underground this year?' My birthday! Why of course; last year I had celebrated it (if I may use that phrase) in the chasm – I made a mental calculation and suddenly exclaimed: 'Good heavens, no! Don't suggest such a thing; there are twelve days to go.'

Half an hour later I was going down again quite normally and at a fair speed. Lépineux talked to me over the phone, ready with advice and encouragement until I reached the bottom.

Despite the weight of my baggage, I had to admit that I had been most skilfully harnessed; I was almost comfortable. Moreover, Robert Lévi, who is for ever improving and perfecting, had substituted for the usual groin-straps and webbing of parachute harness a wooden seat and canvas back-strap. This was a distinct advantage; for whereas a parachute drop very rarely lasts more than a few minutes, our journeys might take several hours, during which the old equipment was liable to cause cramp, or at least a good deal of discomfort. Seated in the 'bosun's chair', I arrived at –257, and was glad to find that Lépineux had thoroughly cleaned up the sloping balcony. I unfastened my talisman, the board, and fixed it in position with a few sharp hammer blows. There it would constitute a little barrier which would stop and hold further falls of stones. I stepped over it, hung in mid-air, and gave the word, 'Lower away!' But some 12 feet lower down I ran into trouble.

'Stop! Stop!' I called.

'What's the matter?'

'Nothing serious, but I'm stuck in a crevice,' I replied, making violent efforts to free myself.

'Casteret, you've lost your way,' said Lépineux who knew 'his' pothole by heart; 'you should have taken the right fork, not the left.'

'I know; but these blasted kitbags have dragged me off the path down here. Haul me up a couple of yards.'

That was better; I had managed to release myself, and descended without further mishap to –425 where the shaft is full of crevices, fissures, and small ledges piled with rubble which I swept down into the void as I passed by.

While thus engaged I witnessed a phenomenon which, though not uncommon, is most alarming, particularly in that situation. My headlamp suddenly revealed a lump of rock poised on a balcony that sloped inwards. It stood on a bed of sand and wet gravel. Was I . . . No, there was no illusion; the thing was moving. The inclination of the shelf, and the water trickling over it, had caused the gravel-bed to shift. It began cascading over the edge, followed almost immediately by the projectile itself, which must have weighed about 12 lb. Instinctively, but to no purpose here, since I was alone in the shaft, I shouted, 'Stone! Stone!' then smiled at my own nervousness as I heard the missile ricochet and break to pieces far below . . .

From this point the shaft was very damp; the walls oozed moisture, and whenever I touched them with bare hands, I received a slight but most unpleasant electric shock through my earphones. I learned afterwards that it was due to defective insulation, which was remedied by Rossini, our electrician. Thus tormented, I came at length to –699. At first I hardly knew where I was, so greatly had the place altered since last year.

If Lépineux had been surprised yesterday at –257, I was staggered now by the pile of debris on this next 'balcony'. With only a small geologist's hammer slung from my belt, I experienced a sense of frustration, helplessness. Besides, there were those accursed bags hanging at my sides; they tired and almost paralysed me. Each of them weighed quite 44 lb, and I began to wonder what on earth Lévi had stuffed them with. It seemed he had packed me off with provisions for a month!

Never mind; I had my job to do, and I must get on with it. No less than two hours were necessary to complete this exhausting labour. During that time I struggled with feet and hands to dislodge, lift, and throw down rocks and small stones. The pile seemed never to diminish, and I was obliged at intervals to stop work and lie down, panting, between my sacks. I guessed they were becoming impatient up above; the delay must have appeared interminable, and they might well be asking whether I should ever reach the bottom. Thanks, however, to a loudspeaker erected near the winch, everyone could hear those avalanches of stone which I unleashed, and which incidentally were undermining my morale. It is not good to have to let loose repeated showers of rock inside a shaft, for they awaken the most dismal echoes which end by scaring even the most hardened explorer. As for the impatience of the surface team with those below, and vice versa, it is familiar to all speleologists.

Lépineux, who had spent more time in the chasm than on the surface, understood the difficulty of my task. He never lost his kindly calm.

'Hello! Lépineux. I've had to stop for a few moments to get breath. I can't go on.'

'That's quite okay. Take it easy; don't hurry,' he answered quietly.

At last, at the end of two hours harassing toil, I was ready to resume my journey. My next ordeal would be the waterfall, and then that horrible spinning motion which Queffelec had predicted. From now onwards I would be suspended in mid-air at the end of a new steel cable which, so they said, was going to turn unceasingly. But I was so relieved to have completed the previous chore, and so eager to get to the bottom, that I was not greatly disturbed by the prospect of a cold douche and whirligig.

'Hello, Lépineux, I'm just approaching the cascade.'

'Are you? Is it running strong?'

'No, it's extraordinary – a mere trickle.'

Yes, in spite of the heavy winter snows and a rainy spring, the cascade which had caused us so much discomfort on previous occasions, was insignificant. My beautiful rubber cape, thank heaven, was unnecessary! Of course I got wet; the water rattled on my helmet and shoulders, but nothing like so heavily as last year.

Lépineux asked me: 'By the way, are you spinning round?'

'Me? No, not at all.'

'Queffelec says you'll jolly soon be doing so.'

'Good, then I'll occupy myself counting the turns.'

As a matter of fact, on reaching the point where gyration formerly began, I started turning, but slowly, very slowly, then more slowly still – and it was over. I had counted only a few turns as against hundreds the year before. This new cable, which had been expected to twist so much, was very well designed and quite anti-gyratory. One should really not anticipate misfortune! And with that comforting thought I landed amid the huge boulders of the Salle Lépineux.

'Thanks, Queffelec, you've got me here in an armchair!'

The journey had taken me exactly three hours, and I was all in. I stumbled a few paces down to the bivouac, where I was at last able to relieve myself of my two bags and harness, and to exchange the ponderous flying helmet for my usual tin hat. I had entered again into possession of these halls which I had left twelve months ago.

At the foot of an enormous rock 65 feet high and 100 feet long, I found our reserve of tinned foods, calcium carbide, various accessories, and a few oddments. Nothing had changed, all was just the same as if we had been here a few days before. There was also a roll of telephone-wire; and I now attached one end of it to the terminal buckle of the cable, which would hence-forward be in almost continual motion between the Salle Lépineux and the surface. These journeys necessitated constant vigilance. Members of the team were for the most part lowered and brought up without a hitch; but in past years we had had a deal of trouble with the loose cable owing to friction and fouling, and to prevent these delays we had to keep it taut. I was doing that now, paying out the wire a little at a time as the cable rose, and holding it straight.

While the cable was being wound up, my telephone was out of use; but as soon as that operation was finished I could unpack an instrument from my kitbag and connect it to the wire. Alas! last year's mishap was repeated. I was carefully unrolling the wire, like an angler paying out his line, when I felt it go limp in my hand. That well-known whistling sound gave warning, and pierced me to the heart. The wire, of course, had broken; it fell at my feet looking like a tangled wig.

I was now cut off altogether. I wondered, too, whether the cable was continuing its upward journey, or was jammed some-where in a crevice. I should have to kick my heels until the next man arrived; and he might be delayed for a host of reasons. All I knew was that my first companion would be Robert Lévi, than whom it would have been impossible to find a more strenuous and conscientious leader. He had insisted on coming down to consider the difficulties of exhumation, to take part in it, and to assess the problem of raising the container.

For want of something better to do, I started to unpack my kitbags, and was immediately grateful for Lévi's solicitude and experience. There was a butane gas stove, a thermix heater, a telephone instrument (at the moment useless), and a heap of foodstuffs ('iron rations') . . . Suddenly I dropped everything and made a dive for the wall. I had caught sight of a magnificent amber-coloured beetle; it was scared, and moved rapidly, but I caught it in a matchbox. Not being an entomologist, I had none of the correct glass tubes. But lying on the ground was a used bottle of excellent Martinique punch left over from last year. Sufficient liquid remained in which to drown the insect. It was a splendid specimen of the extremely rare *Aphaenops Loubensi* which Prof. Jeannel of the Musée de Paris had classified in 1953 as a new species.

The disposal of my luggage and the capture of the insect was not enough to occupy my leisured solitude, so I decided to relax for a quarter of an hour and take a rest. I was suffering from fatigue and nervous tension, but the effect of stretching myself out on the floor was opposite to that which I expected. I became more than ever on edge; besides, the low temperature and dampness of the chasm is intolerable unless one keeps moving about. I got up and walked down to the tomb, and from there went on to the site of last year's camp. The same bits and pieces lay scattered about; a battered helmet, a torn mattress, some empty tins, etc. . . . It was all very dreary, so I climbed back to the bivouac, stopping for a moment and holding my breath to listen for a voice or a falling stone in the great shaft. Nothing moved. I then decided to fill in time with a meal . . . Some lumps of rock came whistling down, and I ducked behind a large boulder. A mouthful of food had given me new heart, and those flying fragments told me that someone was coming down. It was 6 p.m.; I waited anxiously for the least sound, and felt glad that Lévi would soon land at my side.

But at midnight I was still waiting, and asked myself for the hundredth time that inevitable question: 'What the hell are they doing up there?'

In desperation, I put on an extra sweater under my overalls, lay down on a slab of rock, extinguished my lamp, and tried to sleep. Lévi's descent must have been postponed for some good reason until tomorrow.

At 2 a.m., as I tossed and turned on my rocky bed, there was a feeble cry far up in the shaft. Half an hour later Robert Lévi touched down. At last! I had been expecting him for fifteen hours, and had almost given up hope. He told me that he had been delayed time after time, but had determined to get down, no matter what the cost.

Sunday, 8 August Returning to the bivouac at about 9 a.m., we were able to phone the surface; for the cable had not been wound up again since Lévi's arrival. When the time came for its departure, we again unrolled the guide-wire. Again it broke, leaving us in isolation!

We were resigned to our situation, hoping the cable would reach its destination before long, and certain of our programme. Delteil was to come down next; he had volunteered for the delicate and unpleasant task of bringing down the metal coffin . . .

At about 8 o'clock that evening a small avalanche of stones informed us of Delteil's approach.

Flushed with excitement after his memorable journey, Delteil was magnificent. He had battled all alone in the great shaft for three hours, and looked like a *poilu* at Verdun, with feverish eyes, his face lined with fatigue, his harness in disorder, his overalls torn, and one of his hands bleeding.

Our next job was to bear the coffin to the tomb. After slipping and stumbling from top to bottom of the slope, we got it into position ready for the exhumation, which was to take place as soon as we were joined by Dr Mairey and Louis Ballandraux, who would not be down until tomorrow. It was now 11 p.m. We had done enough for one day, and therefore withdrew, dead-beat, to a little tent which was scarcely large enough for three. Although packed like sardines, we were soon fast asleep.

Monday, 9 August I awoke with a feeling that it was time to get up, and took a peep at my companions. Delteil, as usual was snoring hard, but Lévi, to judge by his breathing, was awake.

'Lévi, what's the time?' I whispered, switching on my torch discreetly veiled in a handkerchief.

My neighbour stretched himself, looked at his wristwatch, and then put it sharply to his ear. 'It says 11 o'clock, but it's not going,' he replied. 'It must have stopped last evening.'

I had left my watch in a suit of overalls that were in my haversack, and this lay some distance from the tent which was too small to hold anything but us three. Having extricated myself from my sleeping-bag, I crawled out of the tent, pulled on my boots, and eventually retrieved my watch. Good heavens! . . . yes; the second-hand was moving, so the thing had definitely not stopped.

'Guess,' I said to Lévi.

'It's at least 8 o'clock in the morning,' he answered.

'Don't be absurd,' protested Delteil, who had just woken up. 'It's the dead of night!'

'Dead dark, certainly,' I rejoined, 'but believe me or not, it's midday!'

Neither of them would believe me at first; they thought I was joking. But it was a fact; down there in the chasm, where the temperature was no more than 7° Fahrenheit and the humidity 100 per cent, we had slept fully clothed in a tiny tent for thirteen hours! None of us had ever done anything like it, and we fell to discussing so memorable a feat. We were cut short by a formidable shower of stones.

'Hark! there's someone on the stairs,' said Lévi quietly.

'Another bloke dropping in for lunch,' added Delteil.

We hurried immediately to the bivouac, where Louis Ballandraux had just touched down, carrying two outsize kitbags in addition to his normal load.

During the afternoon we were joined by Doctor Mairey, who brought his medicine-chest, several pairs of rubber gloves, and various accessories. We now prepared to carry out the work of exhumation, and were shortly afterwards gathered at the tomb. In that unstable mass of rock, it took us several hours to construct a horizontal platform on which to lay the container and walk about.

There were only four pairs of gloves, so it was agreed that Delteil, who had badly lacerated hands, should be excused from touching the body. At 6 p.m. we began demolishing stone by stone, the great tumulus beneath which Marcel had been lying for two years, arrayed, as he had fallen, like a medieval knight. He wore his helmet, and, in place of the sword, a torch lay on his breast.

At 9 p.m., exhausted with fatigue and emotion, we removed our gloves. Delteil screwed down the lid, and we put forth what was left of our strength and determination to drag the heavy coffin to a point immediately below the shaft where in due course it could be attached to the end of the cable.

We had fulfilled our task, and it was now the turn of those who were to prepare the shaft for the container's upward journey. Lépineux and Bidegain went down to –257, Labeyrie and Rossini to –699. It had been calculated that their job would take two days.

The preparation of the balconies consisted in erecting near the rim of each a metal lattice girder 6 feet 6 inches long. These were meant to steer the container clear of overhangs, and thus avoid it becoming hung up or jammed in a crevice – events which might prove dangerous if not disastrous. Each girder was made of duralumin sections (another of Lépineux's ideas), and was fitted at its base with a spindle enabling it to swing from side to side, and at the opposite end with a stout wooden pulley to facilitate the cable's passage. Numerous stays, carefully placed and tightly stretched, assured the firmness and rigidity of the girder. Driving *pitons* into the rocky walls, in situations no less perilous than inconvenient, was a job whose difficulty was increased by the fact that our men were obliged to work beneath small but icy-cold cascades, consequent upon a series of violent storms which had transformed the shaft into an aqueduct. It was even necessary on several occasions to interrupt the work and hurriedly bring up the teams – for fear of lightning, which is attracted by potholes. The long steel cable hanging in the shaft would prove a dangerous conductor. On the evening of the exhumation, after pitching a tent for Mairey and Ballandraux, we were roused from sleep at about midnight by the roll of thunder which grew minute by minute; and the cascade in the shaft, swollen by an exceptionally heavy downpour, allowed us a glimpse of its awful possibilities. At the same time, another sound, even more alarming, rose from the depths. This was the subterranean torrent in flood, growling below the chaos of rock. Hence the internal changes of the chasm – those traces of extensive flooding which we observed last year, and the collapse of boulders. The whole place roared, vibrated, and there were falls of stone. Pierre Saint-Martin was in labour; we were in a living chasm in full process of evolution.

Lying in absolute darkness, wrapped in our sleeping-bags under the frail and illusory shelter of our canvas tents, the consciousness of our weak and helpless state in the presence of this awful demonstration taught us an eloquent lesson of humility.

All things considered, we were lucky to escape with nothing worse than a restless night. Mairey and Ballandraux were in worse danger than the rest for their tent was pitched on a stretch of gravel, clearly the bed of a river which might at any moment have reappeared but was, in fact, absorbed by its own deposit before reaching our camp.

Tuesday, 10 August At 9 a.m. I went up to the bivouac with Louis Ballandraux who had brought down a wireless transmitter and was anxious to establish communication with the surface, for the telephone was still cut off. He managed to converse with Fr. Attout, thanks largely to the cable, which had been lowered to –699 and served as a conductor for the waves between that point and the outside world. Among other things, we learned that Mauer would be joining us later in the day. He landed at noon, carrying another two kitbags and a large roll of telephone-wire. Lévi, as chief of the expedition, was now required on the surface; he went up trailing this after him, and we looked forward to re-establishing contact with those above.

In the normal course of events three more of us would have followed Lévi without further delay; only two men would be needed to attach the coffin to the cable and assist at its take-off when the moment arrived. As it was, however, we had other plans.

We had been categorically forbidden to do any more exploring, and were supposed to limit our activities to recovering Loubens's body. From the very start we had considered these instructions as an unjustifiable abuse of authority; we had signed no undertaking, and it was therefore with an easy conscience that I decided upon my own responsibility to ignore them.

The finding of this pothole had been the climax of a search begun by E. A. Martel in 1908, and continued at intervals between 1925 and 1950 by the Groupe Spéléologique de la Pierre Saint-Martin led by Max Cosyns and myself. Lépineux had actually made the discovery; Loubens, another member of the group, had died here; and Dr Mairey had been the victim of what might easily have been a fatal accident. So Pierre Saint-Martin was in a very real sense 'ours', and to go home without trying to explore upstream would have been a miserable surrender of our rights. In any case, we could not have restrained the determination of fellows like Mairey, Mauer and Ballandraux. Besides, to finish the job was surely the noblest honour we could render to poor Loubens's memory.

A party set out at 4 o'clock in the afternoon; it consisted of Mairey, Ballandraux and Mauer. I stayed behind with Delteil, one of whose hands had been badly lacerated.

I had no fears as I watched the other three disappear from sight. All were highly trained and well-tried speleologists.

Our companions had been gone an hour when I climbed that mass of cyclopean boulders in the Salle Lépineux which they had now left behind, and through which Mairey and I had begun our journey upstream (due south into Spanish territory) twelve months ago. My immediate purpose was to revisit a platform of rock where I knew there was a colony of diptera, a kind of mosquito. Lost in this immensity, they had for some unknown cause, taken up residence just here, where I soon found them. Isolated from one another, and quite motionless, they look so easy to catch, but as soon as you approach with a light, they scurry sideways over the rock – like crabs. When they become conscious of imminent danger, they take to flight and then you begin to appreciate their unwillingness to use their wings. They are poor flyers, with an uncertain, dipping movement; and they soon come to rest on the floor or on another rock, but always below their starting-point. Their clumsy flight is due, of course, to atrophy of the wings consequent upon their surroundings, and I have no doubt that in another few thousand years these strange mosquitoes of Pierre Saint-Martin will be wingless. The few that I caught were destined for the microscopes in the Musée de Paris.

During my stroll I came across a short strip of Scotch-light, a piece of cloth treated with reflecting material in the form of powdered catadioptric glass. It was a guide-mark left by Mairey and his companions. These objects, when strategically placed, enable one to go ahead without fear of losing one's way on the return journey through the complicated maze of debris. I followed the trail of these guideposts until I heard the voices of my friends. They were looking for a road to the head-waters, but repeatedly found their passage blocked by boulders reaching to the ceiling. I felt certain, as they did, that once they had overcome these difficulties, and pierced some gap in the wall, they would find the chasm extended for some considerable distance.

I returned to the bivouac. Delteil was busy patching his overalls; they had suffered badly during his descent with the container and were actually in rags. We employ somewhat original tailoring methods at Pierre Saint-Martin; holes are made in the material with the point of a knife, and telephone-wire takes the place of thread. While Delteil was thus engaged I sat on the ground beside him and made a few entries in my notebook. Suddenly we heard a noise high up in the shaft, as of someone falling. It grew louder; and as we ducked, a body landed with a terrifying crash at a distance of 13 or 14 feet on the debris slope. From there it rolled out of sight. Horror-struck and trembling, we jumped up and hurried down to find the unhappy man who had just been killed before our very eyes. Delteil pulled up sharply and bent over a contorted mass. Then he stood erect with a shout of laughter. Thank God! The victim of that dreadful fall was only a large kitbag which had escaped from its owner at –699 and fallen 436 feet to the bottom. It had burst open, and we picked up a number of articles, including a camera (which as you may guess, was useless). We knew then that the bag belonged to Vergnes. Having recovered from the shock, we resumed our peaceful if trivial occupations.

Presently Robert Vergnes himself came down and joined us. His arrival was far more sedate than that of his kitbag. Mairey, Mauer and Ballandraux returned soon afterwards, pleased with their reconnaissance and tremendously excited. They had managed with some difficulty to pass the danger zone, where rocks and ceiling met, and found, as I had predicted, that the gigantic wilderness of rock extended much farther.

Our commandos had done a fine job, and had turned back in order to make their report. I was thrilled, and determined to lead a party on the following day as far as it was possible to go.

Wednesday, 11 August This was to be the day of days – if one may speak of 'day' in places where there is no dawn. It would provide an answer to that question we had left unanswered for a year: did the chasm reach into Spanish territory; and if so, how far?

Pierre Saint-Martin consists of a shaft, 1,135 feet deep, giving access to an enormous cavity through which flows a subterranean river. In 1953 we had travelled downstream for a distance of nearly two miles and to a depth of 2,388 feet in French territory. How far would we get today, through the chaos of its head-waters, into Spain?

The whole team, excepting Vergnes and Delteil, set off at 8 a.m. We expected to be absent for at least a day, perhaps two if all went well. On leaving the bivouac we had to climb in heavy kit up that mountain of boulders, which stands at the near end of the Salle Lépineux, and then descend the opposite face, guided by Scotch-lights which Mairey had laid yesterday. Presently the doctor pointed out one of these signposts lying on a rock which was not on our present track. It was of a pattern used last year, and I recognized it as marking the spot where he and I had forced our way into the heart of the wilderness.

Mairey smiled as we passed that Scotch-light which had so nearly marked the end of his career as a speleologist; and before long we reached the summit of a rise which we had to descend with the help of an electron ladder. This manoeuvre brought us out from the labyrinth into a colossal chamber, so vast and tortuous that we could make out neither its size nor its shape. It was perfectly stupendous, exceeding all conceivable dimensions, far transcending human architecture.

'Since we are now in Spain,' I said, 'let us call this prodigious chamber "Salle de Navarre"; territorially the name is correct, and it will be a gesture towards our Spanish friends who had hoped to be with us on this occasion.'

I have travelled a good deal in Spain, especially in the mountainous province of Navarre, but I can safely say that I have never seen in the whole of the Peninsula so wild a stretch of country as that through which we now advanced by lamplight. Here Earth's structure, which so fascinates Delteil, is set forth on the grandest scale. The journey became so arduous and complicated that we had to make alternate use of ropes and wire ladders in order to negotiate precipice-roads or steep cliffs.

Mauer was lagging behind when he suddenly called for help. We turned round and saw him kneeling, apparently in difficulties on the sloping ground. But there was nothing wrong; he was interested in something quite different from the recovery of his balance. Considering this fearful desert of rock, his eyesight was most remarkable, for he had noticed an insect – a superb *Aphaenops Loubensi* which Mairey recognized as a giant of the species. Taking from his entomologist's pack a small wet paintbrush, he caught the beetle, and put it in a tube of alcohol. It was the fifth specimen to fall into our hands in two years. Animal life, of course, does not abound here; conditions are too severe to make existence anything but precarious.

We should really have been gaining height, since we were travelling upstream. In point of fact, however, we had spent most of our time going downhill. Ballandraux was walking ahead; or rather he was tumbling and jumping from rock to rock, for the ground seemed to consist mainly of pits, fissures and crevasses. He had just made a neat landing on top of a great tubular rock, when we realized with horror that the thing had begun to swing forwards. Then, as in a dream, we saw Ballandraux raised higher and higher into the air. Here was an example of those swaying boulders known as 'Crazy Stones'.

Having recovered from his surprise, Ballandraux purposely renewed the see-saw movement, the effect of which was amplified by the height and mass of the rock. We called 1 'Roche Ballandraux', and each enjoyed a spell of its majestic oscillation.

We might also have exercised the privilege of pioneers and named the huge gallery through which we now proceeded over jagged ground. Our attention, however, was riveted upon the difficulties of progress and of finding our direction, so that we had neither the leisure nor the freedom of imagination to assign names and titles to the places through which we passed.

At this point the torrent flows quite close to the surface, but is still hidden by great boulders beneath which you can hear it rumbling. We were already moving uphill; but the way before us involved an exhausting climb to the level of the ceiling, so we decided to call a halt and have some lunch. Nearby was a small cascade, issuing from the wall; it was a tributary of the main stream, but with a temperature of 7° Fahrenheit it was not much use for diluting the concentrated milk, of which Mairey had produced several tubes from his haversack. I proceeded to distribute pieces of sausage, which Ballandraux cut into rounds with the blade of a metal saw. Having no bread, we rounded off our meal with two packets of dry cake, and then moved on. Presently my companions led me into a narrow passage, on the ceiling of which there were numerous stalactites which did not greatly impress me. I told them so quite frankly; they were shocked, and put me down as blasé!

Yesterday's journey had ended at this point. But the system extended farther in undiminished grandeur; the way continued rough and downhill. We now separated, and each took a different path in order to check up on and eliminate blind alleys. After several reconnaissances and a brief council of war at the rallying point, it was clear that Mauer had found the right track. We followed him over some very rough ground into a winding corridor where we found the river. We advanced first on one bank and then on the other, sometimes on natural bridges and perilous overhangs. It was a strenuous and exciting journey, and we longed to know where it would lead us. At every bend, at every barrier of rock, we quickened our pace to seek what might lie beyond, and to assure ourselves that yet more distant perspectives opened out beneath those mysterious vaults. So far, however, we had kept our heads. The obstacle which now met our gaze was enough to daunt the bravest of the brave.

We had been walking for some minutes on banks that narrowed steadily above foaming rapids. Suddenly the river became deep, and flowed between vertical walls of smooth rock. We could go no farther, except by swimming in that icy water at a temperature of about 20° F, sufficient to cool the most determined hot-head! We had no collapsible boat, not even a raft; but we managed to balance ourselves on an isthmus of rock, which enabled us to advance a few yards and ascertain that 40 or 50 feet beyond that point the stream made a right-angled bend; its far bank was a sheer wall of stone. Considering its enormous width elsewhere, this section of the gallery was relatively small – 16 or 20 feet wide by about 13 feet in height. The contraction set up a violent current of cold air, a regular hurricane, which pierced us to the bone, extinguished our lamps, and churned the surface of the water. This wind, blowing at gale force, proves that the cavern extends for a great distance upstream; but the depth of the river constitutes an impassable barrier unless one has means of navigation. We had come as far as would be possible this year.

We had already started to retrace our steps, when I caught sight of a corridor running upstream and parallel with the river. I hurried in, hoping against hope that it might by-pass the deep water; but after walking for about 55 yards, I found that the ceiling came down to meet the floor while the walls huddled closer together. 'It's a cul-de-sac! There's no road here,' I shouted back to my companions who were ferreting about in a maze of secondary passages.

'Casteret! Come and look. Here are some wonderful stalactites.'

It was Mairey's voice. Stalactites! Fancy thinking about stalactites when we had just been brought to a halt in the most incredible cavern I had ever seen! Sadly, I turned back, conquered by deep water on one side and by a cul-de-sac on the other. My three companions, on the other hand, seemed already to have forgotten their disappointment; they were talking excitedly and admiring their 'wonderful stalactites'.

'Casteret, do come here,' Mairey insisted, 'and tell us what you think of them.' I rejoined them, feeling not a little sceptical. In fact, I was in no mood to share their enthusiasm. But on raising my eyes to the ceiling, I quickly changed my tune. 'Good for you!' I cried, 'they're magnificent, extraordinary.' It is impossible to describe an outcrop of helictites; perfection is always indescribable. But as an expert crystallographer, who has visited more than one thousand caves, I unhesitatingly award the prize for rarity and delicacy to the stalactites of Pierre Saint-Martin.

It was growing late. We cast a final glance at the helictites, a final glance too at the deep water, and resumed our journey. At one stage Ballandraux, having unpacked his drawing pad, compasses and pencil, proceeded to map the chasm. Mairey and Mauer went ahead with the lamp upon which our surveyor based his readings. I stayed behind for the time being to give him light and a helping hand in awkward places. Between the four of us we worked out approximate distances and contours. Our reckoning was probably not far out, especially as sights were for the most part fairly short.

Our journey through the Salle de Navarre gave rise to some differences of opinion as to its real dimensions. In order to clear the matter up, I undertook a solitary excursion which led me over ridges of rock, gigantic crags, and 'Crazy Stones' that seemed ready to crash down at any moment. Finally, I lost myself in a veritable labyrinth of boulders, the end of which I could not see; and it was some time before I succeeded in rejoining my companions who, in spite of the Scotch-lights, had resorted once again to hair-raising feats of acrobatics in order to escape from the labyrinth.

We returned to the bivouac at 6 p.m. after a forced march and a regular display of acrobatics. It had taken us eight hours to cover the 1¼ miles there and back, which should give some idea of the difficulties involved. The cavern extended for 1,100 yards into Spanish territory; and that distance added to two miles on the French side, gives a 4,620-yard stretch of uninterrupted chaos so far explored.

Delteil and Vergnes, who had anxiously awaited the result of our expedition, informed us that work in the shaft was more or less up to schedule, although it was proving a most delicate and awkward business. It seemed, then, that the entire chasm had been a hive of activity. We sat around the oven and chatted while our one hot meal of the day was cooking.

But our joy and satisfaction was tempered by the presence of the coffin which shone through the gloom. It had never ceased to dominate our thoughts.

Thursday, 12 August Early this morning there was much ado in the tent occupied by Mairey, Mauer and Ballandraux. They rose, dressed, trimmed their acetylene lamps, drew their rations, and prepared to set off. The three of them were going to revisit the bottom of the chasm, which some of us had reached in 1953. Dr Mairey, who had formed one of the party on that occasion, and was therefore acquainted with the road, would take charge now. The newcomers, Mauer and Ballandraux, had been longing to make the journey; but this was to be more than just a pleasure-trip, and before they started I ran over the subjects upon which they were to make notes: topography, temperature, humidity, air currents, barometric pressure, and biology. They were also to take photographs.

Vergnes was bitterly disappointed that he was not going with them, but his camera was out of action, so he could do nothing in the way of making a film. He was to return to the surface some time this morning. The cable would soon be lowered, for we had been informed by telephone that someone else was coming down to join us. He arrived an hour later, and Vergnes went up almost immediately. Our visitor was Fr. Jacques Attout, who with Lorian of Charleroi formed the Belgian element which we always included in our Group. He confirmed Delteil's news that preparation of the balconies was well advanced in spite of difficulties. Numerous *pitons* were required to secure the girders, but storms on the surface were delaying work, which had frequently to be broken off. This year's campaign had been inaugurated under the sign of foul weather.

Fr. Attout and I traversed the Salle Lépineux from end to end and from side to side. Looking down into the shaft which gives access to the Salle Elizabeth Casteret, we saw a wire ladder; Mairey, Mauer and Ballandraux had fixed it there earlier in the day. An icy wind howled ceaselessly in this place, and was no encouragement to stay for long, so we returned to the bivouac where Delteil mounted solitary guard at the telephone.

'Father, there's a message for you,' he said as we approached.

'What about?'

'Your bishop has appointed you parish priest of some out-of-the-way place – I've forgotten its name.'

It was perfectly true; so you see the Pierre Saint-Martin telephone had its uses – when it worked!

At about 7 p.m. Fr. Attout unpacked a small case containing his priestly vestments, an altar stone, a chalice and other necessities for the celebration of mass. The altar was an irregular slab of rock. The servers wedged themselves uncomfortably between a vertical wall and a heap of boulders; Delteil lit the two small candles, and I laid the tiny cruets at my feet. Over his alb, etc. the priest donned a beautiful white chasuble with green orphreys; it was almost startling amid that wild, dark scenery. But if the altar was a wretched makeshift affair, and if we ourselves were ragged, dirty and unshaven after a week underground, 'it is the spirit that quickeneth'.

The celebrant told us that he was going to offer the Holy Sacrifice for the repose of Marcel Loubens's soul and for the success of the dangerous undertaking to which we had pledged ourselves. Mass then began, the coffin lying only a few feet from the altar.

An hour later Mairey's team came back, haggard and exhausted, but flushed with success. They had carried out their programme in full: having crossed the seven huge chambers and travelled more than 3 miles through an unimaginable chaos, they had reached the bottom of the cavern where the altimeter confirmed last year's reading of 2,388 feet.

Friday, 13 August I spent a restless night. At midnight and 1 a.m. Bidegain phoned to keep me informed of progress. At 2 o'clock he told me that work on the balconies was complete. Between then and 6 a.m. the men responsible for this achievement were raised to the surface. It was now the turn of those at the bottom, excepting two who were to attach the container to the cable and guide it past the great boulders of the Salle Lépineux after the take-off.

We had much difficulty with the cable on its downward journey, in spite of the guide-wire which was handled from below. Over and over again it became entangled on projections of rock, and had to be pulled this way and that before it was freed. At long last, however, it was in position, and I prepared to leave the cavern.

I had spent hours of alternate joy and sorrow, but one decision had yet to be made: what to do with a small crucifix hanging on the wall. On 13 August 1952, as Marcel lay dying at the bottom of the shaft, Father Atauri, a Spanish priest from San Sebastian who was among a crowd of spectators on the surface, had detached this cross from his rosary and asked Dr Mairey to lay it on the stretcher. Mairey had in fact nailed it to the wall nearby, and it had hung there ever since – a lonely symbol in the waste of that tremendous chasm. I was aware that it belonged to a rosary given to Fr. Atauri by his mother and of great sentimental value in his eyes, so I took it down and slipped it into my pocket-book.

At 2 o'clock in the afternoon I linked the snap-hook of my harness to the cable, gave the signal by telephone, and felt myself raised from the ground, turning, swaying in mid-air. On this my seventh consecutive day underground, I had reason to feel satisfied, but I was distinctly off-colour after that long sojourn in a cold, damp atmosphere, during which my diet had been, to say the least, unorthodox. Lack of sunlight, on the other hand, which is often supposed to cause lassitude and even claustrophobia, had had no ill effects. My eyesight had, if anything, improved; I had the vision of a cat by night.

Within fifty minutes I was out of the shaft, standing in bright sunshine beneath an azure sky. Willing hands stripped me of my harness; I climbed those last few yards of rope-ladder, and sat down by the winding-gear. Queffelec was still at the helm, cheerful, confident, and bold as brass. Nearby was a party of girls dressed in shorts, members of a holiday-camp, who eyed me with unfeigned curiosity from top to toe. Unwashed, unshaven, my drawn face smeared with clay, and overalls in shreds, I must have seemed to them a miserable specimen of humanity. Questions crowded one upon another, but I have only the haziest recollection of that half-hour.

I then strolled up to the camp, and was greeted at the cookhouse by Henri Périllous, who gave me the first proper meal I had been able to enjoy since entering the chasm. I returned to the winch and saw Henri Brosset go down to help Ballandraux attach the coffin. Delteil was then hauled to the surface, followed by Mairey. Father Attout was delayed by a tremendous storm which obliged us to postpone operations until next day.

Saturday, 14 August Fr. Attout came up at 6 a.m. during a hailstorm and in dense fog. Mauer was then hauled to the balcony at –699; Lépineux and Bidegain went down to join him.

This was Judgement Day, to which we had looked forward with hope and yet with dread. My thoughts were with Lépineux, Mauer and Bidegain making their last inspection of the gear. Queffelec adjusted his engine and the winch. It was almost zero hour. Lévi, wearing earphones, spoke hurriedly with the lads at –699, and then with the Salle Lépineux. Labeyrie crouched over the radio, ready to take over if the telephone should fail. Ballandraux and Brosset had just attached the cable to the head of the container, and the girder at –699 was in position. The stage was set.

At exactly 5 p.m. Lévi passed Lépineux's signal to the engineers, and Queffelec threw his engine into gear. The rise of tension was alarming; the machinery vibrated and slipped, the dynamometer showed 1,100 lb. But the container was off the ground, clear of the huge boulders, and was rising slowly. Every available member of the party stood by, as well as a few journalists. There were about fifteen of us all told, huddling together round the winch beneath the shelter of a canvas awning, while rain and hail poured down in torrents, driven by great gusts of wind. In spite of the weather, our attention was concentrated entirely upon the dynamometer and upon the cable as it wound slowly on the drum. We dare not speak. All eyes turned towards Queffelec whose smile had given place to a grim and anxious look. Gradually, however, he relaxed; his countenance cleared, and he gave his assistant Isola a friendly pat on the back.

'Well, it's coming up all right,' he said.

Yes, it was coming up all right. Progress was slow and painful, but it was progress, and our faces showed a lessening of fear.

We had regarded this phase of the journey as most critical; the initial haul had counted for so much, and the container had seemed at that moment so very far away. On second thoughts, however, the situation appeared different. Until now the manoeuvre had involved no danger of contact with the walls . . . The dynamometer jerked several times and startled us.

'It's nothing,' said Lévi. 'It's bumping against the wall every now and again, but there's worse than that to come.'

Holding the receiver of his telephone to the loudspeaker, he enabled us to hear the dismal sound of the container; it resembled a cracked bell. He spoke again into the mouthpiece:

'Approaching –699. Hello, Lépineux! Let me know as soon as you catch sight of it.'

'I see nothing yet; there's that sea of cloud below us . . . oh yes! Here it comes, like a ghost out of the mist.'

There was a dull, heavy sound; the container was in contact with the girder, and a few seconds later it had cleared that dangerous overhang. Lépineux and Mauer had had some anxious moments. One of the *pitons* had come loose; the girder had leaned over, and they had to use all their strength to avoid an accident and, perhaps, disaster.

The container was now dragged on to the balcony and made fast while Lépineux unhooked the cable and attached it to his own harness. Bidegain followed; they were going up to –257 to help with the remainder of the operation. Mauer was to remain alone at –699 and re-attach the container as soon as the cable had been lowered. His situation was fraught with peril. If there were a fall of stones, if the cable snapped, or if some other untoward incident occurred, he would be in the direct line of fire.

Lépineux had joined Bidegain and Rossini at –257 and together they made final preparations for the arrival and reception of the container. On the surface, bad weather continued unabated; we were drenched to the skin and buffeted by an icy gale. The Spanish *carabiniers*, of their charity and unasked, brought us great logs of dead pine wood. They managed also to light a brazier which bore us company throughout that night.

All subterranean work is terribly slow and complicated, and it was some time before the cable was lowered again and Mauer attached it to the nose of the container. Fortunately the telephone was working well; all messages were passed and repeated between –699, –257, and the winch. The next stage of the journey could begin. But just as Lévi was about to give Queffelec the signal, I motioned him to wait. I had glanced at the clock on the instrument board: it was precisely 10 p.m. 'Two years ago today at this very hour,' I said, 'Marcel died. Let's pause for a few moments.' Lévi nodded assent and passed my message to those underground. The whole party observed a minute's silence, drawing from the recollection of that tragedy in 1952 a stern resolve to succeed in their present task. Those of us on the surface were little more than passive, helpless spectators of the drama which now approached its climax.

Mauer had bidden farewell to the container. He was alone now at –699 where he was doomed to remain and suffer through long hours. Lépineux shall now take up the tale. Crouched with José Bidegain and Rossini at –257, he had checked up on the girder.

'The cable was rising; our eyes were glued to the pulley. "It must be getting close now, José," I remarked. "We shan't have long to wait." Rossini phoned the surface to ask for position. Queffelec answered that the container was at –525. At that critical point there was an angle of rock under which it might easily become jammed, and we began to have serious misgivings about the next stage of the journey.

'Almost immediately we were startled by a loud noise, and the cable stopped vibrating. Rossini snatched the telephone . . . The winch had ceased to turn, and the dynamometer had risen from 880 to 2,200 lb. Three times I had the container lowered and raised; three times it jammed, making a tremendous din. Lévi's voice held a note of grave anxiety: "What do you propose doing?" José and I looked at one another. Then I said: "Eat and think. We've got to take our time over this. How late is it?" "Nearly midnight," Lévi replied.'

Sunday, 15 August The crisis was upon us. The wind howled unceasingly, and rain gave place to heavy snow which froze us to the marrow. A journalist, crouching at my side, leaned over and said: 'Nature has unleashed all her forces; the storm, the mountain and the chasm are allied against you. It seems as if the malignant spirits of the place refuse to yield up their prey and Loubens back to you.'

It was clear to those underground, as it was to us gathered round the winch, that there was only one thing to be done: the auto-hoist was a last resource whose use had been foreseen as possible, although we had entertained secret hopes that it would not prove necessary. This appliance was devised by Queffelec. It was a sort of pulley-block, hanging from which a man could raise or lower himself by hand along a steel-wire cable – rather like a plasterer on the façade of a building. It has been very seldom used by speleologists, and requires special training. Before this expedition, Bidegain, Lépineux and I had agreed to practise with it in a small chasm and so familiarize ourselves with its use. As things turned out I had not been able to take part in these exercises on account of a fall while climbing. Lépineux had been obliged therefore to act as Bidegain's assistant; hence no one but José had so far used the apparatus, which requires a good deal of practice. As a precaution, all this gear had been stored on the balcony at –257. Here, then, Lépineux drove in expanding *pitons* to which the cable of the hoist was to be fixed. Bidegain now made himself fast, and his two companions watched him sink slowly out of sight.

Thanks be to God, the only member of the team qualified to use the hoist was a man of calm courage and herculean strength. He alone could have accomplished that overwhelming task. The lot had fallen upon him; he accepted it, and carried it out at the peril of his life and to the limit of physical endurance.

Having reached the container, he would have to release it and escort it on its way, hauling himself up meanwhile yard by yard, hugging the thing to himself and never letting go. I will let him tell the tale; his words far surpass any that I could write.

'On my way down I was haunted by one fear: would the great cable cross my slender thread, squeeze it against a rock, and cut it through? If that happened, there could be no hope: I must inevitably hurtle into space. I recalled Casteret's grave warning as he returned to the surface: "It is going to be a very dangerous operation . . . and I know what I'm talking about." However, I arrived safely at my destination, level with the coffin wedged beneath that cursed overhang. After some manoeuvring, which I directed by telephone, I succeeded in placing it in the position from which I judged it easiest to pass the ledge. Now for it: "Up!"

'With my back to the wall, pushing the massive weight with hands and feet, I got it past the obstacle. It was crushing me but it was going up. Foot by foot we rose together.'

Up there by the winch, half buried in the snow, we shared in spirit the torment of his gradual ascent. The acoustics were such that we could hear the coffin grind against the rock, the hand-chain of the hoist clicking as it moved, the heavy breathing of the man who worked it. Every now and then he would joke or try to joke, and even sang to cheer himself and reassure his wife, who was with us at the winding-gear and showed high courage notwithstanding mortal anguish in her eyes.

The engineers, however, were more worried than any of us. They understood the machinery and just how little more it could endure. At any moment it might fail, or the cable snap, and then . . . We guessed into what purgatory José's heart was plunged;

for not one of us understood more clearly than did he how near Death was hovering.

At times there was despair in his exclamations and his laboured breathing. Even more pathetic was the voice of faith, when he suddenly called out in Basque the Psalmist's words: 'Lord, from the depths I cry to Thee!'

His journey had begun at 1 a.m. At 4 o'clock the nose of the container touched the underside of the balcony where Lépineux and Rossini stood waiting. It had taken three hours to climb 257 feet.

Bidegain shall now resume his story.

'My next job was to steer the coffin past the edge of this platform. The girder, leaning to my left, showed me what I must do. Thrusting all my weight on to the right guy-wire, I dragged the girder into position.

'"Up!" shouted Rossini into the telephone, and the container rose accordingly. The *pitons* were bending, and I wondered would they hold. At long last, however, my burden rested on the balcony: I had made it! Then I collapsed, exhausted but triumphant.'

Yes, he had brought the container so far; but at what cost! The next stage of the journey must soon begin – the most difficult of all, for from this point to the surface the great shaft is a mass of points and blades of rock.

Before the convoy could set out on the last length of its ascent, we had to bring Mauer up. He was still at –699, and I must confess that during the excitement of the last few hours he had been well-nigh forgotten. Lévi shouted to him, but there was no reply. It was a dreadful moment.

'Hello, –257! Try to contact Mauer; he's not answering.'

Still there was no sound. Poor fellow, he had endured so long beneath those icy, pitiless cascades (against which he had unwisely failed to provide himself with waterproof clothing), that he was now half dead with cold. Bolted to the wall on a narrow ledge, he was in a state of prostration and practically unconscious. Aroused at length from his torpor, he was warned that the cable was on its way to pick him up; but it was repeatedly entangled or otherwise delayed, and took a very long time to reach him. Meanwhile, he suffered a relapse. Utterly exhausted and on the verge of desperation, he scarcely answered Lévi's frantic calls ... Eventually, however, at 7 a.m. he informed us that he had closed his snaphook on the cable and was ready to start. He was helped out of the shaft at 8.30 in a pitiful condition; but he had reached the bottom of the chasm, and held on through thick and thin.

Rossini came to the surface at 9 o'clock. Worn out, drenched to the skin, and numb with cold, he was assisted to his tent through a curtain of alternate rain and snow.

Apart from Brosset and Ballandraux (with whom for the moment we were not concerned, for they had turned in and were fast asleep in the Salle Lépineux) only two men remained in the shaft – Bidegain and Lépineux.

They were at –257, with the container tied down on the balcony; and there at about 9 a.m. a most extraordinary scene was enacted. These two bosom friends were heard over the telephone in acrimonious dispute. Lépineux was of opinion that Bidegain had done more than his fair share and was in no condition to proceed. He wanted to take José's place and escort the container with the hoist. Bidegain protested that he was perfectly fit, and that in any case no one but himself knew how to handle the apparatus. José won the day. Lépineux agreed to be hauled up. His face bore the marks of extreme weariness, cold, and nervous tension.

The rest is briefly told; Bidegain completed the terrible ascent, locked in combat with his tragic burden; but the difficulties appeared to increase in proportion as his endurance ebbed away. The container was repeatedly held up by one obstacle after another.

'Up a yard! . . . Stop!' he would say into the microphone.

'Another yard! . . . Stop!'

'Down a yard! . . . Stop! . . .'

And so it went on, José striving desperately to release the coffin, steering it with his body while he worked the hoist. His hands were bleeding; he was in dreadful pain; but he moved like an automaton rising yard by yard, foot by foot, through that last stretch of calvary. Another would have given in; Bidegain fought on to the bitter end. Immediately he reached the surface he collapsed. It was 2 p.m. Twenty hours had elapsed since the coffin started on its journey, and Bidegain had done battle with it for thirteen of those hours.

RAPTURE

JACQUES-YVES COUSTEAU
(1910–1997)

French naval officer, underwater explorer and film-maker. The inventor
of the aqualung, Cousteau used the apparatus to explore, in 1946, the
mysterious inland water cave of the Fountain of Vaucluse, near Avignon.

Our worst experience in five thousand dives befell us not in the
sea but in an inland water-cave, the famous Fountain of Vaucluse
near Avignon. The renowned spring is a quiet pool, a crater under
a six-hundred-foot limestone cliff above the river Sorgue. A trickle
flows from it the year round, until March comes when the
Fountain of Vaucluse erupts in a rage of water which swells the
Sorgue to a flood. It pumps furiously for five weeks then subsides.
The phenomenon has occurred every year in recorded history.

The fountain has evoked the fancy of poets since the Middle
Ages. Petrarch wrote sonnets to Laura by the Fountain of Vaucluse
in the fourteenth century. Frederic Mistral, a Provençal poet, was
another admirer of the spring. Generations of hydrologists have
leaned over the fountain, evolving dozens of theories. They have
measured the rainfall on the plateau above, mapped the potholes
in it, analysed the water, and determined that it is invariably 55°
Fahrenheit all the year round. But no one knew what happened to
discharge the amazing flood.

One principle of intermittent natural fountains is that of an
underground syphon, which taps a pool of water lying higher

inside the hill than the water level of the surface pool. Simple overflows of the inner pool by heavy rain seeping through the porous limestone did not explain Vaucluse, because it did not entirely respond to rainfall. There was either a huge inner reservoir or a series of inner caverns and a system of syphons. Scientific theories had no more validity than Mistral's explanation: 'One day the fairy of the fountain changed herself into a beautiful maiden and took an old strolling minstrel by the hand and led him down through Vaucluse's waters to an underground prairie, where seven huge diamonds plugged seven holes. "See these diamonds?" said the fairy. "When I lift the seventh, the fountain rises to the roots of the fig tree that drinks only once a year."' Mistral's theory, as a matter of fact, possessed one more piece of tangible evidence than the scientific guesses. There is a rachitic hundred-year-old fig tree hooked on the vertical wall at the water-line of the annual flood. Its roots are watered but once a year.

A retired army officer, Commandant Brunet, who had settled in the nearby village of Apt, became an addict of the Fountain as had Petrarch six hundred years before. The Commandant suggested that the Undersea Research Group dive into the Fountain and learn the secret of the mechanism. In 1946 the Navy gave us permission to try. We journeyed to Vaucluse on 24 August, when the spring was quiescent. There seemed to be no point in entering a violent flood if its source might be discovered when the Fountain was quiet.

The arrival of uniformed naval officers and sailors in trucks loaded with diving equipment started a commotion in Vaucluse. We were overwhelmed by boys, vying for the privilege of carrying our air cylinders, portable decompression chamber, aqualungs, and diving dresses, up the wooded trail to the Fountain. Half the town, led by Mayor Garcin, stopped work and accompanied us. They told us about the formidable dive into the Fountain by Señor Negri in 1936. He seemed to have been a remarkably bold type, for we were informed that he had descended in a diving suit with a microphone inside the helmet through which he broadcast a running account of his incredible rigours as he plunged one hundred and twenty feet to the lower elbow of the siphon. Our friends of Vaucluse recalled with a thrill the dramatic moment when the voice from the depths announced that Señor Negri had found Ottonelli's zinc boat!

We already knew about Negri and Ottonelli, the two men who had preceded us into the Fountain, Ottonelli in 1878. We greatly admired Ottonelli's dive in the primitive equipment of his era. We were somewhat mystified by Señor Negri, a Marseille salvage contractor, who had avoided seeing us on several occasions when we sought first-hand information on the topography of the Fountain. We had read his diving report, but we felt deprived of the details he might have given us personally.

The helmet divers described certain features to be found in the Fountain. Ottonelli's report stated that he had alighted on the bottom of a basin forty-five feet down and reached a depth of ninety feet in a sloping tunnel under a huge triangular stone. During the dive his zinc boat had capsized in the pool and slid down through the shaft. Negri said he had gone to one hundred and twenty feet, to the elbow of a siphon leading uphill, and found the zinc boat. The corrosion-proof metal had, of course, survived sixty years immersion. Negri reported he could proceed no further because his air pipe was dragging against a great boulder, precariously balanced on a pivot. The slightest move might have toppled the rock and pinned him down to a gruesome death.

We had predicated our tactical planning on the physical features described by the pioneer divers. Dumas and I were to form the first *cordée* – we used the mountain climber's term because we were to be tied together by a thirty-foot cord attached to our belts. Negri's measurements determined the length of our guide rope – four hundred feet – and the weights we carried on our belts, which were unusually heavy to allow us to penetrate the tunnel he had described and to plant ourselves against currents inside the siphon.

What we could not know until we had gone inside the Fountain was that Negri was over-imaginative. The topography of the cavern was completely unlike his description. Señor Negri's dramatic broadcast was probably delivered just out of sight of the watchers, about fifty feet down. Dumas and I all but gave our lives to learn that Ottonelli's boat never existed. That misinformation was not the only burden we carried into the Fountain: the new air compressor with which we filled the breathing cylinders had prepared a fantastic fate for us.

We adjusted our eyes to the gloom of the crater. Monsieur Garcin had lent us a Canadian canoe, which was floated over the throat of the Fountain, to anchor the guide rope. There was a heavy pig-iron weight on the end of the rope, which we wanted lowered beforehand as far as it would go down. The underwater entry was partially blocked by a huge stone buttress, but we managed to lower the pig-iron fifty-five feet. Chief Petty Officer Jean Pinard volunteered to dive without a protective suit to attempt to roll the pig-iron down as far as it was possible. Pinard returned lobster-red with cold and reported he had shoved the weight down to ninety feet. He did not suspect that he had been down further than Negri.

I donned my constant-volume diving dress over long woollens under the eyes of an appreciative audience perched round the rocky lip of the crater. My wife was among them, not liking this venture at all. Dumas wore an Italian Navy frogman outfit. We were loaded like donkeys. Each wore a three-cylinder lung, rubber foot fins, a heavy dagger, and two large waterproof flashlights, one in hand and one on the belt. Over my left arm was coiled three hundred feet of line in three pieces. Dumas carried an emergency micro-aqualung on his belt, a depth gauge, and a *piolet*, the alpinist's ice-axe. There were rock slopes to be negotiated: with our heavy ballast we might need the *piolet*.

The surface commander was the late Lieutenant Maurice Fargues, our resourceful equipment officer. He was to keep his hand on the guide line as we transported the pig-iron down with us. The guide rope was our only communication with the surface. We had memorized a signal code. One tug from below requested Fargues to tighten the rope to clear snags. Three tugs meant pay out more line. Six tugs was the emergency signal for Fargues to haul us up as quickly as possible.

When the *cordée* reached Negri's syphon, we planned to station the pig-iron, and attach to it one of the lengths of rope I carried over my arm. As we climbed on into the syphon, I would unreel this line behind me. We believed that our goal would be found past Negri's see-sawing rock, up a long sloping arm of the syphon, in an air cave, where in some manner unknown Vaucluse's annual eruption was launched.

Embarrassed by the wealth of gadgets we had hanging on to us, and needing our comrades' support, we waded into the pool. We looked around for the last time. I saw the reassuring silhouette of Fargues and the crowd round the amphitheatre. In their forefront was a young abbé, who had no doubt come to be of service in a certain eventuality.

As we submerged, the water liberated us from weight. We stayed motionless in the pool for a minute to test our ballast and communications system. Under my flexible helmet I had a special mouthpiece which allowed me to articulate underwater. Dumas had no speaking facility, but could answer me with nods and gestures.

I turned face down and plunged through the dark door. I rapidly passed the buttress into the shaft, unworried about Dumas' keeping pace on the thirty-foot cord at my waist. He can outswim me any time. Our dive was a trial run: we were the first *cordée* of a series. We intended to waste no time on details of topography but to proceed directly to the pig-iron and take it on to the elbow of Negri's syphon, from which we would quickly take up a new thread into the secret of the Fountain. In retrospect, I also find that my subconscious mechanism was anxious to conclude the first dive as soon as possible.

I glanced back and saw Didi gliding easily through the door

against a faint green haze. The sky was no longer our business. We belonged now to a world where no light had ever struck. I could not see my flashlight beam beneath me in the frightening dark – the water had no suspended motes to reflect light. A disc of light blinked on and off in the darkness when my flashlight beam hit rock. I went head down with tigerish speed, sinking by my overballast, unmindful of Dumas. Suddenly I was held by the belt and stones rattled past me. Heavier borne than I, Dumas was trying to brake his fall with his feet. His suit was filling with water. Big limestone blocks came loose and rumbled down round me. A stone bounced off my shoulder. I remotely realized I should try to think. I could not think.

Ninety feet down I found the pig-iron standing on a ledge. It did not appear in the torch beam as an object from the world above, but as something germane to this place. Dimly I recalled that I must do something about the pig-iron. I shoved it down the slope. It roared down with Dumas' stones. During this blurred effort I did not notice that I had lost the lines coiled on my arm. I did not know that I had failed to give Fargues three tugs on the line to pay out the weight. I had forgotten Fargues and everything behind us. The tunnel broke into a sharper decline. I circled my right hand continuously, playing the torch in spirals on the clean and polished walls. I was travelling at two knots. I was in the Paris subway. I met nobody. There was nobody in the Metro, not a single rock bass. No fish at all.

At that time of year our ears are well trained to pressure after a summer's diving. *Why did my ears ache so?* Something was happening. The light no longer ran around the tunnel walls. The beam spread on a flat bottom, covered with pebbles. It was earth, not rock, the detritus of the chasm. I could find no walls. I was on the floor of a vast drowned cave. I found the pig-iron, but no zinc boat, no syphon, and no precariously balanced rock. My head ached. I was drained of initiative.

I returned to our purpose, to learn the geography of the immensity that had no visible roof or walls, but rolled away down at a forty-five-degree incline. I could not surface without searching the ceiling for the hole that led up to the inner cavern of our theory.

I was attached to something, I remembered. The flashlight picked out a rope which curled off to a strange form floating supine above the pebbles. Dumas hung there in his cumbersome equipment, holding his torch like a ridiculous glow-worm. Only his arms were moving. He was sleepily trying to tie his *piolet* to the pig-iron line. His black frogman suit was filling with water. He struggled weakly to inflate it with compressed air. I swam to him and looked at his depth gauge. It read one hundred and fifty feet. The dial was flooded. We were deeper than that. We were at least two hundred feet down, four hundred feet away from the surface at the bottom of a crooked slanting tunnel.

We had rapture of the depths, but not the familiar drunkenness. We felt heavy and anxious, instead of exuberant. Dumas was stricken worse than I. I thought: *This is not how I should feel at this depth . . . I can't go back until I learn where we are. Why don't I feel a current? The pig-iron line is our only way home. What if we lose it? Where is the rope I had on my arm?* I was able in that instant to recall that I had lost the line somewhere above. I took Dumas' hand and closed it round the guide line. 'Stay here,' I shouted. 'I'll find the shaft.' Dumas understood me to mean I had no air and needed the safety aqualung. I sent the beam of the flashlight round in search of the roof of the cave. I found no ceiling.

Dumas was passing under heavy narcosis. He thought I was the one in danger. He fumbled to release the emergency lung. As he tugged hopelessly at his belt, he scudded across the drowned shingle and abandoned the guide line to the surface. The rope dissolved in the dark. I was swimming above, mulishly seeking for a wall or a ceiling, when I felt his weight tugging me back like a drifting anchor, restraining my search.

Above us somewhere were seventy fathoms of tunnel and crumbling rock. My weakened brain found the power to conjure up our fate. When our air ran out we would grope along the ceiling and suffocate in dulled agony. I shook off this thought and swam down to the ebbing glow of Dumas' flashlight.

He had almost lost consciousness. When I touched him, he grabbed my wrist with awful strength and hauled me towards him for a final experience of life, an embrace that would take me with him. I twisted out of his hold and backed away. I examined Dumas with the torch. I saw his protruding eyes rolling inside the mask.

The cave was quiet between my gasping breaths. I marshalled all my remaining brain power to consider the situation. Fortunately there was no current to carry Dumas away from the pig-iron. If there had been the least current, we would have been lost. *The pig-iron must be near*. I looked for that rusted metal block, more precious than gold. And suddenly there it was, stolid and reassuring. Its line flew away into the dark, towards the hope of life.

In his stupor, Didi lost control of his jaws and his mouthpiece slipped from his teeth. He swallowed water and took some in his lungs before he somehow got the grip back into his mouth. Now, with the guide line beckoning, I realized that I could not swim to the surface, carrying the inert Dumas, who weighed at least twenty-five pounds in his waterlogged suit. I was in a state of exhaustion from the mysterious effect of the cave. We had not exercised strenuously, yet Dumas was helpless and I was becoming idiotic.

I would climb the rope, dragging Dumas with me. I grasped the pig-iron rope and started up, hand-over-hand, with Dumas drifting below, along the smooth vertical rock.

My first three hand-holds on the line were interpreted correctly by Fargues as the signal to pay out more rope. He did so, with a will. With utter dismay I saw the rope slackening and made super-human efforts to climb it. Fargues smartly fed me rope when he felt my traction. It took an eternal minute for me to work out the right tactics, namely that I should continue to haul down the rope, until the end of it came into Fargues' hand. He would never let go. I hauled the rope in dull glee.

Four hundred feet of rope passed through my hands and curled into the cave. And a knot came into my hands. Fargues was giving us more rope to penetrate the ultimate gallery of Vaucluse. He had efficiently tied on another length to encourage us to pass deeper.

I dropped the rope like an enemy. I would have to climb the tunnel slope like an alpinist. Foot by foot I climbed the finger-holds of rock, stopping when I lost my respiratory rhythm by exertion and was near to fainting. I drove myself on, and felt that I was making progress. I reached for a good hand-hold, standing on the tips of my fins. The crag eluded my fingers and I was dragged down by the weight of Dumas.

The shock turned my mind to the rope again and I suddenly recalled our signals: six tugs meant pull everything up. I grabbed the line and jerked it, confident that I could count to six. The line was slack and snagged on obstacles in the four hundred feet to Maurice Fargues. *Fargues, do you not understand my situation?* I was at the end of my strength. Dumas was hanging on me.

Why doesn't Dumas understand how bad he is for me? Dumas, you will die, anyway. Maybe you are already gone. Didi, I hate to do it, but you are dead and you will not let me live. Go away, Didi. I reached for my belt dagger and prepared to cut the cord to Dumas.

Even in my incompetence there was something that held the knife in its holster. *Before I cut you off, Didi, I will try again to reach Fargues.* I took the line and repeated the distress signal, again and again. *Didi, I am doing all a man can do. I am dying too.*

On shore, Fargues stood in perplexed concentration. The first *cordée* had not been down for the full period of the plan, but the strange pattern of our signals disturbed him. His hard but sensitive hand on the rope had felt no clear signals since the episode a few minutes back when suddenly we wanted lots of rope. He had given it to us, eagerly adding another length. *They must have found something tremendous down there,* thought Fargues. He was eager to penetrate the mystery himself on a later dive. Yet he was uneasy about the lifelessness of the rope in the last few minutes. He frowned and fingered the rope like a pulse, and waited.

Up from the lag of rope, four hundred feet across the friction of rocks, and through the surface, a faint vibration tickled Fargue's finger. He reacted by standing and grumbling, half to himself, half to the cave watchers, '*Qu'est-ce que je risque? De me faire engueuler?*' (What do I risk? Being sworn at?) With a set face he hauled the pig-iron in.

I felt the rope tighten. I jerked my hand off the dagger and hung on. Dumas' air cylinders rang on the rocks as we were borne swiftly up. A hundred feet above I saw a faint triangle of green light, where hope lay. In less than a minute Fargues pulled us out into the pool and leaped in the water after the senseless Dumas. Tailliez and Pinard waded in after me. I gathered what strength I had left to control my emotions, not to break down. I managed to walk out of the pool. Dumas lay on his stomach and vomited. Our friends stripped off our rubber suits. I warmed myself round a cauldron of flaming petrol. Fargues and the doctor worked over Dumas. In five minutes he was on his feet, standing by the fire. I handed him a bottle of brandy. He took a drink and said, 'I'm going down again.' I wondered where Simone was.

The Mayor said, 'When your air bubbles stopped coming to the surface, your wife ran down the hill. She said she could not stand it.' Poor Simone had raced to a café in Vaucluse and ordered the most powerful spirit in the house. A rumour-monger raced through the village, yelling that one of the divers was drowned. Simone cried, 'Which one? What colour was his mask?'

'Red,' said the harbinger.

Simone gasped with relief – my mask was blue. Then she thought of Didi in his red mask and her joy collapsed. She returned distractedly up the trail to the Fountain. There stood Didi, a miracle to her.

Dumas' recuperative powers soon brought his colour back and his mind cleared. He wanted to know why we had been drugged in the cavern. In the afternoon another *cordée*, Tailliez and Guy Morandiere, prepared to dive, without the junk we had carried. They wore only long underwear and light ballast, which made them slightly buoyant. They planned to go to the cavern and reconnoitre for the passage which led to the secret of Vaucluse. As soon as they found it, they would immediately return and sketch the layout for the third *cordée*, which would make the final plunge.

From the diving logs of Captain Tailliez and Morandiere, I am able to recount their experience, which was almost as appalling as ours. Certainly it took greater courage than ours to enter the Fountain from which we had been so luckily saved. In the few minutes they spent just under the surface of the pool, getting used to the water, Morandiere felt intense cold. They entered the tunnel abreast, roped together. Second *cordée* tactics were to swim down side by side along the ceiling.

When they encountered humps sticking down from the roof, they were to duck under them and then return to follow the ceiling closely. Each hump they met promised to level off beyond, but never did. They went down and down. Our only depth gauge had been ruined, but the veteran Tailliez had a sharp physiological sense of depth. At an estimated one hundred and twenty feet he halted the march so they might study their subjective sensations. Tailliez felt the first inviting throbs of rapture of the depths. He knew that to be impossible at a mere twenty fathoms. However, the symptoms were pronounced.

He called to Morandiere that they should turn back. Morandiere manoeuvred himself and the rope to facilitate Tailliez's turnabout. As he did so, he heard that Tailliez's respiratory rhythm was disorderly, and faced his partner so that Tailliez could see him give six pulls on the pig-iron rope. Unable to exchange words underwater, the team had to depend on errant flashlight beams and understanding to accomplish the turn. Morandiere stationed himself below Tailliez to conduct the Captain to the surface. Tailliez construed these activities to mean that Morandiere was in trouble. Both men were slipping into the blank rapture that had almost finished the first *cordée*.

Tailliez carefully climbed the guide line. The rope behind

drifted aimlessly in the water, and a loop hung round his shoulders. Tailliez felt he had to sever the rope before it entangled him. He whipped out his dagger and cut it away. Morandiere, swimming freely below him, was afraid his mate was passing out. The confused second *cordée* ascended to the green hall light of the Fountain. Morandiere closed in, took Tailliez's feet, and gave him a strong boost through the narrow door. The effort upset Morandiere's breathing cycle.

We saw Tailliez emerge in his white underwear, Morandiere following through the underwater door. Tailliez broke the surface, found a footing, and walked out of the water, erect and wild-eyed. In his right hand he held his dagger, upside down. His fingers were cut to the bone by the blade and blood was flowing down his sodden woollens. He did not feel it.

We resolved to call it a day with a shallow plunge to map the entrance of the Fountain. We made sure that Didi, in his anger against the cave, could not slip down to the drowned cavern that had nearly been our tomb. Fargues lashed a 150-foot line to Dumas' waist and took Didi's dagger to prevent him cutting himself loose and going down further. The final reconnaissance of the entrance shaft passed without incident.

It was an emotional day. That evening in Vaucluse the first and second *cordées* made a subjective comparison of cognac narcosis and rapture of the Fountain. None of us could relax, thinking of the enigmatic stupor that had overtaken us. We knew the berserk intoxication of *l'ivresse des grandes profondeurs* at two hundred and fifty feet in the sea, but why did this clear, lifeless limestone water cheat a man's mind in a different way?

Simone, Didi and I drove back to Toulon that night, thinking hard, despite fatigue and headache. Long silences were spaced by occasional suggestions. Didi said, 'Narcotic effects aren't the only cause of diving accidents. There are social and subjective fears, the air you breathe . . .' I jumped at the idea. 'The air you breathe!' I said. 'Let's run a lab test on the air left in the lungs.'

The next morning we sampled the cylinders. The analysis

showed 1/2000 of carbon monoxide. At a depth of one hundred and sixty feet the effect of carbon monoxide is sixfold. The amount we were breathing may kill a man in twenty minutes. We started our new Diesel-powered free-piston air compressor. We saw the compressor sucking in its own exhaust fumes. We had all been breathing lethal doses of carbon monoxide.

Deserts

DYING OF THIRST

SVEN HEDIN
(1865–1952)

Swedish explorer and geographer, the leader of many expeditions to Tibet, China and Central Asia. The incident below took place in the Gobi Desert in 1895.

That night I wrote what I supposed were to be my last lines in my diary: 'Halted on a high dune, where the camels dropped. We examined the east through the field glasses: mountains of sand in all directions, not a straw, no life. All, men as well as camels, are extremely weak. God help us!' May Day, a springtime feast of joy and light at home in Sweden, was for us the heaviest day on our *via dolorosa* through the desert.

The night had been quiet, clear and cold; but the sun was hardly above the horizon when it grew warm. The men squeezed the last drops of the rancid oil out of a goatskin and gave them to the camels. The day before I had not had a single drop of water, and the day before that, only two cups. I was suffering from thirst; and when by chance I found the bottle in which we kept the Chinese spirits for the Primus stove, I could not resist the temptation to drink some of it. It was a foolish thing to do; but nevertheless I drank half the bottle. Yoldash heard the gurgling sound and came toward me, wagging his tail. I let him have a sniff. He snorted and went away sadly. I threw the bottle away and the rest of the liquid flowed out into the sand.

That treacherous drink finished me. I tried to rise but my legs would not support me. The caravan broke camp but I remained behind. Islam Bai led, compass in hand, going due east. The sun was already burning hot. My men probably thought I would die where I lay. They went on slowly, like snails. The sound of the bells grew fainter and finally died away altogether. On every dune-crest the caravan reappeared like a dark spot, smaller and smaller; in every hollow between the dunes it remained concealed for a while. Finally I saw it no more. But the deep trail, with its dark shadows from the sun, which was still low, reminded me of the danger of my situation. I had not strength enough to follow the others. They had left me. The horrible desert extended in all directions. The sun was burning and blinding; there was not a breath of air.

Then a terrible thought struck me. What if this was the quiet preceding a storm? At any moment, then, I might see the black streak across the horizon in the east, which heralded the approach of a sandstorm. The trail of the caravan would then be obliterated in a few moments, and I would never find my men and camels again, those wrecks of the ships of the desert. I exerted all my will-power, got up, reeled, fell, crawled for a while along the trail, got up again, dragged myself along, and crawled. One hour passed, and then another. From the ridge of a dune I saw the caravan. It was standing still. The bells had ceased tinkling. By superhuman efforts I managed to reach it.

Islam stood on a ridge, scanning the eastern horizon and shading his eyes with his hand. Again he asked permission to hurry eastward with the jugs. But seeing my condition he quickly abandoned the idea. Mohammed Shah was lying on his face, sobbingly invoking Allah. Kasim sat in the shadow of a camel, his face covered with his hands. He told me that Mohammed Shah had been raving about water all the way. Yolchi lay on the sand as if he were dead.

Islam suggested that we continue and look for a spot of hard clay ground, where we might dig for water. All the camels were lying down. I climbed on the white one. Like the others, he refused to get up. Our plight was desperate. Here we were to die. Mohammed Shah lay babbling, toying with the sand and raving about water. I realized that we had reached the last act of our desert drama. But I was not yet ready to give in altogether.

The sun was now glowing like an oven. 'When the sun has gone down,' I said to Islam, 'we will break camp and march all night. Up with the tent!' The camels were freed from their burdens and lay in the blazing sun all day. Islam and Kasim pitched the tent. I crawled in, undressed completely, and lay down on a blanket, my head pillowed on a sack. Islam, Kasim, Yoldash and the sheep went into the shade, while Mohammed Shah and Yolchi stayed where they had fallen. The hens were the only ones to keep up their spirits. This death-camp was the unhappiest I lived through in all my wanderings in Asia.

It was only half past nine in the morning, and we had hardly traversed three miles. I was absolutely done up and unable to move a finger. I thought I was dying. I imagined myself already lying in a mortuary chapel. The church bells had stopped tolling for the funeral. My whole life flew past me like a dream. There were not many hours left me on the threshold of eternity. But most of all, I was tormented by the thought of the anxiety and uncertainty which I would cause my parents and brother and sisters. When I should be reported missing, Consul Petrovsky would make investigations. He would learn that I had left Merket on 10 April. All traces after that, however, would then have been swept away; for several storms would have passed over the desert since then. They would wait and wait at home. One year would pass after another. But no news would come, and finally they would cease hoping.

About noon the slack flaps of the tent began to bulge, and a faint southerly breeze moved over the desert. It blew stronger, and after a couple of hours it was so fresh that I rolled myself up in my blanket.

And now a miracle happened! My debility vanished and my

strength returned! If ever I longed for the sunset it was now. I did not want to die: I *would not* die in this miserable, sandy desert! I could run, walk, crawl on my hands and feet. My men might not survive, but I had to find water! The sun lay like a red-hot cannon-ball on a dune in the west. I was in the best of condition. I dressed and ordered Islam and Kasim to prepare for departure. The sunset glow spread its purple light over the dunes. Mohammed Shah and Yolchi were in the same position as in the morning. The former had already begun his death-struggle, and he never regained consciousness. But the latter woke to life in the cool of the evening. With his hands clenched he crawled up to me and cried pitifully: 'Water! Give us water, sir! Only a drop of water!' Then he crawled away.

'Is there no liquid here, whatever?' I said.

'Why, the rooster!' So they cut off the rooster's head and drank his blood. But that was only a drop in the bucket. Their eyes fell on the sheep, which had followed us as faithfully as a dog without complaining. Everyone hesitated. It would be murder to kill the sheep to prolong our lives for only one day. But Islam led it away, turned its head towards Mecca and slashed its carotids. The blood, reddish-brown and ill-smelling, flowed slowly and thickly. It coagulated immediately into a cake, which the men gulped down. I tried it, too; but it was nauseous, and the mucous membrane of my throat was so dry that it stuck there, and I had to get rid of it quickly.

Mad with thirst, Islam and Yolchi collected camel's urine in a receptacle, mixed it with sugar and vinegar, held their noses, and drank. Kasim and I declined to join in this drinking-bout. The two who had drunk this poison were totally incapacitated. They were overcome with violent cramps and vomiting, and lay writhing and groaning on the sand.

Islam recovered slightly. Before darkness fell we went over our baggage. I laid everything that was irreplaceable in one pile: notebooks, itineraries, maps, instruments, pencils and paper, arms and ammunition, the Chinese silver (about £260), lanterns, candles, a pail, a shovel, provisions for three days, some tobacco and a few other things. A pocket Bible was the only book included. Among the things abandoned were the cameras and about a thousand plates, of which about one hundred had already been exposed, the medicine-chest, saddles, clothes, presents intended for the natives, and much besides. I removed a suit of clean clothing from the pile of discarded things and changed everything from head to foot; for if I was to die and be buried by the sandstorms in the eternal desert, I would at least be robed in a clean, new shroud.

The things we had decided to take along were packed in soft saddle-bags, and these were fastened to the camels. All the pack-saddles were discarded, as they would only have added unnecessary weight.

Yolchi had crawled into the tent to lie down on my blanket. He looked repulsive, soiled as he was with blood from the lungs of the sheep. I tried to brace him up and advised him to follow our track during the night. He did not answer. Mohammed Shah was already delirious. In his delirium he muttered the name of Allah. I tried to make his head comfortable, passed my hand over his burning forehead, begged him to crawl along our trail as far as he could, and told him that we would return to rescue him as soon as we found water.

The two men eventually died in the death-camp, or near it. They were never heard of; and when, after a year had elapsed, they were still missing, I gave a sum of money to their respective widows and children.

All five camels were induced to get up, and they were tied to one another in single file. Islam led and Kasim brought up the rear. We did not take the two dying men along, because the camels were too weak to carry them; and, indeed, in their deplorable condition, they could not have kept their seats between the humps. We also cherished the hope that we would find water, in which case we were going to fill the two goatskins that we still carried, and hurry back to save the unfortunate ones.

The hens, having satisfied their keen hunger with the dead sheep's blood, had gone to rest. A silence more profound than that of the grave prevailed around the tent. As twilight was about to merge into darkness, the bronze bells sounded for the last time. We headed eastward as usual, avoiding the highest ridges. After a few minutes' walk I turned about, and gave a farewell glance at the death-camp. The tent stood out distinctly in the vanishing daylight that still lingered in the west. It was a relief to get away from this ghastly place. It was soon swallowed up by the night . . .

Thus we walked on through the night and the sand. After two hours of it, we were so exhausted from fatigue and from lack of sleep, that we flung ourselves headlong on the sand, and dozed off. I was wearing thin, white, cotton clothes, and was soon awakened by the cold night air. Then we walked again, till the limit of our endurance was reached. We slept once more on a dune. My stiff-topped boots, reaching to my knees, made progress difficult. I was on the point of throwing them away several times, but fortunately I did not do so.

After another halt we walked on for five hours more, that is, from four to nine in the morning. This was on 2 May. Then one hour's rest again, and one and a half hour's slow march. The sun was blazing. All became black before our eyes as we sank down on the sand. Kasim dug out, from a northerly slope, sand which was still cold from the night. I stripped and laid myself down in it, while Kasim shovelled sand over me up to my neck. He did the same for himself. Our heads were quite close to each other, and we shaded ourselves from the sun by hanging our clothes on the spade, which we had stuck in the ground.

All day long we lay like this, speaking not a word, and not getting a wink of sleep. The turquoise-blue sky arched over us, and the yellow sea of the desert extended around us, stretching to the horizon.

When the ball of the sun again rested on the ridge of a dune in the west, we got up, shook off the sand, dressed, and dragged ourselves slowly with innumerable interruptions, towards the east, until one o'clock in the morning.

The sand-bath, although cooling and pleasant during the heat of the day, was also weakening. Our strength was ebbing. We could not cover as much ground as the night before. Thirst did not torment us, as it had done during the first days, for the mouth-cavity had become as dry as the outside skin, and the craving was dulled. An increasing feebleness set in instead. The functioning of all the glands was reduced. Our blood got thicker and flowed through the capillaries with increasing sluggishness. Sooner or later this process of drying-up would reach its climax in death.

From one o'clock until half past four in the morning, on 3 May, we lay inanimate; and not even the cold night air could rouse us to go on. But at dawn we dragged ourselves forwards again. We would take a couple of steps intermittently. We managed to get down the sandy slopes fairly well, but climbing the waves of sand was heavy work.

At sunrise, Kasim caught me by the shoulder, stared, and pointed east, without saying a word.

'What is it?' I whispered.

'A tamarisk,' he gasped.

A sign of vegetation at last! God be praised! Our hopes, which had been close to extinction, flamed up once more. We walked, dragged ourselves, and staggered for three hours, before we reached that first bush – an olive branch intimating that the sea of the desert had a shore. We thanked God for this blessed gift, as we chewed the bitter green needles of the tamarisk. Like a water lily the bush stood on its wave of sand, basking in the sun. But how far below was the water that nourished its roots?

About ten o'clock, we found another tamarisk; and we saw several more in the east. But our strength was gone. We undressed, buried ourselves in the sand, and hung our clothes on the branches of the tamarisk to make shade.

We lay in silence for nine hours. The hot desert air dried our faces into parchment. At seven o'clock, we dressed and continued onward. We went more slowly than ever. After three hours' walk in the dark, Kasim stopped short, and whispered: 'Poplars!'

Between two dunes there appeared three poplars, standing close together. We sank down at their base, exhausted with fatigue. Their roots, too, must derive nourishment from below. We took hold of the spade, intending to dig a well, but the spade slipped from our hands. We had no strength left. We lay down and scratched the ground with our nails, but gave up the attempt as useless.

Instead, we tore off the fresh leaves and rubbed them into our skins. Then we collected dry, fallen twigs, and made a fire on the nearest crest as a signal to Islam, should he prove to be still alive, which I very much doubted. The fire might also, perhaps, attract the attention of a shepherd in the woods along the Khotan-daria. But even if a shepherd should see this fire in an area of deathly silence, he was more likely to become frightened and believe it was the desert spirit who haunted the place and practised witchcraft. For fully two hours we kept the fire going, regarding it as a companion, a friend, and a chance of rescue. Nowadays, those who are shipwrecked at sea have other means of sending out their SOS in moments of extreme danger. We had only this fire, and our eyes were glued to its flames.

The night was coming to an end, and the sun, our worst enemy, would soon rise again above the dunes on the eastern horizon, to torment us anew. At four on the morning of 4 May we started off, stumbling along for five hours. Then our strength gave out. Our hope was again on the decline. In the east there were no more poplars, no more tamarisks, to stimulate our dying vitality with their verdure. Only mounds of sand, as far as the eye could reach.

We collapsed on the slope of a dune. Kasim's ability to dig out cold sand for me was gone. I had to help myself as best I could. For fully ten hours we lay silent in the sand. It was strange that we were still alive. Would we have strength enough to drag ourselves through one more night – our last one?

I rose at twilight and urged Kasim to come. Hardly audible was his gasp: 'I can't go on.' And so I left the last remnant of the caravan behind and continued on alone. I dragged myself along, and fell. I crawled up slopes, and staggered down the other side. I lay quiet for long periods, listening. Not a sound! The stars shone like electric torches. I wondered whether I was still on earth, or whether this was the valley of the shadow of death. I lit my last cigarette. Kasim had always received the butts, but now I was alone, and so I smoked this one to the end. It afforded me a little relief and distraction.

Six hours had passed since the beginning of my solitary journey, when, totally overcome with feebleness, I sank down by a new tamarisk, and went off into the doze which I feared, for death might come while I was asleep. As a matter of fact, I hardly slept at all. All the time, in the grave-like silence, I heard the beating of my heart and the ticking of the chronometers. And after a couple of hours I heard the swish of steps in the sand, and saw a phantom stagger and struggle to my side.

'Is that you, Kasim?' I whispered.

'Yes, sir.'

'Come! We have not far to go!'

Heartened by our reunion, we struggled on. We slid down the dunes; we struggled upwards. We would lie motionless where we fell, in our battle against the insidious desire for sleep. We slackened our pace, and grew more and more indolent. We were like sleep walkers; but still we fought for our lives.

Suddenly Kasim grabbed my arm and pointed downwards at the sand. There were distinct tracks of human beings!

In a twinkling we were wide awake. It was plain that the river *must* be near! It was possible that some shepherds had noticed our fire and had come to investigate. Or maybe a sheep, astray in the desert, had been searched for by these men who had so recently passed over the sand.

Kasim bent down, examined the prints, and gasped:

'It is our own trail!'

In our listless, somnolent state, we had described a circle

without knowing it. That was enough for a while; we could not endure any more. We collapsed on the trail and fell asleep. It was half past two in the morning.

When the new day dawned, on 5 May, we rose heavily, and with difficulty. Kasim looked terrible. His tongue was white and swollen, his lips blue, his cheeks were hollow, and his eyes had a dying glassy lustre. He was tortured by a kind of death-hiccup, which shook his whole frame. When the body is so completely dried up that the joints almost creak, every movement is an effort.

It grew lighter. The sun rose. From the top of a dune, where nothing obstructed the view towards the east, we noticed that the horizon, which for two weeks had revealed a row of yellow saw-teeth, now disclosed an absolutely even, dark-green line. We stopped short, as though petrified, and exclaimed simultaneously: 'The forest!' And I added: 'The Khotan-daria! Water!'

Again we collected what little strength we had left and struggled along eastward. The dunes grew lower, we passed a depression in the ground at the bottom of which we tried to dig; but we were still too weak. We went on. The dark-green line grew, the dunes diminished, stopped altogether, and were replaced by level soft ground. We were but a few hundred yards from the forest. At half past five we reached the first poplars, and wearied, sank down in their shade. We enjoyed the fragrance of the forest. We saw flowers growing between the trees, and heard the birds sing and the flies and gadflies hum. At seven o'clock we continued. The forest grew thinner. We came upon a path, showing traces of men, sheep, and horses, and we thought it might lead to the river. After following it for two hours, we collapsed in the shade of a poplar grove.

We were too weak to move. Kasim lay on his back. He looked as if he were going to die. The river *must* be quite near. But we were as if nailed down. A tropical heat surrounded us. Would the day never come to an end? Every hour that passed brought us closer to certain death. We would have to drag ourselves on to the river before it got too late! But the sun did not go down. We breathed heavily and with effort. The will to live was about to desert us.

At seven p.m. I was able to get up . . . Again I urged Kasim to accompany me to the river to drink. He signalled with his hand that he could not rise, and he whispered that he would soon die under the poplars.

Alone I pulled myself along through the forest. Thickets of thorny bushes, and dry fallen branches obstructed my way. I tore my thin clothes and scratched my hands, but gradually I worked my way through. I rested frequently, crawled part of the way on all-fours, and noticed with anxiety how the darkness grew denser in the woods. Finally the new night came – the last one. I could not have survived another day.

The forest ended abruptly, as though burnt by a fire. I found myself on the edge of a six-foot-high terrace, which descended almost perpendicularly to an absolutely even plain, devoid of vegetation. The ground was packed hard. A withered leafless twig was sticking out of it. I saw that it was a piece of driftwood, and that I was in the riverbed of the Khotan-daria. And it was dry, as dry as the sandy desert behind me! Was I to die of thirst in the very bed of the river, after having fought my way so successfully to its bank? No! I was not going to lie down and die without first crossing the Khotan-daria and assuring myself that the whole bed was dry, and that all hope was irretrievably gone . . .

Like the beds of all desert-rivers in Central Asia, that of the Khotan-daria is very wide, flat, and shallow. A light haze floated over the desolate landscape. I had gone about one mile when the outlines of the forest on the eastern shore appeared below the moon. Dense thickets of bushes and reeds grew on the terraced shore. A fallen poplar stretched its dark trunk down towards the riverbed. It looked like the body of a crocodile. The bed still remained as dry as before. It was not far to the shore where I must lie down and die. My life hung on a hair.

Suddenly I started, and stopped short. A water-bird, a wild duck or goose, rose on whirring wings, and I heard a splash. The next moment, I stood on the edge of a pool, seventy feet long and fifteen feet wide! The water looked as black as ink in the moonlight. The overturned poplar-trunk was reflected in its depths.

In the silent night I thanked God for my miraculous deliverance. Had I continued eastward I should have been lost. In fact, if I had touched shore only a hundred yards north or south of the pool, I would have believed the entire riverbed to be dry. I knew that the freshets from melting snowfields and glaciers in northern Tibet flowed down through the Khotan-daria bed only in the beginning of June, to dry up in the late summer and autumn, leaving the bed dry during the winter and spring. I had also heard that in certain places, separated sometimes by a day's journey or more, the river forms eddies, which scoop the bed into greater depths, and that the water may remain the year round in these hollows near the terraced shore. And now I had come upon one of these extremely rare bodies of water!

I sat down calmly on the bank and felt my pulse. It was so weak that it was hardly noticeable – only forty-nine beats. Then I drank, and drank again. I drank without restraint. The water was cold, clear as crystal, and as sweet as the best spring water. And then I drank again. My dried-up body absorbed the moisture like a sponge. All my joints softened, all my movements became easier. My skin, hard as parchment before, now became softened. My forehead grew moist. The pulse increased in strength; and after a few minutes it was fifty-six. The blood flowed more freely in my veins. I had a feeling of well-being and comfort. I drank again, and sat caressing the water in this blessed pool. Later on, I christened this pool Khoda-verdi-kol, or 'the Pool of God's Gift' . . .

My thoughts now flew to Kasim, who lay faint from thirst on the edge of the wood on the western shore. Of the stately caravan of three weeks ago, I, a European, was the only one that had held out till the moment of rescue. If I did not waste my minutes, perhaps Kasim, too, might be saved. But in what was I to carry the water? Why, in my waterproof boots! There was, in fact, no other receptacle. I filled them to the top, suspended them at either end of the spade handle, and carefully recrossed the riverbed. Though the moon was low, my old track was plainly visible. I reached the forest. The moon went down, and dense darkness descended among the trees. I lost my trail, and went astray among thorny bushes and thickets, which would not give under my stockinged feet. From time to time, I called 'Kasim!' at the top of my voice. But the sound died away among the tree trunks; and I got no answer but the 'clevitt' of a frightened night owl.

If I lost my way, perhaps I would never again find the trail and then Kasim would be lost. I stopped at an impenetrable thicket of dry branches and brush, set fire to the whole thing, and enjoyed seeing the flames lick and scorch the nearest poplars. Kasim could not be far away; he was certain both to hear and to see the fire. But he did not come. I had no choice but to await the dawn. At the foot of a poplar, out of reach of the fire. I lay down and slept for some hours. The fire protected me against any prowling wild beasts.

When dawn came the night fire was still glowing, and a black column of smoke was rising above the forest. It was easy now to find my trail and the place where Kasim lay. He was still in the same position as the night before. Upon seeing me, he whispered: 'I am dying!' 'Will you have some water?' I asked, letting him hear the splashing sound. He sat up, dazed and staring. I handed him one of the boots. He lifted it to his lips and emptied it to the last drop. After a short pause he emptied the other one, too.

CROSSING THE EMPTY QUARTER

BERTRAM THOMAS
(1892–1950)

*Thomas, an English explorer, made the first crossing of the Empty
Quarter or Rub al Khali, 1930–1.*

Never before had the great South Arabian desert of Rub 'al Khali
been crossed by white man, and the ambition to be its pioneer
seized me as it had seized every adventurous Englishman whose
lot has been cast in Arabia. But before I tell of the manner of my
camel crossing and of the things that befell, I must briefly intro-
duce the reader who is uninitiated in matters Arabian to the lie of
the land.

'The World,' said the medieval Moslem geographer, 'is in
shape like a ball, and it floats in the circumambient ocean like an
egg in water, half in and half out. Of the exposed portion one
half constitutes the Inhabited Quarter, while the remaining half
is the Empty Quarter, the Rub 'al Khali placed in the barren
wastes of Arabia.'

An extravagant estimate, this, of the place of our wanderings;
yet it is no mean desert that approaches an area as big as England
and France together. That it should have remained *terra incognita*
till after the icy Polar regions, the tropic sources of the Amazon,
and the vast interior spaces of Asia and Africa had been made to
yield up their secrets to Western curiosity, is strange. An Arabian
explanation was given to the traveller Charles Doughty, by his

genial companion Zayed as Shaykhan, that worthy, with his finger upon a page of Arab script, declaring the matter in this wise: 'God has given two of the four parts of the earth to the children of Adam, the third part He has given to Gog and Magog, the fourth is the Rub 'al Khali void of the breath of life.'

Lack of rain and merciless heat indeed make of this a place where the Persian poet would have us believe 'the panting sinner receives a foretaste of his future destiny'. Certainly human life can be but spasmodically supported, and then mostly round the desert's fringes, where, among semi-barbarous nomadic tribes, hunger and the raid are Nature's pruning-hooks.

Native suspicion and an insular outlook combine with insecurity of life to keep the infidel intruder at arm's length, and he who would travel hopefully and usefully requires some apprenticeship and acclimatisation: needs must he speak the tongue, know the mind, grow a beard, dress and act like his desert companions, betraying, for instance, no squeamishness over drinking water, pestiferous though it might be, drawn from unsampled water-holes come upon in the burning sands, and not improved by churning in strong-smelling animal-skins carried on the march. But to our story!

On the 5 October 1931, the SS *British Grenadier*, homeward bound from Persia, arrived off Muscat harbour at dawn, and there picked me up, by arrangement, from a small boat. Two nights later I was dropped, clothed in native dress, into an Arab dhow we sighted riding at anchor off the central-south Arabian shore. Landing, I made my way to the rendezvous where I had expected a trusted Arab chieftain who had served me on an earlier desert expedition, but I found neither him nor his promised string of riding camels.

Experience had taught me the need of not disclosing my plans to anyone in a land where secrecy of movement at the outset is imperative. My hopes of even making a start were thus dashed, and, sick at my bad luck, I turned up into the Qara Mountains to think and to scheme, while I explored and hunted their forested slopes. More than two impatient months passed before despair gave way to reviving hope.

It was the 10 December when at last I set out from Dhufar with a party of desert Arabs that included the famous Sheikh Salih, of the Rashid (Kathir) tribe, twenty-six warriors – nearly all of whom could show the scars of wounds, none of whom had I set eyes on before – and forty camels. The first day's march was as usual cut short, some of the men returning to the booths to buy a trifling gimcrack with which to gladden the eyes of their beauties far away in the black tents, some for a final watering at the sweet well of the mosque, while skins in which we carried our water were oiled and made watertight, and crude, improvised sacks, which did for pack-saddles, were given a final look over.

Our northerly course, on the morrow, led upward through the dense jungles of the Qara escarpment, where I had reaped a bountiful harvest for the Museum – hyenas, wolves and coneys, snakes and lizards, chameleons, birds and butterflies; and at Qatan I looked back for a last glimpse of the blue Indian Ocean 3,000 feet below. Waving yellow meadows that crowned the uplands gave place to libaniferous shrubs as we wended our way down the far side, amid red and rugged rocks wherein were groves of the frankincense and myrrh trees that gave rise to the fame of the Arabia of antiquity, of which we gain echoes in the Bible. Never could campfires have been more luxuriantly fragrant.

Soon we were to bid farewell to this pleasant countryside of rippling brooks and gay bird life, the decorative stork by day and the eerie sound of the tree-bat by night. The pebbly gorge of Dauka, by which we descended, grew shallower as we went, and became but a sandy, serpentine depression in the arid wilderness beyond. In such ancient dried-up riverbeds as this is the secret of life, for the night dews that here collect give rise to an arterial way of desert flora across the barren plain and the route of the caravan.

The foothills of the southern mountains soon sank below our horizon in rear, and the vast clean spaces of a flint-strewn steppe stretched northward before us. Sand-devils, slender columns of whirling sand, sometimes swept hither and thither; sometimes the skyline danced before us in a hot, shimmering mirage, distorting a faraway bush into an expansive copse, an antelope into some monstrous creature, and generally playing tricks with lakes of illusory water.

For the next two months the stars were my only roof, for I travelled, like my companions, without a tent; and as the thermometer almost immediately fell to 45° Fahrenheit at night, one felt bitterly cold after the hot days in the saddle, wearing the same clothes day and night. The luxury of a tent had to be eschewed, in order to keep camel-loads at a minimum, for there were certain indispensable things to carry – rations of rice, sugar, native fat and dates; mapping instruments: a compass, sextant, artificial horizon, chronometers, barometers and hydrometer; natural-history skinning instruments, killing-bottles and preserving chests; a rifle, for none goes unarmed in these parts, it being held neither safe nor respectable; and to pay my way, gunnybags stuffed with 3,000 Maria Theresa dollars, which I kept under my saddle by day and my pillow by night.

I had to be careful to conceal my sextant and keep my star observations unobserved, lest I be suspected of magic or worse, and to this end I always contrived to sleep some thirty or forty yards away from the camp and wait till my companions had settled down for the night. This they did after prayers and hobbling their camels over the best pastures available, lying sprawling around the flickering campfires with their rifle as their only bedding.

A few days' march northward across the gently declining steppe brought us to the waterhole of Shisur, where we dallied for two days to rest our camels preparatory to a nine-days' water-less and hungry stretch westward. This was to be the most dangerous part of my journey, for it is a no-man's-land with a bloody reputation for raiding and counter-raiding between the various tribes of these southern borderlands; and as I was moving with Rashidi tribesmen, I was particularly apprehensive of a collision with a party of the Sa'ar tribe, their hereditary enemies, for whom, moreover, the money I carried would doubtless have acted as a magnet.

Yellow sand dunes rose tier upon tier, backing the western reaches of Umm al Hait, the mighty, dried-up river system I had discovered and mapped on an earlier journey; and hummocky summits were crowned with tamarisk, which in these hungry marches brought our camels running up at the glad sight. It is impossible to carry fodder over these long trails, and camels have to fend for themselves, or rather, a small, well-mounted reconnaissance party goes off to discover the best pastures in the neighbourhood before a general move.

Hence the route taken by the desert traveller cannot with certainty be determined; his course will most likely not be the straightest and shortest one between two points, as with an aeroplane in the air or a ship at sea. And thus it came about that although my plan was to cross the sands northward from sea to sea, I here found myself travelling from east to west along the southern bulwark of the sands.

The full force of the tropical afternoon sun in our faces made me appreciate the Bedouin headdress, the long kerchief which can be wound round the face being merciful indeed as a protection from the sun's burning rays, though my lips and nostrils rarely escaped. Glare glasses I never used, for the reason of possible queer effects on my companions' unaccustomed minds.

'Look, sahib!' said the Arabs riding at my side, one afternoon, and pointing to the ground. 'There is the road to Ubar. Ubar was a great city that our fathers have told us existed in olden times; a city that possessed much treasure and had date gardens and a fort of red silver (gold); it now lies buried beneath the sands, men say in the Rumlait Shu'ait, maybe a few days to the north.'

I had heard of Ubar, an ancient Atlantis of the sands, as it were, from Arab companions of an earlier expedition in the eastern desert, but none could tell of its location. Where my notice was now directed there were deep impressions as of ancient caravan tracks in the hard steppe surface, leading away only to be lost under a wall of sand.

Desiccation of climate through the ages and the extension of the sands, ever encroaching southward, could have brought about its disuse, for it can have led to nowhere worth leading to in historic times, and is now good for nothing. If this local tradition is well founded, Ubar may preserve a memory of the famed land of Ophir, long since lost in the mists of antiquity.

Our course, now trending more to the south, past the dunes of Yibaila and Yadila, was interesting for large, silvery patches in the hollows suggesting a dried-up sea, but which turned out to be sheets of gypsum; though, curiously enough, all along this border-land between sand and steppe, 1,000 feet and more above sea level and today more than 100 miles from the coast, the surface was strewn with oyster and other shell fossils, suggesting that this desert was once an ocean bed.

Beyond Yadila I was next to experience what is extremely rare even for an Arabian explorer, and that was singing sands. As we were floundering along through heavy dune country, the silence was suddenly broken and I was startled for a moment, not knowing what the interruption was or whence it came. 'Listen to that ridge bellowing,' said a Badu* at my side, and looking to where he pointed I saw away on our right hand a steepish sand-cliff about a hundred feet high.

I was too deeply absorbed in the sound to talk, and there was nothing unusual to the eye. The hour was 4.15, and a slight northerly wind blew from the rear of the cliff. I must often have observed similar conditions, but never before heard any accompanying bellowing, only the spectacle of a film of sand smoking over the sand ridges to build up a shape recalling a centurion's helmet. But here the leeward side of the cliff, facing us, was a fairly steep sloping wall, and maybe the surface sands were sliding; certainly some mysterious friction was in progress on a vast scale to produce such starrling loud booming. The noise was comparable to a deep pedal-note of an organ, or the siren of a ship heard, say, from a couple of cables distant. It

* Singular of Bedouin.

continued for about two minutes and then ended as abruptly as it had begun.

The term 'singing sands' seems hardly the most satisfactory one to describe a loud and single note, but it is too firmly established to cavil over, for singing sands are mentioned by quite early Chinese writers, and Marco Polo, who crossed the Great Gobi Desert in the thirteenth century, wrote: 'Sometimes you shall hear the sound of musical instruments and still more commonly the sound of drums.'

We bade adieu to hungry and shivering steppe borderlands, and, turning northward, struck into the body of the sands. The scene before us was magnificent. The sands became almost Alpine in architectural structure, towering mountainously above us, and from the summits we were rewarded with the most glorious panoramas of purest rose-red colour. This Uruq region of the central south must surely be the loftiest throughout all the great ocean of sands.

Our camels climbed arduously the soft slopes, and, slithering knee-deep, made slow progress. No one remained mounted. Indeed, there were places where we had to dig footholds in the sands to enable our animals to climb, other places where we turned back to find an easier way. No horse could have negotiated these southern sands, even if brought here, and the waterless marches behind us, with many consecutive days of ten hours in the saddle, would have made the bringing impossible. A motor-car, too, would surely have charged these slopes in vain.

'The gift of God' – that is the illuminating name by which the Arab nomad knows the camel; and how great is his consideration for her! Time and time again I found myself the only member of our party in the saddle, the Arabs preferring to walk and so spare their mounts, running hither and thither to collect a juicy tuft of camelthorn with which to feed the hungry brutes as we marched along. In the deserts, halts are called, not in accordance with a European watch, but where Nature has, for the nonce, blessed the site with camel pastures. The great ungainly beasts, which you start by despising and learn greatly to admire, are the only means by which you move forward to success or back and out to safety. If camels perish in the remoter waterless wastes, their masters must perish with them.

Christmas Eve was to be a night of excitement and false alarm. We had arrived late in camp, camels had been hobbled and shooed off to the scant bushes, from behind some of which came the brisk noises of merry campfire parties. There was a sudden scream. To me it was like the hooting of an owl or the whining of some wild beast.

'*Gom! Gom!* – Raiders! Raiders!' shouted the excitable Bedouin, leaping to their feet, their rifles at the ready; and my Arab servant came running across to me with my Winchester and ammunition. Our *rabias* (safe-escorts) of the Awamir and Karab tribes rushed out in different directions into the night, shouting – 'We are alert! We are alert! We are So-and-so (giving their names) of such-and-such tribes. These are our party and are under our protection.'*

The object of this was to save us from raiders of their own particular tribes, if such they were, for these would then stay their hand. The cry, I gathered, is never abused: certainly in 1928 I had owed my life, during a journey through the south-eastern border-lands, to my Harsusi *rabia*, who saved us from ambush by members of his own tribe after these had already opened fire at short range.

Our camels were now played out. Their humps, plump and large at the outset, told a story; for the hump is the barometer of the camel's condition, and ours had fallen miserably away. To move onwards involved raising fresh camels, a contingency that had been foreseen, and Shaikh Salih sent ahead to search the Rashidi habitat. He and I had at the outset counted on the need of four relays, but in the event three proved sufficient.

---

* The night's vigil proved to have been unnecessary, for at dawn the tracks of a sand-wolf were traced near by; its whoop had been mistaken for the war-cry of raiders in the final act.

Propitious rains (over great areas rain does not fall throughout the year) of last season in the sands of Dakaka had given rise to superior pastures, and to that area, therefore, the herds had this year gravitated. At the waterhole of Khor Dhahiyah we acquired a new caravan and pushed leisurely westward towards where our third caravan for the final northward dash across the sands was to assemble.

My companions scanned the sands for sign of friend or foe.

'Look, sahib! that's So-and-so,' my men said, pointing to a camel's foot impression that looked, to me, like any other. 'See! she is gone with calf: look how deep are the impressions of her tracks!' And so, following these in the sands, we came up with the object of our quest.

The accuracy of their divination was fascinating. Reading sand-imprints recalled fingerprint identifying in the West, except that it is far less laborious and slow, and not at all the technical job of a highly trained specialist. In fact, every Badu bred in these sands reads the sand-imprints with the readiest facility, for all creation goes unshod, except on an occasion when a Badu wears socks against extreme heat or cold – this being rare, because it is considered effeminate.

The sands are thus an open diary, and he who runs may read. Every one of my companions not only knew at a glance the foot impression of every man and every camel in my caravan, but claimed to know every one of his tribe and not a few of his enemies. No bird may alight, no wild beast or insect pass but needs must leave its history in the sands, and the record lasts until the next wind rises and obliterates it. To tell-tale sand-tracks a sand-fox and many snakes, hares, and lizards, which I added to my collection, owed their undoing, for their hiding-places were in vain.

Whenever, in future, we halted for the night, generally just before sunset, Hamad, my Murra *rabia*, would slink back over our tracks for a few miles with my telescope to ensure that we were not being tracked by an enemy, and return just after nightfall with the good news that campfires could now be safely lighted.

I picked up fragments of ostrich eggs, often in a semi-petrified condition, and members of my party had shot ostriches hereabouts in their youth, though these birds appear now to be extinct. So also the *rim* or white gazelle is becoming rare, though I saw horns lying about, while the common red gazelle and the larger edible lizards are inhabitants of the bordering steppe rather than of the sands, as is the antelope, specimens of which I shot, besides bringing home a young live one.

It is the antelope whose long, straight horns occasionally appear to be a single spear when she runs across your front, thus giving rise, as some suppose, to the ancient myth of the unicorn. This legendary guardian of chastity allowed none but virtuous maidens to approach it, when its anger turned to joy; and, singularly, today in these southern marches the only musical instrument known is a pipe made of antelope horn, which the Arab maiden plays on the joyful occasions of marriage and circumcision.

Of animal life in the sands, a small sand-coloured wolf is said to be met with in parts where subsoil water, however brackish, can be reached by pawing; a sand-coloured fox and a lynx – relatively non-drinking varieties – are commoner; and the hare, the most widespread mammal, is hunted by the Bedouin's *salugi** dog. Of birds I saw very few – bustards, sand-larks, sand-grouse, owls, and the most common, a black raven, while old eggs in a gigantic nest show that the Abyssinian tawny eagle comes on important visits.

The full moon before the fast month of Ramadhan found us at the waterhole of Shanna, where my third, last, and much-reduced caravan (13 men and 5 pack animals) was to rendezvous. One of our old camels was ailing, and there is only one way with a worn-out camel in the desert – namely, to kill and eat it. The law of Leviticus is also the law of Islam: flesh not lawfully slaughtered is sinful to eat; wherefore the hats went round, and 56 dollars, plus her earnings due from me, satisfied the owner of the almost blind 40-year-old Fatira. The beast was slaughtered, jointed, and

* Familiar to British breeders as the Salukhi hound.

divided into heaps after the Arabs had all had a good swig at the contents of her bladder – they had done the same to the antelope's bladder – and for the joints the Bedouin now cast lots.

In the steppe, where stones availed, they would have grilled the carcass on a heap of heated stones with a fire beneath – the Stone Age manner, surely! Here as much as sufficed for a meal was boiled in brackish water, and the rest they allowed to remain uncooked, and so carried it exposed on their saddles, where all the cooking that it received was drying from the heat of the sun. These saddle-dainties the Bedouin were to nibble with great relish in the marches ahead, and to declare to be very good. My own view, I confess, was one to be concealed!

The zero hour for the dash northward had arrived. Star sights and traverse-plotting showed my position on the 10 January, 1932, to be lat. 19° N, long. 50° 45' E. My objective, Qatar, on the Persian Gulf, was thus bearing slightly to the east of north, about 330 miles in a straight line across the mysterious sands. Two only of my thirteen Bedouin – the Murras – claimed to have been over this line of desert before. I had rations left for but twenty-five days.

Clearly, no one could afford to fall ill. A hold-up for ten days, an insufficient rate of progress, a meeting with a party of raiders outnumbering us – any of these might spell disaster. Throughout my journey I was screened from any Arab encampments, that, for all I knew, might have been just over the skyline, the single exception being a tiny encampment of Murra, kinsmen of my guide, where an old man lay dying.

It was made up of one or two miserably small tents, roughly spun – doubtless by the womenfolk – of brown and white camel's hair; tent-pegs that once had been the horns of an antelope; a hammer and a leathern bucket or two – these perhaps typical of the belongings of poor nomadic folk, among whom wealth is counted, primarily, in the noble possessions of camel herds and firearms.

Marching north, the character of the desert sands changed; from the sweeping red landscapes of Dakaka we passed through the region of Suwahib, of lighter hue and characteristic parallel ridges in echelon formation; then the white ocean calms of the central sands, succeeded by a rolling swell of redder colour; and with these changing belts the desert flora changed too, the height above sea level falling progressively.

Contrary to expectation, the great central sand ocean was found to be not waterless. We dug down to water at quite shallow depths – a fathom and a half or so; but it was so brackish as to be almost undrinkable – not unlike Epsom salts both in taste and in its effect on man and beast. There are places where even the camel cannot drink the water, though normally when pastures bring nomads to these parts their camels play the part of distillers, for they drink the water and their masters drink their milk.

The shallow waterholes of the southern sands are sometimes filled in, after water, to hinder a possible pursuer, but in the low, shallowing sands of the north, where patches of hard floor made their first appearance, the waterholes were regular wells, sometimes seventeen fathoms and more deep. They are rare and precious, too, apart from their sweeter contents, for great labour and skill have gone to their making. Both making and cleaning out, which must be done periodically, exact a toll of life, for the soft sides are prone to slip in and entomb the miners, and all that avails for revetment is the branches of dwarf sand-bushes.

Onwards through these great silent wastes my little party moved ever northwards, and my bones no longer ached at the daily demand of eight hours in the saddle. On setting out in the morning the Badu with his first foot forward would mumble some pious invocation – a constant reminder of the great uncertainty and insecurity which shadows him:

> In the name of God the Merciful, the Compassionate,
> Reliance is upon Thee.
> There is none other and none equal to Thee.
> In the name of God the Merciful.
> Deliverance from the slinking devil;
> And on Him we rely.

Their inborn philosophy of life is strictly fatalistic, holding that whatever comes to pass is according to a Divine and inscrutable Will. Their attitude to me, at first sullen and suspicious, changed with growing intimacy as the days passed, and they could be, with a few exceptions, cheerful and friendly companions. Under the stimulating effects of a juicy patch of camel pasture come upon unexpectedly, they would break forth into merry chanting, while around the night campfire they never tired of telling me stories from their entrancing folklore.

22 January brought the first of a series of sandstorms, and I passed many fitful nights. The hissing of the sand-laden wind, the rattling of pack-cordage, and icy cold feet – for the night temperature often fell to within five degrees of freezing point – made sleeping out of doors, without a roof over one's head, intolerable.

Eagerly one waited for the dawn. The wind then dropped, and campfires were the scene of huddled, shivering Bedouin who now roused their camels that had been rounded up overnight for safety, and the wretched beasts shuffled off to graze and feel the warmth of the rising sun. For me the nights had tragic results, the sand-drifts having buried my instruments, making some of them of little further use.

But I was on the last lap. And though for many days sweeping, stinging, blinding winds enveloped us in a blanket of yellow mist, a fine morning came when, climbing the towering sandhill of Nakhala, I beheld before me a silver streak of sea along the faraway skyline. Success was in sight. Keeping the coast a day's march, by report, on our right hand, our northerly course carried us through quarry-like country abounding in fossil shells, the aneroid recording below sea-level readings.

And here we came upon an interesting discovery – a lake in this wilderness. For several miles we marched along its western shore. The Bedouin, walking to the edge, brought away large chunks of rock salt that for a width of twenty feet lined its border. There along the water's edge, too, was a line of dead white locusts, desiccated specimens of the large red variety which, collected and thrown alive on to the hot ash of the campfire, sizzles into one of the few delicacies of the Bedouin. Wretched creatures, these locusts, for they seem to delight in swarming out from the thirsty desert in springtime, only to take a suicidal plunge into the first water they come to.

Our lake behind us, we trekked on through bleak stony country, the haunt of owl and wolf, that proved to be the base of the Qatar peninsula. A Gulf *sbamal* was blowing, but its attendant cold and drizzling rain were powerless to damp the enthusiasm of my poor companions on the eve of a rare payday. They chanted the water-chants which, alas! I should be hearing for the last time, and our thirsty camels pricked up their ears with eager knowingness. And so, at last, we came to the fort of Qatar's ruler standing bold and beckoning on the rim of the sea. The dim luxury of a bath and a square meal was at hand. I had lost a stone and a half in weight on my 650-mile camel journey, but the great south Arabian desert, hitherto a blank on our maps, had ceased to be an enigma and a reproach.

SLOW DEATH AT COOPER'S CREEK

WILLIAM JOHN WILLS
(1834–61)

Wills was an English surveyor who emigrated to Australia, where he served as second in command to Robert O'Hara Burke, on the Victorian Exploration Expedition. After leaving Melbourne on 21 August 1860, the expedition made fast progress to Cooper's Creek, where a depot was left, together with most of the men. Four members – Wills, Burke, Gray and King – continued to the Gulf of Carpentaria, which they reached on 4 February 1861, thus completing the first transcontinental crossing of Australia. On the return journey Gray died of privation, and when the others reached the Cooper's Creek depot they found it deserted. On 23 April 1861, Wills, Burke and King started for Adelaide, via Mount Hopeless.

Tuesday, 23 April 1861 Having collected together all the odds and ends that seemed likely to be of use to us, in addition to provisions left in the plant, we started at 9.15 a.m., keeping down the southern bank of the creek; we only went about five miles, and camped at 11.30 on a billibong, where the feed was pretty good. We find the change of diet already making a great improvement in our spirits and strength. The weather is delightful, days agreeably warm, but the nights very chilly. The latter is more noticeable from our deficiency in clothing, the depot party having taken all the reserve things back with them to the Darling. – To Camp No. 1.

Wednesday, 24 April 1861 As we were about to start this morning, some blacks came by, from whom we were fortunate enough to get about twelve pounds of fish for a few pieces of straps and some matches, etc. This is a great treat for us, as well as a valuable addition to our rations. We started at 8.15 p.m. on our way down the creek, the blacks going in the opposite direction. – To Camp No. 2.

Thursday, 25 April, 1861 Awoke at five o'clock after a most refreshing night's rest – the sky was beautifully clear, and the air rather chilly. We had scarcely finished breakfast, when our friends the blacks, from whom we obtained the fish, made their appearance with a few more, and seemed inclined to go with us and keep up the supply. We gave them some sugar, with which they were greatly pleased – they are by far the most well-behaved blacks we have seen on Cooper's Creek. We did not get away from the camp until 9.30 a.m., continuing our course down the most southern branch of the creek, which keeps a general south-west course. – To Camp No. 3. The waterhole at this camp is a very fine one, being several miles long. The waterfowl are numerous, but rather shy, not nearly so much so, however, as those on the creeks between here and Carpentaria.

Friday, 26 April 1861 We loaded the camels by moonlight this morning, and started at a quarter to six: striking off to the south of the creek, we soon got on a native path which leaves the creek just below the stony ground, and takes a course nearly west across a piece of open country. Leaving the path on our right at a distance of three miles, we turned up a small creek, which passes down between some sandhills, and, finding a nice patch of feed for the camels at a waterhole, we halted at 7.15 for breakfast. We started again at 9.50 a.m., continuing our westerly course along the path: we crossed to the south of the watercourse above the water, and proceeded over the most splendid salt-bush country that one could wish to see, bounded on the left by sandhills, whilst to the right the peculiar-looking flat-topped sandstone ranges form an extensive amphitheatre, through the far side of the arena of which may be traced the dark line of creek timber. At twelve o'clock we camped in the bed of the creek at Camp No. [3], our last camp on the road down from the Gulf, having taken four days to do what we then did in one. This comparative rest and the change in diet have also worked wonders, however, the leg-tied feeling is now entirely gone, and I believe that in less than a week we shall be fit to undergo any fatigue whatever. The camels are improving, and seem capable of doing all that we are likely to require of them. – To Camp No. 4.

Saturday, 27 April 1861 We started at six o'clock, and, following the native path, which at about a mile from our camp takes a southerly direction, we soon came to the high sandy alluvial deposit which separates the creek at this point from the stony rises. Here we struck off from the path, keeping well to the south of the creek, in order that we might mess in a branch of it that took a southerly direction. At 9.20 we came in on the creek again where it runs due south, and halted for breakfast at a fine waterhole with fine fresh feed for the camels. Here we remained until noon, when we moved on again, and camped at one o'clock on a general course, having been throughout the morning SW eight miles.

Sunday, 28 April 1861 Morning fine and calm, but rather chilly. Started at 4.45 a.m., following down the bed of a creek in a westerly direction by moonlight. Our stage was, however, very short for about a mile – one of the camels (Landa) got bogged by the side of a waterhole, and although we tried every means in our power, we found it impossible to get him out. All the ground beneath the surface was a bottomless quicksand, through which the beast sank too rapidly for us to get bushes of timber fairly beneath him; and being of a very sluggish stupid nature he could never be got to make sufficiently strenuous efforts towards extricating himself. In the evening, as a last chance, we let the water in from the creek, so as to buoy him up and at the same time soften the ground about his legs; but it was of no avail. The brute lay quietly in it, as if he quite enjoyed his position. – To Camp No. 6.

Monday, 29 April 1861 Finding Landa still in the hole, we made a few attempts at extricating him, and then shot him, and after breakfast commenced cutting off what flesh we could get at for jerking.

Tuesday, 30 April 1861 Remained here today for the purpose of drying the meat, for which process the weather is not very favourable.

Wednesday, 1 May 1861 Started at 8.40, having loaded our only camel, Rajah, with the most necessary and useful articles, and packed up a small swag each, of bedding and clothing for our own shoulders. We kept on the right bank of the creek for about a mile, and then crossed over at a native camp to the left, where we got on a path running due west, the creek having turned to the north. Following the path we crossed an open plain, and then some sand ridges, whence we saw the creek straight ahead of us running nearly south again: the path took us to the southernmost point of the bend in a distance of about two and a half miles from where we had crossed the creek, thereby saving us from three to four miles, as it cannot be less than six miles round by the creek. – To Camp No. 7.

Thursday, 2 May 1861 Breakfasted by moonlight and started at 6.30. Following down the left bank of the creek in a westerly direction, we came at a distance of six miles on a lot of natives who were camped on the bed of a creek. They seemed to have just breakfasted, and were most liberal in their presentations of fish and cake. We could only return the compliment by some fish-hooks and sugar. About a mile farther on we came to a separation of the creek, where what looked like the main branch turned towards the south. This channel we followed, not however without some misgivings as to its character, which were soon increased by the small and unfavourable appearance that the creek assumed. On our continuing along it a little farther it began to improve and widened out with fine waterholes of considerable depth. The banks were very steep, and a belt of scrub lined it on either side. This made it very inconvenient for travelling, especially as the bed of the creek was full of water for a considerable distance. At 11 a.m. we halted, until 1.30 p.m., and then moved on again, taking a SSW course for about two miles, when at the end of a very long waterhole it breaks into billibongs, which continue splitting into sandy channels until they are all lost in the earthy soil of a box forest. Seeing little chance of water ahead, we turned back to the end of the long waterhole and camped for the night. On our way back Rajah showed signs of being done up. He had been trembling greatly all the morning. On this account his load was further lightened to the amount of a few pounds by the doing away with the sugar, ginger, tea, cocoa, and two or three tin plates. – To Camp No. 8.

Friday, 3 May 1861 Started at seven a.m., striking off in a northerly direction for the main creek.

Saturday, 4 May 1861 Rajah was so stiff this morning as to be scarcely able to get up with his load. Started to return down the creek at 6.45, and halted for breakfast at 9 a.m., at the same spot as we breakfasted at yesterday. Proceeding from there down the creek we soon found a repetition of the features that were exhibited by the creek examined on Thursday. At a mile and a half we came to the last waterhole, and below that the channel became more sandy and shallow, and continued to send off billibongs to the south and west, slightly changing its course each time until it disappeared altogether in a north-westerly direction. Leaving King with the camel, we went on a mile or two to see if we could find water, and being unsuccessful we were obliged to return to where we had breakfasted as being the best place for feed and water.

Sunday, 5 May 1861 Started by myself to reconnoitre the country in a southerly direction, leaving Mr Burke and King with the camel at Camp No. 10. Travelled SW by S for two hours, following the course of the most southerly billibongs; found the earthy soil becoming more loose and cracked up, and the box track gradually disappearing. Changed course to west for a high sand ridge, which I reached in one hour and a half, and continuing in the same direction to one still higher, obtained from it a good view of the surrounding country. To the north were the extensive box forests bounding the creek on either side. To the east earthy plains intersected by watercourses and lines of timber, and bounded in the distance by sand ridges. To the south the projection of the sand ridge partially intercepted the view; the rest was composed of earthy plains, apparently clothed with chrysanthemums. To the westward another but smaller plain was bounded also by high sand ridges running nearly parallel with the one on which I was standing.

This dreary prospect offering no encouragement to proceed, I returned to Camp 10 by a more direct and better route than I had come.

Monday, 6 May 1861 Moved up the creek again to Camp No. 9, at the junction, to breakfast, and remained the day there. The present state of things is not calculated to raise our spirits much; the rations are rapidly diminishing; our clothing, especially the boots, are all going to pieces, and we have not the materials for repairing them properly; the camel is completely done up and can scarcely get along, although he has the best of feed and is resting half his time. I suppose this will end in our having to live like the blacks for a few months.

Tuesday, 7 May 1861 Breakfasted at daylight; but when about to start found that the camel would not rise even without any load on his back. After making every attempt to get him up, we were obliged to leave him to himself.

Mr Burke and I started down the creek to reconnoitre; at about eleven miles we came to some blacks fishing; they gave us some half a dozen fish each, for luncheon, and intimated that if we would go to their camp we should have some more and some bread. I tore in two a piece of macintosh stuff that I had, and Mr Burke gave one piece and I the other. We then went on to their camp about three miles farther. On our arrival they led us to a spot to camp on, and soon afterwards brought a lot of fish, and a kind of bread which they call nardoo. The lighting a fire with matches delights them, but they do not care about having them. In the evening various members of the tribe came down with lumps of nardoo and hand-fuls of fish, until we were positively unable to eat any more. They also gave us some stuff they call bedgery or pedgery; it has a highly intoxicating effect when chewed even in small quantities. It appears to be the dried stems and leaves of some shrub.

Wednesday, 8 May 1861 Left the blacks' camp at 7.30, Mr Burke returning to the junction, whilst I proceeded to trace down the creek. This I found a shorter task than I had expected, for it soon showed signs of running out, and at the same time kept consider-ably to the north of west. There were several fine waterholes within about four miles of the camp I had left, but not a drop all the way beyond that, a distance of seven miles. Finding that the creek turned greatly towards the north, I returned to the blacks' encampment, and as I was about to pass they invited me to stay; I did so, and was even more hospitably entertained than before.

Thursday, 9 May 1861 Parted from my friends, the blacks, at 7.30, and started for Camp No. 9.

Friday, 10 May 1861 Mr Burke and King employed in jerking the camel's flesh, whilst I went to look for the nardoo seed for making bread: in this I was unsuccessful, not being able to find a single tree of it in the neighborhood of the camp. I, however, tried boiling the large kind of bean which the blacks call padlu; they boil easily, and when shelled are very sweet, much resembling in taste the French chestnut; they are to be found in large quantities nearly everywhere.

Saturday, 11 May 1861 Today Mr Burke and King started down the creek to the blacks' camp, determined to ascertain all particulars about the nardoo. I have now my turn at the meat jerking, and must devise some means for trapping the birds and rats, which is a pleasant prospect after our dashing trip to Carpentaria, having to hang about Cooper's Creek, living like the blacks.

Sunday, 12 May 1861 Mr Burke and King returned this morning having been unsuccessful in their search for the blacks, who it seems have moved over to the other branch of the creek.

Tuesday, 14 May 1861 Mr Burke and King gone up the creek to look for blacks with four days' provisions. Self-employed in preparing for a final start on their return.

This evening Mr Burke and King returned, having been some considerable distance up the creek and found no blacks. It is now settled that we plant the things, and all start together the day after tomorrow.

Wednesday, 15 May 1861 Planting the things and preparing to leave the creek for Mount Hopeless.

Thursday, 16th May 1861 Having completed our planting, etc., started up the creek for the second blacks' camp, a distance of about eight miles: finding our loads rather too heavy we made a small plant here of such articles as could best be spared.

Nardoo, Friday, 17 May 1861 Started this morning on a blacks' path, leaving the creek on our left, our intention being to keep a south-easterly direction until we should cut some likely looking creek, and then to follow it down. On approaching the foot of the first sandhill, King caught sight in the flat of some nardoo seeds, and we soon found that the flat was covered with them. This discovery caused somewhat of a revolution in our feelings, for we considered that with the knowledge of this plant we were in a position to support ourselves, even if we were destined to remain on the creek and wait for assistance from town.

Friday, 24 May 1861 Started with King to celebrate the Queen's birthday by fetching from Nardoo Creek what is now to us the staff of life; returned at a little after two p.m. with a fair supply, but find the collecting of the seed a slower and more troublesome process than could be desired.

Monday, 27 May 1861 Started up the creek this morning for the depot, in order to deposit journals and a record of the state of affairs here. On reaching the sandhills below where Landa was bogged, I passed some blacks on a flat collecting nardoo seed. Never saw such an abundance of the seed before. The ground in some parts was quite black with it. There were only two or three gins* and children, and they directed me on, as if to their camp, in the direction I was before going; but I had not gone far over the first sandhill when I was overtaken by about twenty blacks, bent on taking me back to their camp, and promising any quantity of nardoo and fish. On my going with them, one carried the shovel, and another insisted on taking my swag in such a friendly manner that I could not refuse them. They were greatly amused with the various little things I had with me. In the evening they supplied me with abundance of nardoo and fish, and one of the old men, Poko Tinnamira, shared his gunyah with me.

---

* Native women.

Tuesday, 28 May 1861 Left the blacks' camp, and proceeded up the creek; obtained some mussels near where Landa died, and halted for breakfast. Still feel very unwell.

Wednesday, 29 May Started at seven a.m., and went on to the duck-holes, where we breakfasted coming down. Halted there at 9.30 a.m. for a feed, and then moved on. At the stones saw a lot of crows quarrelling about something near the water; found it to be a large fish, of which they had eaten a considerable portion. As it was quite fresh and good, I decided the quarrel by taking it with me. It proved a most valuable addition to my otherwise scanty supper of nardoo porridge. This evening I camped very comfortably in a mia-mia, about eleven miles from the depot. The night was very cold, although not entirely cloudless.

Thursday, 30 May 1861 Reached the depot this morning at eleven a.m.; no traces of anyone except blacks having been here since we left. Deposited some journals and a notice of our present condition. Started back in the afternoon, and camped at the first waterhole. Last night, being cloudy, was unusually warm and pleasant.

Friday, 31 May 1861 Decamped at 7.30 a.m., having first break-fasted; passed between the sandhills at nine a.m., and reached the blanket mia-mias at 10.40 a.m.; from there proceeded on to the rocks, where I arrived at 1.30 p.m., having delayed about half an hour on the road in gathering some portulac. It had been a fine morning, but the sky now became overcast, and threatened to set in for steady rain; and as I felt very weak and tired, I only moved on about a mile further, and camped in a sheltered gully under some bushes.

Saturday, 1 June 1861 Started at 7.45 a.m.; passed the duckholes at ten a.m. and my second camp up, at two p.m., having rested in the meantime about forty-five minutes. Thought to have reached the blacks' camp, or at least where Landa was bogged, but found myself altogether too weak and exhausted; in fact, had extreme difficulty in getting across the numerous little gullies, and was at last obliged to camp from sheer fatigue.

Sunday, 2 June 1861 Started at half past six, thinking to breakfast at the blacks' camp below Landa's grave. Found myself very much fagged, and did not arrive at their camp until ten a.m., and then found myself disappointed as to a good breakfast, the camp being deserted. Having rested awhile and eaten a few fishbones, I moved down the creek, hoping by a late march to be able to reach our own camp; but I soon found, from my extreme weakness, that that would be out of the question. A certain amount of good luck, however, still stuck to me, for on going along by a large waterhole I was so fortunate as to find a large fish, about a pound and a half in weight, which was just being choked by another which it had tried to swallow, but which had stuck in its throat. I soon had a fire lit, and both of the fish cooked and eaten: the large one was in good condition. Moving on again after my late breakfast, I passed Camp No. 67 of the journey to Carpentaria, and camped for the night under some polygonum bushes.

Monday, 3 June 1861 Started at seven o'clock, and keeping on the south bank of the creek was rather encouraged at about three miles by the sound of numerous crows ahead; presently fancied I could see smoke, and was shortly afterwards set at my ease by hearing a cooey from Pitchery, who stood on the opposite bank, and directed me round the lower end of the waterhole, continually repeating his assurance of abundance of fish and bread. Having with some considerable difficulty managed to ascend the sandy path that led to the camp, I was conducted by the chief to a fire where a large pile of fish were just being cooked in the most approved style. These I imagined to be for the general consumption of the half-dozen natives gathered around, but it turned out that they had already had their breakfast. I was expected to dispose of this lot – a task which, to my own astonishment, I soon accomplished, keeping two or three blacks pretty steadily at work extracting the bones for me. The fish being disposed of, next came a supply of nardoo cake and water until I was so full as to be unable to eat any more; when Pitchery, allowing me a short time to recover myself, fetched a large bowl of the raw nardoo flour mixed to a thin paste, a most insinuating article, and one that they appear to esteem a great delicacy. I was then invited to stop the night there, but this I declined, and proceeded on my way home.

Tuesday, 4 June 1861 Started for the blacks' camp intending to test the practicability of living with them, and to see what I could learn as to their ways and manners.

Wednesday, 5 June 1861 Remained with the blacks. Light rain during the greater part of the night, and more or less throughout the day in showers. Wind blowing in squalls from south.

Thursday, 6 June 1861 Returned to our own camp: found that Mr Burke and King had been well supplied with fish by the blacks. Made preparation for shifting our camp nearer theirs on the morrow.

Friday, 7 June 1861 Started in the afternoon for the blacks' camp with such things as we could take; found ourselves all very weak in spite of the abundant supply of fish that we have lately had. I myself, could scarcely get along, although carrying the lightest swag, only about thirty pounds. Found that the blacks had decamped, so determined on proceeding tomorrow up to the next camp, near the nardoo field.

Saturday, 8 June 1861 With the greatest fatigue and difficulty we reached the nardoo camp. No blacks, greatly to our disappointment; took possession of their best mia-mia and rested for the remainder of the day.

Sunday, 9 June 1861 King and I proceeded to collect nardoo, leaving Mr Burke at home.

Monday, 10 June 1861 Mr Burke and King collecting nardoo; self at home too weak to go out; was fortunate enough to shoot a crow.

Tuesday, 11 June 1861 King out for nardoo; Mr Burke up the creek to look for the blacks.

Wednesday, 12 June 1861 King out collecting nardoo; Mr Burke and I at home pounding and cleaning. I still feel myself, if anything, weaker in the legs, although the nardoo appears to be more thoroughly digested.

Thursday, 13 June 1861 Mr Burke and King out for nardoo; self weaker than ever; scarcely able to go to the waterhole for water.

Friday, 14 June 1861 Night alternately clear and cloudy; no wind; beautifully mild for the time of year; in the morning some heavy clouds on the horizon. King out for nardoo; brought in a good supply. Mr Burke and I at home, pounding and cleaning seed. I feel weaker than ever, and both Mr B. and King are beginning to feel very unsteady in the legs.

Saturday, 15 June 1861 Night clear, calm, and cold; morning very fine, with a light breath of air from NE. King out for nardoo; brought in a fine supply. Mr Burke and I pounding and cleaning; he finds himself getting very weak, and I am not a bit stronger.

Sunday, 16 June 1861 We finished up the remains of the camel Rajah yesterday, for dinner; King was fortunate enough to shoot a crow this morning.

The rain kept all hands in, pounding and cleaning seed during the morning. The weather cleared up towards the middle of the day, and a brisk breeze sprang up in the south, lasting till near sunset, but rather irregular in its force. Distant thunder was audible to westward and southward frequently during the afternoon.

Monday, 17 June 1861 Night very boisterous and stormy; northerly wind blowing in squalls, and heavy showers of rain, with thunder in the north and west. King out in the afternoon for nardoo.

Tuesday, 18 June 1861 Exceedingly cold night; sky clear, slight breeze, very chilly and changeable; very heavy dew, warmer towards noon.

Wednesday, 19 June 1861 About eight o'clock a strong southerly wind sprung up, which enabled King to blow the dust out of our nardoo seed, but made me too weak to render him any assistance.

Thursday, 20th June, 1861 Night and morning very cold, sky clear. I am completely reduced by the effects of the cold and starvation. King gone out for nardoo; Mr Burke at home pounding seed; he finds himself getting very weak in the legs. King holds out by far the best; the food seems to agree with him pretty well.

Finding the sun come out pretty warm towards noon, I took a sponging all over; but it seemed to do little good beyond the cleaning effects, for my weakness is so great that I could not do it with proper expedition.

I cannot understand this nardoo at all – it certainly will not agree with me in any form; we are now reduced to it alone, and we manage to consume from four to five pounds per day between us; it appears to be quite indigestible, and cannot possibly be sufficiently nutritious to sustain life by itself.

Friday, 21 June 1861 Last night was cold and clear, winding up with a strong wind from NE in the morning. I feel much weaker than ever and can scarcely crawl out of the mia-mia. Unless relief comes in some form or other, I cannot possibly last more than a fortnight.

It is a great consolation, at least, in this position of ours, to know that we have done all we could, and that our deaths will rather be the result of the mismanagement of others than of any rash acts of our own. Had we come to grief elsewhere, we could only have blamed ourselves; but here we are returned to Cooper's Creek, where we had every reason to look for provisions and clothing; and yet we have to die of starvation, in spite of the explicit instructions given by Mr Burke – 'That the depot party should await our return'; and the strong recommendation to the Committee 'that we should be followed up by a party from Menindie'.

Saturday, 22 June 1861 There were a few drops of rain during the night, and in the morning, about nine a.m., there was every prospect of more rain until towards noon, when the sky cleared up for a time.

Mr Burke and King are out for nardoo; the former returned much fatigued. I am so weak today as to be unable to get on my feet.

Sunday, 23 June 1861 All hands at home. I am so weak as to be incapable of crawling out of the mia-mia. King holds out well, but Mr Burke finds himself weaker every day.

Monday, 24 June 1861 A fearful night. At about an hour before sunset, a southerly gale sprung up and continued throughout the greater portion of the night; the cold was intense, and it seemed as if one would be shrivelled up. Towards morning it fortunately lulled a little, but a strong cold breeze continued till near sunset, after which it became perfectly calm.

King went out for nardoo in spite of the wind, and came in with a good load; but he himself terribly cut up. He says that he can no longer keep up the work, and as he and Mr Burke are both getting rapidly weaker, we have but a slight chance of anything but starvation, unless we can get hold of some blacks.

Tuesday, 25 June 1861 Night calm, clear, and intensely cold, especially towards morning. Near daybreak, King reported seeing a moon in the east, with a haze of light stretching up from it; he declared it to be quite as large as the moon, and not dim at the edges. I am so weak that any attempt to get a sight of it was out of the question; but I think it must have been Venus in the Zodiacal Light that he saw, with a corona around her.

Wednesday, 26 June Mr Burke and King remain at home cleaning and pounding seed; they are both getting weaker every day; the cold plays the deuce with us, from the small amount of clothing we have: my wardrobe consists of a wide-awake, a merino shirt, a regatta shirt without sleeves, the remains of a pair of flannel trousers, two pairs of socks in rags, and a waistcoat, of which I have managed to keep the pockets together. The others are no better off. Besides these, we have between us, for bedding, two small camel pads, some horsehair, two or three little bits of rag, and pieces of oilcloth saved from the fire.

The day turned out nice and warm.

Thursday, 28 June 1861 Mr Burke and King are preparing to go up the creek in search of the blacks; they will leave me some nardoo, wood, and water, with which I must do the best I can until they return. *I think this is almost our only chance.* I feel myself, if anything, rather better, but I cannot say stronger: the nardoo is beginning to agree better with me; but without some change I see little chance for any of us. They have both shown great hesitation and reluctance with regard to leaving me, and have repeatedly desired my candid opinion in the matter. I could only repeat, however, that I considered it our only chance, for I could not last long on the nardoo, even if a supply could be kept up.

Friday, 29 June 1861 Clear, cold night, slight breeze from the east, day beautifully warm and pleasant. Mr Burke suffers greatly from the cold and is getting extremely weak; he and King start tomorrow up the creek to look for the blacks; it is the only chance we have of being saved from starvation. I am weaker than ever, although I have a good appetite and relish the nardoo much; but it seems to give us no nutriment, and the birds here are so shy as not to be got at. Even if we got a good supply of fish, I doubt whether we could do much work on them and the nardoo alone. Nothing now but the greatest good luck can save any of us; and as for myself I may live four or five days if the weather continues warm. My pulse is at forty-eight, and very weak, and my legs and arms are nearly skin and bone. I can only look out, like Mr Micawber, 'for *something to turn up*'; starvation on nardoo is by no means very unpleasant, but for the weakness one feels, and the utter inability to move one's self; for as far as appetite is concerned, it gives the greatest satisfaction.

(*Signed*) W. J. WILLS

Wills's journal was found lying beside his corpse. Burke also died of starvation. King managed to find an aboriginal band and was eventually rescued.

THE CROSSING

NICK DANZIGER
(1958–)

*Anglo-American travel writer and artist. As part of a journey behind
the forbidden borders of Asia, he left Soviet-occupied Afghanistan in
1984 with a mujahedeen jeep convoy for Pakistan.*

The journey, as we bucked and bumped our way across the desert,
was quite back-breaking, but I felt that I could take it pretty
uncomplainingly, for after all it would only be another couple of
nights, and then . . . Then, goodbye helicopters, MiGs, RPGs and
barren desert. Why, in 72 hours' time I would be relaxing in the
swimming pool of a sumptuous hotel.

My daydreams were abruptly overwhelmed by the sight of
another burnt-out Symorgh. It was the fifth wreck we had passed.
How many dead, I wondered, just in this little struggle for control
of the road. Clearly it was not firmly back in mujahedeen hands.

We were going to have to travel for a short stretch along the
main road that links Kabul and Kandahar, and we had sent
scouts ahead to check if it was clear. Now, we pulled over to
await their return. It was a tense time, and I found myself having
to breathe deeply and regularly to contain my excitement. I did
not think I could bear it if they were to return and say '*Ra band*'
– the way is closed.

'When can we expect them?' I asked one of my companions – a
rather better-off young man, who had feigned sickness off and on

in the hope of getting me to give him some pills, which I think he took to be like sweets.

'Two hours,' he said promptly. I decided to expect them in four. In fact, they returned in precisely two hours, and you could tell by their faces what they were going to say.

'*Ra band.*'

We spent the rest of that night and the whole of the next day holed up tensely at an oasis, marking time under the shadow of the trees, while the scouts were dispatched yet again to keep an eye on the situation. Restlessly, we once again discussed alternative possibilities. As we did so, Abdul Mohmy, his usual tireless self, went to bake bread for us at a nearby hamlet.

'Could we walk?' I asked.

'It would take five days – if we could get through.'

'No water,' said Abdul Rahman. He was more restless than anyone else, and clearly couldn't relax.

'What's the matter with him? Is he ill?' I asked Zahir, my minder.

'I think he must be afraid,' replied Zahir.

With two hours of daylight left the scouts returned, this time with the heartening but almost unbelievable news that the road was once again '*ra azad*'. I hoped it would still be so by the time we reached it. We headed off at once.

We had only just cleared the first hill and begun to travel along a dry river bed when someone near me began to scream,

'*Tiare!*'

The panicky word caught on, and soon they were all yelling it, craning for a sight of the sky from the packed jeep. They had spotted a plane.

The jeep slowed violently, and we struggled to bail out, but there were many unable to jump when the jeep decided to take off at full speed. We were the middle jeep. The leader had carried on apparently unaware; the last one had seen the panic ahead and reversed up a hill. Ours had come to a halt some way off and the driver and the mechanic were throwing a tarpaulin over it. We had all rushed up a steep incline and now crouched huddled together, taking refuge in whatever crevice we could find – all, that is, except for one man who had taken off in the other direction – into the open – where, to my total disbelief, he now knelt and proceeded to pray. We strained our ears for the noise of the returning jet, but we must have been just in time to get out of its way, for the sound of its engine faded and finally died.

Once the danger was over, the whole group settled down to pray – I have to say that I found this vexing, given how urgent our situation was. Our driver seemed to pray for an inordinately long time.

We caught up with the first jeep. They, too, had heard the plane, and had rounded a bend and pulled up close to the cliff-wall of the valley we had been passing through.

'Thank God for that valley,' the mechanic said.

'Thank God we weren't five minutes further along the track,' said the driver. 'Then we would have been in open desert.'

During the long days of marching before Nouzad, I had learned to tell the time by measuring the length of my shadow cast by the sun. Now I tried to teach myself how to get my bearings by the stars. I always kept an eye on where the nearest mountains were, and remembered the location of the last oasis we had visited. This wasn't easy. We never took a direct route, but were forever weaving around the desert. I was most impressed by our drivers' uncanny sense of direction, but perhaps the close brush with the aeroplane had disconcerted them more than somewhat, for all at once the three jeeps pulled up together and the drivers announced that they were lost. It was by now dark, and to go on without a guide would have been foolhardy. Luckily, and as always happens in the Afghan desert, other life appeared within a matter of moments, in the form of a tractor and its driver.

Immediately our drivers started to argue with our commanders about who was going to pay this guide for his services. Each side was trying to outdo the other, of course, and there was lot of lip-curling and 'Call yourselves Muslims?' going on. Meantime valuable minutes ticked by, and my nerves were becoming frayed.

'How much are you arguing about?' I asked.

'He wants one thousand *Afghanis*.'

About £7! I was about to pull out the money in *Afghanis*, thinking, to hell with this, I'll pay, but then I stopped. I knew that such a gesture would be hopeless. It would also betray me and endanger my companions. So I sat and seethed until the argument was resolved, trying to calm myself with the thought that for an Afghan, £7 is a considerable sum.

The tractor-driver guided us down a dirt track to a village where dozens and dozens of children milled about, despite the fact that by now it was the middle of the night. We stopped for the mechanics to overhaul the jeeps as far as they could, and for our drivers to find out how far we were still from the Kabul–Kandahar road.

'Three hours,' came the inevitable reply. Gloomily, we refuelled the jeeps from the oil drums they carried and set off again – but at snail's pace, for the track ahead was full of pitfalls, and we had to send two mujahedeen ahead of each vehicle to guide us. However, at length we reached the road. Our tractor-driving guide left us, and I was about to breathe a sigh of relief. Then one of the jeeps broke down. It took half an hour to repair it, by which time I estimated that we had a bare hour of darkness left to travel in. But now, instead of taking to the road, our drivers took off along a track to the left of it.

The track led us to a bowl-shaped area surrounded on three sides by precipitous mountains.

'What are we doing here?' I asked Abdul Rahman as calmly as I could.

Abdul Rahman had recovered quite a lot of his composure. 'We will camp here tonight, and then in the morning we will climb to the guerrilla stronghold at the top of that hill,' he said.

During all my time in Afghanistan, I tried to place my faith in the people in whose hands my safety lay. I had had no difficulty in doing this with Ismail Khan, but I felt doubtful about Abdul Rahman. I decided that I would try to panic him. Fortuitously, high overhead, a large plane flew by. It was still dark enough to see its red landing light flashing clearly.

'Do you see that?' I asked him.

'Yes.'

'That light is a camera. The Russians are taking photographs of us every time it flashes.'

I had hoped that he would order an immediate evacuation. Instead he looked rather pleased and wandered off. I was nonplussed but a few minutes later I was surrounded by delighted mujahedeen.

'Did you see that plane?' they chorused.

'Yes.'

'It was taking pictures of us. Isn't that something?' they announced proudly. 'Abdul Rahman told us. Truly, he is a great commander, to know such things.'

I did discover that the mujahedeen stronghold we had invited ourselves to belonged to a group called Jabhe. In the freezing dawn of 13 September we threw tarpaulins over the jeeps, parked, as I now saw, among several other similarly shrouded vehicles. Then, wrapped in our patous, we climbed the path uphill. We hadn't gone far when,

'Halt! Who goes there?' demanded a young mujahed, popping up from behind a rock, complete with Kalashnikov, which he proceeded to fire, once, into the air. We were frisked and disarmed, and only then allowed to proceed. We were told not to stray from the path, which was clearly marked with black flags, and on either side of which drivers and passengers lay sleeping in niches and crevices in the rocks. We came to a halt at the top of an improvised waiting area-cum-mosque. The holy *mirhab* of the mosque was simply marked out in a semicircle of stones. Here, Abdul Mohmy spent several hours in prayer – an action which gave me serious and grave concern. Mohmy was highly intelligent and genuinely tough. He would not pray so long and so earnestly without good reason. I noticed too that high morale and good humour had somehow evaporated overnight. To my horror, it looked as though the trip to Pakistan had finally been abandoned, though I could not fathom why.

Later the reason became clear. There had been a report on the BBC the night before that the Russians intended to seal the border once and for all. Most of the day was spent brooding, or in *sotto voce* discussion, but by late afternoon a decision appeared to have been reached, and we all trooped down to the jeeps. Hope rose in me before I could suppress it.

'What's happening?' I asked Aminullah, a brazen commander who had joined us on the road.

'Tonight we will try for the border,' he said. 'Tonight it will be make or break.'

Our party was joined by eight heavily armed Jabhe mujahedeen in their own Symorgh. They were mean-looking characters, and one of them still sported his sunglasses, though the light had long since faded; but any demonstration of extra support was reassuring, as we would have to join the main road at a junction by a village where a Russian garrison was situated. We left after a lengthy prayer meeting, but finally the engines roared, beards were wiped, Allah was invoked, and off we went.

The extra Symorgh carrying the eight guerrillas took up the rear. We never saw them again.

On reaching the Kabul–Kandahar road we were confronted by a tumult. Our headlights caught a crowd of mujahedeen running hither and thither, brandishing their guns and shouting frantically. Not far beyond them loomed the sinister shapes of buildings. The first jeep roared off down the road, and the second jeep and ours followed closely, while we passengers either kept a lookout for mines or bent our heads in prayer. We could in fact have been travelling faster, but we dared not, for fear of not being able to brake in time to avoid a pothole or a mine. I wondered if we could have avoided a mine anyway, but then I realised that the local mujahedeen had sent scouts up ahead and these had lit signal flares to tell us that a particular stretch of road was clear. Proceeding like this, from signal to signal, we travelled some way. After a time, we braked hard and swerved off the road down a steep bank to the right. Lights ablaze, we headed for the foothills, but we paused briefly with a group of mujahedeen who proudly showed us the mines they had collected. Mines are simply placed on the tarmac by the army, and the same technique is employed by the mujahedeen when they manage to collect them, rather than being blown up by them. But I hadn't got time to try to make sense out of this, for I was worrying now about why we still had our lights on as we headed across country. What if the Russians had landed heli-borne troops ahead to ambush us? Sometimes I wished I hadn't such a vivid imagination.

Soon the track we were following petered out, and several mujahedeen with torches were dispatched to find it again in the darkness ahead. This was done amid several arguments about the relative correctness of the route we'd chosen. We made slow progress, but soon it became evident that the route was impassable.

But impassable or not, there was no turning back now. We all left the vehicles to walk. Maybe with no load, the drivers could coax the jeeps through the slippery uphill scree. This they did, but we had to gather rocks to build some kind of grippable surface for the tyres ahead, and progress became agonisingly slow. Sometimes a jeep would get stuck and we would have to construct a winch to haul it forwards – a process that took several hours. Our hands and feet were bleeding from the rocks, and we were covered with dust.

This went on for two despairing days, but just as our water was running out, the terrain eased. We made a relatively trouble-free descent to a dry river bed, gratefully climbed into the jeeps again and roared off. The river bed was as good as a motorway after what we'd been through, but still better was to come: a village had been sighted ahead.

'Afghanistan! Afghanistan!' my companions all shouted in relieved triumph.

The only obligatory halts were those made for prayers, though even then only a few people descended – most of us were too impatient. Our driver took ages, and grated on everyone's nerves.

'Do it later,' people shouted at him. 'We're nearly there!'

Placidly, he completed his prayers. Then and not before did we head off again. We were the last jeep. The others had already disappeared from view and we were on our way at speed to catch up. It was dawn, and soon we could be easily spotted by enemy aircraft.

'Never mind – we'll be in Pakistan in an hour,' someone said confidently.

I was still doubtful, but the mujahedeen could hardly contain their jubilation. Another village had appeared on the horizon. Could it be that that village was in Pakistan? It seemed likely, people thought. Closer and closer we came to it. Then our engine seized.

The order was quickly given to make a run for the village, while the driver and mechanic stayed with the vehicle to see what was wrong. The village was soon reached. No, this wasn't Pakistan, they told us. Pakistan was an hour away.

At least we were sheltered and reunited with the other two vehicles. Ours limped into the village soon after, and all three were covered to prevent them from being spotted from the air. There was nothing to do now but kill time until nightfall, so we spent the day either in prayer or eating pomegranates. I'd never eaten one in my life before I travelled to Afghanistan. Now I was developing quite a taste for them. Kandahar airport was to our west, and we could see in the distance the ominous roving of helicopters and MiGs. The area we were in, however, seemed to have been untouched by the violence of the war. This may have been due to the policies of the local Russian commander.

As usual, estimates varied about how long it would actually take us to reach the border. One hour was the most optimistic, six hours the most pessimistic, but the general consensus was that we would have to spend an hour and a half driving through a narrow gorge, mined by the Russians, and here an additional danger existed. Here indeed the Russians sometimes landed heli-borne troops to ambush those entering or leaving the country by the strip of road that threaded it.

A village scout had been sent ahead to spy out the land but by late afternoon he still hadn't returned.

'He'll be back,' Abdul Rahman said.

'I hope so. If he doesn't return, it'll mean he's been either killed or captured – and both those things mean the enemy is around,' I said. I thought about what Rahman had said to me when I'd broached the possibility of walking across – 'They'll either catch you in the open or you'll die of thirst' – he was probably right. I had better stick with the jeep, come what may, I thought.

We were all exhausted by now, after all the struggles and dashed hopes, but we still felt anxious and everyone prayed vigorously. Dusk fell, and there was still no sign of the scout. They decided to leave it in God's hands – 'Insha Allah' – and piled into the jeeps.

Our jeep hadn't gone a hundred yards before the engine stalled again. They'd obviously made a botched job of the repair – what was needed was a new starter motor, of which we carried a spare – and now – when we had least time – they would have to do the job properly.

As they worked I watched them in exasperation. Then an old man appeared wraith-like out of the darkness.

'The tanks are coming,' he announced.

My heart stopped. But he had spoken Pashtu, of which I only understood a little, and perhaps I had misheard him.

'Did he say the tanks are coming?' I asked Abdul Rahman.

'No,' replied Rahman. 'He said the tanks aren't coming.' But it seemed to me unlikely that the old man would have gone to the effort of following us out into the darkness to impart such non-news. Besides, one of the drivers' little boys had started to wail bitterly.

'How's the starter motor going?'

'Nearly there,' came a muffled and frantic reply, which might have meant anything.

I looked around desperately. I couldn't believe our bad luck. Everyone was crowding round the open bonnet to conceal as far as possible the torchlight which was illuminating the mechanic's work. Our armed escort, bringing his rifle to the ready, ordered some of our men to prime the grenades for the RPG, but then it transpired that no one knew how to. What a way to perish, I thought bitterly. By now we could hear the ominous rumble of tanks quite clearly. The little boy whimpered. The rest of us were silent, gazing fearfully into the night behind us.

And then the engine fired. I think that the noise of that engine will remain the sweetest sound I shall ever hear. We piled in before you could say 'Allah' and, praying that nothing else would go wrong, bolted down the road after our companion jeeps.

Incredibly, the other jeeps had waited for us. Irrespective of danger and the possibility of escaping, I noticed that no one was ever abandoned. A frenzied search now began among the other mechanics to find the requisite nuts and bolts from their own tool-kits to bolt our new starter motor securely into place. We were in open desert, and a kilometre away we could see the faint glimmer of the lights of the tanks. Oh, God, I thought . . . so near and yet so far . . . please don't let them get us now . . . All at once I found myself repeating the *kalimeh*, and it comforted me.

The two little boys clung to each other and wept, while the mujahedeen awkwardly tried to comfort them. I watched the tanks. Surely they could see us with their nightsights?

And then I realised that they were not heading towards us, but away from us. The patrol hadn't seen us. All of a sudden a red tracer bullet soared high into the air to the south. We couldn't make out what was going on, but one thing was certain: the Russians' attention was focused elsewhere.

An hour later we reached the mouth of the gorge. We switched our headlights off, and the jeeps filled with the murmur of prayers. I, too, cupped my hands and repeated '*Bismillah Rahman-i-Rahim* . . .'

once again. The tension was overpowering as we gazed up at the looming sides of the gorge, soon lost in the thick darkness.

Allah must have been with us. This last part of the journey was a kind of summation of all that was Afghanistan for me: whether the scout had actually come this far, whether he had returned or gone off somewhere else, I would never know. We had allies though: the goats and sheep gently foraging for food, and with them – a shepherd. Where the terrain was so rough that apart from this strip of road the only access troops could find to it was by helicopter, a shepherd stood alone somewhere above us on the walls of the gorge. We could not see him – indeed, we never saw him – but his voice drifted down to us like a god's – and it provided, as all Afghans do, information. After the usual formal exchange of greetings, he told us that another vehicle had passed safely through not two hours earlier. There had been no activity since. Therefore there were probably no mines, and there could be no ambush. Our hearts leapt.

Further on there was a grim reminder that others had not been so lucky. The wreck of a burnt-out jeep lay by the side of the road.

We emerged from the gorge feeling that truly nothing could stop us now. And as if to confirm our confidence, there on the horizon we could see the twinkling electric lights of Chaman, just inside the Pakistan border. It had been two months since I had seen electric light, and even at this distance it seemed strangely miraculous, and bright.

THE SANDS OF THE GOBI

NIKOLAI NIKHAILOVICH
PRZHEVALSKI
(1839–88)

Russian soldier and traveller. He led several expeditions to Central
Asia, amassing a collection of flora and fauna, including the wild horse
named after him.

The second week in June [1873] we left the high lands of Kan-su
and crossed the threshold of the desert of Ala-shan. The sand
drifts now lay before us like a boundless sea, and it was not
without sundry misgivings that we entered this forbidding realm.

Without sufficient means to enable us to hire a guide, we went
alone, risking all dangers and difficulties, the more imminent
because the year before, while travelling with the Tangutan
caravan, I could only note down by stealth, and often at haphazard, the landmarks and direction of the route. This itinerary was
of course inaccurate, but now it served as our only guide.

We were fifteen days marching from Tajing to Din-yuan-ing,
and safely accomplished this difficult journey, only once nearly
losing ourselves in the desert. This happened on 21 June
between Lake Serik-dolon and the well of Shangin-dalai. Having
left Serik-dolon early in the morning, we marched through
miles of loose sands, and at last came to an expanse of clay
where the track divided. We had not noticed this spot on the
outward journey, and had therefore to guess which of the two
roads would lead to our destination. What made it worse was

that the angle of bifurcation being acute, we could not decide, even with the aid of a compass, which we ought to take. The track to the right being more beaten, we determined to follow it, but after all we were mistaken, for having gone a few miles a number of other tracks crossed ours. This fairly puzzled us; however, we still pressed forward, till at length a well-beaten road joined the one we had first chosen. This we durst not follow, for it went we knew not whither, nor could we return to the place where the roads first branched off. Choosing the lesser of two evils, we resolved to persevere in our first route, hoping soon to see the group of hills at whose foot lies the well of Shangin-dalai. But it was midday, and the intense heat obliged us to halt for two or three hours. On resuming our march, with the aid of the compass we steered in the same direction as before, till at length we discerned a small group of hills to our right. These we supposed to be the landmark of the Shangin-dalai, but they were still a long way off, and the dust which pervaded the atmosphere the whole day prevented our seeing their outline distinctly even with a glass.

Evening fell and we halted for the night, fully confident that these hills were indeed those we were in search of. But on project-ing our line of march on the map, I became aware how far we had diverged to the right of our proper course, and doubts arose as to whether we were really on the right road or not. In the meanwhile only five gallons of water were left for the night; our horses had had none, and were suffering such agonies of thirst that they could hardly move their legs. The question of finding the well on the morrow became one of life and death. How can I describe our feelings as we lay down to rest! Fortunately the wind fell and the dust in the air cleared off. In the morning, with the first glimmer of light, I climbed on to the top of the pile of boxes containing our collections, and carefully scanned the horizon with a glass. I could see distinctly the group of hills we had remarked the previous day, but in a direction due north of our halting-place: I could also distinguish the summit of another, which might perhaps be that of Shangin-dalai. Towards which should we direct our steps? Having taken careful bearings of the latter, and having compared its position on the map with that noted down last year, we decided to march in that direction.

In doubt and anxiety we loaded our camels and started, the hill now and then visible above the low ridges, and now and again hidden from sight. In vain we strained our eyes through the glass to see the cairn of stones ('obo') piled upon its summit; the distance was still too great to distinguish anything so small. At length, after having gone nearly seven miles from the halting-place, we descried what we sought; with strength renewed by hope we pressed onwards; and in a few more hours we stood by the side of the well, to which our animals, tortured with thirst, rushed eagerly forward.

On one of the marches through Southern Ala-shan we met a caravan of Mongol pilgrims on their way from Urga to Lhassa . . . The pilgrims were marching in echelons, some distance apart, having agreed to rendezvous at Koko-nor. As the foremost files met us, they exclaimed, 'See where our brave fellows have got to!' and could hardly believe at first that we four had actually penetrated into Tibet. But what must have been the appearance of the Russian *molodtsi*? Exhausted with fatigue, half starved, unkempt, with ragged clothes and boots worn into holes, we were regular tatterde-malions! So completely had we lost the European aspect that when we arrived at Din-yuan-ing the natives remarked that we were the very image of their own people! – i.e. of the Mongols . . .

In accordance with the plan we had previously sketched, we purposed marching straight to Urga from Din-yuan-ing, by way of the Central Gobi, a route which had never before been travelled by any European, and was therefore of the greatest scientific inter-est. Before starting, however, we determined to rest, and to take this opportunity of exploring more thoroughly than last time the mountains of Ala-shan . . . Here we stayed three weeks, and finally came to the conclusion that the mountains of Ala-shan are rich neither in flora nor in fauna . . .

In such arid mountains as these one would have supposed that we should not have incurred the slightest risk from water; but fate willed that we should experience every misfortune which can possibly overtake the traveller in these countries, for, without giving us the slightest warning, a deluge, such as we never remember to have seen, swept suddenly down upon us.

It was on the morning of 13 July; the summits of the mountains were enveloped in mist, a sure indication of rain. Towards midday, however, it became perfectly clear and gave every promise of a fine day, when, three hours later, all of a sudden, clouds began to settle on the mountains, and the rain poured down in buckets. Our tent was soon soaked through, and we dug small trenches to drain off the water which made its way into the interior. This continued for an hour without showing any sign of abatement, although the sky did not look threatening. The rainfall was so great that it was more than could be absorbed by the soil or retained on the steep slopes of the mountains; the consequence was that streams formed in every cleft and gorge, even falling from the precipitous cliffs, and uniting in the principal ravine, where our tent happened to be pitched, descended in an impetuous torrent with terrific roar and speed. Dull echoes high up in the mountains warned us of its approach, and in a few minutes the deep bed of our ravine was inundated with a turbid, coffee-coloured stream, carrying with it rocks and heaps of smaller fragments, while it dashed with such violence against the sides that the very ground trembled as though with the shock of an earthquake. Above the roar of the waters we could hear the clash of great boulders as they met in their headlong course. From the loose banks and from the upper parts of the defile whole masses of smaller stones were detached by the force of the current and thrown up on either side of the channel, whilst trees were torn up by their roots and rent into splinters ... Barely twenty feet from our tent rushed the torrent, destroying everything in its course. Another minute, another foot of water, and our collections, the fruit of our expedition, were irrevocably gone! ...

Fortune, however, again befriended us. Before our tent was a small projecting ledge of rock upon which the waves threw up stones which soon formed a breakwater, and this saved us. Towards evening the rain slackened, the torrent quickly subsided, and the following morning beheld only a small stream flowing where the day before the waters of a mighty river had swept along . . .

On returning to Din-yuan-ing we equipped our caravan, bartered away our bad camels, bought new ones, and on the morning of 26 July started on our journey. Thanks to our Peking passport and still more to the presents we bestowed on the *tosal-akchi* who acted as regent during the Prince's* absence, we were able to hire two guides to escort us to the border of Ala-shan, where we were to obtain others, and for this purpose the yamen (or magistracy) of Ala-shan issued an official document: in this way we continued to obtain guides from one banner to another; a matter of great importance, for our road lay through the wildest part of the Gobi, in a meridional direction from Ala-shan to Urga, and we could not possibly have found our way without them.

Another long series of hardships now awaited us. We suffered most from the July heat, which at midday rose to 113° Fahr. in the shade, and at night was never less than 73°. No sooner did the sun appear above the horizon than it scorched us mercilessly. In the daytime the heat enveloped us on all sides, above from the sun, below from the burning ground; the wind, instead of cooling the atmosphere, stirred the lower strata and made it even more intolerable. On these days the cloudless sky was of a dirty hue, the soil heated to 145° Fahr., and even higher where the sands were entirely bare, whilst at a depth of two feet from the surface it was 79°.

Our tent was no protection, for it was hotter within than without, although the sides were raised. We tried pouring water

---

* The Prince of Ala-shan.

on it, and on the ground inside, but this was useless, in half an hour everything was as dry as before, and we knew not whither to turn for relief.

The air, too, was terribly dry; no dew fell, and rain clouds dispersed without sending more than a few drops to earth ... Thunderstorms rarely occurred, but the wind was incessant night and day, and sometimes blew with great violence, chiefly from the south-east and south-west. On calm days tornadoes were frequent about the middle of the day or a little later. To avoid the heat as much as possible we rose before daybreak; tea-drinking and loading the camels, however, took up so much time that we never got away before four or even five o'clock in the morning. We might have lightened the fatigue considerably by night-marching, but in that case we should have had to forgo the survey which formed so important a part of our labours ...

The commencement of our journey was unpropitious, for on the sixth day after we left Din-yuan-ing, we lost our faithful friend Faust,* and we ourselves nearly perished in the sands.

It was on 31 July; we had left Djaratai-dabas and had taken the direction of the Khan-ula mountains; our guide having informed us that a march of eighteen miles lay before us that day, but that we should pass two wells about five miles apart.

Having accomplished that distance, we arrived at the first, and after watering our animals, proceeded, in the full expectation of finding the second, where we intended to halt; for though it was only seven in the morning, the heat was overpowering. So confident were we that the Cossacks proposed to throw away the supply of water that we had taken in the casks, in order not to burden our camels needlessly, but fortunately I forbade their doing this. After nearly seven miles more, no well was to be seen, and the guide announced that we had gone out of our road. So he proceeded to the top of a hillock in the immediate neighbour-hood to obtain a view over the surrounding country, and soon

---

* Colonel Prejevalesky's setter.

afterwards beckoned to us to follow. On rejoining him, he assured us that although we had missed the second well, a third, where he purposed passing the night, was scarcely four miles farther. We took the direction indicated. In the meanwhile it was near midday and the heat intolerable. A strong wind stirred the hot lower atmosphere, enveloping us in sand and saline dust. Our animals suffered frightfully; especially the dogs, obliged to walk over the burning sand. We stopped several times to give them drink, and to moisten their heads as well as our own. But the supply of water now failed! Less than a gallon remained, and this we reserved for the last extremity. 'How much farther is it?' was the question we constantly put to our guide, who invariably answered that it was near, that we should see it from the next sandhill or the one after; and so we passed on upwards of seven miles without having seen a sign of the promised well. In the meanwhile the unfortunate Faust lay down and moaned, giving us to understand that he was quite unable to walk. I then told my companion and guide to ride on, charging the latter to take Faust on his camel as he was completely exhausted. After they had ridden a mile in advance of the caravan the guide pointed out the spot where he said the well should be, apparently about three miles off. Poor Faust's doom was sealed; he was seized with fits, and Mr Pyltseff, finding it was impossible to hurry on, and too far to ride back to the caravan for a glass of water, waited till we came up, laying Faust under a clump of *saxaul* and covering him with saddle-felt. The poor dog became less conscious every minute, gasped two or three times, and expired. Placing his body on one of the packs, we moved on again, sorely doubting whether there were really any well in the place pointed out to us by the guide, for he had already deceived us more than once. Our situation at this moment was desperate. Only a few glasses of water left, of which we took into our mouths just enough to moisten our parched tongues; our bodies seemed on fire, our heads swam, and we were close upon fainting. In this last extremity I desired a Cossack to take a small vessel and to ride as hard as he could to the well, accompanied by the guide, ordering him to fire at the latter if he attempted to run away. They were soon hidden in a cloud of dust which filled the air, and we toiled onwards in their tracks in the most anxious suspense. At length, after half an hour, the Cossack appeared. What news does he bring? and spurring our jaded horses, which could hardly move their legs to meet him, we learned with the joy of a man who has been snatched from the jaws of death that the well had been found! After a draught of fresh water from the vesselful that he brought, and, having wet our heads, we rode in the direction pointed out, and soon reached the well of Boro-Sondji. It was now two o'clock in the afternoon; we had, therefore, been exposed for nine consecutive hours to frightful heat, and had ridden upwards of twenty miles.

After unloading the camels, I sent a Cossack back with the Mongol for the pack which had been left on the road, by the side of which our other (Mongol) dog, who had been with us nearly two years, was laid. The poor brute had lain down underneath the pack but was still alive, and after getting a draught of water he was able to follow the men back to camp. Notwithstanding the complete prostration of our physical and moral energies, we felt the loss of Faust so keenly that we could eat nothing, and slept but little all night. The following morning we dug a small grave and buried in it the remains of our faithful friend. As we discharged this last duty to him my companion and I wept like children. Faust had been our friend in every sense of the word! How often in moments of trouble had we caressed and played with him, half forgetting our griefs! For nearly three years had he served us faithfully through the frost and storms of Tibet, the rain and snow of Kan-su, and the wearisome marches of many thousand miles, and at last had fallen a victim to the burning heat of the desert; this too within two months of the termination of the expedition!

The route taken by most of the caravans of pilgrims from Urga to Ala-shan on their way to Tibet turns a little to the west at the Khan-ula mountains, afterwards taking the direction of the

Khalka country. We did not follow this road because the wells along it were not sufficiently numerous ... Our course lay due north, and after crossing some spurs of the Kara-narin-ula entered the country of the Urutes, which lies wedge-shaped between Ala-shan and the Khalka country.

This country is considerably higher than Ala-shan, but soon begins to sink towards the Galpin Gobi plain, where the elevation is only 3,200 feet; north of this again it rises towards the Hurku mountains which form a distinct definition between the barren desert on the south and the more steppe-like region on the north. There is also a slope from the ranges bordering the valley of the Hoang-ho westward to the Galpin Gobi, which forms a depressed basin, no higher than Djaratai-dabas, extending as we were informed by the Mongols, for twenty-five days' march from east to west.

The soil of the Galpin Gobi, in that eastern portion of it which we crossed, consists of small pebbles or of saline clay almost devoid of vegetation; the whole expanse of country to the Hurku range being a desert as wild and barren as that of Ala-shan, but of a somewhat different character. The sand drifts, so vast in the latter country, are here of comparatively small extent, and in their stead we find bare clay, shingle, and naked crumbling rocks (chiefly gneiss) scattered in low groups. Vegetation consists of stunted, half-withered clumps of *saxaul, karmyk, budarhana*, and a few herbaceous plants, the chief amongst which is the *sulhir*; the elms are the most striking features in the Urute country, forming in places small clumps; bushes of wild peach are also occasionally met with, such as are never seen in the desert of Ala-shan. Animal life in these regions is very scant; birds and mammals are the same as in Ala-shan. You may often ride for hours together without seeing a bird, not even a stone-chat or a *kolodjoro*; nevertheless, wherever there are wells or springs, Mongols are to be found, with a few camels, and large numbers of sheep and goats.

During our progress through this country, in the latter half of August, the heat was excessive, although never so high as in

Ala-shan. Winds blew ceaselessly night and day, often increasing to the violence of a gale, and filling the air with clouds of saline dust and sand, the latter choking up many of the wells; but these were more frequently destroyed by the rains, which, although rare, came down with terrific force, and for an hour or two afterwards large rivers continued to flow, silting up the wells (always dug on the lower ground) with mud and sand. It would be impossible to travel here without a guide thoroughly acquainted with the country; for destruction lies in wait for you at every step. In fact this desert, like that of Ala-shan, is so terrible that, in comparison with it, the deserts of Northern Tibet may be called fruitful. There, at all events, you may often find water and good pastureland in the valleys; here, there is neither the one nor the other, not even a single oasis; everywhere the silence of the valley of death.

The well-known Sahara can hardly be more terrible than these deserts, which extend for many hundreds of miles in length and breadth. The Hurku hills, where we crossed, are the northern definition of the wildest and most sterile part of the Gobi, and form a distinct chain with a direction from SE to WNW; how far either way we could not say positively; but, according to the information we received from the natives, they are prolonged for a great distance towards the south-east, reaching the mountains bordering the valley of the Hoang-ho, while on the west they extend, with a few interruptions, to other far distant mountains of no great elevation. If the latter statement may be relied upon, we may conclude that they unite with the Thian Shan, and supply, as it were, a connecting link between that range and the In-shan system; an extremely interesting fact and one worthy of the attention of future explorers.

Their width where we crossed them is a little over seven miles, and their apparent height hardly above a thousand feet . . .

South of the Hurku lies the great trade route from Peking, via Kuku-khoto and Bautu, to Hami, Urumchi and Kulja, branching off near the spring of Bortson, where we encamped for the night . . .

On crossing the frontier of the Khalka country we entered the principality of Tushetu-khan, and hastened by forced marches to Urga, which was now the goal we were so desirous of reaching. Nearly three years of wanderings, attended by every kind of privation and hardship, had so worn us out physically and morally that we felt most anxious for a speedy termination of our journey; besides which, we were now travelling through the wildest part of the Gobi, where want of water, heat, storms of wind, in short every adverse condition combined against us, and day by day undermined what little of our strength remained . . .

The mirage, that evil genius of the desert, mocked us almost daily, and conjured up such tantalising visions of tremulous water that even the rocks of the neighbouring hills appeared as though reflected in it. Severe heat and frequent storms of wind prevented our sleeping quietly at night, much as we needed rest after the arduous day's march.

But not to us alone was the desert of Mongolia an enemy. Birds which began to make their appearance in the latter half of August suffered equally from thirst and hunger. We saw flocks of geese and ducks resting at the smallest pools, and small birds flew to our tent so exhausted with starvation as to allow us to catch them in the hand. We found several of these feathered wanderers quite dead, and in all probability numbers of them perish in their flight across the desert.

The chief migration of birds was in September, and by the 13th of that month we had counted twenty-four varieties. From our observations the geese directed their flight not due south but south-east towards the northern bend of the Hoang-ho.

Eighty-seven miles north of the Hurku hills we crossed another trade route from Kuku-khoto to Uliassutai; practicable for carts although the traffic is mostly on camels . . .

Northwards the character of the Gobi again changes, and this time for the better. The sterile desert becomes a steppe, more and more fruitful as we advance to the north. The shingle and gravel are in turn succeeded by sand mixed in small quantities with clay.

The country becomes extremely undulating. The gradual slopes of low hills intersect one another in every possible direction, and earn for this region the Mongol name *Kangai* – i.e. hilly. This continues for upwards of a hundred miles to the north of the Uliassutai post road, when the waterless steppe touches the margin of the basin of Lake Baikal; here finally, at Hangindaban, you find yourself among groups and ridges of rocky hills, beyond which lie the well-watered districts of Northern Mongolia . . .

Our impatience to reach Urga kept ever increasing as we approached it, and we counted the time no longer by months or weeks but by days. At length after crossing the Hangin-daban range we arrived on the banks of the Tola, the first river we had made acquaintance with in Mongolia. For 870 miles, i.e. between Kan-su and this river, we had not seen a single stream or lake, only stagnant pools of brackish rainwater. Forests now appeared, darkening the steep slopes of the Mount Khan-ola. Under these grateful circumstances we at last accomplished our final march, and on 17 September entered Urga, where we received a warm welcome from our Consul. I will not undertake to describe the moment when we heard our mother-tongue, when we met again our countrymen, and experienced once more European comforts. We inquired eagerly what was going on in the civilised world; we devoured the contents of the letters awaiting us; we gave vent to our joy like children; it was only after a few days that we came to ourselves and began to realise the luxury to which our wanderings had rendered us for so long a time strangers . . . After resting a week at Urga, we proceeded to Kiakhta, which we reached on 1 October 1873.

Our journey was ended. Its success had surpassed all the hopes we entertained when we crossed for the first time the borders of Mongolia. Then an uncertain future lay before us; now, as we called to mind all the difficulties and dangers we had gone through, we could not help wondering at the good fortune which had invariably attended us everywhere. Yes! in the most adverse circumstances, Fortune had been ever constant, and ensured the success of our undertaking: many a time when it hung on a thread a happy destiny rescued us, and gave us the means of accomplishing, as far as our strength would permit, the exploration of the least known and most inaccessible countries of Inner Asia.

ESCAPE FROM THE OUTBACK

ERNEST GILES
(1835–97)

English explorer. During an 1874 expedition to Australia, he was forced to separate from his companion, Gibson.

We were now 90 miles from the Circus water, and 110 from Fort McKellar. The horizon to the west was still obstructed by another rise three or four miles away; but to the west-north-west I could see a line of low stony ridges, ten miles off. To the south was an isolated little hill, six or seven miles away. I determined to go to the ridges, when Gibson complained that his horse could never reach them, and suggested that the next rise to the west might reveal something better in front. The ridges were five miles away, and there were others still further preventing a view. When we reached them we had come 98 miles from the Circus. Here Gibson, who was always behind, called out and said his horse was going to die, or knock up, which are synonymous terms in this region . . . The hills to the west were 25–30 miles away, and it was with extreme regret I was compelled to relinquish a further attempt to reach them. Oh, how ardently I longed for a camel! how ardently I gazed upon this scene! At this moment I would even my jewel eternal have sold for power to span the gulf that lay between! But it could not be, situated as I was; compelled to retreat – of course with the intention of coming again with a larger supply of water – now the sooner I retreated the better. These far-off hills were named the Alfred and Marie Range, in honour of their Royal Highnesses the Duke and Duchess of Edinburgh. Gibson's horse having got so bad had placed us both in a great dilemma; indeed, ours was a most critical position. We turned back upon our tracks, when the cob refused to carry his rider any further and tried to lie down. We drove him another mile on foot, and down he fell to die. My mare, the Fair Maid of Perth, was only too willing to return; she had now to carry Gibson's saddle and things, and we went away walking and riding by turns of half an hour. The cob, no doubt, died where he fell; not a second thought could be bestowed on him.

When we got back to about thirty miles from the Kegs I was walking, and having concluded in my mind what course to pursue, I called to Gibson to halt till I walked up to him. We were both excessively thirsty, for walking had made us so, and we had scarcely a pint of water left between us. However, of what we had we each took a mouthful, which finished the supply, and I then said – for I couldn't speak before – 'Look here, Gibson, you see we are in a most terrible fix with only one horse, therefore only one can ride, and one must remain behind. I shall remain; and now listen to me. If the mare does not get water soon she will die; therefore ride right on; get to the Kegs, if possible, tonight, and give her water. Now the cob is dead there'll be all the more for her; let her rest for an hour or two, and then get over a few more miles by morning, so that early tomorrow you will sight the Rawlinson, at twenty-five miles from the Kegs. Stick to the tracks, and never leave them. Leave as much water in one keg for me as you can afford after watering the mare and filling up your own bags, and, remember, I depend upon you to bring me relief. Rouse Mr Tietkens, get fresh horses and more water bags, and return as soon as you possibly can. I shall of course endeavour to get down the tracks also.'

He then said if he had a compass he thought he could go better at night. I knew he didn't understand anything about compasses, as I had often tried to explain them to him. The one I had was a

Gregory's Patent; of a totally different construction from ordinary instruments of the kind, and I was very loath to part with it, as it was the only one I had. However, he was so anxious for it that I gave it him, and he departed. I sent one final shout after him to stick to the tracks, to which he replied, 'All right', and the mare carried him out of sight almost immediately. That was the last ever seen of Gibson.

I walked slowly on, and the further I walked the more thirsty I became. I had thirty miles to go to reach the Kegs, which I could not reach until late tomorrow at the rate I was travelling, and I did not feel sure that I could keep on at that . . .

24 April to 1 May So soon as it was light I was again upon the horse tracks, and reached the Kegs about the middle of the day. Gibson had been here, and watered the mare, and gone on. He had left me a little over two gallons of water in one keg, and it may be imagined how glad I was to get a drink. I could have drunk my whole supply in half an hour, but was compelled to economy, for I could not tell how many days would elapse before assistance could come: it could not be less than five, it might be many more. After quenching my thirst a little I felt ravenously hungry, and on searching among the bags, all the food I could find was eleven sticks of dirty, sandy, smoked horse, averaging about an ounce and a half each, at the bottom of a pack bag. I was rather staggered to find that I had little more than a pound weight of meat to last me until assistance came. However, I was compelled to eat some at once, and devoured two sticks raw, as I had no water to spare to boil them in.

After this I sat in what shade the trees afforded, and reflected on the precariousness of my position. I was 60 miles from water, and 80 from food, my messenger could hardly return before six days, and I began to think it highly probable that I should be dead of hunger and thirst long before anybody could possibly arrive. I looked at the keg; it was an awkward thing to carry empty. There was nothing else to carry water in, as Gibson had taken all the smaller water bags, and the large ones would require several gallons of water to soak the canvas before they began to tighten enough to hold water. The keg when empty, with its rings and straps, weighed fifteen pounds, and now it had twenty pounds of water in it. I could not carry it without a blanket for a pad for my shoulder, so that with my revolver and cartridge pouch, knife, and one or two other small things on my belt, I staggered under a weight of about fifty pounds when I put the keg on my back. I only had fourteen matches.

After I had thoroughly digested all points of my situation. I concluded that if I did not help myself Providence wouldn't help me. I started, bent double by the keg, and could only travel so slowly that I thought it scarcely worthwhile to travel at all. I became so thirsty at each step I took, that I longed to drink up every drop of water I had in the keg, but it was the elixir of death I was burdened with, and to drink it was to die, so I restrained myself. By next morning I had only got about three miles away from the Kegs, and to do that I travelled mostly in the moonlight. The next few days I can only pass over as they seemed to pass with me, for I was quite unconscious half the time, and I only got over about five miles a day.

To people who cannot comprehend such a region it may seem absurd that a man could not travel faster than that. All I can say is, there may be men who could do so, but most men in the position I was in would simply have died of hunger and thirst, for by the third or fourth day – couldn't tell which – my horsemeat was all gone. I had to remain in what scanty shade I could find during the day, and I could only travel by night.

When I lay down in the shade in the morning I lost all consciousness, and when I recovered my senses I could not tell whether one day or two or three had passed. At one place I am sure I must have remained over 48 hours. At a certain place on the road – that is to say, on the horse tracks – at about 15 miles from the Kegs – at 25 miles the Rawlinson could again be sighted – I saw that the tracks of the two loose horses we had turned back from there had left the main line of tracks, which ran east and west, and had turned about east-south-east, and the tracks of the Fair Maid of Perth, I was grieved to see, had gone on them also. I felt sure Gibson would soon find his error, and return to the main line. I was unable to investigate this any further in my present position. I followed them about a mile, and then returned to the proper line, anxiously looking at every step to see if Gibson's horse tracks returned into them.

They never did, nor did the loose horse tracks either. Generally speaking, whenever I saw a shady desert oak tree there was an enormous bull-dog ants' nest under it, and I was prevented from sitting in its shade. On what I thought was the 27th I almost gave up the thought of walking any further, for the exertion in this dreadful region, where the triodia was almost as high as myself, and as thick as it could grow, was quite overpowering, and being starved, I felt quite light-headed. After sitting down, on every occasion when I tried to get up again, my head would swim round, and I would fall down oblivious for some time. Being in a chronic state of burning thirst, my general plight was dreadful in the extreme. A bare and level sandy waste would have been Paradise to walk over compared to this. My arms, legs, thighs, both before and behind, were so punctured with spines, it was agony only to exist; the slightest movement and in went more spines, where they broke off in the clothes and flesh, causing the whole of the body that was punctured to gather into minute pustules, which were continually growing and bursting. My clothes, especially inside my trousers, were a perfect mass of prickly points.

My great hope and consolation now was that I might soon meet the relief party. But where was the relief party? Echo could only answer – where? About the 29th I had emptied the keg, and was still over 20 miles from the Circus. Ah! who can imagine what 20 miles means in such a case? But in this April's ivory moonlight I plodded on, desolate indeed, but all undaunted, on this lone, unhallowed shore. At last I reached the Circus, just at the dawn of day. Oh, how I drank! how I reeled! how hungry I was! how thankful I was that I had so far at least escaped from the jaws of that howling wilderness, for I was once more upon the range, though still 20 miles from home. There was no sign of the tracks, of anyone having been here since I left it. The water was all but gone. The solitary eagle still was there. I wondered what could have become of Gibson; he certainly had never come here, and how could he reach the fort without doing so?

I was in such a miserable state of mind and body that I refrained from more vexatious speculations as to what had delayed him: I stayed here, drinking and drinking, until about 10 a.m., when I crawled away over the stones down from the water. I was very footsore, and could only go at a snail's pace. Just as I got clear of the bank of the creek. I heard a faint squeak, and looking about I saw, and immediately caught, a small dying wallaby, whose marsupial mother had evidently thrown it from her pouch. It only weighed about two ounces, and was scarcely furnished yet with fur. The instant I saw it, like an eagle I pounced upon it and ate it, living, raw, dying – fur, skin, bones, skull, and all. The delicious taste of that creature I shall never forget. I only wished I had its mother and father to serve in the same way. I had become so weak that by late at night, I had only accomplished 11 miles, and I lay down about 5 miles from the Gorge of Tarns, again choking for water. While lying down here, I thought I heard the sound of the footfalls of a galloping horse going campwards, and vague ideas of Gibson on the Fair Maid – or she without him – entered my head. I stood up and listened, but the sound had died away upon the midnight air. On the 1st of May, as I afterwards found, at one o'clock in the morning, I was walking again, and reached the Gorge of Tarns long before daylight, and could again indulge in as much water as I desired; but it was exhaustion I suffered from, and I could hardly move.

My reader may imagine with what intense feelings of relief I stepped over the little bridge across the water, staggered into the camp at daylight, and woke Mr Tietkens, who stared at me as though I had been one new risen from the dead. I asked him had he seen Gibson, and to give me some food. I was of course prepared to hear that Gibson had never reached the camp; indeed, I could see but two people in their blankets the moment I entered the fort, and by that I knew he could not be there. None of the horses had come back, and it appeared that I was the only one of six living creatures – two men and four horses – that had returned, or were now ever likely to return, from that desert, for it was now, as I found, nine days since I last saw Gibson.

THE PITILESS SUN

PETER FLEMING
(1907–71)

English travel writer and explorer who, in 1935, made an 'undeservedly successful' overland trek from Peking to Kashmir. He was accompanied on the 3,500-mile journey by the Swiss journalist, Ella 'Kini' Maillart.

At the foot of the last pass we halted for a short rest, then climbed it very slowly. I took charge of the camels, for on these narrow and vertiginous tracks the donkeys needed all the men's attention. The Pearl was moving stiffly and eyed the world with distaste, but when we reached the last razor-backed ridge it was pleasant to look back on the peaks massed behind us round the towering snows of the Tokuz Dawan and to reflect that from now on it would be all downhill. Below us, hidden by a dust haze, lay the desert.

We plunged down sharply by the zigzag track into a tremendous gorge, a huge gash in the side of the mountain between whose high enclosing walls we marched with the unfamiliar sense of being shut in, of no longer having distances about us. At four o'clock we made camp near a little salty water hole, after a good stage of ten hours.

The next day, 13 June, was a long one. Soon after dawn we moved off down the narrow, winding gorge, following a dried-up stream-bed through a succession of highly romantic grottoes. Presently it widened, and we passed clumps of flowering tamarisk at which the camels snatched greedily. Everything was deathly still; only a little bird from time to time uttered a short and plaintive song whose sweet notes echoed anomalously under those frowning cliffs. The silence, the tortuous and hidden way, made me feel as if we were engaged on a surprise attack.

After five hours we came to a place which both our map and our guides called Muna Bulak. But once more '*adam yok*', the looked-for tents were absent, and there was only a little spring of very salt and brackish water. We filled the keg and went on for two more hours, debouching from the gorge into a huge desert of sand and piedmont gravel which stretched as far as the eye could see. The mountains with which for so long we had struggled at close quarters were relegated to a hazy backcloth.

At one o'clock we halted, cooked a meal, and wolfed great lumps of boiled mutton. The sun beat down on us savagely and we propped a felt up with tent-poles to make a little shade; this was a sharp contrast to the uplands. We drank a great deal of curiously tasting tea.

At dusk we started off again, marching north-west through a waste of tufted dunes. As the light faded the low patches of scrub took on strange shapes, became dark monsters which, as you watched them, moved; it was all very like that night-march with the Prince of Dzun. We were a long way from water and the men took the caravan along at a good pace. Presently we came out of the dunes into stark desert, as flat and naked and unfriendly as a sheet of ice. The camels were groaning with exhaustion and had to be tugged along. There was no landmark, no incident, to mark the passing of the hours; the stars looked down dispassionately on the small and battered company lungeing blindly forward in the darkness. I whooped mechanically at the camels till my voice went. The Turkis were imprecise about our programme, and we wished that we knew how much longer the ordeal would last.

It ended at half past one in the morning. We had done two stages of more than seven hours each and the camels were dead beat. They slumped down in their tracks and we unloaded and lay down in the lee of the baggage, refreshing ourselves with the dregs of the last brandy bottle and a little salt water. Then we slept, sprawling like corpses on the iron-hard ground.

After two hours Tuzun woke us. Feeling stiff and stale, we made tea with the last of the water, loaded up, and moved off. Sunrise showed a discouragingly empty world; even the mountains were already lost behind the dust haze which is chronic in the Tarim Basin. We stumbled muzzily on, uncomfortably aware that it would soon be very hot.

Presently we heard a kind of roaring sound. Kini, who had crossed the Kizil Kum and claimed to know something of deserts, said it was the wind in some sand dunes we could see to the north. Happily she was wrong; another half-mile brought us to the lip of a low cliff beneath which a wide stony bed was noisily threaded by the channel of the Cherchen Darya. We scrambled down and watered the animals in a current that was opaque with yellow silt and looked as thick as paint.

Tuzun spoke hopefully of reaching Cherchen that day, and we climbed out of the riverbed for the last lap. The sun was well up now; the heat seemed to us terrific and was in fact considerable. The world around us jigged liquidly in a haze. Before long we hit a bad belt of dunes about a mile wide. The soft sand was cruel going for tired animals; once Number Two lost his balance and collapsed sideways, and we had to unload him before he could rise. When we struggled out again on to hard desert there was not much life left in any of us. We crawled on for an hour or two, but the sun was pitiless and at last Tuzun called a halt on a little bluff above the river.

Here we lay up for five hours, and I disgraced myself by drinking a whole kettle of tea while Kini was bathing in the river. She came back so glowing and self-righteous that in the end I went and bathed too, wallowing in the swift khaki water and speculating lazily about Cherchen. Our ignorance, our chronic lack of advance information, must be unexampled in the annals of modern travel. We had neither of us, before starting, read one in

twenty of the books that we ought to have read, and our precon-
ceptions of what a place was going to be like were never based, as
they usefully could have been, on the experience of our few but
illustrious predecessors in these regions. Cherchen, for all we
knew or could find out, might be a walled city, or a cluster of
tents, or almost any other variation on the urban theme. This state
of affairs reflected discreditably on us but was not without its
compensations. It was pleasant, in a way, to be journeying always
into the blue, with no Baedeker to eliminate surprise and marshal
our first impressions in advance; it was pleasant, now, to be within
one march of Cherchen and to have not the very slightest idea
what Cherchen was going to look like.

We enjoyed the halt. The felt gave very little shade, and a light
wind that had sprung up coated our somnolence with half an inch
of sand; but at least we were no longer moving, no longer pressing forward. We dreaded – passionately but surreptitiously, as
children dread the end of holidays – the imminent beginning of
another night-march of indeterminable length.

At four o'clock, though it was still vindictively hot, we began to
load up. The skeleton camels – whose thick wool now appeared,
and was, anomalous but who had had no time to shed it – knelt
and rose again not without protest. With far-fetched prudence,
fearing an examination of our effects like the one in Lanchow, I
removed from my bundled overcoat, which came from Samarkand
and should properly have clothed a cavalry officer in the Red
Army of the Soviet Union, buttons embossed with the hammer
and sickle. At half past four we started.

Men and animals moved groggily; this was our fourth stage in
thirty-six hours, and even Tuzun, who had started fresh five days
ago, showed signs of wear and tear. Very soon we came into dunes
again; the animals floundered awkwardly and the march lost
momentum. The camels showed signs of distress; one of the
donkeys was dead lame and another, from sheer weakness,
bowled over like a shot rabbit on a downhill slope. A kind of
creeping paralysis was overtaking the expedition.

We knew that we were near Cherchen, but there comes a point, while you are suffering hardship or fatigue, when you cannot see beyond the urgent business of endurance. This point we had reached. We might have been a month's journey from our goal, instead of a very few hours, for all the difference that its proximity now made to us. We could no more think than we could see beyond the next ridge of dunes; our reprieve, no doubt, had been signed, but we were still in prison. Our minds told us that this was the last lap; but our hearts and our bodies could take only an academic kind of comfort from the assurance. We were absorbed in the task of finishing a difficult stage.

The sun began to set. The donkeys tottered along very reluctantly, and the tired camels wore that kind of dignity which you associate with defeat; it was clear that we should not make Cherchen that night. Then, suddenly, from the top of a high dune, my eye caught a strip of queer eruptions on the horizon to the north-west; the skyline, for months either flat and featureless or jagged and stark, was here pimpled with something that did not suggest a geological formation. I got out my field-glasses . . .

It was like spying on another planet. The green of the trees, with the approach of dusk, had turned a soft and bluish grey; but they were trees beyond a doubt – a deep, serried phalanx, pricked here and there with the lance-heads of tall poplars. For all that we had been expecting a phenomenon, it was incredible; we had grown so accustomed to the life of nomads in an empty winter world that we had not bargained for so concrete, so delightful an intimation of spring and domesticity. The peaceful and luxuriant silhouette before us suggested a kind of life to which we had overlong been strangers.

PRISONERS OF THE SAND

ANTOINE DE SAINT-EXUPÉRY
(1900–44)

French pilot and writer. During a commercial crossing of the Libyan desert his aircraft crashed, leaving himself and his co-pilot 250 miles from habitation. This experience he recounted in Wind, Sand and Stars *(1939) but it also led to his famous allegorical children's story,* Le Petit Prince *(1942), about a boy from another planet who befriends an airman stranded in the desert. Saint-Exupéry was posted missing after a reconnaissance flight in the Second World War.*

A man can go nineteen hours without water, and what have we drunk since last night? A few drops of dew at dawn. But the north-east wind is still blowing, still slowing up the process of our evaporation. To it, also, we owe the continued accumulation of high clouds. If only they would drift straight overhead and break into rain! But it never rains in the desert.

'Look here, Prévot. Let's rip up one of the parachutes and spread the sections out on the ground, weighed down with stones. If the wind stays in the same quarter till morning, they'll catch the dew and we can wring them out into one of the tanks.'

We spread six triangular sections of parachute under the stars, and Prévot unhooked a fuel tank. This was as much as we could do for ourselves till dawn. But, miracle of miracles! Prévot had come upon an orange while working over the tank. We share it, and though it was little enough to men who could have used a few gallons of sweet water, still I was overcome with relief.

Stretched out beside the fire I looked at the glowing fruit and said to myself that men did not know what an orange was. 'Here we are, condemned to death,' I said to myself, 'and still the certainty of dying cannot compare with the pleasure I am feeling. The joy I take from this half of an orange which I am holding in my hand is one of the greatest joys I have ever known.'

I lay flat on my back, sucking my orange and counting the shooting stars. Here I was, for one minute infinitely happy. 'Nobody can know anything of the world in which the individual moves and has his being,' I reflected. 'There is no guessing it. Only the man locked up in it can know what it is.'

For the first time I understood the cigarette and glass of rum that are handed to the criminal about to be executed. I used to think that for a man to accept these wretched gifts at the foot of the gallows was beneath human dignity. Now I was learning that he took pleasure from them. People thought him courageous when he smiled as he smoked or drank. I knew now that he smiled because the taste gave him pleasure. People could not see that his perspective had changed, and that for him the last hour of his life was a life in itself.

We collected an enormous quantity of water – perhaps as much as two quarts. Never again would we be thirsty! We were saved; we had a liquid to drink!

I dipped my tin cup into the tank and brought up a beautifully yellow-green liquid the first mouthful of which nauseated me so that despite my thirst I had to catch my breath before swallowing it. I would have swallowed mud, I swear; but this taste of poisonous metal cut keener than thirst.

I glanced at Prévot and saw him going round and round with his eyes fixed to the ground as if looking for something. Suddenly he leaned forward and began to vomit without interrupting his spinning. Half a minute later it was my turn. I was seized by such convulsions that I went down on my knees and dug my fingers into the sand while I puked. Neither of us spoke, and for a quarter of an hour we remained thus shaken, bringing up nothing but a little bile.

After a time it passed and all I felt was a vague, distant nausea. But our last hope had fled. Whether our bad luck was due to a sizing on the parachute or to the magnesium lining of the tank, I never found out. Certain it was that we needed either another set of cloths or another receptacle.

Well, it was broad daylight and time we were on our way. This time we should strike out as fast as we could, leave this cursed plateau, and tramp till we dropped in our tracks . . .

I don't remember anything about that day. I remember only my haste. I was hurrying desperately towards something – towards some finality. I remember also that I walked with my eyes to the ground, for the mirages were more than I could bear. From time to time we would correct our course by the compass, and now and again we would lie down to catch our breath. I remember having flung away my waterproof, which I had held on to as covering for the night. That is as much as I recall about the day. Of what happened when the chill of evening came, I remember more. But during the day I had simply turned to sand and was a being without mind.

When the sun set we decided to make camp. Oh, I knew as well as anybody that we should push on, that this one waterless night would finish us off. But we had brought along the bits of parachute, and if the poison was not in the sizing, we might get a sip of water next morning. Once again we spread our trap for the dew under the stars.

But the sky in the north was cloudless. The wind no longer had the same taste on the lip. It had moved into another quarter. Something was rustling against us, but this time it seemed to be the desert itself. The wild beast was stalking us, had us in its power. I could feel its breath in my face, could feel it lick my face and hands. Suppose I walked on: at the best I could do five or six miles more. Remember that in three days I had covered one hundred miles, practically without water.

And then, just as we stopped, Prévot said:

'I swear to you I see a lake!'

'You're crazy.'

'Have you ever heard of a mirage after sunset?' he challenged.

I didn't seem able to answer him. I had long ago given up believing my own eyes. Perhaps it was not a mirage; but in that case it was a hallucination. How could Prévot go on believing? But he was stubborn about it.

'It's only twenty minutes off. I'll go have a look.'

His mulishness got on my nerves.

'Go ahead!' I shouted. 'Take your little constitutional. Nothing better for a man. But let me tell you, if your lake exists it is salt. And whether it's salt or not, it's a devil of a way off. And besides, there is no damned lake!'

Prévot was already on his way, his eyes glassy. I knew the strength of these irresistible obsessions. I was thinking: 'There are somnambulists who walk straight into locomotives.' And I knew that Prévot would not come back. He would be seized by the vertigo of empty space and would be unable to turn back. And then he would keel over. He somewhere, and I somewhere else. Not that it was important . . .

Night fell. The moon had swollen since I last saw it. Prévot was still not back. I stretched out on my back and turned these few data over in my mind. A familiar impression came over me, and I tried to seize it. I was . . . I was . . . I was at sea. I was on a ship going to South America and was stretched out, exactly like this, on the boat deck. The tip of the mast was swaying to and fro, very slowly, among the stars. That mast was missing tonight, but again I was at sea, bound for a port I was to make without raising a finger. Slave traders had flung me on this ship.

I thought of Prévot who was still not back. Not once had I heard him complain. That was a good thing. To hear him whine would have been unbearable. Prévot was a man.

What was that? Five hundred yards ahead of me I could see the light of his lamp. He had lost his way. I had no lamp with which to signal back. I stood up and shouted, but he could not hear me.

A second lamp, and then a third! God in Heaven! It was a search party and it was me they were hunting!

'Hi! Hi!' I shouted.

But they had not heard me. The three lamps were still signalling me.

'Tonight I am sane,' I said to myself. 'I am relaxed. I am not out of my head. Those are certainly three lamps and they are about five hundred yards off.' I stared at them and shouted again, and again I gathered that they could not hear me.

Then, for the first and only time, I was really seized with panic. I could still run, I thought. 'Wait! Wait!' I screamed. They seemed to be turning away from me, going off, hunting me elsewhere! And I stood tottering, tottering on the brink of life when there were arms out there ready to catch me! I shouted and screamed again and again.

They had heard me! An answering shout had come. I was strangling, suffocating, but I ran on, shouting as I ran, until I saw Prévot and keeled over.

When I could speak again I said: 'Whew! When I saw all those lights . . .'

'What lights?'

God in Heaven, it was true! He was alone!

This time I was beyond despair. I was filled with a sort of dumb fury.

'What about your lake?' I rasped.

'As fast as I moved towards it, it moved back. I walked after it for about half an hour. Then it seemed still too far away, so I came back. But I am positive, now, that it is a lake.'

'You're crazy. Absolutely crazy. Why did you do it? Tell me. Why?'

What had he done? Why had he done it? I was ready to weep with indignation, yet I scarcely knew why I was so indignant. Prévot mumbled his excuse:

'I felt I had to find some water. You . . . your lips were awfully pale.'

Well! My anger died within me. I passed my hand over my forehead as if I were waking out of sleep. I was suddenly sad. I said:

'There was no mistake about it. I saw them as clearly as I see you now. Three lights there were. I tell you, Prévot, I saw them!'

Prévot made no comment.

'Well,' he said finally, 'I guess we're in a bad way.'

In this air devoid of moisture the soil is swift to give off its temperature. It was already very cold. I stood up and stamped about. But soon a violent fit of trembling came over me. My dehydrated blood was moving sluggishly and I was pierced by a freezing chill which was not merely the chill of night. My teeth were chattering and my whole body had begun to twitch. My hand shook so that I could not hold an electric torch. I who had never been sensitive to cold was about to die of cold. What a strange effect thirst can have!

Somewhere, tired of carrying it in the sun, I had let my waterproof drop. Now the wind was growing bitter and I was learning that in the desert there is no place of refuge. The desert is as smooth as marble. By day it throws no shadow; by night it hands you over naked to the wind. Not a tree, not a hedge, not a rock behind which I could seek shelter. The wind was charging me like a troop of cavalry across open country. I turned and twisted to escape it: I lay down, stood up, lay down again, and still I was exposed to its freezing lash. I had no strength to run from the assassin and under the sabre-stroke I tumbled to my knees, my head between my hands.

A little later I pieced these bits together and remembered that I had struggled to my feet and had started to walk on, shivering as I went. I had started forward wondering where I was and then I had heard Prévot. His shouting had jolted me into consciousness.

I went back towards him, still trembling from head to foot – quivering with the attack of hiccups that was convulsing my whole body. To myself I said: 'It isn't the cold. It's something else. It's the end.' The simple fact was that I hadn't enough water in me. I had tramped too far yesterday and the day before when I was off by myself, and I was dehydrated.

The thought of dying of the cold hurt me. I preferred the phantoms of my mind, the cross, the trees, the lamps. At least they would have killed me by enchantment. But to be whipped to death like a slave! . . .

Confound it! Down on my knees again! We had with us a little store of medicines – a hundred grammes of ninety per cent alcohol, the same of pure ether, and a small bottle of iodine. I tried to swallow a little of the ether: it was like swallowing a knife. Then I tried the alcohol: it contracted my gullet. I dug a pit in the sand, lay down in it, and flung handfuls of sand over me until all but my face was buried in it.

Prévot was able to collect a few twigs, and he lit a fire which soon burnt itself out. He wouldn't bury himself in the sand, but preferred to stamp round and round in a circle. That was foolish.

My throat stayed shut, and though I knew that was a bad sign, I felt better. I felt calm. I felt a peace that was beyond all hope. Once more, despite myself, I was journeying, trussed up on the deck of my slave ship under the stars. It seemed to me that I was perhaps not in such a bad pass after all.

So long as I lay absolutely motionless, I no longer felt the cold. This allowed me to forget my body buried in the sand. I said to myself that I would not budge an inch, and would therefore never suffer again. As a matter of fact, we really suffer very little. Back of all these torments there is the orchestration of fatigue or of delirium, and we live on in a kind of picture book, a slightly cruel fairy tale.

A little while ago the wind had been after me with whip and spur, and I was running in circles like a frightened fox. After that came a time when I couldn't breathe. A great knee was crushing in my chest. A knee. I was writhing in vain to free myself from the weight of the angel who had overthrown me. There had not been a moment when I was alone in this desert. But now I have ceased strives to outwit the forces of nature. He stares in expectancy for the coming of dawn the way a gardener awaits the coming of spring. He looks forward to port as to a promised land, and truth for him is what lives in the stars . . .

I have nothing to complain of. For three days I have tramped the desert, have known the pangs of thirst, have followed false scents in the sand, have pinned my faith on the dew. I have struggled to rejoin my kind, whose very existence on earth I had forgotten. These are the cares of men alive in every fibre, and I cannot help thinking them more important than the fretful choosing of a nightclub in which to spend the evening. Compare the one life with the other, and all things considered this is luxury! I have no regrets. I have gambled and lost. It was all in the day's work. At least I have had the unforgettable taste of the sea on my lips.

I am not talking about living dangerously. Such words are meaningless to me. The toreador does not stir me to enthusiasm. It is not danger I love. I know what I love. It is life.

The sky seemed to me faintly bright. I drew up one arm through the sand. There was a bit of the torn parachute within reach, and I ran my hand over it. It was bone dry. Let's see. Dew falls at dawn. Here was dawn risen and no moisture on the cloth. My mind was befuddled and I heard myself say: 'There is a dry heart here, a dry heart that cannot know the relief of tears.'

I scrambled to my feet. 'We're off, Prévot,' I said. 'Our throats are still open. Get along, man!'

The wind that shrivels up a man in nineteen hours was now blowing out of the west. My gullet was not yet shut, but it was hard and painful and I could feel that there was a rasp in it. Soon that cough would begin that I had been told about and was now expecting. My tongue was becoming a nuisance. But most serious of all, I was beginning to see shining spots before my eyes. When those spots changed into flames, I should simply lie down.

The first morning hours were cool and we took advantage of them to get on at a good pace. We knew that once the sun was high there would be no more walking for us. We no longer had the right to sweat. Certainly not to stop and catch our breath. This coolness was merely the coolness of low humidity. The prevailing wind was coming from the desert, and under its soft and treacherous caress the blood was being dried out of us.

Our first day's nourishment had been a few grapes. In the next three days each of us ate half an orange and a bit of cake. If we had had anything left now, we couldn't have eaten it because we had no saliva with which to masticate it. But I had stopped being hungry. Thirsty I was, yes, and it seemed to me that I was suffering less from thirst itself than from the effects of thirst. Gullet hard. Tongue like plaster of Paris. A rasping in the throat. A horrible taste in the mouth.

All these sensations were new to me, and though I believed water could rid me of them, nothing in my memory associated them with water. Thirst had become more and more a disease and less and less a craving. I began to realize that the thought of water and fruit was now less agonizing than it had been. I was forgetting the radiance of the orange, just as I was forgetting the eyes under the hat brim. Perhaps I was forgetting everything.

We had sat down after all, but it could not be for long. Nevertheless, it was impossible to go five hundred yards without our legs giving way. To stretch out on the sand would be marvellous – but it could not be.

The landscape had begun to change. Rocky places grew rarer and the sand was now firm beneath our feet. A mile ahead stood dunes and on those dunes we could see a scrubby vegetation. At least this sand was preferable to the steely surface over which we had been trudging. This was the golden desert. This might have been the Sahara. It was in a sense my country.

Two hundred yards had now become our limit, but we had determined to carry on until we reached the vegetation. Better than that we could not hope to do. A week later, when we went back over our traces in a car to have a look at the *Simoon*, I measured this last lap and found that it was just short of fifty miles. All told we had done one hundred and twenty-four miles.

The previous day I had tramped without hope. Today the word 'hope' had grown meaningless. Today we were tramping simply because we were tramping. Probably oxen work for the same reason. Yesterday I had dreamed of a paradise of orange trees. Today I would not give a button for paradise; I did not believe oranges existed. When I thought about myself I found in me nothing but a heart squeezed dry. I was tottering but emotionless. I felt no distress whatever, and in a way I regretted it: misery would have seemed to me as sweet as water. I might then have felt sorry for myself and commiserated with myself as with a friend. But I had not a friend left on earth.

Later, when we were rescued, seeing our burnt-out eyes men thought we must have called aloud and wept and suffered. But cries of despair, misery, sobbing grief are a kind of wealth, and we possessed no wealth. When a young girl is disappointed in love she weeps and knows sorrow. Sorrow is one of the vibrations that prove the fact of living. I felt no sorrow. I was the desert. I could no longer bring up a little saliva; neither could I any longer summon those moving visions towards which I should have loved to stretch forth arms. The sun had dried up the springs of tears in me.

And yet, what was that? A ripple of hope went through me like a faint breeze over a lake. What was this sign that had awakened my instinct before knocking on the door of my consciousness? Nothing had changed, and yet everything was changed. This sheet of sand, these low hummocks and sparse tufts of verdure that had been a landscape, were now become a stage setting. Thus far the stage was empty, but the scene was set. I looked at Prévot. The same astonishing thing had happened to him as to me, but he was as far from guessing its significance as I was.

I swear to you that something is about to happen. I swear that life has sprung in this desert. I swear that this emptiness, this stillness, has suddenly become more stirring than a tumult on a public square.

'Prévot! Footprints! We are saved!'

We had wandered from the trail of the human species; we had cast ourselves forth from the tribe; we had found ourselves alone on earth and forgotten by the universal migration; and here, imprinted in the sand, were the divine and naked feet of man!

'Look, Prévot, here two men stood together and then separated.'

'Here a camel knelt.'

'Here . . .'

But it was not true that we were already saved. It was not enough to squat down and wait. Before long we should be past saving. Once the cough has begun, the progress made by thirst is swift.

Still, I believed in that caravan swaying somewhere in the desert, heavy with its cargo of treasure.

We went on. Suddenly I heard a cock crow. I remembered what Guillaumet had told me: 'Towards the end I heard cocks crowing in the Andes. And I heard the railway train.' The instant the cock crowed I thought of Guillaumet and I said to myself: 'First it was my eyes that played tricks on me. I suppose this is another of the effects of thirst. Probably my ears have merely held out longer than my eyes.' But Prévot grabbed my arm:

'Did you hear that?'

'What?'

'The cock.'

'Why . . . why, yes, I did.'

To myself I said: 'Fool! Get it through your head! This means life!'

I had one last hallucination – three dogs chasing one another. Prévot looked, but could not see them. However, both of us waved our arms at a Bedouin. Both of us shouted with all the breath in our bodies, and laughed for happiness.

But our voices could not carry thirty yards. The Bedouin on his slow-moving camel had come into view from behind a dune and now he was moving slowly out of sight. The man was probably the only Arab in this desert, sent by a demon to materialize and vanish before the eyes of us who could not run.

We saw in profile on the dune another Arab. We shouted, but our shouts were whispers. We waved our arms and it seemed to us that they must fill the sky with monstrous signals. Still the Bedouin stared with averted face away from us.

At last, slowly, slowly he began a right-angle turn in our direction. At the very second when he came face to face with us, I thought, the curtain would come down. At the very second when his eyes met ours, thirst would vanish and by this man would death and the mirages be wiped out. Let this man but make a quarter-turn left and the world is changed. Let him but bring his torso round, but sweep the scene with a glance, and like a god he can create life.

The miracle had come to pass. He was walking towards us over the sand like a god over the waves.

The Arab looked at us without a word. He placed his hands upon our shoulders and we obeyed him: we stretched out upon the sand. Race, language, religion were forgotten. There was only this humble nomad with the hands of an archangel on our shoulders.

Face to the sand, we waited. And when the water came, we drank like calves with our faces in the basin, and with a greediness which alarmed the Bedouin so that from time to time he pulled us up. But as soon as his hand fell away from us we plunged our faces anew into the water.

Jungles

AMAZONIA EXTREMIS

HENRY SAVAGE LANDOR
(1865–1924)

British explorer and author. He led a expedition to Amazonia in 1910, on his return writing Across Unknown South America.

We started once more across the virgin forest, directing our steps due west. Filippe this time undertook to open the *picada*, while I, compass in hand, marched directly behind him, Benedicto following me. If I had let him go, he would have described circle after circle upon himself instead of going in a straight line.

From that point our march across the forest became tragic. Perhaps I can do nothing better than reproduce almost word by word the entries in my diary.

We ate that morning what little there remained of the *mutum* we had shot the previous evening. Little we knew then that we were not to taste fresh meat again for nearly a month from that date.

During 3 September we made fairly good progress, cutting our way through incessantly. We went that day 20 kil. We had no lunch, and it was only in the evening that we opened the last of the three small boxes of sardines, our entire dinner consisting of three and a half sardines each.

On 4 September we were confronted, soon after our departure, with a mountainous country with deep ravines and furrows, most trying for us owing to their steepness. We went over five ranges of hills from 100 to 300 ft in height, and we crossed five streamlets in the depressions between those successive ranges.

Filippe was again suffering greatly from an attack of fever, and I had to support him all the time, as he had the greatest difficulty in walking. Benedicto had that day been entrusted with the big knife for cutting the *picada*.

We went some 20 kil. that day, with nothing whatever to eat, as we had already finished the three boxes of sardines, and I was reserving the box of anchovies for the moment when we could stand hunger no longer.

On 5 September we had another very terrible march over broken country, hilly for a good portion of the distance, but quite level in some parts.

The man Benedicto, who was a great eater, now collapsed altogether, saying that he could no longer carry his load and could not go on any farther without food.

The entire day our eyes had roamed in all directions, trying to discover some wild fruit which was edible, or some animal we might shoot, but there was the silence of death all around us. Not a branch, not a leaf was moved by a living thing; no fruit of any kind was to be seen anywhere.

Our appetite was keen, and it certainly had one good effect – it stopped Filippe's fever and, in fact, cured it altogether.

The two men were tormenting me the whole day, saying they had no faith in the compass: how could a brass box – that is what they called it – tell us where we could find *feijão*? It was beyond them to understand it. They bemoaned themselves incessantly, swearing at the day they had been persuaded to come along with me and leave their happy homes in order to die of starvation in the forest with a mad Englishman! And why did we go across the forest at all, where there was no trail, when we could have gone down by the river on a trading boat?

On 6 September it was all I could do to wake up my men. When they did wake, they would not get up, for they said the only object in getting up was to eat, and as there was nothing to eat there was no use in getting up. They wanted to remain there and die.

I had to use a great deal of gentle persuasion, and even told them a big story – that my *agulha* or needle (the compass) was telling me that morning that there was plenty of *feijão* ahead of us.

We struggled on kilometre after kilometre, one or another of us collapsing under our loads every few hundred metres. We went over very hilly country, crossing eight hill ranges that day with steep ravines between. In fact, all that country must once have been a low tableland which had been fissured and then eroded by water, leaving large cracks. At the bottom of each we found brooks and streamlets of delicious water. Of the eight rivulets found that day one only was fairly large. It fell in little cascades over rock. We could see no fish in its waters.

The forest was fairly clean underneath, and we had no great difficulty in getting through, a cut every now and then with the knife being sufficient to make a passage for us. I had by that time entirely given up the idea of opening a regular *picada*, over which I could eventually take the men and baggage I had left behind.

We found that day a palm with a bunch of small nuts which Benedicto called *coco do matto*; he said they were delicious to eat, so we proceeded to cut down the tall palm tree. When we came to split open the small *cocos* our disappointment was great, for they merely contained water. There was nothing whatever to eat inside the hard shells. We spent some two hours that evening cracking the *cocos* – some two hundred of them – each nut about the size of a cherry. They were extremely hard to crack, and our expectant eyes were disappointed two hundred times in succession as we opened every one and found nothing whatever to eat in them.

We were beginning to feel extremely weak, with a continuous feeling of emptiness in our insides. Personally, I felt no actual pain. The mental strain, perhaps, was the most trying thing for me, for I had no idea when we might find food. I was beginning to feel more than ever the responsibility of taking those poor fellows there to suffer for my sake. On their side they certainly never let one moment go by during the day or night without reminding me of the fact.

On 7 September I had the greatest difficulty in getting the men out of their hammocks. They were so exhausted that I could not rouse them. We had had a terrific storm during the night, which had added misery to our other sufferings. Innumerable ants were now causing us a lot of damage. Filippe's coat, which had dropped out of his hammock, was found in the morning entirely destroyed. Those miniature demons also cut the string to which I had suspended my shoes in mid-air, and no sooner had they fallen to the ground than the ants started on their mischievous work. When I woke up in the morning all that remained of my shoes were the two leather soles, the upper part having been completely destroyed.

Going through the forest, where thorns of all sizes were innumerable, another torture was now in store for me. With pieces of string I turned the soles of the shoes into primitive sandals; but when I started on the march I found that they hurt me much more than if I walked barefooted. After marching a couple of kilometres, my renovated foot gear hurt me so much in going up and down the steep ravines that I took off the sandals altogether and flung them away.

That day we went over eleven successive hill ranges and crossed as many little streamlets between them. My men were terribly downhearted. We had with us a Mauser and two hundred cartridges, but although we did nothing all day long but look for something to kill we never heard a sound of a living animal. Only one day at the beginning of our fast did I see a big *mutum* – larger than a big turkey. The bird had never seen a human being, and sat placidly perched on the branch of a tree, looking at us with curiosity, singing gaily. I tried to fire with the Mauser at the bird, which was only about seven or eight metres away, but cartridge after cartridge missed fire. I certainly spent not less than twenty minutes constantly replenishing the magazine, and not a single cartridge went off. They had evidently absorbed so much moisture on our many accidents in the river and in the heavy rainstorms we had had of late, that they had become useless.

While I was pointing the gun the bird apparently took the greatest interest in my doings, looked at me, stooping down gracefully each time that the rifle missed fire, singing dainty notes almost as if it were laughing at me. The funny part of it all was that we eventually had to go away disappointed, leaving the bird perched on that very same branch.

As the days went by and we could find nothing to eat, my two men lost their courage entirely. They now refused to suffer any longer. They said they had not the strength to go back, so they wanted to lie down and die. Many times a day did I have to lift them up again and persuade them gently to come on another few hundred metres or so. Perhaps then we might find the great river Madeira, where we should certainly meet traders from whom we could get food.

Late in the afternoon of 7 September, as we were on a high point above the last range of hills met that day, a large panorama opened before us, which we could just see between the trees and foliage of the forest.

To obtain a full view of the scenery it was necessary to climb up a tree. I knew well that we could not yet have reached the river we were looking for, but perhaps we were not far from some large tributary of the Madeira, such as the Secundury.

Climbing up trees in the Brazilian forest was easier said than done, even when you possessed your full strength. So many were the ants of all sizes which attacked you with fury the moment you embraced the tree, that it was not easy to get up more than a few feet.

When we drew lots as to whom of us should climb the tree, Benedicto was the one selected by fate. Benedicto was certainly born under an unlucky star; when anything nasty or unpleasant happened to anybody it was always to poor Benedicto. After a lot of pressing he proceeded to go up the tree, uttering piercing yells as every moment great *sauba* ants bit his arms, legs or body. He was brave enough, and slowly continued his way up until he reached a height of some 30 ft above the ground, from which eminence he gave us the interesting news that there were some high hills standing before us to the west, while to the north-west was a great flat surface covered by dense forest.

No sooner had Benedicto supplied us with this information from his high point of vantage than we heard an agonising yell and saw him spread flat on the ground, having made a record descent.

Filippe and I, although suffering considerably, were in fits of laughter at Benedicto, who did not laugh at all, but pawed himself all over, saying he must have broken some bones. When I proceeded to examine him I found upon his body over a hundred *sauba* ants clinging to his skin with their powerful clippers.

Aching all over, poor Benedicto got up once more. I put the load upon his back and we resumed our journey, making a precipitous descent almost *à pic* down the hillside. Our knees were so weak that we fell many times and rolled down long distances on that steep incline. At last we got to the bottom, rejoicing in our hearts that we had no more hills to climb, as I had made up my mind that I would now march slightly to the north-west, so as to avoid the hilly region which Benedicto had discovered to the west.

My men had an idea that the great river we were looking for must be in that plain. For a few hours they seemed to have regained their courage. We heard some piercing shrieks, and we at once proceeded in their direction, as we knew they came from monkeys. In fact we found an enormously high tree, some 5ft in diameter. Up on its summit some beautiful yellow fruit stared us in the face. Four tiny monkeys were busy eating the fruit. Benedicto, who had by that time become very religious, joined his hands and offered prayers to the Virgin that the monkeys might drop some fruit down, but they went on eating while we gazed at them from below. We tried to fire at them with the Mauser, but again not a single cartridge went off. Eventually the monkeys dropped down the empty shells of the fruit they had eaten. With our ravenous appetite we rushed for them and with our teeth scraped off the few grains of sweet substance which remained attached to the inside of the shells. We waited and waited under that tree for a long time, Filippe now joining also in the prayers. Each time a shell dropped our palates rejoiced for a few moments at the infinitesimal taste we got from the discarded shells. It was out of the question to climb up such a big tree or to cut it down, as we had no strength left.

We went on until sunset; my men once more having lost heart. Brazilians lose heart very easily. At the sight of small hills before them, a steep descent, or a deep river to cross, they would lie down and say they wanted to remain there and die. Filippe and Benedicto did not carry more than 20 lb each of my own baggage, but their hammocks weighed some 20 lb each, so that their loads weighed altogether about 40 lb.

We went on, crossing five more streamlets that afternoon, of which one, 2 m wide, had beautifully limpid water. We nevertheless went on, until eventually after sunset we had to camp near a stream of filthy water.

As we had now been four entire days without eating anything at all, I thought it was high time to open the valuable tin of anchovies – the only one in our possession. We had a terrible disappointment when I opened the tin. I had purchased it in S. Manoel from Mr Barretto. To our great distress we discovered that instead of food it contained merely some salt and a piece of slate. This was a great blow to us. The box was a Brazilian counterfeit of a tin of anchovies. How disheartening to discover the fraud at so inopportune a moment! I had reserved the tin until the last as I did not like the look of it from the outside. We kept the salt – which was of the coarsest description.

On 8 September we were slightly more fortunate, as the country was flatter. I was steering a course of 290° b. m. (NW). I found that farther south we would have encountered too mountainous a country.

We crossed several streamlets, the largest 3 m wide, all of which flowed south. We had no particular adventure that day, and considering all things, we marched fairly well – some 20 kil. Towards the evening we camped on a hill. When we got there we were so exhausted that we made our camp on the summit, although there was no water near.

On 9 September, after marching for half an hour we arrived at a stream 15m. wide, which I took at first to be the river Secundury, a tributary of the Madeira River. Near the banks of that stream we found indications that human beings had visited that spot – perhaps the Indians we had heard so much about. The marks we found, however, were, I estimated, about one year old. Although these signs should have given us a little courage to go on, we were so famished and exhausted that my men sat down on the river-bank and would not proceed. By that time we had got accustomed even to the fierce bites of the ants. We had no more strength to defend ourselves. In vain we strained our eyes all the time in search of wild fruit. In the river we saw plenty of fish; we had a fishing line with us, but no bait whatever that we could use. There are, of course, no worms underground where ants are so numerous. We could not make snares in the river, as it was much too deep. So we sat with covetous eyes, watching the fish go by. It was most tantalising, and made us ten times more hungry than ever to be so near food and not be able to get it.

It is curious how hunger works on your brain. I am not at all a glutton, and never think of food under ordinary circumstances. But while I was starving I could see before me from morning till night, in my imagination, all kinds of delicacies – caviare, Russian soups, macaroni au gratin, all kinds of refreshing ice creams, and plum pudding. Curiously enough, some days I had a perfect craving for one particular thing, and would have given anything I possessed in the world to obtain a morsel of it. The next day I did not care for that at all, in my imagination, but wanted something else very badly. The three things which I mostly craved for while I was starving were caviare, galantine of chicken, and ice cream – the latter particularly.

People say that with money you can do anything you like in the world. I had at that time on my person some £6,000 sterling, of which £4,000 was in actual cash. If anybody had placed before me a morsel of any food I would gladly have given the entire sum to have it. But no, indeed; no such luck! How many times during those days did I vividly dream of delightful dinner and supper parties at the Savoy, the Carlton, or the Ritz, in London, Paris, and New York! How many times did I think of the delicious meals I had had when a boy in the home of my dear father and mother! I could reconstruct in my imagination all those meals, and thought what an idiot I was to have come there out of my own free will to suffer like that. My own dreams were constantly interrupted by Benedicto and Filippe, who also had similar dreams of the wonderful meals they had had in their own houses, and the wonderful ways in which their *feijãozinho* – a term of endearment used by them for their beloved beans – had been cooked at home by their sweathearts or their temporary wives.

'Why did we leave our *feijãozinho*' – and here they smacked their lips – 'to come and die in this rotten country?'

All day I heard them talk of *feijãozinho, feijãozinho*, until I was wearied to distraction by that word – particularly as, even when starving, I had no desire whatever to eat the beastly stuff.

The negro Filippe and Benedicto were really brave in a way. I tried to induce them all the time to march as much as we could, so as to get somewhere; but every few moments they sat or fell down, and much valuable time was wasted.

As the days went by and our strength got less and less every hour, I decided not to cut the forest any more, but to go through without that extra exertion. As I could not trust my men with the big knife, I had to carry it myself, as occasionally it had to be used – especially near streams, where the vegetation was always more or less entangled.

That evening (9 September) we had halted at sunset – simply dead with fatigue and exhaustion. The *sauba* ants had cut nearly all the strings of Filippe's hammock; while he was resting peacefully on it the remainder of the strings broke, and he had a bad fall. He was so exhausted that he remained lying on the ground, swarming all over with ants and moaning the whole time, having no strength to repair the hammock.

When Filippe eventually fell into a sound slumber I had a curious experience in the middle of the night. I was sleeping in my improvised hammock, when I felt two paws resting on my body and something sniffing in my face. When I opened my eyes I found a jaguar, standing up on its hind paws, staring me straight in the face. The moment I moved, the astonished animal, which had evidently never seen a human being before, leapt away and disappeared.

I find that people have strange ideas about wild animals. It is far from true that wild beasts are vicious. I have always found them as gentle as possible. Although I have seen nearly every wild beast that it is possible for man to see in the world, I have never once been attacked by them, although on dozens of occasions I have come into close contact with them. I invariably found all wild animals – expect the African buffalo – quite timid and almost gentle, unless, of course, they have been worried or wounded. These remarks do not apply to wild animals in captivity.

On 10 September – that was the seventh day of our involuntary fast – we had another dreary march, again without a morsel of food. My men were so downhearted that I really thought they would not last much longer. Hunger was playing on them in a curious way. They said that they could hear voices all round them and people firing rifles. I could hear nothing at all. I well knew that their minds were beginning to go, and that it was a pure hallucination. Benedicto and Filippe, who originally were both atheists of an advanced type, had now become extremely religious, and were muttering fervent prayers all the time. They made a vow that if we escaped alive they would each give £5 sterling out of their pay to have a big mass celebrated in the first church they saw.

At this place I abandoned the few cartridges we had, as they were absolutely useless. They were Mauser cartridges which I had bought in Rio de Janeiro, and it is quite possible that they were counterfeits.

Taking things all round, my men behaved very well, but these were moments of the greatest anxiety for me, and I myself was praying fervently to God to get us out of that difficulty. My strength was failing more and more daily, and although I was suffering no actual pain, yet the weakness was simply appalling. It was all I could do to stand up on my legs. What was worse for me was that my head was still in good working order, and I fully realised our position all the time.

The country we were travelling over was fairly hilly, up and down most of the time, over no great elevations. We passed two large tributaries of the main stream we had found before, and a number of minor ones. The main stream was strewn with fallen trees, and was not navigable during the dry season. The erosion of the banks by the water had caused so many trees to fall down across it that no canoe could possibly go through.

I noticed in one or two places along the river traces of human beings having been there some years before.

In the afternoon we again wasted much energy in knocking down two palm trees on the summit of which were great bunches of *coco do matto*. Again we had a bitter disappointment. One after the other we split the nuts open, but they merely contained water inside shells that were much harder to crack than wood. My craving for food was such that in despair I took two or three *sauba* ants and proceeded to eat them. When I ground them under my teeth their taste was so acidly bitter that it made me quite ill. Not only that, but one *sauba* bit my tongue so badly that it swelled up to a great size, and remained like that for several days.

On 11 September we had another terrible march, the forest being very dense and much entangled along the stream. We had great trouble in getting through, as there were many palms and ferns, and we had no more strength to cut down our way. We came to a big tree, which was hollow inside up to a great height, and round which were millions of bees.

Benedicto, who was a great connoisseur in such matters, said that high up inside the tree there must be honey. The bees round that tree were unfortunately stinging bees. We drew lots as to who should go inside the tree to get the honey. It fell to Benedicto. We took off most of our clothes and wrapped up his head and legs so that he might proceed to the attack. The job was not an easy one, for in the first reconnaissance he made with his head inside the tree he discovered that the honey must be not less than 20 ft above the ground, and it was necessary to climb up to that height inside the tree before he could get it. In order to hasten matters – as Benedicto was reluctant in carrying out the job – I tried my hand at it, but I was stung badly by hundreds of bees behind my head, on my eyelids, on my arms and legs. When I came out of the tree I was simply covered with angry bees, which stung me all over. So I told Benedicto that, as Fate had called upon him to do the work, he had better do it.

Benedicto was certainly very plucky that day. All of a sudden he dashed inside the tree and proceeded to climb up. We heard wild screams for some minutes; evidently the bees were protecting their home well. While Filippe and I were seated outside, smiling faintly at poor Benedicto's plight, he reappeared. We hardly recognized him when he emerged from the tree, so badly stung and swollen was his face, notwithstanding the protection he had over it. All he brought back was a small piece of the honeycomb about as large as a florin. What little honey there was inside was quite putrid, but we divided it into three equal parts and devoured it ravenously, bees and all. A moment later all three of us were seized with vomiting, so that the meagre meal was worse than nothing to us.

We were then in a region of innumerable liane, which hung from the trees and caught our feet and heads, and wound themselves round us when we tried to shift them from their position. Nearly all the trees in that part had long and powerful spikes.

Then near water there were huge palms close together, the sharp-edged leaves of which cut our hands, faces and legs as we pushed our way through.

A violent storm broke out in the afternoon. The rain was torrential, making our march extremely difficult. It was just like marching under a heavy shower-bath. The rain lasted for some three hours. We crossed one large stream flowing west into the Secundury, and also two other good-sized streamlets.

We had a miserable night, drenched as we were and unable to light a fire, the box of matches having got wet and the entire forest being soaked by the torrential storm. During the night another storm arrived and poured regular buckets of water upon us.

On 12 September we drowsily got up from our hammocks in a dejected state. By that time we had lost all hope of finding food, and no longer took the trouble to look round for anything to eat. We went on a few hundred metres at a time, now Benedicto fainting from exhaustion, then Filippe, then myself. While one or another was unconscious much time was wasted. Marching under those conditions was horrible, as either one or other of us collapsed every few hundred metres.

Another violent storm broke out, and we all lay on the ground helpless, the skin of our hands and feet getting shrivelled up with the moisture.

My feet were much swollen owing to the innumerable thorns which had got into them while walking barefooted. It was most painful to march, as I was not accustomed to walk without shoes.

We went only ten kilometres on 12 September. We crossed two small rivers and one large, flowing west and south, evidently into the Secundury.

On 13 September we had another painful march, my men struggling along, stumbling and falling every little while. They were dreadfully depressed. Towards the evening we came to a big tree, at the foot of which we found some discarded shells, such as we had once seen before, of fruit eaten by monkeys. My men and I tried to scrape with our teeth some of the sweet substance which still adhered to the shells. We saw some of the fruit, which was fit to eat, at a great height upon the tree, but we had not the strength to climb up or cut down that enormous tree.

All the visions of good meals which I had had until then had now vanished altogether on that tenth day of fasting, and I experienced a sickly feeling in my inside which gave me an absolute dislike for food of any kind. My head was beginning to sway, and I had difficulty in collecting my ideas. My memory seemed to be gone all of a sudden. I could no longer remember in what country I was travelling, nor could I remember anything distinctly. Only some lucid intervals came every now and then, in which I realised our tragic position; but those did not last long, all I could remember being that I must go to the west. I could not remember why nor where I intended to come out.

Everything seemed to be against us. We were there during the height of the rainy season. Towards sunset rain came down once more in bucketfuls and lasted the entire night, the water dripping from our hammocks as it would from a small cascade. We were soaked, and shivering, although the temperature was not low. I had my maximum and minimum thermometers with me, but my exhaustion was such that I had not the strength to unpack them every night and morning and set them.

We crossed two streamlets flowing west. Benedicto and Filippe were in such a bad way that it was breaking my heart to look at them. Every time they fell down in a faint I never knew whether it was for the last time that they had closed their eyes. When I felt their hearts with my hand they beat so faintly that once or twice I really thought they were dead. That day I myself fainted, and fell with the left side of my face resting on the ground. When I recovered consciousness some time later, I touched my face, which was hurting me, and found that nearly the whole skin of my cheek had been eaten up by small ants, the lower lid of the eye having suffered particularly. A nasty sore remained on my face for some two months after that experience, the bites of those ants being very poisonous.

Bad as they were, there is no doubt that to a great extent we owed our salvation to those terrible ants. Had it not been for them and the incessant torture they inflicted on us when we fell down upon the ground, we should have perhaps lain there and never got up again.

I offered Benedicto and Filippe a large reward if they continued marching without abandoning the precious loads. Brazilians have a great greed for money, and for it they will do many things which they would not do otherwise.

On 14 September we made another most painful march of 20 kil., again up and down high hills, some as much as 300 ft. above the level land of that country, and all with steep, indeed, almost vertical, sides, extremely difficult for us to climb in our exhausted condition. We saw several streamlets flowing west. When evening came we had before us a high hill, which we ascended. When we reached the top we just lay upon the ground like so many corpses, and, ants or no ants biting us, we had not the energy to get up again. Once more did the rain come down in torrents that night, and to a certain extent washed the ants from our bodies.

My surprise was really great the next morning when I woke up. I felt myself fading away fast. Every time I closed my eyes I expected never to open them again.

On 15 September we made another trying march, collapsing under our loads every few hundred metres. My men were constantly looking for something to eat in all directions, but could find nothing. Benedicto and Filippe were now all the time contemplating suicide. The mental strain of perpetually keeping an eye on them was great.

We were sitting down, too tired to get up, when Filippe amazed me considerably by the following words, which he spoke in a kind of reverie:

'It would be very easy,' he said, 'now that you have no more strength yourself, for us two to get the big knife and cut your throat. We know that you have a big, big sum of money upon you, and if we robbed you we would be rich for ever. But we do not want to do it. It would not be much use to us, as we could not get out of the forest alone. I believe we shall all die together, and all that money will go to waste.'

Filippe said this in quite a good-natured manner. The two poor fellows were so depressed that one had to forgive them for anything they said.

As the river seemed to describe a big loop, I had left it three days before, seeing plainly by the conformation of the country that we should strike it again sooner or later. We were marching once more by compass. My men, who had no faith whatever in the magnetic needle, were again almost paralysed with fear that we might not encounter the stream again. A thousand times a day they accused me of foolishness in leaving the river, as they said it would have been better to follow its tortuous course – notwithstanding the trouble we had in following it, owing to the dense vegetation near the water – rather than strike once more across country. They were beginning to lose heart altogether, when I told them I could see by the vegetation that we were once more near the water. Anybody accustomed as I am to marching through the forest could tell easily by the appearance of the vegetation some miles before actually getting to a stream.

I reassured my companions, saying that within a few hours we should certainly meet the 'big water' again. In fact, not more than half an hour afterwards we suddenly found ourselves once more on the large stream – at that point 70 metres wide.

My men were so amazed and delighted that they embraced me and sobbed over my shoulders for some time. From that moment their admiration for the compass was unbounded; they expected me to find anything with it.

MAN-EATER

COLONEL JIM CORBETT
(1875–1955)

*Anglo-Indian soldier, naturalist and big-game hunter. A wildlife reserve
in the Indian state of Uttar Pradesh bears his name.*

I had wounded the tigress on 7 April, and it was now the 10th. As
a general rule a tiger is not considered to be dangerous – that is,
liable to charge at sight – twenty-four hours after being wounded.
A lot depends on the nature of the wound, however, and on the
temper of the wounded individual. Twenty-four hours after
receiving a light flesh wound a tiger usually moves away on being
approached, whereas a tiger with a painful body wound might
continue to be dangerous for several days. I did not know the
nature of the wound the tigress was suffering from, and as she
had made no attempt to attack me the previous day I believed I
could now ignore the fact that she was wounded and look upon
her only as a man-eater, and a very hungry man-eater at that, for
she had eaten nothing since killing the woman whom she had
shared with the cubs.

Where the tigress had crossed the stream there was a channel,
three feet wide and two feet deep, washed out by rainwater. Up
this channel, which was bordered by dense brushwood, the tigress
had gone. Following her tracks I came to a cattle path. Here she
had left the channel and gone along the path to the right. Three
hundred yards along was a tree with heavy foliage and under this

tree the tigress had lain all night. Her wound had troubled her and she had tossed about, but on the leaves on which she had been lying there was neither blood nor any discharge from her wound. From this point on I followed her fresh tracks, taking every precaution not to walk into an ambush. By evening I had tracked her for several miles along cattle paths, water channels, and game tracks, without having set eyes on so much as the tip of her tail. At sunset I collected my men, and as we returned to camp they told me they had been able to follow the movements of the tigress through the jungle by the animals and birds that had called at her, but that they too had seen nothing of her.

When hunting unwounded man-eating tigers the greatest danger, when walking into the wind, is of an attack from behind, and to a lesser extent from either side. When the wind is from behind, the danger is from either side. In the same way, if the wind is blowing from the right the danger is from the left and from behind, and if blowing from the left the danger is from the right and from behind. In none of these cases is there any appreciable danger of an attack from in front, for in my experience all unwounded tigers, whether man-eaters or not, are disinclined to make a head-on attack. Under normal conditions man-eating tigers limit the range of their attack to the distance they can spring, and for this reason they are more difficult to cope with than wounded tigers, who invariably launch an attack from a little distance, maybe only ten or twenty yards, but possibly as much as a hundred yards. This means that whereas the former have to be dealt with in a matter of split seconds, the latter give one time to raise a rifle and align the sights. In either case it means rapid shooting and a fervent prayer that an ounce or two of lead will stop a few hundred pounds of muscle and bone.

In the case of the tigress I was hunting, I knew that her wound would not admit of her springing and that if I kept out of her reach I would be comparatively safe. The possibility that she had recovered from her wound in the four days that had elapsed since I had last seen her had, however, to be taken into account. When therefore I started out alone on the morning of 11 April to take up the tracks where I had left them the previous evening, I resolved to keep clear of any rock, bush, tree, or other object behind which the tigress might be lying up in wait for me.

She had been moving the previous evening in the direction of the Tanakpur road. I again found where she had spent the night, this time on a soft bed of dry grass, and from this point I followed her fresh tracks. Avoiding dense cover – possibly because she could not move through it silently – she was keeping to water channels and game tracks and it became apparent that she was not moving about aimlessly but was looking for something to kill and eat. Presently, in one of these water channels she found and killed a few-weeks-old *kakar*. She had come on the young deer as it was lying asleep in the sun on a bed of sand, and had eaten every scrap of it, rejecting nothing but the tiny hooves. I was now only a minute or two behind her, and knowing that the morsel would have done no more than whet her appetite, I redoubled my precautions. In places the channels and game tracks to which the tigress was keeping twisted and turned and ran through dense cover or past rocks. Had my condition been normal I would have followed on her footsteps and possibly been able to catch up with her, but unfortunately I was far from normal. The swelling on my head, face, and neck, had now increased to such proportions that I was no longer able to move my head up or down or from side to side, and my left eye was closed. However, I still had one good eye, fortunately my right one, and I could still hear a little.

During the whole of that day I followed the tigress without seeing her and without, I believe, her seeing me. Where she had gone along water channels, game tracks, or cattle paths that ran through dense cover I skirted round the cover and picked up her pug-marks on the far side. Not knowing the ground was a very great handicap, for not only did it necessitate walking more miles than I need have done, but it also prevented my anticipating the movements of the tigress and ambushing her. When I finally gave up the chase for the day, the tigress was moving up the valley in the direction of the village.

Back in camp I realized that the 'bad time' I had foreseen and dreaded was approaching. Electric shocks were stabbing through the enormous abscess, and the hammer blows were increasing in intensity. Sleepless nights and a diet of tea had made a coward of me, and I could not face the prospect of sitting on my bed through another long night, racked with pain and waiting for something, I knew not what, to happen. I had come to Talla Des to try to rid the hill people of the terror that menaced them and to tide over my bad time, and all that I had accomplished so far was to make their condition worse. Deprived of the ability to secure her natural prey, the tigress, who in eight years had only killed a hundred and fifty people would now, unless she recovered from her wound, look to her easiest prey – human beings – to provide her with most of the food she needed. There was therefore an account to be settled between the tigress and myself, and that night was as suitable a time as any to settle it.

Calling for a cup of tea – made hill-fashion with milk – which served me as dinner, I drank it while standing in the moonlight. Then, calling my eight men together, I instructed them to wait for me in the village until the following evening, and if I did not return by then to pack up my things and start early the next morning for Naini Tal. Having done this I picked up my rifle from where I put it on my bed, and headed down the valley. My men, all of whom had been with me for years, said not a word either to ask me where I was going or to try to dissuade me from going. They just stood silent in a group and watched me walk away. Maybe the glint I saw on their cheeks was only imagination, or maybe it was only the reflection of the moon. Anyway, when I looked back not a man had moved. They were just standing in a group as I had left them . . .

One of the advantages of making detailed mental maps of ground covered is that finding the way back to any given spot presents no difficulty. Picking up the pug-marks of my quarry where I had left them, I resumed my tracking, which was now only possible on game tracks and on cattle paths, to which the tigress was, fortunately, keeping. *Sambhar* and *kakar* had now come out on to the open glades, some to feed and others for protection, and though I could not pinpoint their alarm calls they let me know when the tigress was on the move and gave me a rough idea of the direction in which she was moving.

On a narrow, winding cattle path running through dense cover I left the pug-marks of the tigress and worked round through scattered brushwood to try to pick them up on the far side. The way round was longer than I had anticipated, and I eventually came out on an open stretch of ground with short grass and dotted about with big oak trees. Here I came to a halt in the shadow of a big tree. Presently, by a movement of this shadow, I realized that the tree above me was tenanted by a troop of *langurs*. I had covered a lot of ground during the eighteen hours I had been on my feet that day, and here now was a safe place for me to rest awhile, for the *langurs* above would give warning of danger. Sitting with my back against the tree and facing the cover round which I had skirted, I had been resting for half an hour when an old *langur* gave his alarm call; the tigress had come out into the open and the *langur* had caught sight of her. Presently I, too, caught sight of the tigress just as she started to lie down. She was a hundred yards to my right and ten yards from the cover, and she lay down broadside on to me with her head turned looking up at the calling *langur*.

I have had a lot of practice in night shooting, for during the winter months I assisted our tenants at Kaladhungi to protect their crops against marauding animals such as pig and deer. On a clear moonlight night I can usually count on hitting an animal up to a range of about a hundred yards. Like most people who have taught themselves to shoot, I keep both eyes open when shooting. This enables me to keep the target in view with one eye, while aligning the sights of the rifle with the other. At any other time I would have waited for the tigress to stand up and then fired at her, but unfortunately my left eye was now closed and a hundred yards was too far to risk a shot with only one eye. On the two previous nights the tigress had lain in the one spot and had possibly slept most of the night, and she might do the same now. If she lay right down on her side – she was now lying on her stomach with her head up – and went to sleep I could either go back to the cattle path on which I had left her pug-marks and follow her tracks to the edge of the cover and get to within ten yards of her, or I could creep up to her over the open ground until I got close enough to make sure of my shot. Anyway, for the present I could do nothing but sit perfectly still until the tigress made up her mind what she was going to do.

For a long time, possibly half an hour or a little longer, the tigress lay in the one position, occasionally moving her head from side to side, while the old *langur* in a sleepy voice continued to give his alarm call. Finally she got to her feet and very slowly and very painfully started to walk away to my right. Directly in the line in which she was going there was an open ravine ten to fifteen feet deep and twenty to twenty-five yards wide, which I had crossed lower down when coming to the spot where I now was. When the tigress had increased the distance between us to a hundred and fifty yards, and the chances of her seeing me had decreased, I started to follow her. Slipping from tree to tree, and moving a little faster than she, I reduced her lead to fifty yards by the time she reached the edge of the ravine. She was now in range, but was standing in shadow, and her tail end was a very small mark to fire at. For a long and anxious minute she stood in the one position and then, having made up her mind to cross the ravine, very gently went over the edge.

As the tigress disappeared from view I bent down and ran forwards on silent feet. Bending my head down and running was a very stupid mistake for me to have made, and I had only run a few yards when I was overcome by vertigo. Near me were two oak saplings, a few feet apart and with interlaced branches. Laying down my rifle I climbed up the saplings to a height of ten or twelve feet. Here I found a branch to sit on, another for my feet, and yet other small branches for me to rest against. Crossing my arms on the branches in front of me, I laid my head on them, and at that moment the abscess burst, not into my brain as I feared it would, but out through my nose and left ear.

'No greater happiness can man know, than the sudden cessation of great pain', was said by someone who had suffered and suffered greatly, and who knew the happiness of sudden relief. It was round about midnight when relief came to me, and the grey light was just beginning to show in the east when I raised my head from my crossed arms. Cramp in my legs resulting from my having sat on a thin branch for four hours had roused me, and for a little while I did not know where I was or what had happened to me. Realization was not long in coming. The great swelling on my head, face, and neck had gone and with it had gone the pain. I could now move my head as I liked, my left eye was open, and I could swallow without discomfort. I had lost an opportunity of shooting the tigress, but what did that matter now, for I was over my bad time and no matter where or how far the tigress went I would follow her, and sooner or later I would surely get another chance.

When I last saw the tigress she was heading in the direction of the village. Swinging down from the saplings, up which I had climbed with such difficulty, I retrieved my rifle and headed in the same direction. At the stream I stopped and washed and cleaned myself and my clothes as best I could. My men had not spent the night in the village as I had instructed them to, but had sat round a fire near my tent keeping a kettle of water on the boil. As, dripping with water, they saw me coming towards them they sprang up with a glad cry of 'Sahib! Sahib! You have come back, and you are well.' 'Yes', I answered, 'I have come back, and I am now well.' When an Indian gives his loyalty, he gives it unstintingly and without counting the cost. When we arrived at Talla Kote the headman put two rooms at the disposal of my men, for it was dangerous to sleep anywhere except behind locked doors. On this my bad night, and fully alive to the danger, my men had sat out in the open in case they could be of any help to me, and to keep a kettle on the boil for my tea – if I should return. I cannot remember if I drank the tea, but I can remember my shoes being drawn off by willing hands, and a rug spread over me as I lay down on my bed.

Hours and hours of peaceful sleep, and then a dream. Someone was urgently calling me, and someone was as urgently saying I must not be disturbed. Over and over again the dream was repeated with slight variations, but with no less urgency, until the words penetrated through the fog of sleep and became a reality. 'You *must* wake him or he will be very angry.' And the rejoinder, 'We will *not* wake him for he is very tired.' Ganga Ram was the last speaker, so I called out and told him to bring the man to me. In a minute my tent was besieged by an excited throng of men and boys all eager to tell me that the man-eater had just killed six goats on the far side of the village. While pulling on my shoes I looked over the throng and on seeing Dungar Singh, the lad who was with me when I shot the cubs, I asked him if he knew where the goats had been killed and if he could take me to the spot. 'Yes, yes,' he answered eagerly, 'I know where they were killed and I can take you there.' Telling the headman to keep the crowd back, I armed myself with my .275 rifle and, accompanied by Dungar Singh, set off through the village.

On the way down the hill the lad had told me that round about midday a large flock of goats in charge of ten or fifteen boys was feeding in the hollow, when a tiger – which they suspected was the man-eater – suddenly appeared among them and struck down six goats. On seeing the tiger the boys started yelling and were joined by some men collecting firewood near by. In the general confusion of goats dashing about and human beings yelling, the tiger moved off and no one appeared to have seen in which direction it went. Grabbing hold of three dead goats the men and boys dashed back to the village to give me the news, leaving three goats with broken backs in the hollow.

That the killer of the goats was the wounded man-eater there could be no question, for when I last saw her the previous night she was going straight towards the village. Further, my men told me that an hour or so before my return to camp a *kakar* had barked near the stream, a hundred yards from where they were sitting, and thinking that the animal had barked on seeing me they had built up the fire. It was fortunate that they had done so, for I later found the pug-marks of the tigress where she had skirted round the fire and had then gone through the village, obviously with the object of securing a human victim. Having failed in her quest she had evidently taken cover near the village, and at the first opportunity of securing food had struck down the goats. This she had done in a matter of seconds, while suffering from a wound that had made her limp badly.

As I was not familiar with the ground, I asked Dungar Singh in which direction he thought the tigress had gone. Pointing down the valley he said she had probably gone in that direction, for there was heavy jungle farther down. While I was questioning him about this jungle, with the idea of going down and looking for the tigress, a *kalege* pheasant started chattering. On hearing this the lad turned round and looked up the hill, giving me an indication of the direction in which the bird was calling. To our left the hill went up steeply, and growing on it were a few bushes and stunted trees. I knew the tigress would not have attempted to climb this hill, and on seeing me looking at it Dungar Singh said the pheasant was not calling on the hill but in a ravine round the shoulder of it. As we were not within sight of the pheasant, there was only one thing that could have alarmed it, and that was the tigress. Telling Dungar Singh to leave me and run back to the village as fast as he could go, I covered his retreat with my rifle until I considered he was clear of the danger zone and then turned round to look for a suitable place in which to sit.

The only trees in this part of the valley were enormous pines which, as they had no branches for thirty or forty feet, it would be quite impossible to climb. So of necessity I would have to sit on the ground. This would be all right during daylight, but if the tigress delayed her return until nightfall, and preferred human flesh to mutton, I would need a lot of luck to carry me through the hour or two of darkness before the moon rose.

On the low ridge running from left to right on the near side of the hollow was a big flat rock. Near it was another and smaller one. By sitting on this smaller rock I found I could shelter behind the bigger, exposing only my head to the side from which I expected the tigress to come. So here I decided to sit. In front of me was a hollow some forty yards in width with a twenty-foot-high bank on the far side. Above this bank was a ten- to twenty-yard-wide flat stretch of ground sloping down to the right. Beyond this the hill went up steeply. The three goats in the hollow, which were alive when the boys and men ran away, were now dead. When striking them down the tigress had ripped the skin on the back of one of them.

The *kalege* pheasant had now stopped chattering, and I speculated as to whether it had called at the tigress as she was going up the ravine after the lad and I had arrived or whether it had called on seeing the tigress coming back. In the one case it would mean a long wait for me, and in the other a short one. I had taken up my position at 2 p.m., and half an hour later a pair of blue Himalayan magpies came up the valley. These beautiful birds, which do a lot of destruction in the nesting season among tits and other small birds, have an uncanny instinct for finding in a jungle anything that is dead. I heard the magpies long before I saw them, for they are very vocal. On catching sight of the goats they stopped chattering and very cautiously approached. After several false alarms they alighted on the goat with the ripped back and started to feed. For some time a king vulture had been quartering the sky, and now, on seeing the magpies on the goat, he came sailing down and landed as lightly as a feather on the dead branch of a pine tree. These king vultures with their white shirt-fronts, black coats, and red heads and legs, are always the first of the vultures to find a kill. Being smaller than other vultures it is essential for them to be first at the table, for when the others arrive they have to take a back seat.

I welcomed the vulture's coming, for he would provide me with information I lacked. From his perch high up on the pine tree he had an extensive view, and if he came down and joined the magpies it would mean that the tigress had gone, whereas if he remained where he was it would mean that she was lying up somewhere close by. For the next half hour the scene remained unchanged – the magpies continued to feed, and the vulture sat on the dead branch – and then the sun was blotted out by heavy rain clouds. Shortly after, the *kalege* pheasant started chattering again and the magpies flew screaming down the valley. The tigress was coming, and here, sooner than I had expected, was the chance of shooting her that I had lost the previous night when overcome by vertigo.

A few light bushes on the shoulder of the hill partly obstructed my view in the direction of the ravine, and presently through these bushes I saw the tigress. She was coming, very slowly, along the flat bit of ground above the twenty-foot-high bank and was looking straight towards me. With only head exposed and my soft hat pulled down to my eyes, I knew she would not notice me if I made no movement. So, with the rifle resting on the flat rock, I sat perfectly still. When she had come opposite to me the tigress sat down, with the bole of a big pine tree directly between us. I could see her head on one side of the tree and her tail and part of her hindquarters on the other. Here she sat for minutes, snapping at the flies that, attracted by her wound, were tormenting her . . .

The people of Talla Des had suffered and suffered grievously from the tigress, and for the suffering she had inflicted she was now paying in full. To put her out of her misery I several times aligned the sights of my rifle on her head, but the light, owing to the heavy clouds, was not good enough for me to make sure of hitting a comparatively small object at sixty yards.

Eventually the tigress stood up, took three steps and then stood broadside on to me, looking down at the goats. With my elbows resting on the flat rock I took careful aim at the spot where I thought her heart would be, pressed the trigger, and saw a spurt of dust go up on the hill on the far side of her. On seeing the dust the thought flashed through my mind that not only had I missed the tigress's heart, but that I had missed the whole animal. And yet, after my careful aim, that could not be. What undoubtedly had happened was that my bullet had gone clean through her without meeting any resistance. At my shot the tigress sprang forward, raced over the flat ground like a very frightened but unwounded animal, and before I could get in another shot disappeared from view.

Mad with myself for not having killed the tigress when she had given me such a good shot, I was determined now that she would not escape from me. Jumping down from the rock, I sprinted across the hollow, up the twenty-foot bank and along the flat ground until I came to the spot where the tigress had disappeared. Here I found there was a steep forty-foot drop down a loose shale scree. Down this the tigress had gone in great bounds. Afraid to do the same for fear of spraining my ankles, I sat down on my heels and tobogganed to the bottom. At the foot of the scree was a well-used footpath, along which I felt sure the tigress had gone, though the surface was too hard to show pugmarks. To the right of the path was a boulder-strewn stream, the one that Dungar Singh and I had crossed farther up, and flanking the stream was a steep grassy hill. To the left of the path was a hill with a few pine trees growing on it. The path for some distance was straight, and I had run along it for fifty or more yards when I heard a *ghooral* give its alarm sneeze. There was only one place where the *ghooral* could be and that was on the grassy hill to my right. Thinking that the tigress had possibly crossed the stream and gone up this hill, I pulled up to see if I could see her. As I did so, I thought I heard men shouting. Turning round I looked up in the direction of the village and saw a crowd of men standing on the saddle of the hill. On seeing me look round they shouted again and waved me on, *on*, straight along the path. In a moment I was on the run again, and on turning a corner found fresh blood on the path.

The skin of animals is loose. When an animal that is standing still is hit in the body by a bullet and it dashes away at full speed, the hole made in the skin does not coincide with the hole in the flesh, with the result that, as long as the animal is running at speed, little if any blood flows from the wound. When, however, the animal slows down and the two holes come closer together, blood flows and continues to flow more freely the slower the animal goes. When there is any uncertainty as to whether an animal that has been fired at has been hit or not, the point can be very easily cleared up by going to the exact spot where the animal was when fired at, and looking for cut hairs. These will indicate that the animal was hit, whereas the absence of such hairs will show that it was clean missed.

After going round the corner the tigress had slowed down, but she was still running, as I could see from the blood splashes, and in order to catch up with her I put on a spurt. I had not gone very far when I came to a spur jutting out from the hill on my left. Here the path bent back at a very acute angle, and not being able to stop myself, and there being nothing for me to seize hold of on the hill-side, I went over the edge of the narrow path, all standing. Ten to fifteen feet below was a small rhododendron sapling, and below the sapling a sheer drop into a dark and evil-looking ravine where the stream, turning at right angles, had cut away the toe of the hill. As I passed the sapling with my heels cutting furrows in the soft earth, I gripped it under my right arm. The sapling, fortunately, was not uprooted, and though it bent it did not break. Easing myself round very gently, I started to kick footholds in the soft loamy hill-face which had a luxuriant growth of maidenhair fern.

The opportunity of catching up with the tigress had gone, but I now had a well-defined blood trail to follow, so there was no longer any need for me to hurry. The footpath which at first had run north now ran west along the north face of a steep and well-wooded hill. When I had gone for another two hundred yards along the path, I came to flat ground on a shoulder of the hill. This was the limit I would have expected a tiger shot through the body to have travelled, so I approached the flat ground, on which there was a heavy growth of bracken and scattered bushes, very cautiously.

A tiger that has made up its mind to avenge an injury is the most terrifying animal to be met with in an Indian jungle. The tigress had a very recent injury to avenge and she had demonstrated – by striking down six goats and by springing and dashing away when I fired at her – that the leg wound she had received five days before was no handicap to rapid movement. I felt sure, therefore, that as soon as she became aware that I was following her and she considered that I was within her reach, she would launch an all-out attack on me, which I would possibly have to meet with a single bullet. Drawing back the bolt of the rifle, I examined the cartridge very carefully, and satisfied that it was one of a fresh lot I had recently got from Manton in Calcutta, I replaced it in the chamber, put back the bolt, and threw off the safety catch.

The path ran through the bracken, which was waist high and which met over it. The blood trail led along the path into the bracken, and the tigress might be lying up on the path or on the right or the left-hand side of it. So I approached the bracken foot by foot and looking straight ahead for, on these occasions, it is unwise to keep turning the head. When I was within three yards of the bracken I saw a movement a yard from the path on the right. It was the tigress gathering herself together for a spring. Wounded and starving though she was, she was game to fight it out. Her spring, however, was never launched, for, as she rose, my first bullet raked her from end to end, and the second bullet broke her neck.

Days of pain and strain on an empty stomach left me now trembling in every limb, and I had great difficulty in reaching the spot where the path bent back at an acute angle and where, but for the chance dropping of a rhododendron seed, I would have ended my life on the rocks below.

The entire population of the village, plus my own men, were gathered on the saddle of the hill and on either side of it, and I had hardly raised my hat to wave when, shouting at the tops of their voices, the men and boys came swarming down. My six Garhwalis were the first to arrive. Congratulations over, the tigress was lashed to a pole and six of the proudest Garhwalis in Kumaon carried the Talla Des man-eater in triumph to Talla Kote village. Here the tigress was laid down on a bed of straw for the women and children to see, while I went back to my tent for my first solid meal in many weeks. An hour later with a crowd of people round me I skinned the tigress.

The Air

THE SPIRIT OF ST LOUIS

CHARLES A. LINDBERGH
(1902–74)

American aviator who achieved world fame when, in May 1927, he made the first non-stop solo flight from New York to Paris. The flight, which took 33.5 hours, was made in a Ryan monoplane named Spirit of St Louis.

The Eighteenth Hour

The minute hand has just passed 1.00 a.m. It's dawn, one hour after midnight ... With this faint trace of day, the uncontrollable desire to sleep falls over me in quilted layers. I've been staving it off with difficulty during the hours of moonlight. Now it looms all but insurmountable. This is the hour I've been dreading; the hour against which I've tried to steel myself. I know it's the beginning of my greatest test. This will be the worst time of all, this early hour of the second morning – the third morning, it is, since I've slept.

I've lost command of my eyelids. When they start to close, I can't restrain them. They shut, and I shake myself, and lift them with my fingers. I stare at the instruments, wrinkle forehead muscles tense. Lids close again regardless, stick tight as though with glue. My body has revolted from the rule of its mind. Like salt in wounds, the light of day brings back my pains. Every cell of my being is on strike, sulking in protest, claiming that nothing, nothing in the world, could be worth such effort; that man's tissue was never made for such abuse. My back is stiff; my shoulders ache; my face burns; my eyes smart. It seems impossible to go on longer. All I want in life is to throw myself down flat, stretch out – and sleep.

I've struggled with the dawn often enough before, but never with such a background of fatigue. I've got to muster all my reserves, all the tricks I've learned, all remaining strength of mind, for the conflict. If I can hold in air and close to course for one more hour, the sun will be over the horizon and the battle won. Each ray of light is an ally. With each moment after sunrise, vitality will increase.

Shaking my body and stamping my feet no longer has effect. It's more fatiguing than arousing. I'll have to try something else. I push the stick forward and dive down into a high ridge of cloud, pulling up sharply after I clip through its summit. That wakes me a little, but tricks don't help for long. They're only tiring. It's better to sit still and conserve strength.

My mind strays from the cockpit and returns. My eyes close, and open, and close again. But I'm beginning to understand vaguely a new factor which has come to my assistance. It seems I'm made up of three personalities, three elements, each partly dependent and partly independent of the others. There's my body, which knows definitely that what it wants most in the world is sleep. There's my mind, constantly making decisions that my body refuses to comply with, but which itself is weakening in resolution. And there's something else, which seems to become stronger instead of weaker with fatigue, an element of spirit, a directive force that has stepped out from the background and taken control over both mind and body. It seems to guard them as a wise father guards his children; letting them venture to the point of danger, then calling them back, guiding with a firm but tolerant hand.

When my body cries out that it *must* sleep, this third element replies that it may get what rest it can from relaxation, but that sleep is not to be had. When my mind demands that my body stay alert and awake, it is informed that alertness is too much to expect under these circumstances. And when it argues excitedly that to sleep would be to fail, and crash, and drown in the ocean, it is calmly reassured, and told it's right, but that while it must not expect alertness on the body's part, it can be confident there'll be no sleep.

The Nineteenth Hour

When I leave a cloud, drowsiness advances; when I enter the next, it recedes. If I could sleep and wake refreshed, how extraordinary this world of mist would be. But now I only dimly appreciate, only partially realize. The love of flying, the beauty of sunrise, the solitude of the mid-Atlantic sky, are screened from my senses by opaque veils of sleep. All my remaining energy, all the attention I can bring to bear, must be concentrated on the task of simply passing through.

The Twentieth Hour

The nose is down, the wing low, the plane diving and turning. I've been asleep with open eyes. I'm certain they've been open, yet I have all the sensations of waking up – lack of memory of inter-vening time, inability to comprehend the situation for a moment, the return of understanding like blood surging through the body. I kick left rudder and pull the stick back cornerwise. My eyes jump to the altimeter. No danger; I'm at 1,600 feet, a little above my chosen altitude. In a moment, I'll have the plane levelled out. But the turn-indicator leans over the left – the air speed drops – the ball rolls quickly to the side. A climbing turn in the opposite direction! My plane is getting out of control!

The realization is like an electric shock running through my body. It brings instant mental keenness. In a matter of seconds I have the *Spirit of St Louis* back in hand. But even after the needles are in place, the plane seems to be flying on its side. I know what's happening. It's the illusion you sometimes get while flying blind, the illusion that your plane is no longer in level flight, that it's spiralling, stalling, turning, that the instruments are wrong.

There's only one thing to do – shut off feeling from the mind as much as your ability permits. Let a wing stay low as far as bodily senses are concerned. Let the plane seem to manoeuvre as it will, dive, climb, sideslip, or bank; but keep the needles where they belong. Gradually, when the senses find that the plane is continuing on its course, that air isn't screaming through the cowlings as it would in a dive, that wings aren't trembling as they would in a stall, that there's really no pressure on the seat as there would be in a bank, they recover from their confusion and make obeisance to the mind.

As minutes pass and no new incident occurs, I fall into the state of eye-open sleep again. I fly with less anguish when my conscious mind is not awake. At times I'm not sure whether I'm dreaming through life or living through a dream. It seems I've broken down the barrier between the two, and discovered some essential relationship between living and dreaming I never recognized before. Some secret has been opened to me beyond the ordinary consciousness of man. Can I carry it with me beyond this flight, into normal life again? Or is it forbidden knowledge? Will I lose it after I land, as I've so often lost the essence of some midnight's dream?

The Twenty-second Hour

Will the fog never end? Does this storm cover the entire ocean? Except for that small, early morning plot of open sea, I've been in it or above it for nine hours. What happened to the high pressure area that was to give me a sunny sky? The only storms reported were local ones in Europe!

I remind myself again that I didn't wait for confirmation of good weather. Dr Kimball said only that stations along the coast reported clearing, and that a large high-pressure area was moving in over the North Atlantic. He didn't say there'd be no storms. The weather's no worse than I expected when I planned this flight. Why should I complain of a few blind hours in the morning? If the fog lifts by the time I strike the European coast, that's all I should ask. The flight's been as successful as I ever hoped it would be. The only thing that's seriously upset my plans is the sleepless night before I started – those extra twenty-three hours before take-off.

Of course no one thought the weather would break enough to let me start so quickly. But why did I depend on what anyone thought? Why did I take any chance? I didn't have to go to a show that evening. I didn't have to go to New York. This is the price for my amusement, and it's too high. It imperils the entire flight. If this were the first morning without sleep instead of the second, blind flying would be a different matter, and my navigation on a different plane.

The fog dissolves, and the sea appears. Flying two hundred feet higher, I wouldn't have seen it, for the overcast is just above me. There's no sun; only a pocket of clear air. Ahead, is another curtain of mist. Can I get under it this time? I push the stick forward. Waves are mountainous – even higher than before. If I fly close to their crests, maybe I can stay below the next area of fog.

I drop down until I'm flying in salt spray whipped off whitecaps by the wind. I clip five feet above a breaker with my wheels, watch tossing water sweep into the trough beyond. But the fog is too thick. It crowds down between the waves themselves. It merges with their form. A gull couldn't find enough ceiling to fly above this ocean. I climb. The air's rougher than before, swirling like the sea beneath it. I open my throttle wider to hold a margin of speed and power.

Before I reach a thousand feet, waves show again, vaguely – whitecaps veiled and unveiled by low-lying scuds of fog. I nose down; but in a moment they're gone, smothered by mist. I climb.

While I'm staring at the instruments, during an unearthly age of time, both conscious and asleep, the fuselage behind me becomes filled with ghostly presences – vaguely outlined forms, transparent, moving, riding weightless with me in the plane. I feel no surprise at their coming. There's no suddenness to their appearance. Without turning my head, I see them as clearly as though in my normal field of vision. There's no limit to my sight – my skull is one great eye, seeing everywhere at once.

These phantoms speak with human voices – friendly, vapourlike shapes, without substance, able to vanish or appear at will, to pass in and out through the walls of the fuselage as though no walls were there. Now, many are crowded behind me. Now, only a few remain. First one and then another presses forward to my shoulder to speak above the engine's noise, and then draws back among the group behind. At times, voices come out of the air itself, clear yet far away, travelling through distances that can't be measured by the scale of human miles; familiar voices, conversing and advising on my flight, discussing problems of my navigation, reassuring me, giving me messages of importance unattainable in ordinary life.

The Twenty-third Hour

Sea, clouds and sky are all stirred up together – dull grey mist, blinding white mist, patches of blue, mottling of black, a band of sunlight sprinkling diamond facets on the water. There are clouds lying on the ocean, clouds just risen from its surface, clouds floating at every level through twenty thousand feet of sky; some small, some overpowering in size – wisps, masses, layers. It's a breeding ground for mist.

I fly above, below, between the layers, as though following the interstices of a giant sponge; sometimes under a blue sky but over an ocean veiled by thick and drifting mist; sometimes brushing grey clouds with my wings while my wheels are almost rolling in the breakers' foam. It's like playing leapfrog with the weather. These cloud formations help me to stay awake. They give me something on which to fix my eyes in passing, but don't hold my stare too long. Their tremendous, changing, flashing world removes monotony from flight.

Sunlight flashes as I emerge from a cloud. My eyes are drawn to the north. My dreams are startled away. There, under my left wing, only five or six miles distant, a coastline parallels my course – purple, haze-covered hills; clumps of trees; rocky cliffs. Small, wooded islands guard the shore.

But I'm in mid-Atlantic, nearly a thousand miles from land! Half-formed thoughts rush through my mind. Are the compasses completely wrong? Am I hopelessly lost? Is it the coast of Labrador or Greenland that I see? Have I been flying north instead of east?

It's like waking from a sound sleep in strange surroundings, in a room where you've never spent a night before. The wallpaper, the bed, the furniture, the light coming in the window, nothing is as you expected it to be.

I shake my head and look again. There can be no doubt, now, that I'm awake. But the shoreline is still there. Land in mid-Atlantic! Something has gone wrong! I couldn't have been flying north, regardless of the inaccuracy of my compasses. The sun and the moon both rose on my left, and stars confirmed that my general direction was towards Europe. I know there's no land out here in mid-ocean – nothing between Greenland and Iceland to the north, and the Azores to the south. But I look down at the chart for reassurance; for my mind is no longer certain of its knowledge. To find new islands marked on it would hardly be stranger than the flight itself.

No, they must be mirages, fog islands sprung up along my route; here for an hour only to disappear, mushrooms of the sea. But so apparently real, so cruelly deceptive! *Real* clouds cover their higher hills, and pour down into their ravines. How can those bluffs and forests consist of nothing but fog? No islands of the earth could be more perfect.

The Twenty-fourth Hour

Here it's well into midday and my mind's still shirking, still refusing to meet the problems it undertook so willingly in planning for this flight. Are all those months of hard and detailed work to be wasted for lack of a few minutes of concentrated effort? Is my character so weak that I can't pull myself together long enough to lay out a new, considered course? Has landing at Le Bourget become of so little import that I'll trade success for these useless hours of semiconscious relaxation? *No; I must, I will* become alert, and concentrate, and make decisions.

There are measures I haven't yet used – too extreme for normal times. But now it's a case of survival. Anything is justified that has effect. I strike my face sharply with my hand. It hardly feels the blow. I strike again with all the strength I have. My cheek is numb, but there's none of the sharp stinging that I counted on to wake my body. No jump of flesh, no lash on mind. It's no use. Even these methods don't work. Why try more?

But Paris is over a thousand miles away! And there's still a continent to find. I must be prepared to strike a fog-covered European coast hundreds of miles off course; and, if necessary, to fly above clouds all the hours of another night. How can I pass through such ordeals if I can't wake my mind and stir my body? But the alternative is death and failure. Can I complete this flight to Paris? Can I even reach the Irish coast? *But the alternative is death and failure! Death! For the first time in my life, I doubt my ability to endure.*

The stark concept of death has more effect than physical blow or reasoned warning. It imbues me with new power, power strong enough to communicate the emergency to my body's senses, to whip them up from their lethargy and marshall them once more – in straggling ranks, but with some semblance of order and coordination. *It's life, life, life itself at stake.* This time I'm not just saying so. *I know it.*

The Twenty-sixth Hour

Is there something alive down there under my wing? I thought I saw a dark object moving through the water. I search the surface, afraid to hope, lest I lose confidence in vision. Was it a large fish, or were my eyes deceiving me? After the fog islands and the phantoms, I no longer trust my senses. The *Spirit of St Louis* itself might fade away without causing me great surprise. But – yes, there it is again, slightly behind me now, a porpoise – the first living thing I've seen since Newfoundland. Fin and sleek, black body curve gracefully above the surface and slip down out of sight.

The ocean is as desolate as ever. Yet a complete change has taken place. I feel that I've safely recrossed the bridge to life – broken the strands which have been tugging me towards the universe beyond. Why do I find such joy, such encouragement in the sight of a porpoise? What possible bond can I have with a porpoise hundreds of miles at sea, with a strange creature I've never seen before and will never see again? What is there in that flashing glimpse of hide that means so much to me, that even makes it seem a different ocean? Is it simply that I've been looking so long, and seeing nothing? Is it an omen of land ahead? Or is there some common tie between living things that surmounts even the barrier of species?

Can it be that the porpoise was imaginary too, a part of this strange, living dream, like the fuselage's phantoms and the islands which faded into mist? Yet I know there's a difference, a dividing line that still exists between reality and apparition. The porpoise *was* real, like the water itself, like the substance of the cockpit around me, like my face which I can feel when I run my hand across it.

It's twenty-six and a half hours since I took off. That's almost twice as long as the flight between San Diego and St Louis; and that was much the longest flight I ever made. It's asking a lot of an engine to run twenty-six hours without attention. Back on the mail, we check our Liberties at the end of every trip. Are the rocker-arms on my Whirlwind still getting grease? And how long will it keep on going if one of them should freeze?

I shift arms on the stick. My left hand – being free, and apparently disconnected from my mind's control – begins aimlessly exploring the pockets of the chart bag. It pulls the maps of Europe halfway out to reassure my eyes they're there, tucks my helmet and goggles in more neatly, and fingers the shiny little first-aid kit and the dark glasses given me by that doctor on Long Island. Why have I let my eyes burn through the morning? Why have I been squinting for hours and not thought of these glasses before? I hook the wires over my ears and look out on a shaded ocean. It's as though the sky were overcast again. I don't dare use them. They're too comfortable, too pleasant. They make it seem like evening – make me want to sleep.

I slip the glasses back into their pocket, pull out the first-aid kit, and idly snap it open. It contains adhesive tape, compact bandages, and a little pair of scissors. Not enough to do much patching after a crash. Tucked into one corner are several silk-covered, glass capsules of aromatic ammonia. 'For use as Smelling Salts', the labels state. What did the doctor think I could do with smelling salts over the ocean? This kit is made for a child's cut finger, or for some debutante fainting at a ball! I might as well have saved its weight on the take-off, for all the good it will be to me. I put it back in the chart bag – and then pull it out again. If smelling salts revive people who are about to faint, why won't they revive people who are about to fall asleep? Here's a weapon against sleep lying at my side unused, a weapon which has been there all through the morning's deadly hours. A whiff of one of these capsules should sharpen the dullest mind. And no eyes could sleep stinging with the vapour of ammonia.

I'll try one now. The fumes ought to clear my head and keep the compass centered. I crush a capsule between thumb and fingers. A fluid runs out, discolouring the white silk cover. I hold it cautiously, several inches from my nose. There's no odour. I move it closer, slowly, until finally it touches my nostrils. I smell nothing! My eyes don't feel the slightest sting, and no tears come to moisten their dry edges. I inhale again with no effect, and throw the capsule through the window. My mind now begins to realize how deadened my senses have become, how close I must be to the end of my reserves. And yet there may be another sleepless night ahead.

The Twenty-seventh Hour

I'm flying along dreamily when it catches my eyes, that black speck on the water two or three miles southeast. I realize it's there with the same jerk to awareness that comes when the altimeter needle drops too low in flying blind. I squeeze my lids together and look again. A boat! A small boat! Several small boats, scattered over the surface of the ocean!

Seconds pass before my mind takes in the full importance of what my eyes are seeing. Then, all feeling of drowsiness departs. I bank the *Spirit of St Louis* towards the nearest boat and nose down towards the water. I couldn't be wider awake or more keenly aware if the engine had stopped.

Fishing boats! *The coast, the European coast, can't be far away!* The ocean is behind, the flight completed. Those little vessels, those chips on the sea, are Europe. What nationality? Are they Irish, English, Scotch, or French? Can they be from Norway, or from Spain? What fishing bank are they anchored on? How far from the coast do fishing banks extend? It's too early to reach Europe unless a gale blew behind me through the night. Thoughts press forward in confused succession. After fifteen hours of solitude, here's human life and help and safety.

The ocean is no longer a dangerous wilderness. I feel as secure as though I were circling Lambert Field back home. I could land alongside any one of those boats, and someone would throw me a rope and take me on board where there'd be a bunk I could sleep on, and warm food when I woke up.

The first boat is less than a mile ahead – I can see its masts and cabin. I can see it rocking on the water. I close the mixture control and dive down fifty feet above its bow, dropping my wing to get a better view.

But where is the crew? There's no sign of life on deck. Can all the men be out in dories? I climb higher as I circle. No, there aren't any dories. I can see for miles, and the ocean's not rough enough to hide one. Are the fishermen frightened by my plane, swooping down suddenly from the sky? Possibly they never saw a plane before. *Of course* they never saw one out so far over the ocean. Maybe they all hid below the decks when they heard the roar of my engine. Maybe they think I'm some demon from the sky, like those dragons that decorate ancient mariners' charts. But if the crews are so out of contact with the modern world that they hide from the sound of an airplane, they must come from some isolated coastal village above which airplanes never pass. And the boats look too small to have ventured far from home. I have visions of riding the top of a hurricane during the night, with a hundred-mile-an-hour wind drift. Possibly these vessels are anchored north of Ireland, or somewhere in the Bay of Biscay. Then shall I keep on going straight, or turn north, or south?

I fly over to the next boat bobbing up and down on the swells. Its deck is empty too. But as I drop my wing to circle, a man's head appears, thrust out through a cabin porthole, motionless, staring up at me. In the excitement and joy of the moment, in the rush of ideas passing through my reawakened mind, I decide to make that head withdraw from the porthole, come out of the cabin, body and all, and to point towards the Irish coast. No sooner have I made the decision than I realize its futility. Probably that fisherman can't speak English. Even if he can, he'll be too startled to understand my message, and reply. But I'm already turning into position to dive down past the boat. It won't do any harm to try. Why deprive myself of that easy satisfaction? Probably if I fly over it again, the entire crew will come on deck. I've talked to people before from a plane, flying low with throttled engine, and received the answer through some simple gesture – a nod or an outstretched arm.

I glide down within fifty feet of the cabin, close the throttle, and shout as loudly as I can 'WHICH WAY IS IRELAND?'

How extraordinary the silence is with the engine idling! I look back under the tail, watch the fisherman's face for some sign of understanding. But an instant later, all my attention is concentrated on the plane. For I realize that I've lost the 'feel' of flying. I shove the throttle open, and watch the air-speed indicator while I climb and circle. As long as I keep the needle above sixty miles an hour, there's no danger of stalling. Always before, I've known instinctively just what condition my plane was in – whether it had flying speed or whether it was stalling, and how close to the edge it was riding in between. I didn't have to look at the instruments. Now, the pressure of the stick no longer imparts its message clearly to my hand. I can't tell whether air is soft or solid.

When I pass over the boat a third time, the head is still at the porthole. It hasn't moved or changed expression since it first appeared. It came as suddenly as the boats themselves. It seems as lifeless. I didn't notice before how pale it is – or am I now imagining its paleness? It looks like a severed head in that porthole, as though a guillotine had dropped behind it. I feel baffled. After all, a man who dares to show his face would hardly fear to show his body. There's something unreal about these boats. They're as weird as the night's temples, as those misty islands of Atlantis, as the fuselage's phantoms that rode behind my back.

Why don't sailors gather on the decks to watch my plane? Why don't they pay attention to my circling and shouting? What's the matter with this strange flight, where dreams become reality, and reality returns to dreams? But these aren't vessels of cloud and mist. They're tangible, made of real substance like my plane – sails furled, ropes coiled neatly on the decks, masts swaying back and forth with each new swell. Yet the only sign of crew is that single head, hanging motionless through the cabin porthole. It's like 'The Rime of the Ancient Mariner' my mother used to read aloud. These boats remind me of the 'painted ship upon a painted ocean'.

I want to stay, to circle again and again, until that head removes itself from the porthole and the crews come out on deck. I want to see them standing and waving like normal, living people. I've passed through worlds and ages since my last contact with other men. I've been away, far away, planets and heavens away, until only a thread was left to lead me back to earth and life. I've followed that thread with swinging compasses, through lonely canyons, over pitfalls of sleep, past the lure of enchanted islands, fearing that at any moment it would break. And now I've returned to earth, returned to these boats bobbing on the ocean. I want an earthly greeting. I deserve a warmer welcome back to the fellowship of men.

Shall I fly over to another boat and try again to raise the crew? No, I'm wasting minutes of daylight and miles of fuel. There's nothing but frustration to be had by staying longer. It's best to leave. There's something about this fleet that tries my mind and spirit, and lowers confidence with every circle I make. Islands that turn to fog, I understand. Ships without crews, I do not. And that motionless head at the porthole – it's no phantom, and yet it shows no sign of life. I straighten out the *Spirit of St Louis* and fly on eastward.

The Twenty-eighth Hour

Is that a cloud on the northeastern horizon, or a strip of low fog – or – *can it possibly be land*? It looks like land, but I don't intend to be tricked by another mirage. Framed between two grey curtains of rain, not more than ten or fifteen miles away, a purplish blue band has hardened from the haze – flat below, like a waterline – curving on top, as though composed of hills or aged mountains.

I'm only sixteen hours out from Newfoundland. I allowed eighteen and a half hours to strike the Irish coast. If that's Ireland, I'm two and a half hours ahead of schedule. Can this be another, clearer image, like the islands of the morning? Is there something strange about it too, like the fishing fleet and that haunting head? Is each new illusion to become more real until reality itself is meaningless? But my mind is clear. I'm no longer half asleep. I'm awake – alert – aware. The temptation is too great. I can't hold my course any longer. The *Spirit of St Louis* banks over towards the nearest point of land.

I stare at it intently, not daring to believe my eyes, keeping hope in check to avoid another disappointment, watching the shades and contours unfold into a coastline – a coastline coming down from the north – a coastline bending toward the east – a coastline with rugged shores and rolling mountains. It's much too early to strike England, France or Scotland. It's early to be striking Ireland; but that's the nearest land.

A fjorded coast stands out as I approach. Barren islands guard it. Inland, green fields slope up the sides of warted mountains. This *must* be Ireland. It can be no other place than Ireland. The fields are too green for Scotland; the mountains too high for Brittany or Cornwall.

Now, I'm flying above the foam-lined coast, searching for prominent features to fit the chart on my knees. I've climbed to two thousand feet so I can see the contours of the country better. The mountains are old and rounded; the farms small and stony. Rain-glistened dirt roads wind narrowly through hills and fields. Below me lies a great tapering bay; a long, bouldered island; a village. Yes, there's a place on the chart where it all fits – line of ink on line of shore – Valentia and Dingle Bay, *on the south-western coast of Ireland!*

I can hardly believe it's true. I'm almost exactly on my route, closer than I hoped to come in my wildest dreams back in San Diego. What happened to all those detours of the night around the thunderheads? Where has the swinging compass error gone? The wind above the storm clouds must have blown fiercely on my tail. In edging northward, intuition must have been more accurate than reasoned navigation.

The southern tip of Ireland! On course; over two hours ahead of schedule; the sun still well up in the sky; the weather clearing! I circle again, fearful that I'll wake to find this too a phantom, a mirage fading into mid-Atlantic mist. But there's no question about it; every detail on the chart has its counterpart below; each major feature on the ground has its symbol on the chart. The lines correspond exactly. Nothing in that world of dreams and phantoms was like this. I spiral lower, looking down on the little village. There are boats in the harbour, wagons on the stone-fenced roads. People are running out into the streets, looking up and waving. This is earth again, the earth where I've lived and now will live once more. Here are human beings. Here's a human welcome. Not a single detail is wrong. I've never seen such beauty before – fields so green, people so human, a village so attractive, mountains and rocks so mountainous and rocklike.

I bank steeply around and set my course southeastward, cutting across the bouldered fjords, flying low over the hilltop farms, the rock fences and the small, green fields of Kerry. Now, I can check the engine – All cylinders hitting on the left switch – All cylinders hitting on the right – And all instrument readings are normal.

Sheep and cattle graze on their sloping pastures. Horse-drawn carts crawl along their shiny roads. People move across walled-in barnyards, through doorways of the primitive stone buildings. It must be a hard place to gain a living from the soil. And it would be worse than New England for a forced landing.

Even the wish to sleep has left, and with it the phantoms and voices. I didn't notice their absence before; but now, as I settle down for the last six hundred miles to Paris, I realize that they remained behind with the fishing fleet. They vanished with that first strange touch of Europe and of man. Since I sighted those specks on the water, I've been as wide awake as though I started the flight this morning after a warm breakfast and a full night's sleep. The thought of floating off in a bed of feathers has lost its attractiveness.

Time is no longer endless, or the horizon destitute of hope. The strain of take-off, storm, and ocean, lies behind. There'll be no second night above the clouds, no more grappling with misty walls of ice. There's only one more island to cross – only the narrow tip of an island. I look at England's outline on my map. And then, within an hour, I'll see the coast of France; and beyond that, Paris and Le Bourget. As Nova Scotia and Newfoundland were stepping-stones from America, Ireland and England are stepping-stones to Europe. Yesterday, each strip of sea I crossed was an advance messenger of the ocean. Today, these islands down below are heralds to a continent.

It's as though a curtain has fallen behind me, shutting off the stagelike unreality of this transatlantic flight. It's been like a theatre where the play carries you along in time and place until you forget you're only a spectator. You grow unaware of the walls around you, of the programme clasped in your hand, even of your body, its breath, pulse, and being. You live with the actors and the setting, in a different age and place. It's not until the curtain drops that consciousness and body reunite. Then, you turn your back on the stage, step out into the cool night, under the lights of streets, between the displays of store windows. You feel life surging in the crowd around you, life as it was when you entered the theatre, hours before. Life is real. It always was real. The stage, of course, was the dream. All that transpired there is now a memory, shut off by the curtain, by the doors of the theatre, by the passing minutes of time.

Striking Ireland was like leaving the doors of a theatre – phantoms for actors; cloud islands and temples for settings; the ocean behind me, an empty stage. The flight across is already like a dream. I'm over villages and fields, back to land and wakefulness and a type of flying that I know. I'm myself again, in earthly skies and over earthly ground. My hands and feet and eyelids move, and I can think as I desire. That third, controlling element has retired to the background. I'm no longer three existences in one. My mind is able to command, and my body follows out its orders with precision.

Ireland, England, France, Paris! The night at Paris! *This* night at Paris – less than six hours from Now – *France and Paris!* It's like a fairy tale. Yesterday I walked on Roosevelt Field; today I'll walk on Le Bourget.

SOURCES & ACKNOWLEDGEMENTS

The editor has made every effort to locate all persons having any rights in the selections appearing in this anthology and to secure permission from the holders of such rights. Any queries regarding the use of material should be addressed to the editor c/o the publishers.

Andrée, S. A., Nils Strindberg, Knut Fraenkel, *The Andrée Diaries*, John Lane The Bodley Head, 1931

Barrington, A. J., 'Diary of a West Coast Prospecting Party', *Early Travellers in New Zealand*, ed. Nancy M. Taylor, Oxford, Clarendon Press, 1959

Blashford-Snell, J., *A Taste for Adventure*, Readers Union, 1979

Bonatti, W., *On the Heights*, Rupert Hart-Davis, 1964

Byrd, R. E., *Alone*, Neville Spearman, 1955

Callahan, S., *Adrift*, Bantam Press, 1986. Copyright © Steven Callahan 1986

Casteret, N., *The Descent of Pierre Saint-Martin*, Dent, 1955

Corbett, J., *The Temple Tiger*, Oxford India Paperbacks, 1997

Cousteau, J., *The Silent World of Jacques Cousteau*, Hamish Hamilton, 1953

Danziger, N., *Danziger's Travels*, Paladin, 1988. Copyright © N. Danziger 1987. Reprinted by Permission of Harper Collins Publishers.

Drummond, E., 'Mirror, Mirror', *Ascent*, 1973

Fiennes, R., *To the Ends of the Earth*, Mandarin, 1995. Copyright © Ranulph Fiennes 1983. Reprinted by permission of Curtis Brown

Fleming, P., *News from Tartary*, Futura, 1980. Reprinted by permission

Giles, E., *Australia Twice Traversed*, 1889

Hedin, S., *My Life as an Explorer*, Cassell, 1926

Herzog, M., *Annapurna*, Jonathan Cape

Heyerdahl, T., *The Kon-Tiki Expedition*, Penguin, 1963

Hillary, E., *High Adventure*, Hodder & Stoughton, 1957

Lindbergh, C., *The Spirit of St Louis*, John Murray 1953

Mawson, D., *The Home of the Blizzard*, Hodder & Stoughton, 1930

Ridgway, J., Blyth, C., *Fighting Chance*, Paul Hamlyn, 1966. Copyright © J. Ridgway & C. Blyth 1966

Roosevelt, T., *Through the Brazilian Wilderness*, John Murray, 1914

Saint-Exupéry, A. de, *Wind, Sand & Stars*, Heinemann, 1939. Trans. copyright © Lewis Galantíre

Scott, R. F., *Scott's Last Expedition*, John Murray, 1923

Shackleton., E., *South*, Lyons Press, 1998

Snow, S., 'Kings of the Equator', *Explorers' And Travellers' Tales*, ed. O. Tcherine, The Adventurers Club, 1963. Copyright © Sebastian Snow 1958

Thomas, B., 'The First Crossing of the Great Souths Arabian Desert', *Explorer's All*, ed. Sir Percy Sykes, George Newnes Ltd, 1938

Van der Post, L., *Venture to the Interior*, The Hogarth Press, 1952

Waterton, C., *Wanderings in South America*, Thomas Nelson & Sons, 1891